Vienna

timeout.com/vienna

Published by Time Out Guides Ltd, a wholly owned subsidiary of Time Out Group Ltd.
Time Out and the Time Out logo are trademarks of Time Out Group Ltd.

© Time Out Group Ltd 2007
Previous editions 2000, 2003, 2005.

10 9 8 7 6 5 4 3 2 1

This edition first published in Great Britain in 2007 by Ebury Publishing
A Random House Group Company
20 Vauxhall Bridge Road, London SW1V 2SA

Random House Australia Pty Limited 20 Alfred Street, Milsons Point, Sydney, New South Wales 2061, Australia
Random House New Zealand Limited 18 Poland Road, Glenfield, Auckland 10, New Zealand
Random House South Africa (Pty) Limited Isle of Houghton, Corner Boundary
Road & Carse O'Gowrie, Houghton 2198, South Africa

Random House UK Limited Reg. No. 954009

For further distribution details, see www.timeout.com

ISBN 10: 1-84670-030-2
ISBN 13: 978184670 0309

A CIP catalogue record for this book is available from the British Library

Printed and bound by Firmengruppe APPL, aprinta druck, Wemding, Germany

The Random House Group Limited makes every effort to ensure that the papers used in our books are made from trees
that have been legally sourced from well-managed and credibly certified forests. Our paper procurement policy can be
found on www.rbooks.co.uk/environment.

Hofburg & Heldenplatz.

Time Out Guides Limited
Universal House
251 Tottenham Court Road
London W1T 7AB
Tel + 44 (0)20 7813 3000
Fax + 44 (0)20 7813 6001
Email guides@timeout.com
www.timeout.com

Editorial
Editor Geraint Williams
Deputy Editor Edoardo Albert
Listings Editor Maite Bachero
Proofreader Patrick Mulkern
Indexer Jonathan Cox

Managing Director Peter Fiennes
Financial Director Gareth Garner
Editorial Director Ruth Jarvis
Deputy Series Editor Dominic Earle
Editorial Manager Holly Pick
Assistant Management Accountant Ija Krasnikova

Design
Art Director Scott Moore
Art Editor Pinelope Kourmouzoglou
Senior Designer Henry Elphick
Graphic Designer Gemma Doyle
Junior Graphic Designer Kei Ishimaru
Digital Imaging Simon Foster
Ad Make-up Jodi Sher

Picture Desk
Picture Editor Jael Marschner
Deputy Picture Editor Tracey Kerrigan
Picture Researcher Helen McFarland

Advertising
Sales Director Mark Phillips
International Advertising Manager Kasimir Berger
International Sales Consultant Ross Canadé
International Sales Executive Charlie Sokol
Advertising Sales (Vienna) Alexandra Meran
Advertising Assistant Kate Staddon

Marketing
Group Marketing Director John Luck
Marketing Manager Yvonne Poon
Sales and Marketing Director North America Lisa Levinson

Production
Group Production Director Mark Lamond
Production Manager Brendan McKeown
Production Coordinator Caroline Bradford
Production Controller Susan Whittaker

Time Out Group
Chairman Tony Elliott
Financial Director Richard Waterlow
Group General Manager/Director Nichola Coulthard
Time Out Magazine Ltd MD Richard Waterlow
Time Out Communications Ltd MD David Pepper
Time Out International MD Cathy Runciman
Group Art Director John Oakey
Group IT Director Simon Chappell

Contributors
Introduction Geraint Williams **History** Nicolas Parsons, Geraint Williams **Vienna Today** Geraint Williams, Joe Remick **Literary Vienna** Oona Strathern, Geraint Williams **Where to Stay** Geraint Williams **Sightseeing** Geraint Williams (*2nd District* Joe Remick) **Restaurants** Geraint Williams **Cafés & Coffee Houses** Geraint Williams **Shops & Services** Geraint Williams **Festivals & Events** Joanna Bostock **Children** Joanna Bostock **Film** Richard Rees Jones, Geraint Williams **Galleries** Nicole Scheyerer **Gay & Lesbian** Geraint Williams **Music: Classical & Opera** Robin Lee **Music: Rock, Roots & Jazz** Richard Rees Jones **Nightlife** Geraint Williams **Sport & Fitness** Katie Binns, Geraint Williams (*Euro 2008* Peterjon Cresswell) **Theatre & Dance** Geraint Williams, Diane Shooman **Trips Out of Town** Geraint Williams **Directory** Maite Bachero, Simone La Rosa Monier, Geraint Williams **Further Reference** Geraint Williams, Richard Rees Jones.

Maps john@jsgraphics.co.uk

Photography by Britta Jaschinski except pages 16, 59 Mozarthaus Vienna/David Peters; page 18 Schloss Schonbrunn, Vienna, Austria/The Bridgeman Art Library; page 21 Getty Images; page 22 Reuters/Heinz-Peter Bader (Austria); page 158 Vukica Mikaća; page 161 Jazz Fest Wien Archive; page 169 MUMOK/Lena Deinhardstein, Lisa Rastl; pages 174, 175 Lisa Rastl; page 183 Wiener Staatsoper; page 189 Rex Features; page 207 Rupert Steiner; page 215 ANTO/Wiesenhofer; pages 216, 217, 219 Austrian National Tourist Office.

The following images were provided by the featured establishments/artists: pages 42, 48, 171.

The Editor would like to thank Maite Bachero, Stephanie Mohr, Simone Coll, Edoardo Albert, Linda Kaszubski, Jutta Kurzmanovski-Jandl, Duncan Larkin, Peter Morgan, Sandra Pfeifer, Francesca von Habsburg, Imke Haasler and the good folk at Delugan Meissl Associated Architects, Stefan Jena, Christopher Bayne, Christopher Green, Roger Cartwright, Stephen McFarlane, Pablo Williams Bachero and all contributors to previous editions of *Time Out Vienna*, whose work forms the basis for parts of this book.

Contents

Oberes Belvedere & Österreichische Galerie. *See p91.*

Introduction

When *Time Out Vienna* first appeared in 2000, the comparable Prague and Budapest guides were already steaming into their fourth editions. Understandably, the post-1989 euphoria had bestowed considerable excitement on the capitals of Vienna's newly liberated eastern neighbours. But why then did it take so long for Vienna itself to be recognised? After all, the city was the last stop on the eastern branch line of Western capitalism and, what's more, for a thousand years it has been at the very centre of European history. Perhaps people thought it simply too boring, too old, too trapped in chocolate cake clichés of bewhiskered emperors and liveried lackies. Other reasons for people to pass up a visit here include the suspicions that the place is too formal, too expensive, too schmaltzy and, even worse, still shrouded in the memory of its complicity with the Nazis in 1938. There are evidently a lot of preconceived ideas about Vienna and these either draw you in or make you reject it outright.

Although Vienna has done very nicely indeed out of flogging Mozart, the Habsburgs, Klimt and choirboys in sailor suits to visitors from five continents, a wander outside its historic centre will show you that the city has moved on. The dynamism of the Naschmarkt, the MuseumsQuartier, the Gürtel bars and the streets of the 7th district is largely powered by the city's more recent arrivals. The musty air of retrospection that still pervades the city – particularly in its coffee houses, shop façades, statuary and stiff handshakes – creates a unique feel that gives Vienna its special character. But now that the city's inhabitants hail from more diverse backgrounds, these trappings of Old Vienna form a backdrop that inspires rather than stifles.

A day in the city offers a wealth of contrasts – exit a deliriously decorated Baroque church and enter an avant-garde gallery; drink locally made wine (Vienna has its own vineyards) at a traditional tavern before settling in for the night at one of the many DJ bars; or switch from Mozart to metal as the mood takes you. You'll find greater variety here than you ever suspected. Like Prague and Budapest, Vienna has been busy reinventing itself.

ABOUT TIME OUT CITY GUIDES

This is the fourth edition of *Time Out Vienna*, one of an expanding series of Time Out guides produced by the people behind the successful listings magazines in London, New York and Chicago. Our guides are all written by resident experts who have striven to provide you with all the most up-to-date information you'll need to explore the city or read up on its background, whether you're a local or a first-time visitor.

THE LIE OF THE LAND

Vienna is divided into 23 districts, spiralling out from the central Innere Stadt. In our listings the first number in each address is the district and the second the street number. So, for example, the address for Café Central is given as 1, Herrengasse 14. This means that it's in the 1st district, at No.14 on Herrengasse. The 1st district is the old heart of the city and contains many of the tourist sights. The 2nd district goes east to the Danube, while districts 3 to 9 run clockwise around the centre and contain most of the rest of Vienna's attractions. See the map on page 54 for more details. In all addresses we've also included phone numbers, websites, postcodes for those venues to which you might want to write and map references that point to our street maps at the back of the guide. For further orientation information, *see p55*.

ESSENTIAL INFORMATION

For all the practical advice you might need for visiting the area – including visa and customs information, details of local transport, a list of emergency numbers, information on local weather and a selection of useful websites – turn to the Directory at the back of this guide. It begins on page 222.

THE LOWDOWN ON THE LISTINGS

We have tried to make this book as easy to use as possible. Addresses, phone numbers, bus information, opening times and admission prices are all included in the listings. However, businesses can change their arrangements at any time. Before you go out of your way, we'd strongly advise you to phone ahead to check opening times and other particulars. While every effort and care has been made to ensure the accuracy of the information contained in this guide, the publishers cannot accept responsibility for any errors it may contain. ▶

□ P R O D U C T S □

TAKE **VIENNA** HOME

WIEN PRODUCTS
Shopping with a difference

A vacation in the cultural metropolis that is Vienna is the best way to discover the newest lifestyle and fashion trends, as well as shopping for a few gifts for friends and family back home. The brochure, "Shopping, Wining & Dining" available at the Vienna Tourist Information Office (Albertinaplatz) is very useful for finding those special items. It includes information on all WIEN PRODUCTS' member companies, who guarantee the highest quality on all their products.

Find a whole range of fine fashion shoppng, from the contemporary bags at "Vienna Bag" to glamorous glasses from "Schau Schau" and stylish "Mühlbauer" hats. "Oesterreichischen Werkstaetten"offer first quality arts and crafts products, made with distinctive Austrian creative flair.

But it's not just about fashion. WIEN PRODUCTS companies also offer the finest tableware, like the glass and porcelain from famous firms such as "Lobmeyr" and "Augarten", as well as a huge range of handcrafted silverware from "Jarosinksy & Vaugoin" and the "Wiener Silberschmiede Werkstaette". "Schwaebische Jungfrau" table linen will set it all off nicely .

All that shopping may make you hungry and as we all know Vienna is world famous for its range of delicious food and drink. Going for a breakfast may seem easy in the city of the "Wiener Kaffeehaus", but one of the best can be found at "Haas & Haas" at the "Stephansdom", where more than 30 varieties of breakfast are available. Another culinary hub for gourmets and connoisseurs is "Julius Meinl am Graben" where the finest ingredients and delicacies from all over the world are displayed over three dazzling floors.

So enjoy your trip to Vienna and take advantage of Vienna's unique shopping!

WIEN PRODUCTS is a project of the Vienna Chamber of Commerce & Industry. It was founded in 1995 with the goal of supporting the export efforts of selected Viennese consumer goods manufacturers. The 50 companies currently associated with WIEN PRODUCTS produce outstanding quality goods provide excellent service, and seek to incorporate Vienna's unique flair and sense of aesthetics into their products.

www.wienproducts.at
+43 I 5I 450 I5I7

Further information about WIEN PRODUCTS is available on the Internet at www.wienproducts.at or from the WIEN PRODUCTS Service Center, tel: +43 1 51 450 1517.

▶ PRICES AND PAYMENT

We have noted where venues such as shops, hotels, restaurants and theatres accept the following credit cards: American Express (AmEx), Diners Club (DC), Discover (Disc), MasterCard (MC) and Visa (V). Many will also accept travellers' cheques, and/or other cards such as Carte Blanche.

The prices we've listed in this guide should be treated as guidelines, not gospel. If prices vary wildly from those we've quoted, ask whether there's a good reason. If not, go elsewhere. Then please let us know. We aim to give the best and most up-to-date advice, so we want to know if you've been badly treated or overcharged.

TELEPHONE NUMBERS

At first glance Austrian phone numbers can seem confusing: there can be as many as ten or as few as three or four digits to each number. There is also the *Durchwahlen* (direct-dial extension numbers) system. This means some numbers are followed by a hyphen and then a digit (usually 0); this tells you there are a number of extensions. Dialling the main number plus the digits following the hyphen will connect you directly to an extension. So, if you know the extension you want, dial the relevant digits after the hyphen. Extension 0 will usually get you through to the main desk/operator, who will then transfer your call if necessary. Likewise, if you dial all the numbers up to the hyphen you will still get through to the same main desk/operator. To make a call to Vienna from elsewhere in Austria, dial 01 and then the number as given in the book. To phone Vienna from abroad, dial 43 for Austria, followed by 1 and then the number. For more on telephones and codes, *see p231*.

MAPS

The map section starts on page 240 and includes an overview of the city, detailed street maps, and train and underground routes. The street maps pinpoint the specific locations of hotels (❶), bars (❶) and restaurants (❶).

LET US KNOW WHAT YOU THINK

We hope you enjoy *Time Out Vienna*, and we'd like to know what you think of it. We welcome tips for places that you consider we should include in future editions and take note of your criticism of our choices. You can email us at guides@timeout.com.

Advertisers

We would like to stress that no establishment has been included in this guide because it has advertised in any of our publications and no payment of any kind has influenced any review. The opinions given in this book are those of Time Out writers and entirely independent.

There is an online version of this book, along with guides to over 100 international cities, at **www.timeout.com**.

DOROTHEUM

SEIT 1707

The leading Auction House in Central Europe

Old Master Paintings, 19th Century Paintings, Modern and
Contemporary Art, Design, Antiques, Jewellery, Collectors Items

Palais Dorotheum, Dorotheergasse 17, 1010 Vienna, Austria
Tel. +43-1-515 60-570, client.services@dorotheum.at
Catalogues: Tel. +43-1-515 60-200, kataloge@dorotheum.at
Online Catalogues: www.dorotheum.com

IA◉
International
Auctioneers

Banksy (born 1975), Gangsta Rat (detail), 2004, Auction May 2007, price realised € 76,800

In Context

Features

**Church of Christ
the Hope of the World.** *See p88.*

Hofburg. *See p14.*

History

A whirl through Viennese history.

Early in the first century AD, the settlement of Vindobona was only a subsidiary outpost of what was known as Carnuntum, the capital of the Roman province of Pannonia Superior. Vindobona, 40 kilometres (25 miles) west of the capital along the Danube, was centred on what is now the Hoher Markt in old Vienna, with a squadron of cavalry based nearby in the modern 3rd district. Carnuntum and Vindobona were part of a Roman defensive line, known as the Limes, built along the Danube to keep out the Germanic barbarians.

From the end of the third century AD, the failure of the Romans to subdue the Germanic tribes, and the constant aggression of Vandals and Goths in particular, made the situation of Vindobona increasingly precarious. At the end of the following century (probably in 395), a fire destroyed the military camp and led to the withdrawal of its Roman legion. Roman influence lingered on, though, until the Eastern Emperor Theodosius II formally ceded Pannonia to the Huns in 433.

THE DARK AGES

When the Romans withdrew southwards, they left behind a small residue of veterans and Romanised inhabitants. These were now at the mercy of repeated waves of invaders, themselves often in flight from powerful adversaries. Despite such disruptions, there was evidently some continuity in organised administration. From at least the eighth century, a governor dispensed justice from the Berghof, which was at the western end of today's Hoher Markt (now recalled by a plaque on the wall). The earliest recorded church in Vienna, the Ruprechtskirche, was built just to the east, probably in the ninth century. Its dedication to Saint Rupert indicates its association with the shippers of salt from the

Salzkammergut; the missionary Saint Rupert, who died around 710, was the first bishop of Salzburg, and the patron saint of salt miners. The eastward spread of Christianity also brought with it Bavarian settlers, the ancestors of the German-Austrians who would form the core population of the region.

By the ninth century, Vindobona had disappeared, and the city's modern name – which first appeared in the Salzburg annals of 881 – had become current. It is supposedly derived from the Illyro-Celtic word Vedunja, meaning a woodland stream. Wenia was situated at the eastern edge of the Carolingian Empire, in a buffer zone periodically overrun by the Magyars from the east. Following the defeat of a Bavarian army at Pressburg (Bratislava) in 907, Wenia was under Magyar control for several decades, but the decisive victory of the German king Otto the Great on the Lechfeld, near Augsburg, in 955 marked a turning point. The Magyars would eventually be pushed back to the River Leitha, now in the Austrian province of Burgenland, which became the permanent frontier.

This hotly disputed border territory between 'West' and 'East' – a role to which it reverted during the Cold War over 1,000 years later – came to be known as Austria. The name first occurs in an imperial document of 996 bestowing lands on the bishop of Freising, described as being 'in a region popularly known as Ostarrichi' ('Eastern Realm', the origin of Österreich). Even before then, in 976, Emperor Otto II had awarded the 'Ottonian Mark' established by his father, between Enns and Traisen, to the Bavarian Margraves (Counts) of Babenberg. This ambitious dynasty, whose members combined shrewd diplomacy with ostentatious piety, would dominate the expanding territories of 'Austria' for 270 years.

THE BABENBERGS

When Leopold I of Babenberg (976-94) first took charge of his new possessions, the seat of his power was in Melk on the Danube. He managed to extend his lands to the east, probably as far as the Wienerwald, but Wenia itself remained in Magyar hands. The Magyars were content to hold the Berghof and maintain a military camp on today's Schwarzenbergplatz, without establishing any permanent settlement.

The Magyars were finally forced back to the Leitha by Adalbert 'the Victorious' (1018-55). The Babenbergs still had to impose their authority over local lords, powers in the area since the Carolingian era. Like their successors the Habsburgs, the Babenbergs reinforced their territorial claims by astute marriages into rival dynasties. Their ambitions were generally

projected eastwards, and the Babenberg seat moved progressively along the Danube from Melk via Klosterneuburg to Vienna.

Saint Leopold III of Babenberg (1096-1135) would become Austria's patron saint (canonised in 1485). He was a man of piety, a peacemaker who refused the German crown, devoting himself instead to founding or refounding abbeys and churches (Heiligenkreuz and Klosterneuburg among them). In 1137, his successor Leopold IV (1136-41) came to an agreement with the bishopric of Passau to build a new church in Vienna, just outside the town boundary. Ten years later, this Romanesque predecessor of the Stephansdom cathedral was completed.

The most significant Babenberg for the history of Vienna was Heinrich II Jasomirgott (1141-77), so called because of his favourite oath ('So help me God!'). He was prevailed upon to renounce the dukedom of Bavaria, acquired by his predecessor in 1139, but was handsomely rewarded by the upgrading of Austria itself in 1156 to an independent dukedom. Equally important was Heinrich's decision to move his court to Vienna in the same year, to the area still known as Am Hof ('At the Court'). In 1155, Irish monks were summoned from his former seat at Regensburg to found the Schottenstift ('Monastery of the Scots', so-called because in medieval Latin Ireland was Scotia Maior).

The town's economic expansion continued under Heinrich's successor, Leopold V (1177-94), who benefited from two windfalls: he inherited much of Styria and Upper Austria in 1192 when their ruler died childless; and he received much of the huge ransom paid to Emperor Heinrich VI for the release of Richard the Lionheart. (The crusading king of England had insulted Leopold and the emperor's representative during the siege of Acre in Palestine, and in 1192 was making his way back to England overland after being shipwrecked on the Adriatic. He was recognised in Vienna and imprisoned in the castle at Dürnstein until March 1193.) Leopold's share was enough to found Wiener Neustadt and extend the fortifications of Vienna and the border town of Hainburg.

Late 12th-century Vienna was booming economically and culturally. Under Leopold VI 'the Glorious' (1198-1230), troubadours, known as *Minnesänger*, were prominent at the Babenberg court, singing the praises of noble ladies and celebrating the duke's glory and virtue. Leopold VI encouraged trade, ingratiating himself with the burghers by allowing guilds to be formed and, most importantly, awarding Vienna its 'staple right', in 1221. This obliged foreign merchants trading on the Danube to sell their goods to local traders within two months of their being landed, effectively guaranteeing the lion's share of the downstream trade to the Viennese. It was a 'right' to make money which the Viennese enthusiastically accepted.

The reign of the last Babenberg, Friedrich II 'the Warlike' (1230-46), saw a decline in the fortunes of the city and the dukedom. After a fierce dispute with the German emperor, Friedrich was killed in 1246 fighting the Hungarians, leaving no male heirs. The resulting power vacuum was filled by the ambitious Ottokar II of Bohemia, who reinforced his claim by marrying Friedrich II's widow at Hainburg in 1252.

THE COMING OF THE HABSBURGS

Ottokar cultivated the Viennese burghers – as well as executing a few who tried to oppose him – and most of the town swung behind him. He gave generously for the rebuilding of the Stephansdom and other edifices after a fire in 1258, and founded a hospital for lepers as well as the Wiener Bürgerspital almshouse. He also initiated the building of the Hofburg, Vienna's future imperial palace, originally as a fairly simple fortress.

The increased sensibility towards the poor and sick that was revealed in the endowment of hospitals coincided with a wave of religious fervour – a recurrent phenomenon in Viennese history. The uncertainties of the age were also reflected in outbreaks of religious enthusiasm: processions of flagellants appeared in the streets of Vienna, complementing the campaigns against impiety by the Dominicans, whose first church in Vienna was consecrated in 1237.

Ottokar's ambiguous position was made precarious by a failed attempt to become King of Germany (king-emperors were elected from among the lesser princes). He was further undermined when Rudolf of Habsburg was chosen as king in his place in 1273. Rudolf, whose original, small domain was in modern Switzerland, was initially seen as a compromise candidate deemed harmless by the other electors, but he soon proved himself far-sighted and shrewd. He set out to challenge Ottokar's power, and by 1276 he had occupied Vienna. They made a temporary peace, but in 1278 Ottokar was killed in the battle of Dürnkrut, on the Marchfeld north-east of Vienna. His embalmed body was displayed in the Minorite monastery, a reminder to the people that those who aspire to climb highest also fall furthest.

The arrival of Rudolf began 640 years of virtually unbroken, if sporadically resisted, Habsburg rule in Austria; Vienna was to be the Residenzstadt of every Habsburg ruler except Maximilian I (1493-1519), whose main seat was Innsbruck, and Rudolf II (1576-1612), who preferred Prague. From 1283, Rudolf left the government of Austria in the hands of his son Albrecht, who made himself unpopular by challenging some burgher privileges, and had to put down a rebellion in the city in 1287-88. In 1298, Albrecht I became the first Habsburg to add to the title of German King that of Holy Roman Emperor which, like Vienna, would in later centuries become virtually synonymous with the dynasty. To accommodate Vienna's new ruling house, the Hofburg would expand continuously through the centuries; even up to the outbreak of war in 1914.

Problems beset the Habsburgs in the first half of the 14th century. In 1310, there was a rising in Vienna against Friedrich 'the Handsome', which had two significant consequences: one of the properties confiscated from the conspirators was handed over to become the first City Hall (Altes Rathaus), and the city's rights and privileges were codified for the first time in the so-called Eisenbuch (1320). During the reign of Albrecht 'the Lame' (1298-1358), plagues of locusts ravaged the Vienna Basin (in 1338 and 1340); and hardly had they disappeared than Vienna was hit by the Black Death, at the height of which, in 1349, 500 people were dying each day. The plague was then followed by a terrible fire.

Vienna's Christian population blamed the Jews for the plague (they were said to have poisoned the wells), and Albrecht had to struggle to prevent major violence. A Jewish community had been established in Vienna since Babenberg times and had reached a considerable size. It was mainly concentrated close to Am Hof, on and around today's Judenplatz. Its location was not accidental, for Jews traditionally enjoyed the ruler's protection; even this, though, was not always enough to spare them from persecution at times of crisis.

DYNASTY BUILDING

Duke Albrecht achieved a shrewd dynastic alliance in 1353, when his son, the future Rudolf IV, married the daughter of Karl IV of Bohemia, Holy Roman Emperor since 1346. Advantageous marriage was thereafter the principal pillar of Habsburg expansionism, aphoristically described in a 16th-century adaptation of a line from Ovid: 'Others make war; you, fortunate Austria, marry!' The magnificence of the Prague ruled by his illustrious father-in-law was a spur to Rudolf's ambitions: masons who had worked on the great cathedral of Saint Vitus in Prague were summoned to work on the Stephansdom, and

The **Plague Monument**. Vienna suffered many outbreaks of the disease over the years.

Rudolf founded a university in Vienna in 1365, clearly inspired by Karl's earlier foundation of the Prague Carolinum.

In the same year, Rudolf died in Milan, aged only 26. He had reigned for a mere seven years, but his ingenious policies ranged from social and monetary reform to the promotion of urban renewal through tax holidays and rent reform. Not for nothing was he known as 'the Founder' (as well as, equally aptly, 'the Cunning').

As a moderniser, Rudolf clashed with vested interests, such as the guilds and the Church. But his attempts to advance the claims of the dynasty over the title of Holy Roman Emperor were embarrassingly ill-judged. A diligently produced forgery known as the *Privilegium Maius* invented a picturesque lineage and even more picturesque titles for the earlier Habsburgs. It was magisterially rubbished by the poet Petrarch, whom the emperor had asked to verify its authenticity. Even more disastrous was Rudolf's institution of a system of power sharing among the male Habsburg heirs (the Rudolfinische Hausordnung). This resulted in a Habsburg equivalent of the Wars of the Roses between the 'Albertine' and 'Leopoldine' lines (named after Rudolf's two quarrelling brothers and joint heirs), which lasted intermittently for four generations.

In 1411, Albrecht V, of the Albertine line, came of age and entered a Vienna under threat from Moravian knights and the Protestant Hussites of Bohemia, who laid waste parts of Lower Austria for several years. Bad harvests and the loss of the wine trade to German merchants contributed to a rancid atmosphere, in which the Jews were, once again, scapegoats.

This time the ruler himself was the instigator of a horrifying pogrom, the Wiener Geserah. In 1420-21, Albrecht stripped Vienna's poorer Jews of their belongings and dispatched them on a raft down the Danube. Richer members of the community were tortured until they revealed where their wealth was hidden, and then burned alive on the Erdberg. Many others opted for mass suicide to escape torture. The centuries-old ghetto by Am Hof was demolished. The reasons for Albrecht's ethnic cleansing have never been fully explained, for it represented a break in the rulers' long tradition of protecting the local Jews, and also removed an important source of ducal finance.

In foreign policy, however, Albrecht V showed the usual Habsburg adroitness. He married the daughter of Emperor Sigismund, and on the latter's death inherited the crown of Hungary. In the same year, 1438, he was also elected Holy Roman Emperor. Excluding a brief

Where the music lived: **Mozarthaus Wien**. *See p20.*

lapse of three years in the 18th century, the Habsburgs would retain this title (protected by bribing the other electors) right up until Napoleon forced its abolition in 1806.

> ## 'Only the heroism of the city's defenders and the early winter saved Vienna.'

Only a year later, though, Albrecht died while fighting the Turks in Hungary. His heir, born after his father's death, was known as Ladislas Posthumus (1440-57). Ladislas's guardian was Friedrich III, of the Leopoldine line, and so the dynasty immediately sank back into its chronic inheritance disputes. Friedrich was crowned Holy Roman Emperor himself in 1452, but his position at home was weak, especially in Vienna. Furious at what they saw as the favouring of other towns by Friedrich, the Viennese merchants forced the release of Ladislas, and declared their loyalty to him. Poor Ladislas died aged only 17 in 1457, whereupon fighting continued between Friedrich and his own brother, Albrecht, the latter supported by the Viennese. This culminated in a seven-week siege of the Hofburg in 1462, when Friedrich was holed up in the castle together with his three-year-old son, the future Maximilian I. He was rescued by the intervention of the Hussite Bohemian king, Jiríz Podebrad, but then had to agree to share power with Albrecht. Only when Albrecht died in 1463 did Friedrich regain control of Vienna.

Friedrich III's ultimate triumph – he effectively ruled for 53 years, dying in 1493 – is often attributed to the fact that he outlived all his rivals, including the much younger Hungarian king Matthias Corvinus, who occupied Vienna from 1485 to 1490. Moreover, the emperor's survival, the extinction of the Albertine line and the removal of the Hungarian threat meant that the way was open to a real concentration and expansion of Habsburg power. Friedrich's son, Maximilian, took up his inheritance at a time of expanding wealth and power, when the seeds of humanist learning planted in Vienna in earlier decades were beginning to bear fruit, amid the pan-European cultural blossoming of the Renaissance.

EMPIRE AND COUNTER-REFORMATION
Maximilian was nicknamed 'the Last Knight', an indication that he lived between two worlds of medieval chivalry and the Renaissance. Possessed of astonishing energy, he performed feats of endurance as a hunter, soldier and athlete. Inspired by the spirit of the

Renaissance, he encouraged the new learning at Innsbruck and Vienna, home to such humanist scholars as Konrad Celtis and Johannes Cuspinianus. The study of pure science, medicine and cartography all began to flourish, although disproportionate attention was dedicated to Habsburg genealogy (the 'House of Austria' was traced back to Noah). In 1498, Maximilian made one of his most memorable contributions to Viennese history when he founded the Hofmusikkapelle, the forerunner of the Vienna Boys' Choir.

Maximilian brought Habsburg marriage diplomacy to its zenith. Through his first wife, Maria of Burgundy, one of the richest territories in Europe (including modern Holland, Belgium and Luxembourg) came under Habsburg control. His son, Philip 'the Fair', married Joanna 'the Mad', daughter of Ferdinand and Isabella of Spain, thus acquiring Castile, Aragon, southern Italy and all the Spanish possessions in the New World for the dynasty. In 1515, Maximilian stood proxy for the marriage of his two young grandchildren to the male and female heirs of the joint throne of Bohemia and Hungary, then ruled by the Jagellonian dynasty. These would also fall to the Habsburgs after the last Jagellonian king, Lajos II, was drowned fleeing the Turks after the disastrous Battle of Mohács, in 1526.

Philip the Fair died before Maximilian, who was thus succeeded by his grandson Karl V, better known in English as Emperor Charles V. On his accession to the imperial throne in 1519, he ruled over an empire 'on which the sun never set' – much too large for one man to direct, and already beset by a stream of problems. The Ottoman advance in south-east Europe seemed unstoppable, and equally ominous, after 1517, was the gathering momentum of the Reformation.

Vienna saw nothing of Karl, who ceded his Austrian possessions to his brother Ferdinand in 1521. The latter was immediately faced with the rapid success of Lutheranism, especially in the towns, coupled in the case of Vienna with demands for more self-government. Ferdinand solved this last difficulty by simply executing Mayor Siebenbürger and six councillors in Wiener Neustadt in 1522, and subjecting the Viennese to absolutist control. He was less successful against the Lutherans and the more radical Anabaptists, despite the punishments meted out to leading Protestants (men were burned at the stake and their wives drowned in the Danube). The increasingly Protestant nobility began to make religious freedom a condition of military assistance against the advancing Turks. Having overrun Hungary, by 1529 the Ottomans were at the gates of Vienna, a vulnerable city

with old-fashioned defences. The morale of Vienna's religiously divided population had been lowered by Ferdinand's vicious rule and a major fire in 1525. Only the heroism of the city's defender, Count Salm, and the early onset of winter prevented Vienna from falling.

The Turks left behind much devastation, but lessons were learned from the siege. Most important was the need to modernise the city's fortifications, which were rebuilt in 1531-66 using the well-proven Italian model of star-shaped bastions. Vienna became a heavily fortified imperial seat, entirely subordinate to the court, but it was also cosmopolitan, as functionaries and petitioners came from all over Europe on imperial business.

HEARTS AND MINDS

From 1551, when Ferdinand summoned the Jesuits to the city, Vienna also became a testing ground for the Counter-Reformation. Evangelisation was led by scholars and preachers such as Peter Canisius, who compiled the catechisms of the Catholic faith to be used in the struggle for hearts and minds in a Vienna that was still 80 per cent Protestant. This struggle was characterised by dogma and paranoia; the Jewish community, which had gradually re-established itself since 1421, was again a convenient target, suffering prohibitions on property owning and trade, as well as the obligation to wear an identifying yellow ring on clothes. This oppressive atmosphere was relaxed a little under Maximilian II (1564-78), who stuck to the letter of the Peace of Augsburg of 1555, which recognised both the Catholic and Lutheran faiths in the Empire, provided that subjects followed the faith of their princes. Lutherans flooded out of Vienna each Sunday to hold services in the chapels of nearby Protestant lords, but as the screw of the Counter-Reformation tightened under Rudolf II (1576-1608) and his brother Matthias, many migrated to more sympathetic parts of Europe.

The dominant figure of the Counter-Reformation in Vienna was Cardinal Khlesl, a Vienna-born convert from Lutheranism, who purged the university of Protestantism, and whose great Klosteroffensive (monastery offensive) led to the second great wave of Catholic foundations in the city (1603-38).

Protestantism was by no means dead among the nobility, however, and as late as 1619 a group of them forced their way into the Hofburg and delivered a list of demands to Ferdinand II (1619-37). The following year saw the defeat of the Bohemian Protestants at the Battle of the White Mountain, the first major engagement of the Thirty Years War (1618-48).

This war and the triumph of Catholicism in southern Germany and Austria would mean the end for Lutheranism in Vienna, even though a Swedish Protestant army threatened the city as late as 1645. In the course of the war, the Jesuits gained control of the university, in 1622, and in 1629 Ferdinand issued his Edict of Restitution, restoring to the Catholic Church 1,555 properties under Protestant control since 1552. In Vienna Protestant laymen were also effectively expropriated by an ingenious catch-22 – only Catholics could become burghers of the city, and only burghers could own property. This was Habsburg religiosity at its most ruthless, with cynical greed and oppression cloaked by a fig leaf of piety.

BAROQUE VIENNA
But this was by no means the only fruit of the Counter-Reformation, for it also produced a great flourishing of the visual arts, architecture, music, drama and literature in the 17th and 18th centuries. Leopold I (1640-1705), known as 'the first baroque emperor', spent lavishly on huge operas and ballets. The gifted could usually expect patronage, whether they came from the Empire or beyond it. Italians long held

Marie Antoinette. See p20.

sway in all the fine arts, music and architecture. Local architects such as Fischer von Erlach and Hildebrandt only came to the fore a generation later – and even they were Italian-trained. The music preferred at court, similarly, was for two centuries Italian-influenced, dominated by a series of Italian composers and librettists from Cesti (1623-69), through Caldara (1670-1736) and Metastasio (1698-1782), to Mozart's great rival Antonio Salieri (1750-1825).

'Nostrils into which three fingers could be stuck'.

Leopold was not an attractive figure: the Turkish traveller Evliya Celebi describes his 'bottle-shaped head', with a nose 'the size of an aubergine from the Morea', displaying 'nostrils into which three fingers could be stuck'. His character was hardly more appealing, even if his deviousness was sometimes dictated by the need to fight wars on two fronts, against the French and the Turks. Educated by bigots, he married an even more bigoted Spanish woman, Margarita Teresa, who blamed her miscarriages on the Jews. In 1669, egged on by Christian Viennese burghers, Leopold ordered a renewed expulsion of the Jews from their settlement on the Unteren Werd. The area was renamed the Leopoldstadt (now Vienna's 2nd district), and Jewish property was given to Christians. Ironically, this district again became a Jewish quarter in the 19th century.

This move so weakened the imperial and city finances, however, that in 1675 the richer Jews had to be invited back. Troubles multiplied with a major outbreak of plague in 1679, whereupon the emperor and nobility scurried off to Prague, leaving the Church authorities to organise relief for the stricken people.

THE SAVING OF CHRISTENDOM
After the plague came the Turks, who besieged Vienna for the second and last time in 1683. The city was rescued only at the last minute, after 62 days, by an army led by Jan Sobieski, king of Poland. Christendom was saved. The Emperor, who had prudently retreated to Passau for the duration, returned to his Residenz to give public, if grudging, acknowledgement to his saviours, and the court artists got to work on bombastic depictions of 'Leopold, the victor over the Turks'.

Leopold's reign lasted 47 years, during which the Empire survived a considerable battering. After an interlude under the promising Joseph I (1705-11), who died of smallpox aged 33, Leopold's younger son Karl became emperor. By this time, the Habsburgs' enemies were in retreat. After a string of victories by Prince Eugène of Savoy, the Peace of Karlowitz of 1699 had restored Hungary, Transylvania and Slavonia to Habsburg rule, and in the War of the Spanish Succession the alliance of Austria, Britain and Holland effectively fought Louis XIV's France to a standstill. Even then, Leopold's duplicitous and cynical treatment of the 'liberated' Magyars managed to provoke a Hungarian war of independence (1704-11) led by Prince Ferenc Rákóczi, whose troops devastated the outskirts of Vienna in 1704.

Afterwards, Prince Eugène advised the erection of a new defensive line, the Linienwall, along the route followed today by Vienna's beltway, the Gürtel. Vienna began to assume the profile it has today, with outlying villages (Vororte) beyond the Gürtel, suburbs (Vorstadt) between the Gürtel and the bastions (replaced by the Ringstrassen in the 19th century), and finally the medieval core of the Altstadt.

After the Hungarian threat had receded, the reign of Karl VI (1711-40) saw a building boom in Vienna: existing churches were Baroque-ised (all 30 Gothic altars of the Stephansdom were replaced) and new Baroque churches were built, notably Hildebrandt's Peterskirche and Fischer von Erlach's Karlskirche. The nobility, with new, undisturbed sources of revenue, were determined to compete with the ruling house, and built magnificent winter and summer palaces – at least 15 between 1685 and 1720, the greatest Hildebrandt's Belvedere, for Prince Eugène. It was a time of triumphalism, bombast and conspicuous consumption by the ruling class and the Church, not balanced by job creation for the rest, although Eugène took care to re-employ his war veterans as labourers and gardeners.

The whey-faced Karl VI showed no interest in the plight of the poor. When he wasn't hunting his energies were spent on efforts to ensure that one of his daughters could inherit the Habsburg throne, despite all the precedents that only permitted male succession. To bolster the position of his eldest daughter, Maria Theresia, he touted a document known as the 'Pragmatic Sanction' round the courts of Europe, where it was politely signed by princes who had not the slightest intention of honouring it.

As soon as Karl died, to general rejoicing in Vienna, the Empire was attacked by Friedrich II of Prussia, who invaded Silesia and launched the War of the Austrian Succession. Encouraged by Friedrich's initial success, Karl Albert of Bavaria then invaded Bohemia, with French support. The situation was saved only by good luck, when Karl Albert died in 1745 and Maria Theresia's husband, Franz Stephan of Lothringen, was elected Holy Roman

Emperor in his place. Another major factor, though, was the remarkable steadfastness of Maria Theresia herself, which so impressed the Hungarian nobles when she appeared before them to seek support in 1741 that they offered their 'life and blood' for their 'King' – since constitutionally she could officially be neither 'Queen' of Hungary nor 'Empress', even though she has often been described as such.

THE AGE OF ABSOLUTISM

Maria Theresia, one of the greatest of the Habsburgs, had one of the most important qualities in a ruler: an ability to choose wise advisers and able administrators. With her support, men like Wenzel von Kaunitz, Friedrich von Haugwitz (a converted Protestant from Saxony), Joseph von Sonnenfels (a converted Jew from Moravia) and Gerard van Swieten (a Dutchman) reformed key elements in the ramshackle machinery of imperial government, including the army. This new approach was labelled 'enlightened absolutism' – although some parts were more enlightened than others: Maria Theresia wouldn't tolerate Jews, unless they converted, and was only with great difficulty persuaded by Sonnenfels that torturing suspects did not contribute to law and order. Motivated perhaps by her Jesuit education, she also introduced a risible Chastity Commission in 1752, which caused Casanova a lot of grief on his visit to Vienna.

Despite such aberrations, Maria Theresia was generally held in affection by the Viennese. She abandoned the stiff Spanish protocol of her forebears and lived relatively informally, if incongruously, in the great Schönbrunn Palace built for her by Nikolaus Pacassi, in emulation of her daughter Marie Antoinette's future home in Versailles. Her encouragement of local manufacturing, the creation of a postal service and even the introduction of house numbering (originally to aid recruiting) were all signs of new thinking. After the death of Franz Stephan in 1765, she ruled jointly with her son, Joseph II (1765-90), who was to take enlightened reforms much further when he ruled alone after her death in 1780.

Joseph had travelled widely and fallen under the influence of the French Enlightenment and even Masonic ideas. His most lasting achievement was his Tolerance Patent of 1781, granting religious freedom to Protestant and Orthodox Christians, followed in 1782 by a more limited Patent for the Jews. In the same year Joseph also dissolved nearly one in five of Austria's monasteries, on the grounds they weren't engaged in activities useful to the state. Also important for Vienna was his foundation of the Allgemeinen Krankenhaus, or

General Hospital, in 1784, and his opening of the imperial picture gallery and parks, such as the Augarten and Prater, to public view.

The age of absolutism had seen the last flourishing of the Baroque style and the transition to a classicism preoccupied with purity of form, although in architecture this did not really emerge until the following century. The change of direction in music was already evident 40 years earlier, in Gluck's ground-breaking 1762 opera *Orfeo*, considered the first opera to subordinate its music to the requirements of the drama, in place of the florid Baroque operas of the Italians. Gluck was followed by the great names of the Wiener Klassik – Haydn (1732-1809) and Mozart (1756-91), who was based in Vienna for the last ten years of his life, which thus coincided almost exactly with the reign of Joseph II. Just as Mozart and Haydn learned from each other, so Ludwig van Beethoven, who lived in Vienna from 1792 to his death in 1827, was influenced by both of them, and in turn had a huge impact on Franz Schubert (1797-1828). This unbroken line of genius, nurtured by the patronage of Austrian aristocrats, the dynasty and the Church, and encouraged by the musical enthusiasm of the Viennese, has not been equalled by any other European city.

NAPOLEON AND BIEDERMEIER

The 19th century began badly for the Habsburg Empire. Joseph's promising successor, Leopold II, died unexpectedly in 1792 after reigning only two years, and was succeeded by his narrow-minded son Franz II (1792-1835). Franz's reactionary views were fuelled by events in France, where his aunt, Marie Antoinette, was executed the year after he ascended the throne. The rise of Napoleon then subjected him to further humiliations, including two occupations of Vienna by French troops (in 1805 and 1809), the enforced marriage of his daughter to the upstart French emperor and finally the bankruptcy of the state.

'The title of Holy Roman Emperor no longer existed.'

The French behaved quite graciously as conquerors (a guard of honour was placed outside Haydn's house as he lay dying, and officers crowded in to hear the première of Beethoven's *Fidelio*), but these setbacks caused the Habsburgs to lose their aura. Conscious of the absurdity of being titular emperor of territories that had been overrun by Napoleon, Franz gave himself the new title of 'Emperor of Austria' in 1804; in 1806, a herald on the balcony of Vienna's Kirche am Hof announced that the title of Holy Roman Emperor, founded by Charlemagne in 800, no longer existed.

Napoleon was eventually defeated in 1814, and the Habsburg capital became the venue for the Congress of Vienna, in which the allied powers – Austria, Prussia, Russia, Britain and many others – thrashed out the frontiers of post-Napoleonic Europe. The shrewd diplomacy of Franz's chancellor, Prince Metternich – as well as the advantage of being hosts – ensured Austria emerged from the wars with dignity intact and a generous territorial settlement.

On the other hand, it now required the repressive apparatus of Metternich's police state to keep the lid on aspirations unleashed in the wake of the French Revolution. Strict censorship meant that even Franz Grillparzer (1791-1872), Austria's greatest dramatist and a Habsburg loyalist to the core, could get into trouble; disrespect for the authorities could be voiced only indirectly, as in the brilliant ad libbing of the comic genius Johann Nestroy (1801-62). Denied any political voice, Viennese burghers were driven into internal exile. They retreated into a world of domesticity, 'in a quiet corner', the characteristic features of the Biedermeier culture (so called after the satirical figure of a solid, middle-class citizen portrayed in a Munich magazine), which predominated from 1814 to 1848.

Painters like Friedrich von Amerling evoked the idealised family life of the bourgeoisie, Ferdinand Raimund conjured an escapist fairy-tale world on the stage and Adalbert Stifter cultivated a quietist philosophy of resignation in his celebrated novel *Indian Summer*. In architecture, Josef Kornhäusel designed neo-classical buildings with a stripped-down, unobtrusive elegance. In music, the revolutionary fervour of Beethoven's *Fidelio* and *Ninth Symphony* gave way to the melodious romanticism of Schubert's introspective *Lieder*.

While such a life was possible for the property-owning and professional class, the burgeoning working-class population of Vienna was at the mercy of the industrial revolution. Overcrowding, unemployment and disease were rife. A cholera epidemic in 1831-32 prompted some remedial measures, but not before typhoid fever from infected water had claimed the life of Schubert, in 1828. Meanwhile, the population of Vienna exploded by 40 per cent between the beginning of the century and 1835, to reach 330,000. Many of the new migrants were former peasants, who had been driven off the land and were searching for work.

The desperation of the famine-stricken working class and the frustrations of the politically impotent middle class erupted in the Revolution of March 1848. At first it seemed as if the old order was doomed: almost the whole Empire was in revolt, the hated Metternich had to flee Vienna and the simple-minded Ferdinand I, who had succeeded Franz in 1835, was forced to concede a new constitution and lift censorship. In Vienna, a provisional city council was set up, freeing the burghers from noble control, and a Civil Guard recruited from local citizens was formed, with the grudging consent of the authorities.

As elsewhere in Europe, in this tumultuous year of revolutions, it was the army that put an end to the uprisings. The great Marshal Radetzky won major victories in northern Italy; the Croatian general Jellacic moved against Hungary (helped by the intervention of Russian troops); and Marshal Windischgraetz subdued Vienna. Habsburg authority seemed to have been restored, but not all the Revolution's achievements could be rescinded: serfdom was abolished throughout the Empire forever, and the mere existence of liberal constitutions, however briefly they had been in force, supplied a new theoretical basis for discussion.

FRANZ JOSEF

Ferdinand abdicated and was succeeded by his 18-year-old nephew Franz Josef I (1848-1916). He began his reign with the executions and repression of former revolutionaries. Yet, by the end of his 68-year rule, he had presided over a gradual emancipation of his people. By 1900, the seemingly anachronistic Habsburg monarchy was in practice no more oppressive than most western European states. In 1867, he approved the *Ausgleich*, or 'Compromise', with Hungary, granting it equal rights in a new 'Dual Monarchy', to be called Austria-Hungary. Universal adult male suffrage was introduced in 1907, earlier than in Britain. What couldn't be controlled, however, were the forces of nationalism, which eventually tore the multi-ethnic empire apart, plunging Europe into war.

For Vienna, Franz Josef's most significant measures were the demolition of the old city bastions in 1857 and the approval of a plan for the area beyond them to be occupied by a magnificent boulevard, the Ringstrasse, on the Parisian model of Baron Hausmann. A symbol of burgeoning civil society, the Ring was to be lined with imposing public buildings, each built in a historicist style symbolic of its function. This great project, which took shape over some 26 years, was to be completed with an 'Imperial Forum' linking the last part of the Hofburg to be built (the Neue Burg) with the neighbouring museums. This was never carried out, but the Ring, with its new museums, city hall, opera,

Adele Bloch-Bauer by Gustav Klimt. *See p23.*

theatres and stock exchange, transformed Vienna into a modern metropolis.

Much of the finance for this reconstruction came from the high bourgeoisie, whose tastes in the arts were conservative. The most generous patronage was given to Hans Makart, who painted overblown historical canvases. Statues of Habsburg rulers and generals peppered the city. The burghers' preference for the now-entrenched musical tradition of the late Wiener Klassik was satisfied by Johannes Brahms, who lived in Vienna from 1878 until his death in 1897. In contrast, Anton Bruckner was subjected to abuse and even ridicule by the critical establishment in Vienna.

The decades from 1860 to 1900 make up the so-called *Gründerzeit*, or 'Founders' Period' (also called the *Ringstrassen* era), and saw the construction of a modern state, economy and society. The administration of Vienna was dominated from 1861 by the liberal bourgeoisie, with money made in industrial development, property speculation and banking. The Liberal City Council, elected by a narrow suffrage of only 3.3 per cent of Vienna's 550,000 inhabitants, followed its own interests, but for a while these coincided in many respects with those of most citizens. Huge infrastructure investment resulted in an improved water

Freedom Party (FPö) poster. *See p26.*

supply, new bridges across the Danube and the much-needed channelling of the river itself. In 1870, Vienna acquired its first trams.

Unbridled capitalism had, of course, its downside. In the catastrophic year of 1873, the stock market crashed, and many financiers were ruined; some committed suicide. The death toll among businesses was equally dramatic, as 60 companies, 48 banks and eight insurance societies went bust. The crisis ensured that Vienna's World Exhibition of that year was a financial disaster, worsened by an outbreak of cholera. For Vienna's Liberals, it was 'never glad confident morning again'. The catastrophe of 1881, when the Ringtheater burned down killing 386 people, was almost the final straw. Felder's successor was held responsible and had to resign.

FIN DE SIÈCLE AND END OF EMPIRE

Turn-of-the-century Vienna has become almost a cliché of sensuality, eroticism and overripe aestheticism. It generated some of the most contrasting movements of the modern era, including militant anti-semitism and Zionism. It also produced psychoanalysis, and several of the greatest masters of early modernism.

A new star rose in city politics in the 1880s, a renegade Liberal called Karl Lueger, who founded his own Christian Social party and consolidated a power base by exposing

corruption (of which there was plenty) and stirring up anti-semitism in a vicious scapegoating of Jews (the dark thread running through Viennese history). Many of the wealthy Liberal magnates were Jewish, and Lueger adroitly focused popular resentment upon them.

His support was boosted by the extension of the franchise to those who paid only five Gulden in taxes, in 1885, and the incorporation of the peripheral settlements (Vororte) into the city in 1892. Vienna more than tripled its area and increased its population by over half a million, to 1,364,000. Immigrants poured into the city (especially Czechs, and Jews from the east), another factor in creating a climate beneficial to Lueger's politics. 'Handsome Karl' was a shrewd populist and gifted administrator, who understood how to turn the envy and discontent of Vienna's petit bourgeoisie to his advantage. The young Adolf Hitler, living in Viennese doss-houses in the 1900s, greatly admired him. Franz Josef, though, did not. Lueger's faction won a majority on the City Council in 1895, but his election as mayor was vetoed three times by the emperor, who among other things feared a flight of Jewish capital. The emperor, however, had to cede in 1897, and Lueger remained in office until 1910.

'The dance became emblematic of hedonistic escapism.'

Lueger was strongly supported by the lesser Catholic clergy, although the more senior churchmen denounced his radical and anti-semitic views in 1895. Pope Leo XIII, however, upheld Lueger's claim that he was merely adhering to the social doctrines of the Church, and that his objections to Jews were doctrinal, not racial. Papal support was decisive, and the Viennese hierarchy gradually backed him. Lueger's policies may be influencing the world indirectly even today: just as the Christian Social majority was being established in the city, the Budapest-born Viennese journalist Theodor Herzl published the first Zionist agenda, *Der Judenstaat* (1896), arguing that the persistence of anti-semitism in central Europe showed that Jews, however assimilated, could not be safe without their own state. This was received with incomprehension and even anger by the highly assimilated Viennese Jewish establishment, but it began the process that led to the foundation of Israel.

In contrast to social tensions, the emollient side of the pleasure-loving Viennese of the 19th century was revealed in the general passion for theatre and music, which made possible the astonishing careers of musicians such as Josef Lanner and the Strauss dynasty. The Viennese waltz was a commercialised and refined version of folk dances, chiefly the *Ländler* of Upper Austria. The dance became emblematic of hedonistic escapism. Its critics pointed out that the Viennese were too busy waltzing to heed the news of the catastrophic defeat of the Habsburg army by the Prussians at Königgrätz (Sadowa) in 1866, a defeat that marked the beginning of the end for the Habsburg Empire.

Even more censorious things were said about the craze for operetta, which began with an Offenbach-influenced work by Franz von Suppé (*Das Pensionat*, 1860) and continued into the 20th century (its last major figure, Robert Stolz, died in 1975).

In the 1890s, Vienna and its peculiar atmosphere generated several new trends. The Secession movement displayed a galaxy of talent. One of the most important figures was the architect Otto Wagner, who departed from the ponderous historicism of his youth to create early-modernist buildings of great functional integrity. A trenchant critic of Wagner, Adolf Loos, rejected Secessionist ornamentation and carried the idea of functionalism still further. The artist Gustav Klimt broke existing taboos to produce masterpieces of sensual eroticism, combined with a pessimistic emphasis on the inevitability of death, a preoccupation he shared with the next generation of expressionists, such as Egon Schiele. Gustav Mahler took over the Imperial Opera and swept away generations of shibboleths he described as *Schlamperei* (sloppiness), to the indignation of the players. The most successful playwright was Arthur Schnitzler, whose bleak depictions of sexual exploitation, societal cynicism and personal trauma were admired by Freud.

Freud's own *Interpretation of Dreams* appeared in 1900, causing not a ripple. His novel treatment for 'hysteria' and new-fangled technique of hypnosis were viewed with indifference or suspicion by colleagues in the medical establishment. The author Karl Kraus wrote that 'psychoanalysis is the disease of which it purports to be the cure'. Kraus edited the journal *Die Fackel* (The Torch), which became an effective counterblast to the belligerent mood that overtook the city after the Empire slithered into war in 1914. Many other modernist writers, such as Hermann Bahr (the self-publicising leader of the Jung Wien literary circle), became ranting war propagandists.

WAR AND 'RED VIENNA'

The assassination of the heir apparent, Archduke Franz Ferdinand, lit the fuse that led to war, and the old emperor, Franz Josef, finally died in 1916. Franz Josef's inexperienced great-nephew Karl I (1916-22) took over the throne, but was unable to end the war on honourable terms. This sealed his fate, and he went into exile in March 1919. World War I killed off the coffee house milieu of turn-of-the-century Vienna, in which Bahr and Kraus had flourished. The brilliant *feuilletons* (meandering cultural essays) perused over coffee, the interminable feuds, the narcissism, the head waiters who acted as unpaid secretaries, the unpaid bills – in short, the whole Bohemian existence seemed anachronistic after Austria and her allies lost the war and the Empire was dismembered in 1918-19.

Vienna's situation was desperate. Deprived of its empire, it had become a *Wasserkopf*, a diseased 'hydrocephalus', in a state reduced from over 50 million to three million people overnight. One-third of the population was in Vienna, including thousands of bureaucrats, many of whose jobs no longer existed, plus unemployed refugees and ex-soldiers. A 'Republic of German Austria' (Deutschösterreich) was proclaimed on 12 November 1918. The name reflected the desire of most Austrians – of all political parties – for an *Anschluss*, or union, with Germany. This proposal, though, was firmly rejected by the Allies, who had not fought a war so that Germany could actually increase in size. So the First Austrian Republic began its peculiarly unwanted existence.

In 1919, the Social Democrats swept to power in the Vienna City Council. The party had been founded in 1889 by Viktor Adler, a Jewish doctor with a strong social conscience, and rapidly expanded its support among workers living in horrific conditions. By 1900, the socialists were able to win 43 per cent of the votes in local elections, although the absurdly discriminatory electoral system gave them only two seats on the City Council. After the war, though, the party's moment finally came. Adler died in the flu epidemic of 1918, but he and gifted Marxist theoreticians such as Otto Bauer had laid the foundation for the period known as *Rotes Wien* (Red Vienna), which followed. It was the first example in the world of a city administered by socialists.

A major difficulty was that Vienna was still officially part of Lower Austria, which was conservative dominated. This mismatch was resolved in 1922, when Vienna became a *Bundesland* (Federal Province) in its own right. The Social Democrats were able to embark on one of the most intensive programmes of housing, welfare and cultural initiatives ever seen in Europe (*see p112* **Monolithic city**).

The City Council's socialist measures and uncompromising *Kulturkampf* (cultural

struggle) with the Church was decisive in the growing polarisation between socialist Austria (principally Vienna) and conservative Catholic Austria (much of the countryside). For most of the 1920s, power was held at national level by a Christian Social government led by a priest, Ignaz Seipel. His greatest achievement was rescuing the country from the disastrous bout of hyper-inflation in 1922, but differences between right and left widened inexorably during his rule. Both sides had their own militias (the conservative Heimwehr and socialist Schutzbund), and a crisis occurred in 1927 when a conservative jury acquitted Heimwehr soldiers who had shot and killed members of the Schutzbund. A mob burned down the Palace of Justice, ignoring pleas for restraint from socialist leaders. Matters worsened as the world economic crisis deepened post-1929 and unemployment rose.

Tensions climaxed in a brief civil war in 1934, in which the relatively well-armed forces of the right easily overcame the socialist militias. During the fighting, the huge Karl-Marx-Hof housing block, a bastion of red support, was shelled into submission. Authoritarian rule was then imposed on Austria, and Vienna's administrative independence was terminated by the regime of Engelbert Dollfuss, a peculiar mix of extreme reactionary Catholicism and home-grown fascism.

THE ANSCHLUSS AND WORLD WAR II

In 1933, Hitler came to power in Germany. Soon he began a drive to increase his influence in the land of his birth, Austria. Shortly after the civil war, the Nazis attempted a coup d'état in Vienna, killing Chancellor Dollfuss. Though an extreme right-winger, he had not been ready to follow Hitler's orders. Dollfuss's successor, Kurt Schuschnigg, soon found himself under pressure from Hitler and local Nazis to accept the *Anschluss* of Austria to the German Reich (the 'Greater Germany' solution most Austrians had wanted at the end of World War I). Schuschnigg tried to rally support by calling a referendum on Austrian independence for 13 March 1938. In order to pre-empt this (which would almost certainly have endorsed independence), German troops crossed the border at dawn on 12 March.

In Vienna the Nazis set about turning the lives of their opponents and the Jews into an inferno. Hitler was ecstatically received when he addressed a crowd of 200,000 in Heldenplatz. The Church hastened to accommodate him – Cardinal-Archbishop Innitzer gave a Nazi salute on his way to meet the Führer and urged the faithful to vote for the *Anschluss* in the subsequent Nazi plebiscite (when he later had second thoughts, Nazi thugs trashed his residence). Soon after the onset of Nazi rule, Jews throughout the Reich were terrorised

during the *Reichskristallnacht* of 9 November 1938. In Vienna the operation lasted several days, with mobs attacking Jews, destroying and stealing their property, and burning down 42 synagogues. Adolf Eichmann (who, like many of the most virulently anti-semitic Nazis, was Austrian-born) opened an office on Prinz Eugen Strasse, where Jews were 'processed': those with sufficient resources could buy their freedom; the rest were sent to the concentration camps. Some 120,000 Jews emigrated, while 60,000 were either to be executed or to die through forced labour. Leading non-Jewish opponents of the Nazis were also interned in camps. On 1 April 1938, the first batch of prominent Austrian politicians (including Leopold Figl) left for Dachau.

More than 30 concentration camps were built in Austria, the most notorious being Mauthausen, on the Danube east of Linz. Between 1938 and 1945, 35,318 out of 197,000 prisoners were executed or worked to death here, quarrying stone for Hitler's project to convert his boyhood hometown, Linz, into the capital of the Reich. Mauthausen is now a memorial (www.mauthausen-memorial.at).

As the catastrophe of World War II unfolded, a kernel of resistance appeared in Vienna, partly spurred by the Allies' 1943 Moscow declaration that Austria's status at the end of the war would depend on her willingness to

rebel. This was the origin of the notion of Austria as 'Hitler's first victim', rather than an equal participant in Nazism: one that remains valid for many Austrians even today.

Lying far to the east, quite a lot of war industry was moved to the Vienna area. This proved fateful, after 7 March 1944, when the Allied bombers could reach the city from Italy. In one air raid, over 400 people died in the cellars of an apartment building behind the Opera. They were never exhumed, and a monument, Against War and Fascism, was erected on the site in 1988.

In spring 1945, the Soviet army took the already devastated city after fierce fighting: 8,769 deaths were caused by Allied bombing and 2,226 from fighting on the ground; 1,184 resistance fighters had been executed, 9,687 died in Gestapo prisons; 36,851 apartments had been destroyed and thousands of other buildings damaged. Over 50,000 Viennese Jews had been slaughtered by the Nazi regime, and a quarter of a million Austrians had died in German uniform.

While some of these statistics might fuel the idea of Austrian 'victimhood', the notion was also politically convenient for the occupying powers as they sought to detach Austria from Germany. The Soviets initially refused to accept Austrian independence until the German question had been tackled. The process was accelerated after Stalin's death and agreement was formally reached with the signing of the *Staatsvertrag* (Austrian State Treaty) in 1955. Based on the principle of permanent Austrian neutrality and covertly on the 'victim' thesis, the treaty ensured that 'de-nazification' in Austria only stigmatised the most prominent Nazis, allowing huge numbers of passive, opportunistic or enthusiastic participants in Hitler's regime to present themselves as mere patriots. Unlike in Germany, this failure to address the reality of the Nazi era created an identity crisis that has returned to haunt post-war Austrian politics and, to some extent, still persists today.

POST-WAR AUSTRIA

Austria therefore became the only European country occupied by the Soviets to regain full independence after 1945. The Staatsvertrag restored Austrian sovereignty by papering over internal political differences, in response to a widespread desire for stability in the post-war period. This was achieved by the establishment of a system known as Proporz, whereby political power was effectively shared out by the two main parties – the conservative People's Party (ÖVP) and the Socialists (SPÖ) – and the various interest groups that were represented by the corresponding Chamber of Commerce and Chamber of Labour.

Supported by UN aid and the Marshall Plan, Austrians displayed great resourcefulness in rebuilding their shattered country – especially considering that the Soviets had dismantled most of Austria's industry and shipped it eastwards as war reparations. The rebuilding of Vienna's burned-out Stephansdom was complete by 1952, and by 1955 both the Burgtheater and the Staatsoper reopened. With cultural renewal, self-irony occasionally reared its head, notably Helmut Qualtinger's brilliant satirical portrait of the typical Viennese petit-bourgeois opportunist, 'Herr Karl', who joined the Nazis for the free sandwiches and beer. Conspicuously absent were the leading lights of pre-war Vienna's literature, stage and music – most of whom had been Jews.

'The Soviets dismantled most of Austria's industry and shipped it eastwards.'

Consensus politics were certainly effective in the reconstruction of Austria, which became, according to Eric Hobsbawm, 'a sort of second Switzerland – a small country committed to neutrality, envied for its persistent prosperity and therefore described (correctly) as "boring"'.

Vienna voted consistently for Social Democrat mayors, and in 1970 the national government itself became socialist under the charismatic if imprudent Bruno Kreisky, chancellor until 1983. It was his achievement that Vienna became a third seat of the United Nations. The city had already hosted the Atomic Energy Commission since 1956, and was to add OPEC (1965) and the monitoring commission for the Helsinki Agreements (OSCE) to its portfolio. This much sought-after world profile also made Vienna a target: the OPEC building was stormed by Arab terrorists in 1975, Palestinian terrorists murdered a city councillor and launched a grenade attack on the Vienna synagogue in 1981, and in 1985 there was a bloody attack on the El Al desk at Schwechat Airport.

In the 1980s, Vienna gradually shed its dour Ostbloc aura and credit for the outward signs of this – renovation of façades, the sprouting of pavement cafés and a rejuvenation of cultural life – was due to the election of new-broom Mayor Helmut Zilk in 1984. However, with the election of Kurt Waldheim as president in 1986, the first cracks appeared in Austria's cosy post-war political cohabitation. Waldheim's impeccable international profile – secretary-general of the UN from 1972 to 1982 – was

dynamited by revelations that he had omitted details of his Wehrmacht service in the Balkans and Salonika, Greece. With the world's media on his trail, Waldheim denied knowledge of Nazi atrocities against Yugoslav partisans and the deportation of Greek Jews, claiming he had been on leave. Austrian voters refused to be swayed by international pressure and duly voted him president. Despite the collateral damage (the US put Waldheim on its 'watch list' of undesirable aliens), the affair rekindled debate on the Nazi period in Austria and reached fever pitch with the arrival of maverick German theatre director Claus Peymann at the Burgtheater in 1986. His feisty productions of plays by Thomas Bernhard scandalised audiences with their taboo-breaking emphasis on Austrian complicity during World War II.

Long-awaited gestures of reconciliation with Vienna's Jewish community also emerged with the opening of a Jewish Museum in 1993, although important issues relating to the restitution of Jewish property were not addressed until 2002, when the findings of the Historians' Commission were published.

EU MEMBERSHIP, BOYCOTT AND THE PRESENT

The fall of the Iron Curtain in 1989 and Austria's entry into the EU in 1995 brought new challenges, and new conflicts. Fears of foreign meddling were exploited by the Freedom Party (FPÖ) of right-wing populist Jörg Haider, which in 1999 ran a virulently xenophobic campaign to poll an astonishing 27.2 per cent of the vote. When ÖVP leader Wolfgang Schüssel announced a coalition with Haider, it led to massive protests and finally widespread international condemnation, culminating in an EU boycott of the new government. Constant infighting led to early elections in 2002 and the FPÖ vote sank to ten per cent, provoking Haider's retreat into regional politics. The coalition resumed but following the formation of a new party by the Haider-wing of the FPÖ, the Alliance for the Future of Austria (BZÖ), the government was in the unprecedented position of having ministers that belonged to a party that had never been formally elected. In October 2006, despite the scandal surrounding the near collapse of a bank belonging to the Austrian unions, the SPÖ achieved a surprising narrow victory. Haider's BZÖ barely maintained a parliamentary presence and the FPÖ, narrowly pushed into fourth position by the Greens, proved that there was still an audience for xenophobic demagogy. After months of negotiations, the habitual SPÖ-ÖVP grand coalition was revived, with social democrat Alfred Gusenbauer as chancellor.

Key events

AD 8 Vindobona becomes part of the Roman province of Pannonia.
212 The civil settlement at Vindobona is raised to the rank of Municipium.
881 'Wenia' appears in the Salzburg annals.
996 First occurrence of the name Ostarrichi (Austria) in an imperial document.
1298 Albrecht I is the first Habsburg to be elected Holy Roman Emperor.
1338-49 Vienna hit by disasters: locust swarms, plague and fire.
1420-21 The Wiener Geserah: the first notorious pogrom against the Jews.
1529 First Turkish siege of Vienna.
1551 The Jesuits are summoned to Vienna. The Counter-Reformation begins.
1577 Protestant worship forbidden in Vienna.
1658-1705 Rule of the 'first baroque emperor', Leopold I.
1669 Second expulsion of Jews from Vienna.
1679 Plague in Vienna.
1683 Second Turkish siege of Vienna.
1704-11 Hungarian War of Independence against Habsburg hegemony.
1740-80 Maria Theresia reforms government, education, law and the army. The age of enlightened absolutism.
1781 Tolerance Patent offers toleration to non-Catholic faiths and later (1782) to Jews.
1780-91 Mozart in Vienna.
1805 & 1809 Vienna occupied by Napoleonic troops.
1814-15 Congress of Vienna settles post-war map of Europe.
1848 Revolution all over the Empire.
1848-49 Franz Josef I becomes Emperor. Defeat of the revolution.
1857 Demolition of city bastions. Building of the Ringstrassen boulevard begins.
1860-1900 Founders' Period (*Gründerzeit*). Liberal political hegemony, industrial expansion.
1861 Liberals take over city hall. Infrastructure investment by Mayor Cajetan Felder (1868-78).
1866 Austrian defeat by the Prussians at Königgrätz (Sadowa).
1870 Vienna Tramway Company set up.
1873 World Exhibition in Vienna. Cholera outbreak. Stock market crashes.
1881 Ringtheater burns down.
1888-89 Viktor Adler founds the Social Democratic Party.

1897-1910 Karl Lueger's term as Mayor of Vienna. Communalisation of public services, anti-semitic populist politics.
1889 Crown Prince Rudolf commits suicide.
1898 The Vienna Secession is founded.
1900 Freud's *Interpretation of Dreams* published.
1914 Franz Ferdinand assassinated.
1914-18 World War I.
1916 Death of Franz Josef I.
12 Nov 1918 Proclamation of the Republic of 'Deutschösterreich'.
March 1919 Franz Josef's successor, Karl I, resigns and leaves the country.
May 1919 Social Democrats take power in Vienna City Council. Period of 'Red Vienna'.
1919 Treaty of St Germain fixes the new borders of Austria, shorn of her Empire.
1922 The Christian Social Chancellor, Ignaz Seipel, rescues the country from hyper-inflation by means of foreign credits.
1927 The Palace of Justice is burned down.
1934 'Civil War' between Catholic Conservative government forces and the Social Democrats ends in victory for the Conservatives and the founding of the Fatherland Front. Attempted Nazi *putsch*. Assassination of Chancellor Dollfuss.
1938 *Anschluss* with Hitler's Reich. Hitler welcomed in Vienna by jubilant crowds.
9 Nov 1938 Reichskristallnacht – Jewish properties burned and looted, Jews beaten.
1939-45 World War II.
1945-55 Occupation by the Allies. Vienna under four-power control.
1955 Austrian State Treaty liberates the country, which becomes neutral.
1965 OPEC offices located in Vienna.
1970 Social Democrats take power under Bruno Kreisky, who is chancellor until 1983.
1981 Vienna becomes the third seat of UNO.
1984 Helmut Zilk becomes Mayor of Vienna.
1989 Fall of the Iron Curtain.
1995 Austria joins the European Union.
2000 Formation of controversial ÖVP/FPÖ coalition means EU sanctions against Austria.
2003 Start of a new ÖVP-FPÖ coalition.
2004 Following the death of Thomas Klestil, Heinz Fischer elected President of Austria.
2006 Social Democrats narrowly win the elections.
2007 An SPÖ-ÖVP coalition is formed with Social Democrat Alfred Gusenbauer as chancellor.

Haas Haus. *See p56.*

Vienna Today

Prosperous and plural.

In 2006 the appalling odyssey of schoolgirl Natascha Kampusch briefly put Vienna on the world stage. She was kidnapped as an eight-year old in 1998 and held prisoner for eight years in the basement of a house in Vienna's northern suburbs until she managed to flee her captor Wolfgang Priklopil and alert help (Priklopil killed himself within hours of her escape). This woeful tale did little to change the common perception of Vienna as a city with a gloomy, navel-gazing disposition, the cradle of investigation into humanity's darkest, most inexplicable motives. Another of Vienna's traumas – its uneasy relationship with the events of Nazi rule and World War II – was partially exorcised in June 2007 with the death of former President Kurt Waldheim. His candidacy for the presidency in 1986, after he was exposed for glossing over his wartime activities in the Wehrmacht during the Nazis' Balkan campaign, unleashed a controversy

that became a watershed in the history of post-war Austria. The 'Waldheim Affair' usefully subjected the convenient thesis of Austrian victimhood to intense public debate and eventually led to Chancellor Vranitzky's public declaration of collective guilt in 1991. While the authorities unanimously praised Waldheim as a major political figure of his era, others were not quite so respectful. Within hours of the news of his death, internet forums on quality daily *Der Standard*'s website were closed due to the 'merciless' nature of the postings.

While few of its inhabitants would dispute the Viennese reputation for melancholy, short tempers and a pathological culture of complaint, there are signs that the city is becoming a more open, communicative and, dare we say, happier place. After all, Vienna is the capital of the fourth richest economy in the EU. Year after year, it is commended in surveys by Mercer Consulting and the

Economist Intelligence Unit as the third most liveable city in the world after Zürich and Geneva. It shares with its Swiss neighbours enviably high standards in education, health care, public transport and safety, but unlike them, it has a vibrant, ever-expanding cultural scene, hands-on political activism, and excellent eating and drinking. The Viennese are also intensely attached to their leisure time – don't try calling an office after 2pm on Friday – and are spoiled with excellent facilities and acres of open space. In addition to traditional pastimes such as skiing, hiking and nude bathing, chances are the average Viennese will be cultivating the tattooed and pierced body beautiful at the local gym or solarium. Other signs that the Viennese are lightening up include the relatively recent interest in the the global cult of wealth and celebrity. The traditionally sober national press has a shrill new tabloid – *Oesterreich* – that closely documents the activities of Austria's first modern celebrity couple: floppy-haired former finance minister Karl-Heinz Grasser and Fiona Swarowski, heir to the jewellery and glass animal empire. Mr 'zero deficit' was happy to expose his nipples beneath a dinner jacket in a photo shoot for Italian *Vogue*, yet went on to sue Condé Nast when the photos resurfaced in a German-language sister publication.

Of its approximately 1,600,000 inhabitants, 30 per cent are first to third generation immigrants and 18.8 per cent are not Austrian citizens. An increasing number of these come from bordering EU states such as Germany and Austrians can barely disguise their glee when being served by a waiter from what used to be their all-powerful neighbour. However, immigration is no laughing matter as the Austrians discovered in 2000. The announcement of a coalition government between the conservative People's Party (ÖVP) and Jörg Haider's right-wing anti-foreigner Freedom Party (FPÖ) led to an EU diplomatic boycott of Austria. Since then Haider has retreated to govern the southern province of Carinthia and split the FPÖ by forming a new party, the Alliance for the Future of Austria (BZÖ). Although the latter almost disappeared from the political map in the 2006 general elections, the FPÖ and its new leader HC Strache still managed to poll 11 per cent. Strache's campaign was strongly reminiscent of Haider's worst excesses, using slogans such as *Daham statt Islam* (Viennese dialect for 'the homeland rather than Islam'). Later photos were published showing a youthful Strache giving a three-fingered neo-Nazi salute – he claimed he was ordering three beers.

The minor miracle of the 2006 elections however was the narrow victory of the Social Democrats (SPÖ). Despite the outgoing government's internationally-lauded economic record and the scandal surrounding the near-collapse of the BAWAG, a bank owned by the labour movement ('Penthouse socialism' was hailed the expression of 2006 by a weekly news magazine), Alfred Gusenbauer became the first SPÖ Chancellor of the new millennium. Forced into a new coalition with the ÖVP, Gusenbauer proceeded to hand the conservatives the major ministries on a plate and formed what must be one of the most eccentric governments in Austrian history. It includes a Minister of Defence who was a conscientious objector and a health minister who modelled at the 2007 Life Ball and revealed to the press that she enjoys a Schweinsbraten and that 'not so long ago' she'd had a few drinks too many. Gusenbauer himself gives school children extra classes two evenings a week to justify his proposal that students should do the same in return for grants. After little more than six months, the coalition looks extremely shaky. Consensus is sorely lacking and issues such as the parliamentary investigation into the purchase of Eurofighter jets provoke intense mud-slinging. The proposed smoking ban and other smaller fry are forever being delayed, so you should be able to smoke with impunity in Vienna until at least January 2008.

'To diffuse the Karlsplatz drug scene, classical music was piped through the area's subways.'

The streets of Vienna have never looked so ethnically mixed. Polish grocers, Russian restaurants and Balkan music clubs are firmly established, attesting to a human influx which will take Vienna's population over the two million mark by 2030, 28 per cent of whom will be from outside Austria. Economist Alexander van der Bellen, the soft-spoken leader of the Greens, believes Austria needs 30,000 new immigrants per year to stave off economic decline, while voices within the FPÖ and, more worryingly, in the ÖVP are talking about a complete stop to immigration. While the parties remain profoundly divided on this issue, the situation for 'illegal' immigrants and asylum seekers, particularly from sub-Saharan Africa and former Soviet Republics such as Chechnya is grave. Austria has Europe's toughest laws on asylum and

Celebrate and enjoy at the heart of Vienna

Located in the heart of Vienna right at the Ringstraße, opposite to the Burgtheater,
the Vienna Rathauskeller (town hall cellar) offers the perfect ambience for a culinary
journey to the traditional Austrian cuisine.

foreigners' rights and Amnesty International and others constantly chide the authorities for not observing international standards and for rough treatment in police custody. Many asylum seekers are either destitute or rely entirely on NGOs such as the Catholic Church and its agencies, or heroic campaigners like Ute Bock, a retired social worker whose tireless efforts on behalf of undocumented foreigners earned her the UNHCR prize for work with refugees in 2000.

Vienna's police force is currently facing a crisis of authority. In the last year, no fewer than three leading police officers have either resigned or been sacked over allegations of accepting underworld favours. This power vacuum at the top is causing resentment among the undermanned lower ranks, many of whom have been waiting years for transfers back to the provinces. Heavy-handed policing is undeniably the *plat du jour* in Vienna – ranging from serious beatings of foreigners to more anecdotal incidents such as the arrest and roughing up of a journalist from *Der Spiegel* for jumping a red light on her bicycle. Ahead of Euro 2008, visitors are advised to approach the local bobbies with extreme care.

Nor are football fans likely to get a warm welcome from Ursula Stenzel, head of the 1st district council. This former newsreader and ÖVP Euro MP is dead against plans to locate a 'fan-mile' on her turf during the championship. Stenzel's crusade to reclaim the Innere Stadt for its residents includes removing Christmas punch stands from Stephansplatz, calls for a ban on public alcohol consumption, resident-only access to the city's parks and even wanting to eject the *Fiaker* horses because of the damage they do to the city's cobbles. One of her contributions to diffusing the Karlsplatz drug scene consists of piping classical music through the area's subways.

Not surprisingly, Vienna's electorate have never voted in a council run by Stenzel's party. Vienna has been governed uninterruptedly by the SPÖ since 1919 (except for the 1934-45 hiatus). They have an outright majority in the city hall and control 16 of Vienna's 23 districts. The remaining seven are divided between the ÖVP with five and the Greens, who increased their tally to two after taking the genteel 8th district from the ÖVP in 2005. Now in his second term, Mayor Michael Häupl (nicknamed *Fiaker* for his resemblance to Vienna's ruddy-faced carriage drivers) is a portly, straight-talking figure who is enormously influential at national level since the mayor is also the governor of the federal region of Vienna. With a long interventionist tradition in social policy symbolised by a commitment to public housing

and rent control, today the SPÖ promotes ambitious schemes that foresee a new central railway station for Vienna and the construction of whole new districts such as the Aspern airfield project over the Danube and corresponding underground connections. With the SPÖ back in parliament, it seems likely that Vienna will find it easier to obtain the investment necessary for this infrastructure. Furthermore, the growing influence of the Greens on the council is steering the SPÖ towards making greater efforts to integrate Vienna's foreign communities. This they hope to achieve by encouraging kindergarten attendance and offering women language courses (*Mama lernt deutsch*) at their children's schools or playgroups. The theme of gender inequalities was given a public profile with the introduction of female pictograms in public signposting. Although tougher Green proposals such as a London-style car tax get the thumbs-down from the voter-conscious SPÖ, the Greens are doing a good job of keeping the Reds on their toes. Nevertheless, anyone doubting popular support for the SPÖ should try to be in Vienna for 1 May when marches from every district descend on the City Hall in a show of fervent red flag waving before drifting off to the Prater for an afternoon of fraternal beer and sausages.

Donau City. *See p88.*

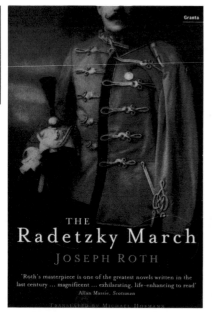

THE
Radetzky March
JOSEPH ROTH

'Roth's masterpiece is one of the greatest novels written in the last century ... magnificent ... exhilarating, life-enhancing to read'
Allan Massie, *Scotsman*

TRANSLATED BY MICHAEL HOFMANN

JOSEPH ROTH
Translated by Michael Hofmann

'Joseph Roth is counted among the great novelists of the twentieth century' *Times Literary Supplement*

Literary Vienna

Unhappily ever after.

The roots of modern Austrian literature can be traced back to Franz Grillparzer. He was, if you are feeling generous, the Shakespeare of Austria. Born in 1791 in Bauernmarkt, in old Vienna, when the city was the cultural capital of the German-speaking world, by the time he died in 1872 the Empire was already in decline. Grillparzer's celebrated 'Shakespearean' feel for tragedy was inspired not just by those turbulent times, but by his own family life. His youngest brother and mother both killed themselves, and he had a long-standing and difficult affair with his cousin's wife, before moving on to fall in love with a 15-year-old girl.

Towards the end of the 19th century, literature fed even more hungrily on the atmosphere of intoxication and melancholy that was intrinsic to the final apocalyptic spurt of the Habsburg Empire. Georg Trakl (1887-1914) has the dubious honour of being one of the unhappiest poets of this time. He was a hypersensitive alcoholic outsider, with frequent moods of 'frantic intoxication and criminal melancholy'. His training as a pharmacist offered him optimum access to drugs, and the advantage he took of this was clearly reflected in his work. A tortured sexual relationship with his sister ('the thousand devils whose thorns drive the flesh frantic') didn't help. He died of a cocaine overdose in 1914. His sister shot herself a few years later. Trakl is notoriously difficult to translate, but he was greatly admired by his contemporaries, such as the great philosopher Ludwig Wittgenstein (1889-1951), who supported him for a time and hailed him a genius.

Another colourful Viennese character was the precocious Hugo von Hofmannsthal (1874-1929), already feted in Viennese intellectual circles at the age of 16. He gave up poetry following a premature midlife crisis, and ended up writing libretti for Richard Strauss. Hofmannsthal died suddenly of a heart attack just before the funeral of his son, who had

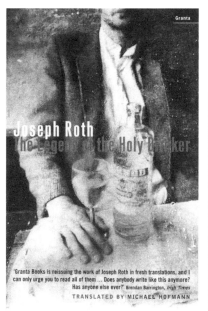

committed suicide. Another, later writer who suffered an equally miserable life was journalist and novelist Joseph Roth (1894-1939). Recently rediscovered and retranslated, he was born on the eastern edge of the Habsburg Empire, today part of the Ukraine, but his work is closely associated with Vienna. Roth's father disappeared before he was born and died in a lunatic asylum, World War I curtailed his education, his wife went mad, and he himself survived on menial jobs and journalism before he died exiled, alcoholic and destitute in Paris, the setting of his now-famous *The Legend of the Holy Drinker*. During the 1920s and 1930s, Roth somehow managed to write the finest chronicles of the death throes of the Empire, *Radetzky March* and *The Emperor's Tomb*, as well as memorable accounts of the Soviet experiment and Mussolini's Italy.

'If I must choose the lesser of two evils, I will choose neither.'

Alongside alcoholism, the literary '-isms' of the turn of the century were impressionism, symbolism and naturalism. Hermann Bahr (1863-1934) decided he was an expressionist, and became the leading spirit of the Jungwien, a literary circle formed by the likes of Arthur

Schnitzler and Hofmannsthal that convened at Café Griensteidl on Michaelerplatz and later nearby at Café Central on Herrengasse. The latter was frequented by poet Peter Altenberg (1859-1919), whose dummy still sits in a corner.

HEDONISM AND HYPOCRISY

The increasing influence of psychological themes in general and psychoanalysis in particular on the writing in these years is most clearly illustrated by Arthur Schnitzler (1862-1931). He became a friend of Freud, though Freud had first avoided meeting him 'from a kind of reluctance to meet my double'. Schnitzler's 1926 *Dream Story*, filmed rather loosely as *Eyes Wide Shut* by Stanley Kubrick, depends heavily on dream psychology, explores the subconscious and, for its time, was, like Freud, a great taboo breaker. Despite its date, it is set firmly in fin de siècle Vienna, and conveys a strange atmosphere of hedonism, bourgeois hypocrisy, and the sexual and psychological frustrations peculiar to that strange time. Schnitzler's other internationally renowned work is the 1900 play *Reigen*, best known in English by its French title *La Ronde*, thanks to Max Ophuls' classic 1950 film. Characteristically pessimistic, the play portrays a circle of sexual encounters through every class of end-of-the-century Vienna. Schnitzler, a Jew who, unlike many at that time, denied his

Jewishness, also documented the anti-semitism of pre-World War II Vienna in his novel *The Road to the Open*.

The use of aphorisms was another trademark of Austrian writing at this time, practised to great effect by Bohemian-born Jewish satirist Karl Kraus (1874-1936). He penned the phrase 'If I must choose the lesser of two evils, I will choose neither', which became a motto for a whole generation of Viennese. Founder, editor and writer of the satirical revue *Die Fackel* (The Torch), Kraus is best known for his anti-war drama *The Last Days of Mankind*.

The novelist Robert Musil (1880-1942) said of Kraus that 'there are two things which one can't fight because they are too long, too fat and have neither head nor foot: Karl Kraus and psychoanalysis'. Professional jealousy aside, Musil was a celebrated essayist, and wrote a beautiful if unusual short story, *The Temptation of Silent Veronica*, about a psychotic woman who appears to have been buggered by a dog, and, more famously, his unfinished three-volume novel *The Man Without Qualities*. Written after World War I, it dealt entirely with the last years of the Empire before 1914. Like many writers, Musil left Austria after the *Anschluss*, and died penniless and anonymous abroad.

> **'Reading Stefan Zweig's autobiography, it is easy to see how, as the social and political climate changed, the disillusionment that led to his suicide set in.'**

Yet another casualty of the curse that seems to hover over literary Vienna and, like the Furies, follow its sons abroad was Ödön von Horváth (1901-38), a friend of Joseph Roth who fled to Paris to escape the Nazis and was killed shortly after by a falling branch on the Champs-Elysées during a freak storm. Meanwhile, the 'almost over-gifted' Jewish writer Stefan Zweig (1881-1942) fled from the Nazis to South America, to kill himself with his wife in Brazil. Utterly cultured, a speaker and translator of several languages, he was a respected figure in literary circles throughout Europe, and for a time in the 1920s his hugely popular biographies and historical books made him the world's most widely translated author. Reading Zweig's autobiography *The World of Yesterday*, it is easy to see how, as the social and political climate changed, the disillusionment that led to his suicide set in.

FOULING THE NEST

If Austria's post-war politicians enthusiastically endorsed the notion of Austrian victimhood, its most celebrated writers begged to differ. For Thomas Bernhard (1931-89), Peter Handke (born 1942) and Elfriede Jelinek (born 1946), the country that emerged from the war is a crass fiction, what Bernhard described as a *Geschäftshaus*, an emporium retailing a schmaltzy blend of Alpine scenery and imperial myths, inhabited by 'six-and-a-half million idiots'. For Jelinek 'internal exile' is the only option: 'Austria is a nation of criminals. This country has a criminal past.' Such vitriol earned them and others the epithet *Nestbeschmutzer* or 'nest foulers'. Whatever the truth of their statements, they nevertheless point to an insurmountable breach between a nation and the representatives of its literature.

Haunted by illegitimacy, maternal rejection, and a series of life-threatening illnesses, Bernhard was an irascible figure, a self-confessed troublemaker whose plays and novels eschew any utopian political activism for meandering repetition and scabrous humour that give the impression we are eavesdropping on a madman. At home, he is remembered for his play *Heldenplatz*, a merciless dissection of the myths surrounding Hitler's annexation of Austria, premiered during Waldheim's presidency. For a glimpse into Bernhard's world, call in at Café Bräuenerhof, where his regular meetings with Paul Wittgenstein, the philosopher's clinically insane nephew, led to his most readable work: *Wittgenstein's Nephew*.

Like Bernhard's, Elfriede Jelinek's work depends heavily on stylistic fireworks that often sit uncomfortably in translation. When she was awarded the 2004 Nobel Prize for Literature, the world responded with a resounding 'who?' and there was a stony silence in Austria. Her name probably registered among those who had read the credits for Michael Haneke's film version of her novel *Die Klavierspielerin* (The Piano Teacher). This fearful portrait of Erika, a frustrated middle-aged piano teacher whose masochistic demands alienate the student she desires as a lover, savagely juxtaposes the Vienna Conservatoire with the Gürtel's peep shows to attack another Austrian sacred cow: the male-dominated world of classical music. Jelinek alleged a 'social phobia' to avoid the Nobel ceremony, lamenting that Bernhard had been overlooked in his lifetime. However, by singling out 'her musical flow of voices and counter-voices in novels and plays that with extraordinary linguistic zeal reveal the absurdity of society's clichés and their subjugating power', the Swedes may well have had Bernhard in mind.

Where to Stay

Pension Altstadt Vienna. *See p47.*

Where to Stay

And it's good night Vienna!

Visitors to Vienna are spoiled for choice in a city that racks up around nine million overnight stays each year. Pick yourself a hotel with history, a plush palace where princes retain rooms, family-run pensions or, more recently, some stripped-down designer digs. Many of these come with quintessential Viennese features – fishbone parquet floors, splendid double doors, windows that close with a resounding clunk and ceilings so high that even the smallest box room appears palatial. While there are few real bargains, bedding down in Vienna needn't break the bank.

Like the majority of Vienna's sights, most accommodation is located in the Innere Stadt, the city's historic centre. If you venture out into districts 2-9, you can often make great savings without skimping on quality, and still be only a short walk from the attractions.

With the current trend for bargain-trawling on the internet, Vienna's hoteliers are reluctant to give firm rates for a period as long as the shelf life of this guide. If you avoid the large congresses that Vienna frequently hosts, rooms may be available at rates well below the prices we quote. New openings and reopenings often provide good deals, while 2008 sees the arrival of the Ring, another Ringstrasse five-star hotel, and the relaunch of the bucolic Hotel im Palais Schwarzenberg. Google the two for deals.

Hotels follow a star rating reflecting amenities and services. Our listings come under the following categories: Deluxe (over

€320 for a double); Expensive (€180-€350); Moderate (€130-€220); Budget (€70-€135); Very cheap (under €75); Seasonal hotels; Hostels; Camping and Long-term accommodation. If you arrive without a reservation, there are helpful offices at the Westbahnhof (west) and Südbahnhof (south) railway stations and at Schwechat airport. In town, the tourist office on Albertinaplatz, behind the Staatsoper, will make bookings for a small fee, or just grab a copy of their hotel guide. You can book online at the tourist office website www.vienna.info or by calling 24555.

1st district

Deluxe

Bristol

1, Kärntner Ring 1 (515 160/www.westin.com/bristol). U1, U2, U4 Karlsplatz/tram 1, 2, D, J. **Rates** €410-€610 single/double; €950-€4,350 suite. **Credit** AmEx, DC, MC, V. **Map** p251 E7/8 ❶
A truly exceptional hotel, the Bristol scores highly on service, history and location. Set on the Ringstrasse across Kärntner Strasse from the Staatsoper, the hotel offers unadulterated, old fashioned luxury. The 140 rooms are decked out in the opulent Viennese style, with some of the smaller rooms overwhelmed by cumbersome furniture. To be on the safe side, book the 350sq m (3,760sq ft) Prince of Wales suite, the largest in Austria! Naturally, state-of-the-art technology and elegant modern bathrooms also feature. The Bristol bar is a traditional and intimate meeting place going back to well before the 1945-55 era, when the hotel was the US military headquarters. The Korso restaurant behind the lobby is also highly prized.
Bar. Business centre. Concierge. Disabled-adapted rooms. Gym. Internet (broadband, wireless). No-smoking rooms. Parking (€28/day). Restaurant. Room service. TV.

Hilton Vienna Plaza

1, Schottenring 11 (313 900/www.hilton.com). U2 Schottentor/Universität/tram 1, 2, D. **Rates** €210 single; €330 double; €450-€2,500 suite. **Credit** AmEx, DC, MC, V. **Map** p250 D5 ❷

---

❶ Green numbers in this chapter correspond to the location of each hotel as shown on the street maps. *See pp242-251.*

The best Hotels

For visiting dignitaries
Imperial (*see p38*).

For gregarious backpackers
Wombat's Vienna the Base (*see p50*).

For love in the afternoon
Hotel Orient (*see p43*).

For design junkies on a budget
Hollmann Beletage (*see p41*).

For well-heeled design junkies
Do&Co Hotel (*see p39*).

Do&Co Hotel. *See p39.*

On the positive side, nearly anything you might want in a luxury hotel you'll find in the Hilton Plaza. Abundant use of cherrywood in contrast to light pastel colours adds an elegant touch. Amenities are complete, service is outgoing, staff friendly and helpful. But you'd be hard pressed to differentiate between this and similar accommodation in any other major city. Even the original art is, well, foreign. The vaguely 1930s-style furniture in the lobby sets the style for the least Viennese of Vienna's top hotels; the 218 rooms and suites are in the main upmarket standard, with marble baths.

The sister Hilton on Stadtpark (Am Stadtpark 3, 717 000) reopened in 2004 after total renovation; in the 2nd, the Danube Hilton (Handelskai 269, 727 770), a cleverly converted warehouse, offers huge Scandinavian-style rooms and a riverside location. *Bar. Business centre. Café. Concierge. Disabled-adapted rooms. Gym. Internet (broadband). No-smoking floors. Parking (€24/day). Restaurant. Room service. TV.*

Hotel Residenz Palais Coburg

1, Coburgbastei 4 (51818-0/www.palais-coburg.com). U3 Stubenring/tram 1, 2. **Rates** €490-€2,140 suite. **Credit** AmEx, DC, JCB, MC, V. **Map** p251 F7 ❸
Built in 1857 for Ferdinand Saxe-Coburg-Gotha (the brother of Queen Victoria's mother), this late neo-Classicist palace opened as a suite hotel in late 2003. The Coburg's owner runs the hotel as a private trust since it houses his Strategic Capital Market Research

institute. He aims at a mere 35% occupancy, and so ensures that the breathtaking public rooms, rooftop pool and garden are never crowded. The entrance is a spectacular sight, hewn out of one of the few remaining chunks of Vienna's city walls. The spacious lobby displays remains of the original Renaissance fortifications in recesses and provides access to the Coburg's excellent bistro and restaurant. Named after various regal blood relations of the Saxe-Coburgs, the huge suites are often used by long-stay guests and all feature fully equipped kitchens, seating areas and balconies. Interiors vary from imperial opulent to modern minimal with lots of high-tech toys, and there are views of the Stadtpark or over the rooftops of old Vienna. *Bar. Business centre. Concierge. Garden. Gym. Internet (broadband, wireless). No-smoking rooms. Parking (valet €35). Pool (indoor). Restaurants (3). Room service. Spa. TV (DVD).*

Imperial

1, Kärntner Ring 16 (501 100/www.luxurycollection. com/imperial). U1, U2, U4 Karlsplatz/tram 1, 2, D, J. **Rates** €640-€830 single/double; €940-€4,950 suite. **Credit** AmEx, DC, JCB, MC, V. **Map** p251 E8 ❹
As the first sight of the Imperial's towering marble-clad lobby confirms, this is the first address for state visitors or anyone else seeking the ultimate in discretion, service and accommodation. Expect the staff to address you by name. Built in 1869, this town palace is one of the Ringstrasse's most imposing

Hotel Residenz Palais Coburg. That's Saxe-Coburg-Gotha to you, mate.

edifices, just round the corner from the Musikverein. The lower floors are given over to luxurious suites festooned with antiques and old masters. Each has a personal butler at your service. The rooms get progressively smaller as you go higher in the hotel but high ceilings, swagged curtains and period details dominate throughout. The bar is a great plush, red velvet affair with piano accompaniment, but the restaurant doesn't live up to its grandiose setting. *Bar. Business centre. Concierge. Disabled-adapted room. Gym. Internet (wireless). No-smoking floor. Restaurant. Parking (valet €30/day). Room service. TV.*

Sacher

1, Philharmonikerstrasse 4 (514 560/www.sacher. com). U1, U2, U4 Karlsplatz. **Rates** €313-€613 single/double; €735-€4,522 suite. **Credit** AmEx, DC, MC, V. **Map** p250 E7 ❺

As befits a hotel of its standing, the Sacher is awash with anecdotes: home of the Sacher-Torte, the world's most famous chocolate cake; patronised by Emperor Franz Josef (after his famously austere banquets at Hofburg, the aristocracy would repair to the Sacher restaurant); and virtually synonymous with the Staatsoper. Privately run since 1876, it also plays a prominent role in Carol Reed's *The Third Man* as it was commandeered as British HQ during the four-power occupation. Renovation work in 2004-05 replaced its tenebrous reception with a more luminous space and created 40 new rooms on two further floors, designed by Pierre Yves Rochon. The latter are minimalist by the Sacher's chintz and velvet standards, but still feature original antiques and all the house's trademark opulence but with more high-tech. There's no fitness centre, but guests have free use of the John Harris Club (*see p204*). The hotel's superb location right behind the Staatsoper, legendary service and the magnificent Blue Bar appeal to lovers of bygone days, but its fame means that its cafés and Sacher-Torte outlet are often packed. *Bar. Business centre. Concierge. Disabled-adapted rooms. Internet (broadband, wireless). No-smoking rooms. Parking (valet €29/day). Restaurant. Room service. Spa. TV.*

Expensive

Ambassador

1, Kärntnerstrasse 22/Neuer Markt 5 (961 610/ www.ambassador.at). U1, U2, U4 Karlsplatz, U1, U3 Stephansplatz. **Rates** €233-€426 single; €245-€534 double; €453-€641 suite. **Credit** AmEx, DC, MC, V. **Map** p251 E7 ❻

In keeping with the general decline of the Kärntnerstrasse, the Ambassador must be the only five-star hotel with a branch of Mango inside. Nevertheless, this grand old place has welcomed everyone from Josephine Baker to Haile Selassie of Ethiopia. The 86 rooms are large and plush with parquet floors and heavy velvet curtains. Rooms are also air-conditioned, which is useful in summer when revellers on the Kärntnerstrasse tend to whoop

it up a bit. If noise bothers you, consider asking for a room on the Neuer Markt side – it's quieter and the view is better. The Ambassador's restaurant is run by local celebrity chef Toni Mörwald. *Bar. Business centre. Concierge. Gym. Internet (broadband, wireless). No-smoking rooms. Parking (garage €30/day). Room service. TV.*

Astoria

1, Kärntner Strasse 32-34 (515 770/www.austria-trend.at/asw). U1, U2, U4 Karlsplatz, U1, U3 Stephansplatz/bus 3a. **Rates** €149 single; €213 double; €269 suite. **Credit** AmEx, DC, MC, V. **Map** p250 E7 ❼

The Astoria is one of the grand old hotels dating from the 19th century, which accounts for the large high-ceilinged rooms along with the slightly musty atmosphere and original Jugendstil accents. Renovations have brought facilities and classic period decor up to date in the 118 rooms. The trade-off for a superb central location and views over the busy pedestrian Kärntner Strasse is street noise, but this is less evident on the upper floors or in those rooms looking on to the side streets. The front-desk management is particularly helpful. *Bar. Internet (broadband). No-smoking rooms. Parking (€26/day). Restaurant. Room service. TV.*

Do&Co Hotel

1, Stephansplatz 12 (24 188/www.doco.com). U1, U3 Stephansplatz. **Rates** €199-€499. **Credit** AmEx, DC, MC, V. **Map** p251 E7 ❽

Super-centrally located and beautifully appointed, the Do&Co is currently the hottest new hotel in the city. If you want to be bang in the centre with a jaw-dropping view of Stephansdom, and hanker after design details, don't hesitate. Occupying architect's Hans Hollein's cylindrical Haas Haus, Dutch design duo FG stijl slotted in the rooms like slices of torte, cladding them in dark woods and suede. B&O flat screens, torrential glassed-off overhead showers and large comfy beds are thrown in for good measure. Staff are exceptionally helpful – a minor miracle considering that the reception and other communal areas are woefully cramped. This is exacerbated by the popularity of the restaurant (*see p117*) and bar: both predate the hotel and are adored by the city's movers and shakers. Breakfast is a pricey, pay-by-item affair, but given the location, there's plenty of choice nearby. **Photo** *p37*. *Bar. Business centre. Internet (broadband, wireless). No-smoking floor. Parking (valet). Room service. Restaurant.*

Le Meridien Vienna

1, Opernring 13-15 (588 900/www.lemeridien-vienna.com). U1, U2, U4 Karlsplatz/tram 1, 2, D, J. **Rates** €195-€395 single/double; €650-€855 suite. **Credit** AmEx, DC, MC, V. **Map** p250 E7 ❾

Five years on from when it opened, Le Meridien has become a firm favourite with visitors to Vienna. The hotel was slotted into the shell of three Ringstrasse town houses by designers Real Studios from London: its public areas are full of highly theatrical

RENAISSANCECASTLE
ROSENBURG

THE MOST ROMANTIC EXPERIENCE JUST OUTSIDE OF VIENNA

FALCONRY ... LUSH ROMANTIC GARDENS ... SHAKESPEARE FESTIVAL

... AVAILABLE ALSO FOR SPECIAL WEDDINGS AND PARTIES ...

A-3573 Rosenburg 1   T. +43(0)2982-2911   www.rosenburg.at

original touches, weird lighting and art installations. Upstairs, the 294 clutter-free rooms offer great modern comfort: specially designed Ligne Roset beds, superb bathrooms, works commissioned from young local artists, large flatscreen TVs (too large for the smaller rooms) and free mini-bar. Apart from the Shambala restaurant (concept by French chef Michel Rostang), there's also a very spacey bar featuring local heroes on the decks and a rather undistinguished repro Viennese café. All these establishments have separate access keeping the lobby free for guests. Check the website for their 'generous daily best available rates'. Note that breakfast (€26) is not included in the room rate, but it's an impressive range that's on offer.
Bar. Business centre. Café. Concierge. Gym. Internet (broadband, wireless). No-smoking floors. Parking (valet, €26/day). Pool (indoor). Restaurant. Room service. TV.

Radisson SAS Palais

1, Parkring 16 (515 170/www.radissonsas.com). U4 Stadtpark/tram 1, 2. **Rates** €189-€260 single/double; €299-€370 suite. **Credit** AmEx, DC, MC, V. **Map** p251 F7 ⑩
Take two turn-of-the-20th century town houses and a clever architect, and the result can be as enticing as the 247-room Radisson SAS Palais. The inner courtyards have been glassed over to form an atrium lobby and open café area enlivened with refreshing touches of greenery, while rooms and baths have been incorporated into the structures. The decor is a blend of Scandinavian modern and Viennese traditional, that manages to retain a comfortable old-world feeling. The best views are out over the park from the front rooms on the upper floors.
Bar. Business centre. Concierge. Disabled-adapted rooms. Gym. Internet (broadband, wireless). No-smoking floors. Parking (€37/day). Restaurant. Room service. Spa. TV.

Radisson Style Hotel

1, Herrengasse 12 (22 780 0/www.radissonsas.com). U3 Herrengasse. **Rates** €255-€310 single/double; €390-€505 suite. **Credit** AmEx, DC, MC, V. **Map** p250 E6 ⑪
Ignore the naff name, the Style is a newish (2005) boutique affair on the palatial Herrengasse, two doors from Café Central. Part of the Radisson chain since 2006, this former bank (the sauna is in the strong room) has 78 spacious rooms and suites. While guests won't find much in the way of breathtaking views (except for the corner suites overlooking Palais Ferstel), the accommodation's sleek styling, marble bathrooms, flatscreen TVs and free mini-bars offer plenty of alternative eye- and head-candy. The circular reception area is adorned with large format photographic images of the city and provides access to Sapori, an Italo-fusion restaurant, and the cool but pricey H12 bar. Breakfast is not included for the cheaper 'Style' rooms.
Bar. Gym. Internet (broadband, wireless). No-smoking rooms. Parking (€23/day). Restaurant. TV (DVD).

Moderate

Amadeus

1, Wildpretmarkt 5 (533 87380/www.hotel-amadeus.at). U1, U3 Stephansplatz/bus 1a, 3a. **Rates** €87-€129 single; €154-€172 double. **Credit** AmEx, DC, MC, V. **Map** p251 E6 ⑫
This intimate hotel is wonderfully central. Rooms are period-furnished, mainly in white and dark red, while bathrooms are pristine white. The smallest singles are compact, the doubles smallish but comfortable. Weekend packages are offered, with double rooms at single rate. Staff are friendly and helpful.
Concierge. Internet (broadband, wireless). Room service. TV.

Hollmann Beletage

1, Köllnerhofgasse 6 (961 1960/www.hollmann-beletage.at). U1, U4 Schwedenplatz. **Rates** €140-€180 double. **Credit** AmEx, DC, MC, V. **Map** p251 F6 ⑬
Housed on the first floor of a 19th-century apartment building, the Hollman's seven airy rooms open up on to a large central reception area with cool white beams, a high-tech log fire and an electric piano (with headphones, so other guests aren't disturbed). Note that reception is unmanned at night, so out of hours the guests use a pre-arranged code to get in, and can help themselves to drinks from the bar. In the spacious rooms, seating areas are minimally elegant, while the bathrooms and TVs are cunningly

Le Meridien Vienna. *See p39.*

hidden behind long pale wood wardrobe units. In late 2006, the hotel opened a stylish restaurant just around the corner (see p118).
Bar. Internet (wireless). No-smoking rooms. Parking (€23/day). Restaurant. Spa. TV.

Kaiserin Elisabeth

1, Weihburggasse 3 (515 26-0/www.kaiserinelisabeth. at). U1, U3 Stephansplatz. **Rates** €109-€122 single; €208-€230 double. **Credit** AmEx, DC, MC, V.
Map p251 E7 ⑭
The venerable Kaiserin has a red velvet and crystal lobby that exudes a slightly decadent imperial atmosphere. The hotel is superbly located, just off Kärntnerstrasse, and many of the 63 rooms have parquet floors and towering ceilings, decorated with oriental carpets and 1950s touches; the newest rooms are beautiful and retain a Viennese feel. The front desk is a decided plus, with very helpful staff.
Bar. Concierge. Internet (broadband). No-smoking rooms. Parking (garage €28/day). Room service. TV.

König von Ungarn

1, Schulerstrasse 10 (515 840/www.kvu.at). U1, U3 Stephansplatz. **Rates** €145 single; €206 double; €283-€333 apartment. **Credit** AmEx, DC, MC, V.
Map p251 F7 ⑮
The 'King of Hungary', in the shadow of the cathedral, is formed out of a 16th-century house (Mozart lived next door). Conversion into a hotel turned the central courtyard into a captivating informal atrium lobby and lounge, complete with tree. Access to the 33 medium-sized rooms on the upper floors is via galleried hallways. Each room is individually decorated, with an emphasis on antique and country furnishings, stripped wood and colourful fabrics.
Bar. Concierge. Internet (broadband). Parking (€28/day). Restaurant. Room service. TV.

Mailberger Hof

1, Annagasse 7 (512 0641-0/www.mailbergerhof.at). U1, U2, U4 Karlsplatz, U1, U3 Stephansplatz. **Rates** €125-€160 single; €180-€210 double; €210-€240 junior suite. **Credit** AmEx, DC, JCB, MC, V.
Map p251 E7 ⑯
Tucked away in two baroqued up Gothic gable houses on a pedestrian side street off Kärntner Strasse, the Mailberger Hof is a favourite with opera stars and other regulars who welcome its discreet, quiet location. The 40 rooms are splendidly decorated in co-ordinated homely style, some teetering on twee, some in elegant period decor. For longer stays, small apartments with kitchenettes are available. A 10% senior discount is offered. The family management is accommodating and helpful, and the hotel's own ticket office is a highly useful service.
Business centre. No-smoking rooms. Restaurant. Room service. TV.

Rathauspark

1, Rathausstrasse 17 (404 12-0/www.austria-trend.at/rhw). U2 Rathaus. **Rates** €138 single; €199 double; €232 junior suite. **Credit** AmEx, DC, MC, V.
Map p250 D6 ⑰

Ideal for a tryst: **Das Triest**. *See p45.*

Lodged in an imposing 19th-century building behind the University, this attractive 117-room hotel oscillates between the elegant stucco ceilings of rooms on the lower floors and more modern styling on the upper floors. The rooms in general are welcoming and decorated in light colours. The American-style full breakfast buffet is great and a variety of tram lines are on the doorstep.
Bar. Business centre. Concierge. Internet (broadband). No-smoking floor. Parking (€21/day). TV.

Starlight Suiten

1, Salzgries 12 (535 9222/all locations: www.starlight hotels.com) U2, U4 Schottenring/tram 1, 2/bus 3a. **Rates** €153-183 single; €183-211 double. **Credit** AmEx, DC, MC, V. **Map** p251 E6 ⑱
When these three hotels hit Vienna in the late 1990s, their functional styling and airy decor were something of a revelation. Each hotel has 45-50 suites that are similar in concept, with living room, bedroom and tiled bathroom and a working area. They all have two phones and two TVs. The locations, totally renovated former apartment buildings, are central yet

relatively quiet. Choose the Salzgries address to be in the thick of the Innere Stadt. Staff are outgoing and helpful with services such as concert tickets. *Bar. Gym. Internet (wireless). No-smoking rooms. Parking (€17/day). TV.*
Other locations 1, Renngasse 13 (533 9989); 3, Am Heumarkt 15 (710 7808).

Budget

Austria

1, Wolfengasse 3/Am Fleischmarkt 20 (515 230/ www.hotelaustria-wien.at). U1, U4 Schwedenplatz/ tram 1, 2, 21, N/bus 2a. **Rates** *€75-€97 single; €101-€149 double; €139-€185 apartment.* **Credit** AmEx, DC, MC, V. **Map** p251 F6 ⑲
This older hotel is located on a blissfully quiet cul-de-sac, convenient for the city centre and transport. Period furnishings, decor and new baths have brought most of the 46 rooms up to a modern standard, but the hotel still has a few bedrooms without baths that fit our 'budget' price range. Despite such touches as oriental carpets and crystal chandeliers, the general atmosphere is one of informal comfort. Staff are particularly friendly and helpful.
Internet (broadband/wireless). No-smoking rooms. Parking (€19/day). Room service. TV.

Hotel Orient

1, Tiefer Graben 30 (533 7307/www.hotelorient.at). U2, U4 Schottenring. **Rates** maximum 3hrs €57-€85 suite; night €160 suite. **Credit** AmEx, DC, MC, V. **Map** p250 E6 ⑳
Originally a tavern for Danube boatmen when a branch of the river flowed along the end of the street, the Orient has functioned as a hotel since 1896. Today it is Vienna's classiest 'love hotel' with suites sold by the hour and the night (Saturdays and Sundays only). Decked out in pure burlesque opulence and overseen with great discretion, the suites sport suggestive names such as the 1001 Nights, Kaisersuite or the newer Rosa Rosa Rosa room. They could all do with some renovation. Former guests such as Orson Welles and Kenneth Anger contribute to the Orient's mythical status in the city. There's a branch, Domizil, a family-oriented 40-room pension behind Stephansdom (Schulerstrasse 14, 513 3199-0, www.hotelpensiondomizil.at).
Bar. Room service.

Kärntnerhof

1, Grashofgasse 4 (512 1923/www.karntnerhof.com). U1, U4 Schwedenplatz/tram 1, 2, 21, N/bus 2a. **Rates** €85-€105 single; €130-€157 double; €205-€247 suite. **Credit** AmEx, DC, MC, V. **Map** p251 F6 ㉑
Hidden in a small cul-de-sac leading into the delightful Heiligenkreuzerhof, the Kärntnerhof's discrete entrance sports a splendid 1950s neon sign. The hotel has 43 modernised yet slightly kitsch rooms and exceptional personal service; no tour groups here. The location is quiet, despite being close to public transport, restaurants, shopping and nightlife.
Bar. Concierge. Disabled-adapted rooms. Parking (€17/day). Room service. TV.

Pension Christina

1, Hafnersteig 7 (533 2961-0/www.pertschy.com). U1, U4 Schwedenplatz/tram 1, 2, 21, N/bus 2a. **Rates** €60-€76 single; €95-€128 double. **Credit** AmEx, DC, MC, V. **Map** p251 F6 ㉒
The 33 rooms here are somewhat on the small side but they are attractively decorated and comfortably furnished. The amenities are few; the main draw lies in a quiet yet central location on a tiny sidestreet. The Pension Christina is part of the local Pertschy group, together with the slightly more expensive Pension Pertschy (*see below*).
No-smoking room. Parking (garage €14/day, street €3.60/day permit). TV.

Pension Nossek

1, Graben 17 (533 7041-0/www.pension-nossek.at). U1, U3 Stephansplatz. **Rates** €50-€77 single; €115 double; €143 suite. **No credit cards. Map** p250 E6 ㉓
The family-owned and managed Pension Nossek on the three middle upper floors of a late 19th-century apartment/office block has been a favourite for generations, both for its friendly service and its superb location in the heart of the city, amid the smart shops. The pedestrian area ensures that the hotel remains relatively quiet. The 32 rooms range from fairly spacious to compact, and the oriental carpets and crystal chandeliers serve to complement the period-style furnishings. Many guests book their stay up to a year in advance.
Parking (€16/day-€35/week). Room service. TV.

Pension Pertschy

1, Habsburgergasse 5 (534 49-0/www.pertschy.com). U1, U3 Stephansplatz. **Rates** €67-€105 single; €102-€177 double. **Credit** AmEx, DC, JCB, MC, V. **Map** p250 E7 ㉔
Easily overlooked in a side street off the Graben, this town palace is typical of the joys that lie behind Vienna's façades. Looking on to a gorgeous inner courtyard (sadly used as a car park), this friendly pension is full of period touches, such as the elegant stairway that guests hardly notice when taking the lift to the first floor reception. Most of the 50 rooms are spacious, with period furniture, the odd antique (a couple still have their original ceramic ovens as showpieces), and some have kitchenettes. Baths, of course, were later additions, and are not luxurious, but generally satisfactory. New rooms (top floor front) are elegant, decorated in rose and cream, with parquet floors and crystal chandeliers. For location and the distant sound of *Fiaker* horses clipclopping by on Habsburgergasse, the Pertschy is an atmospheric choice. It also runs the slightly cheaper Pension Christina (*see above*).
No-smoking rooms. Parking (garage €16/day). TV.

Pension Suzanne

1, Walfischgasse 4 (513 2507/www.pension-suzanne.at). U1, U2, U4 Karlsplatz/tram 1, 2, D, J/bus 3a. **Rates** €77-78 single; €96-€110 double; €117-€119 apartment. **Credit** AmEx, DC, MC, V. **Map** p251 E7 ㉕

Most of the 25 rooms in this 1950s building were originally small apartments, meaning that many have kitchenettes; a few even sport small outside terraces. The rooms are comfortable, with compact bathrooms; those on the courtyard or in the back building are the quietest, although all come with soundproof double-glazing. The central location is within moments of the major shops and the opera. The family-managed Suzanne attracts a host of regulars, so book early. *Concierge. TV.*

Post

1, Fleischmarkt 24 (515 83-0/www.hotel-post-wien.at). U1, U4 Schwedenplatz/tram 1, 2, 21, N/bus 2a. **Rates** €40-€81 single; €66- €122 double. **Credit** AmEx, DC, MC, V. **Map** p251 F6 ⊕

Location is the main attraction here – just steps from the public transport at Schwedenplatz and convenient for shopping and nightlife. The 107 rooms are a bit on the dated side, with standard furniture and occasional oriental rugs on the parquet floors. The few rooms without baths are real bargains. Staff are accommodating if sometimes overstretched. *Café. Internet (dataport, broadband in some rooms). Parking (€18/day). Room service. TV.*

Zur Wiener Staatsoper

1, Krugerstrasse 11 (513 1274-0/www.zurwiener staatsoper.at). U1, U2, U4 Karlsplatz/tram 1, 2, D, J/bus 3a. **Rates** €78-€95 single; €111-€140 double. **Credit** DC, JCB, MC, V. **Map** p251 E7 ⊕

This was novelist John Irving's blueprint for the Vienna hotel in *Hotel New Hampshire*. Don't be misled by the colossi over the entrance and the stuccoed lobby: the hotel's rooms are smallish yet comfortable although with undistinguished decor. But for a loca-

tion just off Kärntnerstrasse and within a baton's throw of the Staatsoper, its rates are remarkable. Don't expect much in the way of facilities, but the staff try their best. The equally well-located sister Hotel Schweizerhof has 55 rooms at the same prices. *Parking (€17/day). TV.*

Other locations Hotel Schweizerhof 1, Bauernmarkt 22 (533 1931).

3rd district

Expensive

InterContinental Wien

3, Johannesgasse 28 (711 220/www.vienna.inter continental.com). U4 Stadtpark. **Rates** €280-€340 single; €280-€340 double; €380-€735 suite. **Credit** AmEx, DC, MC, V. **Map** p251 F8 ⊕

When it went up in the mid 1960s, the 453-room InterContinental gave Vienna its first chain hotel and a major eyesore. But it has worn well, from the velvet and crystal lobby to the more modern, individual style of the rooms – go for the ones at the front with great views over the Stadtpark. For service and accommodation, the hotel remains one of InterContinental's flagships and, in 2006, George W Bush and his entourage took over the whole place for three days. The city centre is about a ten-minute walk away. Both the relaxed lobby café and adjacent bar are popular spots – it was here that fashionable crooner Louis Austen's career took off. Local foodies have never embraced its restaurant. *Bar. Business centre. Concierge. Gym. Internet (broadband). No-smoking floors. Parking (garage €20/day). Restaurant. Room service. TV.*

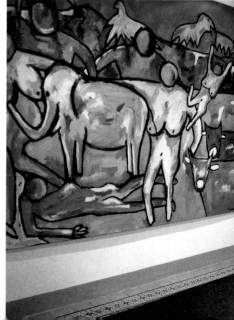

Moderate

Mercure Grand Hotel Biedermeier Wien

*3, Landstrasser Hauptstrasse 28 (716 71-0/
www.mercure.com). U3, U4 Landstrasse, then
bus 74a/tram O.* **Rates** €120-€170 single;
€170-€220 double. **Credit** AmEx, DC, MC, V.
Map p251 G7 ㉙

This jewel of a hotel resulted from the skilful conversion of 19th-century residential buildings into modern accommodation. Here you'll have an instant sense of old Vienna; the 202 rooms and 33 suites are done up in a period style and decor that emphasise comfort with simplicity. The only problem for individual travellers is the tour groups that are also drawn by the authentic Viennese charm. The location is about 20 minutes' walk from the centre, although transport is convenient and frequent. The picturesque narrow alley that divides the hotel is home to boutiques and galleries.
*Bar. Business centre. Concierge. Disabled-adapted
rooms. Internet (broadband, wireless). No-smoking
rooms. Parking (€15/day). Restaurant. TV.*

NH Belvedere

*3, Rennweg 12a (206 11/www.nh-hotels.com). Tram
71.* **Rates** €119-€195 single/double. **Credit** AmEx,
MC, DC, V. **Map** p247 F9 ㉚

Part of the expanding Spanish hotel chain, the brand-new NH Belvedere is housed in a Jugendstil building that was formerly the Austrian government's printing works. Backing on to the Belvedere botanical gardens, it has 114 spanking new rooms at good prices for the location and facilities.

*Bar. Café. Gym. Room service. Disabled-adapted
rooms. Internet (wireless). No-smoking rooms.
Parking (€14/day). TV.*
Other locations NH Wien 7, Mariahilfer Strasse
32-34 (521720); NH Attersee 7, Mariahilfer Strasse 78
(524 5600); NH Airport Hotelstrasse 1-3, A-1300
Flughafen Wien (701510).

4th district

Expensive

Das Triest

*4, Wiedner Hauptstrasse 12 (589 180/www.das
triest.at). U1, U3, U4 Karlsplatz/tram 62, 65.* **Rates**
€206 single; €265 double; €328-€540 suite. **Credit**
AmEx, DC, MC, V. **Map** p247 E8 ㉛

Das Triest is Vienna's original boutique hotel. Conceived by Terence Conran in 1995 in what was a stagecoach inn on the route south to the Habsburg port of Trieste, its portholed windows allude to the name's nautical connotations. Twelve years on, despite its popularity with touring pop stars such as Marilyn Manson, Massive Attack and Robbie Williams (who had a copy of the bar built backstage at his Vienna concert in 2003), the hotel is scuffed in places but generally wearing well. The attractive rooms and lobby are full of fresh flowers and various designer details such as Castiglione lamps, while the inner courtyard garden is bathed in sunshine and a delightful place to sit out catching the rays. In keeping with the theme, you can enjoy good northern Italian cuisine in the chic Collio restaurant or in the courtyard in summer. The Silverbar is one of Vienna's coolest hotel bars (*see p198*). **Photo** *p42*.

Pension Altstadt Vienna.
See p47.

BAR

RESTAURANT

MEETINGS

Stephansplatz 12,
A-1010 Vienna
hotel@doco.com
www.doco.com

DO & CO

HOTEL
VIENNA

Tel: +43 (1) 24 188
Fax: + 43 (1) 24 188 444

EVENTS

Bar. Business centre. Gym. Internet (dataport, broadband, wireless). No-smoking floors. Parking (garage €24/day). Restaurant. Roof-garden (garden suites). Room service. Sauna. TV.

Budget

Carlton Opera

4, Schikanedergasse 4 (587 5302/www.carlton.at). U1, U2, U4 Karlsplatz/U4 Kettenbrückengasse/tram 62, 65. **Rates** €50-€99 single; €73-€130 double. **Credit** AmEx, DC, MC, V. **Map** p247 D8 ⓜ
The façade reveals the 1904 origins of this hotel; fortunately, many of the art nouveau touches inside are also preserved. The 52 rooms are mostly high-ceilinged, many with parquet floors; the larger rooms have kitchenettes. Furnishings are comfortable if undistinguished, the white tiled bathrooms likewise. Single rooms are small but adequate. The Carlton is right beside the Naschmarkt and the Schleifmühlgasse gallery scene, and about a 15-minute walk from the city centre.
Concierge. Internet (wireless). No-smoking rooms. Parking (€15/day). Room service. TV.

6th district

Moderate

Kummer

6, Mariahilfer Strasse 71a (58895-0/www.hotel kummer.at). U3 Neubaugasse/bus 13a, 14a. **Rates** €79-€185 single; €89-€220 double. **Credit** AmEx, DC, MC, V. **Map** p246 C8 ⓜ
Located in the thick of the busy Mariahilfer Strasse, the Kummer is an impressive Historicist building with 95 modern carpeted rooms. While the decor is humdrum, the substantial buffet breakfast and proximity to the shops and nightlife of districts 6 and 7 more than compensate. From the U-Bahn station opposite, it's three stops to Stephansplatz. Or you could walk it in 20 leisurely minutes.
Bar. Disabled-adapted rooms. Internet (dataport, wireless in lobby). No-smoking floors. Parking (garage €20/day). Restaurant. Room service. TV.

Das Tyrol

6, Mariahilfer Strasse 15 (587 5415/www.das-tyrol.at). U2 Museumsquartier/bus 2a. **Rates** €109-€209 single; €149-€239 double; €139-€259 suite. **Credit** AmEx, DC, MC, V. **Map** p250 D8 ⓜ
The renovation of this cosy 30-room hotel gave it a boutiquey town house feel, with dubious contemporary artwork and the odd stick of Thonet and Wittmann furniture. Although rooms have been cleverly fitted into unusual spaces without sacrificing comfort or convenience, some of the decor remains slightly unconvincing; the bathrooms are gleaming white affairs. Located just off Vienna's main retail artery, and just across the street from the Museumsquartier, the Tyrol is also within easy walking distance of the Innere Stadt. There's a sauna and solarium but no gym. Staff here are charming.

Business centre. Concierge. Internet (dataport, highspeed). No-smoking rooms. Parking (garage €18/day). Room service. TV.

7th district

Moderate

K+K Hotel Maria Theresia

7, Kirchberggasse 6 (521 23/www.kkhotels.com). U2, U3 Volkstheater/tram 49/bus 2a. **Rates** €180 single; €240 double; €295 suite. **Credit** AmEx, DC, MC, V. **Map** p250 D7 ⓜ
This K+K hotel in the quaint Spittelberg district is ideal for both the best of the city's museums and some good shopping, and has convenient transport to the city centre, about 15 minutes' walk away. The hotel is spacious and informal, with 123 rooms of standard decor and furnishings. You, thus making it ideal for tour groups. Staff members are friendly and helpful. The sister K+K Palais Hotel offers 66 rooms in a former town house on a quiet Innere Stadt square. Rates for both hotels are the same.
Bar. Business center. Concierge. Gym. Internet (highspeed, wireless). No-smoking rooms. Parking (€15/day). Restaurant. Room service. TV.
Other locations K+K Palais Hotel 1, Rudolfsplatz 11 (533 1353).

Pension Altstadt Vienna

7, Kirchengasse 41 (522 6666/www.altstadt.at). U2, U3 Volkstheater/bus 48a. **Rates** €109-€139 single; €139-€169 double; €169-€189 double (Matteo Thun); €169-€299 suite. **Credit** AmEx, DC, MC, V. **Map** p246 C7 ⓜ
This one-time residential building close to Spittelberg and the MuseumsQuartier is the city's most elegant pension. Of the 37 rooms and suites, nine were redesigned by interiors guru Matteo Thun in 2006. These are a fantastic synthesis of period elegance and contemporary touches, and well worth the supplement. The older rooms look splendid too with great art and furnishings that range from Mies van der Rohe chairs to oriental kilims. The lounge and breakfast room are in the same tone and the management unusually helpful. **Photo** p45.
Bar. Internet (dataport, wireless). No-smoking rooms. Parking (garage €18/day, street €7/day). TV.

Budget

Fürstenhof

7, Neubaugürtel 4 (523 3267-0/www.hotel-fuerstenhof.com). U3, U6 Westbahnhof (exit Westbahnhof)/tram 6, 18. **Rates** €46-€94 single; €65-€110 double. **Credit** AmEx, DC, MC, V. **Map** p246 B8 ⓜ
Walk diagonally left out of the Westbahnhof, across the thick traffic on the Gürtel (or take the pedestrian tunnel to Innere Mariahilfer Strasse) to get to this family managed hotel. The historic façade identifies the building as about a century old. Most of the 58 rooms are large, with comfortable, if somewhat

Levante Parliament.

undistinguished, furnishings and decor. Windows are now soundproofed, but rooms at the side have less traffic noise than those on the front. If you can cope with a toilet and shower down the hall, the few rooms without baths (but with sinks) are two-thirds the price of the others. Staff are friendly and supportive if occasionally seeming rather harried.
Hotel services. Internet (dataport). Parking (€13/day). Room service. TV.

Very cheap

Kugel
7, Siebensterngasse 43 (523 3355/www.hotel kugel.at). U2 Volkstheater, then tram 49. **Rates** €48-€95 single; €85-€105 double. **No credit cards.** **Map** p246 C7/8 ③⑨
The Kugel is in the heart of the 7th district and only a stroll away from the main museums. The 37 attractively decorated rooms with their modern four-poster beds are a real bargain; a few rooms without bath or some just with shower but no toilet are cheaper still. The breakfast room is long overdue for a refit, but ample breakfasts compensate, or you can start your day instead at one of the nearby coffee houses. The family management is chummy and helpful.
Parking (garage €9/day). TV.

8th district

Expensive

Levante Parliament
8, Auerspergstrasse 9 (228 28-0/www.thelevante. com). U2, U3 Volkstheater/tram J, 46. **Rates** €210 single; €275 double; €340 suite. **Credit** AmEx, DC, MC, V. **Map** p250 C6 ③⑨
Barely a year old, this superb conversion of an early 20th-century sandstone building on the fringes of the 8th district is one of Vienna's design hotel highlights. While the tentacular glass sculptures of Romanian artist Ion Nemtoi that adorn the restaurant and massive inner courtyard may not be to everyone's taste, the rooms are elegant and uncluttered. All 65 of them and the five suites are rendered in stone, dark wood and glass in harmony with the building's modernist roots. The nearby Levante Laudon is a chic budget version, useful for longer stays.
Bar. Business centre. Concierge. Disabled adapted rooms. Gym. Internet (broadband, wireless). No-smoking rooms. Parking (€22/day). Restaurant. Room service. TV.
Other locations The Levante Laudon, 8, Laudongasse 8 (407 137-0).

Moderate

Hotel Rathaus Wein & Design
8, Lange Gasse 13 (400 1122/www.hotel-rathaus-wien.at). U2, U3 Volkstheater/tram 46. **Rates** €118-€138 single; €148-€198 double. **Credit** AmEx, DC, MC, V. **Map** p250 C7 ④⓪

The Rathaus, which is run by a Salzburg family and not to be confused with the City Hall, combines interesting boutique styling with the theme of wine. Located in an old apartment building in Vienna's noble 8th district, all 33 rooms are named after top Austrian vintners and bottles of their produce sit temptingly on the dark wood shelving. The creaky wrought-iron lift retains a touch of fin-de-siècle ambience, a nice contrast to the hyper-modern rooms, reception areas and bar. The last of these is naturally wine oriented, does light lunches and will lay on a bit of cheese and antipasti for guests arriving late. Breakfast is extra, at €13.
Bar. Concierge. Internet (broadband). Parking (€14.60/day). Room service. TV.

Budget

Hotel Zipser
8, Lange Gasse 49 (404 54-0/www.zipser.at). U2 Rathaus/tram 5, 33. **Rates** €67-€79 single; €85-€135 double. **Credit** AmEx, DC, MC, V. **Map** p246 C6 ④①
This one-time apartment block behind the town hall in the charming 8th district dates to 1904, but the 47 fair-sized rooms are fresh and inviting, decorated in contemporary colours and furnishings. Some rooms at the back have splendid tree-shaded balconies. The staff are unusually friendly and accommodating.
Bar. Business centre. Internet (wireless). Parking (€13.90/day). TV.

Very cheap

Pension Lehrerhaus
8, Lange Gasse 20 (403 2358-100/www.lhv.at). Tram 46, J. **Rates** €27-€46 single; €50-€76 double; €3 extra for only 1-night stay. **Credit** DC, MC, V. **Map** p250 C6/7 ④②
A modest 40-room hotel, with high-ceilinged rooms of various sizes, all welcomingly decorated (soft colours with light wood furniture) and immaculate. Rates vary depending on facilities; rooms without bath or toilet are real bargains. Breakfast is not included; pay for what you want from coin machines in the breakfast room.
TV (some rooms).

Pension Wild
8, Lange Gasse 10 (406 5174/www.pension-wild.com). U2, U3 Volkstheater/tram 46. **Rates** €37-€65 single; €45-€89 double. **Credit** AmEx, DC, MC, V. **Map** p250 C7 ④③
Combine a relaxed family-managed environment (and one that's gay-friendly, too) with a convenient location, and it's not surprising that this pension is usually fully booked. The 22 rooms are attractively modern with colour co-ordinated fabrics and light wood furniture. Most rooms have been recently redecorated. A buffet breakfast is offered in a cheerful front room and small kitchenettes on each floor are handy for snacking or light meals.
Room service.

Seasonal hotels

During the long summer vacations, many of Vienna's student residences are turned into reasonably priced, if modest, hotels. All of them have single or double rooms, with bath or shower. Furnishings are what you'd expect in a better-class dormitory: adequate but nothing fancy. There's central booking via the Academia (401 76-55 or 401 76-77, fax 401 76-20, www.academia-hotels.co.at) for three hotels grouped in Pfeilgasse; and for the Albertina group (512 7493, fax 512 1968, www.allyou needhotels.at) with two locations, in the 2nd and 4th districts. They generally operate between 1 July and 30 September.

2nd district

AllYouNeed Vienna 2

2, Grosse Schiffgasse 12 (512 74 93/www.allyouneed hotels.at). U2, U4 Schottenring/tram 1, 2/bus 5a. **Rates** €59 single; €88 double. **Credit** AmEx, DC, MC, V. **Map** p251 F5 ④

Newest of the seasonal hotels and belonging to the Albertina group mentioned above, this 122-room three-star hotel might lie across the Danube canal, but it is only a short walk to the city centre.
Bar. Internet. TV.

4th district

AllYouNeed Vienna 4

4, Schäffergasse 2 (512 74 93/www.allyouneed hotels.at). U1 Taubstummengasse/tram 62, 65/bus 59a. **Rates** €59 single; €88 double. **Credit** AmEx, DC, MC, V. **Map** p247 E9 ④

Refurbished and reopened in 2003, this three-star 99-room facility run by the Albertina group is within easy walking distance of the Naschmarkt. The opera and city centre lie some 15 minutes away on foot. *TV.*

7th district

Atlas

7, Lerchenfelder Strasse 1-3 (524 20 40). U2, U3 Volkstheater/tram 46. **Rates** €60 single; €84 double. **Credit** AmEx, DC, MC, V. **Map** p250 C7 ④

It's location that makes the difference to staying at this 182-room three-star Academia group facility; the MuseumsQuartier is a mere two-minute walk away, and the bars and restaurants of the 7th district are nearly as conveniently placed.
Bar. Café. Internet (dataport). Restaurant.

8th district

Academia

8, Pfeilgasse 3a (401 76-0). Tram 46, J. **Rates** €50 single; €66 double. **Credit** AmEx, DC, MC, V. **Map** p246 C7 ④

This 260-room warren in a leafy part of the 8th district is one of the larger and better of the seasonal hotels run by the Academia group. Double rooms are the same size as singles with a second bed added, and adequate if not overly spacious. The adjacent Avis (Pfeilgasse 4) offers 72 somewhat larger rooms at the same rates and shares a coffee bar and breakfast room facilities with the Academia.
Bar. Concierge. Internet (modem).

Hostels

The city's Camping leaflet will give you the addresses and critical details of youth hostels and other similar ultra-cheap accommodation.

Hostel Hütteldorf

13, Schlossberggasse 8 (877 1501/www.hostel.at). U4 Hütteldorf. **Rates** per person €13-€21. **Credit** AmEx, DC, MC, V.

Way out of town but well-connected by U-Bahn, so don't let the site deter you. The place has 60 rooms and 285 beds; rooms hold six to eight beds each. The price includes breakfast.
Internet (wireless). Parking (free).

Jugendherberge Wien-Myrthengasse

7, Myrthengasse 7 (523 6316/www.jugend herberge.at). Tram 46/ bus 48a. **Rates** per person €16-€20. **Credit** AmEx, DC, MC, V. **Map** p246 C7 ④

This is the most centrally located of the city's youth hostels with 68 rooms and 270 beds (four to six beds per room). The price includes breakfast.
Internet.

Westend City Hostel

6, Fügergasse 3 (597 6729/www.westendhostel.at). U3, U6 Westbahnhof (exit Innere Mariahilfer Strasse-Millergasse)/tram 6, 18. **Rates** per person €18.40-€24.20. **No credit cards. Map** p246 B9 ④

Once both a bordello and a hotel, this 27-room, 211-bed hostel is just three minutes from the Westbahnhof rail station. Totally transformed in 2002, the rooms are modestly furnished, but attractive nonetheless, each with a shower/toilet module. All rooms are no-smoking. A deal with a nearby restaurant allows cheap meals, while breakfast is included in the room rate.
Internet. Parking (€13/day).

Wombat's Vienna the Base

15, Grangasse 6 (897 2336/www.wombats.at). U3, U6 Westbahnhof (exit Gerstnerstrasse)/ tram 52, 58. **Rates** per person in 4-6 person rooms €17-€21; doubles €50. **No credit cards**. **Map** p246 ⑤

Voted 'the cleanest hostel in the world' by hostel-world.com, Wombat's City Hostel has been a rousing success. Located behind Westbahnhof, it's convenient for young interrailers who lap up the laid-back atmosphere and the opportunity to trade tales in the bar and lounge. Now they've opened the swish Wombat's Vienna the Lounge in a nearby but

more salubrious location on Mariahilfer Strasse. For those who can't handle too much communal living, there are singles and doubles as well as the usual four-to-six-bed dorms, all no-smoking with a shower and toilet. The buffet breakfast costs just €3.50. *Bar. Disabled-adapted rooms. Internet.*
Other locations Wombat's Vienna the Lounge, 15, Mariahilfer Strasse 157 (897 2336/www.wombats.at).

Camping

Facilities at Viennese campsites are first class, particularly at prime locations such as Neue Donau and Schlosspark Laxenburg. As such, they're much in demand, particularly during the summer peak season, so book early. Check out the sites at www.wien.camping.at.

14th district

Camping Wien West

14, Hüttelbergstrasse 80 (914 2314/www.wien camping.at). Tram 49, then bus 148, 152. **Rates** per person €5.90-€6.90; €3.50-€4 4-15s; €4.50-€5.50 tent; €8.50-€9.50 camper van; €3-€4 electricity hook-up; €25-€29 1-2 person bungalow; €44-€48 3-4 person bungalow. **Open** all year except February. **Credit** AmEx, DC, MC, V.
The site is on the edge of the Wienerwald, 8km (5 miles) west of the city centre. Facilities include lounges, kitchen with cooking facilities, supermarket, buffet, washing machines and dryer. There are disposal facilities for chemical toilets and a motor van service centre. Unsurprisingly, it tends to get packed around about midsummer.

22nd district

Aktiv Camping Neue Donau

22, Am Kleehäufel (202 4010/www.wiencamping.at). U1 Vienna International Centre, then bus 91a to campsite Kleehäufel. **Rates** per person €5.90-€6.90; €3.50-€4 4-15s; €4.50-€6.50 tent; €8.50-€12 camper van; €3-€4 electricity hook-up. **Open** Apr-Sept. **Credit** AmEx, DC, MC, V.
This location is just north of the 'New Danube' recreation area parallel to the main Danube, and there are hiking, cycling, swimming, boating and nude bathing areas nearby. It's about 4km (2.5 miles) north-east of the city centre. Facilities include lounges, kitchens with cooking equipment, a supermarket, a buffet and washing machines. In addition, there are provisions for emptying out chemical toilets and a camper van service centre.

23rd district

Camping Rodaun

23, An der Au 2 (888 4154/www.quickinfo.at/camping-rodaun). Schnellbahn S-1, S-2, S-3 to Liesing, then bus 253, 254, 255. **Rates** per person €5.45; €3.27 3-13s; €4.36 tent; €5.01 camper van. **Open** Mid May-Oct. **Credit** V.

This campsite is about 10km (6 miles) west of the city centre, in the Rodaun suburb. It is on the fringes of the Wienerwald, adjacent to an artificial lake created by a dam across the Liesing river, and so it feels pretty rural. Facilities include electricity outlets and a restaurant.

Long-term accommodation

1st district

Sacher Apartments

1, Rotenturmstrasse 1 (533 3238). U1, U3 Stephansplatz. **Rates** up to 9 days €95-€115 single/double. 10 days or longer €75-€95 single/double. Monthly rates by agreement.
No credit cards. Map p251 E6 ③
This eight-room apartment hotel occupying the upper floor of a post-war office block offers compact but comfortable accommodation. The Sacher is in the heart of the city and there is public transport (and even horse-drawn carriages) at the door. *Internet (dataport). TV.*

Singerstrasse 21-25

1, Singerstrasse 21-25 (514 49-0/www.singerstrasse 2125.at). U1 Stephansplatz, U3 Stubentor/tram 1, 2/bus 1a. **Open** Reception 8am-8pm Mon-Fri. **Rates** *studio* €609-€728/€2,190-€2,635 per wk/mth; *executive suite* €966-€1,071/€3,503-€3,933 per wk/mth. **Credit** AmEx, DC, MC, V. **Map** p251 F7 ㉜
The 77 serviced apartments in this purpose-built complex look fresh in their attractive livery of light grey walls and contrasting natural wood floors. Two sizes each of studio and two-room executive accommodation offer every convenience a longer-term guest could want, from elegantly outfitted bathrooms to compact full kitchenettes complete with glassware, tableware, dishes, pots and pans, toasters, coffee machine, microwave and even a dishwasher. There's a self-service laundrette on site too. *Concierge. Internet (broadband). Parking (garage, €15/day). TV.*

19th district

Kaiser Franz Joseph Apartments

19, Sieveringer Strasse 4a (329 00-0/www.deraghotels.de). U2 Schottentor/tram 1, 2, D, then tram 38 or U4 Heiligenstadt, then bus 39a. **Rates** €102-€165 single; €119-€265 double; €185-€395 suite; from 15 days onward: €35-€63 single apartment; €46-€119 double apartment; €75-€184 suite. **Credit** AmEx, DC, MC, V.
Kaiser Franz Joseph Apartments is a newish facility that holds 95 hotel rooms and 344 serviced apartments. The decor is attractively modern with comfortable furnishings. Set on the fringe of an upmarket residential district that's close to the vineyards, the location has good transport to the city centre. *Bar. Business centre. Gym. Internet (dataport, wireless). No-smoking rooms. Parking (garage €12/day). Restaurant. TV.*

Sightseeing

Features

Belvedere. *See p91.*

Vienna Districts

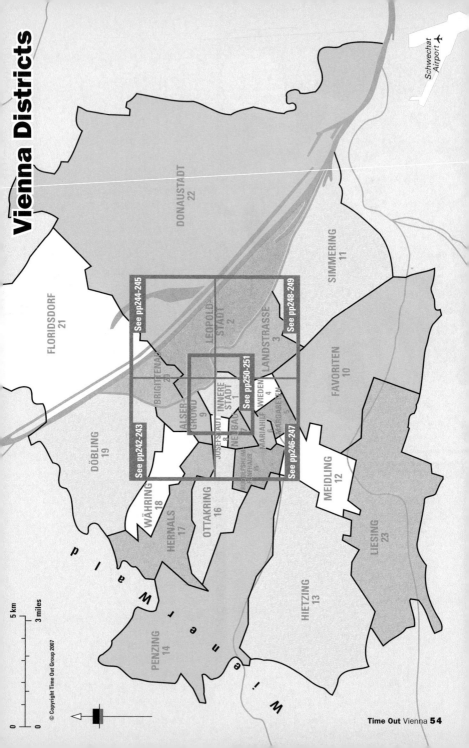

Schwechat Airport

FLORIDSDORF 21

DONAUSTADT 22

DÖBLING 19

See pp242-243

See pp244-245

BRIGITTENAU 20

ALSER GRUND 9

LEOPOLD STADT 2

SIMMERING 11

WÄHRING 18

JUSEFSTADT 8

NEUBAU 7

INNERE STADT 1

See pp250-251

LANDSTRASSE 3

See pp248-249

HERNALS 17

OTTAKRING 16

MARIAHILF 6

WIEDEN 4

MARGARETEN 5

RUDOLFSHEIM FUNFHAUS 15

See pp246-247

FAVORITEN 10

MEIDLING 12

PENZING 14

HIETZING 13

LIESING 23

5 km

3 miles

© Copyright Time Out Group 2007

Introduction

From the grandiose to the gruesome, Vienna's gamut of great sights is a reflection of European history.

Vienna is an ideal destination for the independent traveller with a liking for the arts, intellectual and geopolitical history, or carefree self-indulgence. Outside the dense mesh of sights formed by the Innere Stadt, Vienna's historic centre, and tourist magnets such as Belvedere and Schönbrunn, the rest of the city is a spacious, inviting, magnificently appointed ensemble, ideal for strolling, pausing and taking stock. Given the upheavals it endured and inflicted on itself throughout the 20th century, it's surprising how pristine Vienna has remained. Amid the Baroque palaces and churches, exuberant parks, imposing 19th-century apartment buildings and art nouveau façades, the only thing that occasionally irks is the heavy-handed kitsch wrought by a tourist industry intent on exploiting Vienna's status as former imperial metropolis and European capital of classical music.

Vienna's barrier-free, user-friendly quality is evident when you first encounter its underground system: no turnstiles, no showing tickets, just a short escalator ride to the platforms. Not that you'll need it much. The central core of the Innere Stadt is easily walkable and districts 2-9, where the remainder of the city's sights are located, are more enjoyably reached via tram. Thanks to over a century of rigorous urban planning and enlightened municipal government, Vienna is helpfully divided into 23 clearly delineated *Bezirke* (districts) that surround the historic centre in two concentric circles. The kaleidoscopic central core of the Innere Stadt is hemmed in by the Danube Canal to the north and by the east–west horseshoe of the monumental Ringstrasse, and contains the vast majority of the city's best-known sights. Once you're finished with the inner city, access is easy to districts 2-9, where the remainder of Vienna's most worthwhile sights are located. When you tire of the asphalt, take any of the trams heading north and west, and you emerge in the Vienna Woods (*see p214*) or among the vineyards that line the city's northern fringe.

Tourist-Info Wien

1, Albertinaplatz (211 14-222/www.vienna.info). **U1, U2, U4 Karlsplatz. Open** 9am-7pm daily. **Map** p250 E7.
The main tourist office. It offers superb brochures on all aspects of the city, as well as tickets, maps, tours, an accommodation service and currency exchange.

Museums & galleries

Despite considerable municipal and state largesse in matters of the arts, free entrance to museums is limited to Sundays, and in relatively few places. Those intending to see Vienna's bewildering selection of museums and art galleries from the inside could purchase the **Vienna Card**, which offers entrance discounts to more than 190 museums and sights, and 72 hours' free public transport for €18.50. The card is available at hotels, tourist offices and stations.

Tours

Vienna's history is reflected in numerous walking tours that take in aspects of the city such as Jewish life, imperial history and Viennese art nouveau (Jugendstil). Times and details appear in the monthly *Wien Programm* leaflet, available from tourist offices and hotels. Of particular interest is the *Third Man* tour (usually 4pm Mon-Fri, but phone 774 8901 or check www.viennawalks.com). The tour in English and German takes you to the locations featured in Orson Welles' film, including the sewers. Architecture buffs should consult the Architekturzentrum Wien (www.azw.at) for tours of Vienna's urban fabric.

Sightseeing

1st District: Innere Stadt

The heart of Europe.

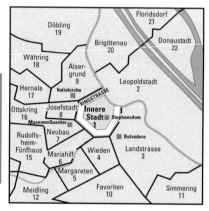

Maps p250 and p251

It's easy to spend a few days in Vienna without leaving its fascinating historic centre. What the Viennese call the first district, the Innere Stadt or the 'city', is an area slightly smaller than New York's Central Park, where they come to shop, stroll, eat, drink and work. And unlike many capitals, a fair few of them live here too. For the visitor, the Innere Stadt contains reflections of the myriad changes that have taken place in Vienna since the Romans founded the garrison town of Vindobona over 2,000 years ago. As you walk though its winding streets and alleys, and along broad 19th-century precincts, you'll come across Roman remains, medieval houses and Baroque palaces and churches. It's architectural texture is also woven with imposing apartment buildings from the age of 19th-century liberalism, and traces of Jugendstil, the local strain of art nouveau, that along with the early Modernism of Adolf Loos recall Vienna's frenzied fin-de-siècle creativity. The reason why so much is crammed into these 3.6 square kilometres (1.39 square miles) lies in the fact that Vienna's city walls remained standing well into the 1850s. Although successive members of the House of Habsburg were the city's most dynamic promoters, it was their enduring fear of Ottoman invasion that stunted Vienna's growth for centuries.

Bisected by the north-south axis of Kärntnerstrasse and Rotenturmstrasse, the Innere Stadt centres on Stephansdom, Vienna's magnificent Gothic cathedral. From Stephansplatz the broad elegant thoroughfare of Graben eventually leads to the vast, rambling Hofburg, the Imperial Palace, headquarters of the Habsburg Empire until its demise in 1918.

Today, the area forms Vienna's classiest retail and residential district, with most of the its top-flight hotels and restaurants, venerable coffee houses and concert halls, and a pavement-café ambience akin to that of the Mediterranean. There's a lot to pack in here, but with its gentle pace and relative serenity, the Innere Stadt is one of the most remarkable, yet liveable city centres of any major European capital.

Stephansplatz

Situated at the junction of two U-Bahn lines (U1 and U3) and two of Vienna's most famous pedestrian streets, Kärntner Strasse and Graben, Stephansplatz and the cathedral are useful landmarks when exploring the Innere Stadt. In addition to the shoppers, commuters and drifters, the square is jammed with tourists crowding around the street performers, and getting collared by costumed students hawking tickets for Mozart evenings of dubious merit. The cathedral's bulk overwhelms the square, whose air is thick with the smells of ice-cream, roasting coffee and the urine of the *Fiaker* horses lined up on the northern side. The buildings that surround **Stephansdom** are a mixture of Baroque and 19th century, housing various agencies of the church, apart from the post-war block facing the main entrance.

On the north side of Stephansplatz is the **Dom- und Diozesanmuseum** (Cathedral and Diocesan Museum). Facing the main entrance to the cathedral, the buildings are nondescript post-war edifices, with some, such as the corner of Rotenturmstrasse, frankly shoddy. The demolition of one such monstrosity made way for Hans Hollein's curvaceous Haas Haus (1990), once the city's most controversial modern building due to its proximity to the venerable cathedral. Having failed miserably as a shopping arcade, it now houses a swish new designer hotel whose fifth-floor bar offers one of the best views of the cathedral.

At the Kärntnerstrasse end of Stephansplatz, the square changes its name to Stock-im-

Sightseeing

The distinctive **Stephansdom** dominates Vienna's skyline.

Eisenplatz ('iron in wood' is a rough translation), where journeymen would hammer a nail into a log to ensure safe passage home after a trip to Vienna. A glass case protecting a stump of larch studded with nails is on the side of the Equitable Palace building (on the corner of Kärntner Strasse), the neo-Baroque 19th-century seat of the famous insurance company. It's worth taking a peek inside at the sumptuous marble cladding of the entrance hall and the courtyard tiled in Hungarian Zsolnay ceramics. To access any locked palatial building in Vienna it usually suffices to ring the bell of any corporate-sounding address and then push open the door.

Dom- und Diozesanmuseum

1, Stephansplatz 6 (515 52 3689/www.dommuseum. at). U1, U3 Stephansplatz. **Open** 10am-5pm Tue-Sat. **Admission** €7; €5.50 concessions; €3 children. **Credit** AmEx, DC, MC, V. **Map** p251 E/F6.
Located in the Baroque Archbishop's Palace, the pricey Cathedral and Diocesan Museum can be truly recommended only to devotees of Baroque painting. Highlights are works by Austrian masters such as Anton Kraus, Franz Maulbertsch and Michael Angelo Unterberger. However, there is the hotch-potch of curiosities typical of ecclesiastical museums: the first European portrait on panel, that of Rudolph IV (1360); a Giotto-esque stained-glass

window (1340) with Jugendstil ornamentation (restored 1900); and the blackened remnants of the cathedral's Gothic carved choir stalls (these were destroyed in a 1945 bombing raid).

Stephansdom

1, Stephansplatz (51552-3526/www.stephans kirche.at). U1, U3 Stephansplatz. **Open** 6am-10pm Mon-Sat; 7am-10pm Sun. **Admission** free. **Tours** *German* €4 10.30am, 3.30pm daily. *English* Apr-Oct €4 3.45pm daily. **No credit cards. Map** p251 E7.
Although originally located beyond the medieval city walls, St Stephen's Cathedral lies at the centre of the present Innere Stadt and dominates the city's skyline. No other building is so unanimously loved and revered by the Viennese as their dear Steffl ('little Stephen' in the local dialect). It is certainly a symbol of endurance, having undergone numerous phases of building and repair due to the ravages of the Turks, the Napoleonic French and the Allies. The last thorough restoration was completed in 1948 after fire destroyed the roof of the nave.

From the outside the cathedral appears divided into three distinct parts. On a sunny day, the geometrically designed tiled roof of the nave, depicting the Habsburg crown protected by chevrons, is magnificent. Dating from the late 13th century, the oldest existing feature is the Romanesque Riesentor (Giants' Gate), the main entrance to the cathedral. The origin of the name is unclear, but the most attractive explanation is that mammoth bones dug

Top ten   Major sights

Belvedere
Splendid city views from the terrace of this Baroque masterpiece. *See p91.*

Hofburg
Europe's largest family home is a treasure trove that breathes history. *See p64.*

Kaisergruft
The imperial crypt is the key to the Viennese way of death. *See p60.*

Karlskirche
Baroque with a Byzantine touch. *See p99.*

MuseumsQuartier
Vienna's sprawling arts complex is winning the locals over. *See p83.*

Ringstrasse
Refresh your knowledge of architectural history on the great bourgeois boulevard. *See p76.*

Schönbrunn
Escape the crowds in the gorgeous gardens of Vienna's number one tourist attraction. *See p106.*

Secession
Temple to the city's once flaming modernity. *See p99.*

Staatsoper
The premier venue of Europe's music capital. *See p183.*

Stephansdom
Vienna's short on Gothic, but this is the city's hoariest steeple. *See p57.*

up during the building work were taken by the good burghers of Vienna to be the remains of a race of giants killed in the biblical flood. The entrance is flanked by the impressive Heidentürme (Pagan Towers), so called because of their tenuous resemblance to minarets, forming a façade peppered with references to the city's history, past and present.

Look out for the circular recess to the left of the entrance, which enabled citizens to check that their local bakers weren't peddling undersized loaves, and on the other side the inscription *O5* – the capital O and the fifth letter (E) – representing the first two letters of Oesterreich – a symbol of the Austrian resistance in World War II. Now protected by Plexiglas, it used to be regularly highlighted in chalk whenever alleged war criminal and ex-Austrian president Kurt Waldheim attended Mass. The icing on the cake is undoubtedly the 137m- (450ft-) high south tower, a magnificently hoary Gothic finger completed in 1433 after 74 years of work. Unfortunately, it is almost permanently obscured by scaffolding. A north tower of similar dimensions was projected in the early 16th century, but austerity measures imposed during the first Turkish siege of 1529 put paid to the idea.

The interior, with its beautiful high vaulting, is surprisingly gloomy and always packed with visitors. Still, it remains very much a place of worship, and during Mass, access is denied to most of the nave. It is worth going inside to see the extraordinary carving of the Pilgram pulpit at the top of the nave, where the sculptor, contravening the usual stonemasons' code of practice, has depicted himself looking out of a window to admire his own work. This motif is repeated under the organ loft on the north side of the nave. Other highlights include the tomb of war hero Eugène of Savoy in the Tirna Chapel, also located to the north of the nave, just inside the main entrance. In an ancestral tradition aimed at creating several focal points of devotion to the Crown, the cathedral's catacombs house the entrails of the principal Habsburgs, while their hearts and corpses dwell in the Augustinerkirche and the Imperial Crypt, respectively. Unless you love contemplating piles of bones and skulls, give the catacombs a miss.

A lift operates from the north side of the nave to the top of the north tower, where the cathedral's enormous bell, the Pummerin ('Boomer'), hangs. For the sense of achievement and to enjoy the splendid views, you could take the 553 steps that lead to the top. Access is from the outside on the south side.

East of Stephansdom

The two principal streets to the east of Stephansdom, Singerstrasse and Domgasse, lead towards Vienna's only remaining medieval quarter. This small but charming labyrinth of streets is practically tourist free and must be one of the most desirable residential areas of any European inner city. The area directly behind the cathedral is known as the Blutviertel (Blood Quarter), which supposedly derives from a massacre of renegade Templar Knights in 1312 on Blutgasse, connecting Singerstrasse and Domgasse. In contrast, the house at Blutgasse 7 has a fine example of the tranquil inner courtyards that abound in this area. At Blutgasse 3 there's a so-called *Pawlatschenhaus* (gallery house – deriving from the Czech *pavlac*), one of several that are found through the city. On Singerstrasse are several 17th-century palaces such as the Neupauer-Breuner (no.16), housing the Vienna branch of Sotheby's, the Woka lighting company (*see p156*), that reproduces modernist classics, and the church and treasury of the fearsome Teutonic Knights (**Schatzkammer des Deutschen Ritterordens**).

One block east, at the junction of Singerstrasse and Grünangergasse, is the imposing Palais Rottal, and in the delightful cobbled Grünangergasse (at no.4) there's Palais Fürstenberg, with two finely carved stone greyhounds over the portal.

Mozarthaus Wien

1, Domgasse 5/Schulerstrasse 8 (512 1791/www. mozarthausvienna.at). U1, U3 Stephansplatz. **Open** 10am-8pm daily. **Admission** €9; €7 concessions; €3 children. **No credit cards. Map** p251 F7.

Mozart's only remaining Viennese residence reopened as a museum on 27 January 2006, the day of his 250th birthday, and is known locally as the Figarohaus (because he wrote *The Marriage of Figaro* here). Mozart lived on the first floor from 1784 to 1787, reputedly his happiest (and most prosperous) years in the city. Laid out on floor levels, the new museum offers a thoroughly documented portrait of Mozart's highly productive years in Vienna, with numerous drawings and paintings of the clan, original sheet music, letters and musical instruments, and a host of interactive audio-visuals. Naturally there are also the obligatory shop and 'Mozart' coffee house. Although most of his personal effects are in his home town of Salzburg, the trustees have done a commendable job of presenting Mozart's achievements.

Schatzkammer des Deutschen Ritterordens

1, Singerstrasse 7 (512 1065/www.deutscher-orden.at). U1, U3 Stephansplatz. **Open** *Church* 7am-6pm daily. *Treasury* 10am-noon Mon, Thur, Sat; 3-5pm Wed, Fri. **Admission** €4; €3 concessions; free under-11s. **No credit cards. Map** p251 E7.

The building on Singerstrasse and those of the adjoining courtyard belong to one of the most powerful orders to emerge from the Crusades. The fearful sounding Teutonic Knights (Deutscher Ritterorden) had the Schatzkammer (church and treasury) constructed in the 14th century as a shelter for the care of the sick and needy: good works that began during the Crusades and continue to this day. The church is recognisably Gothic, but apart from the 16th-century altarpiece and the coats of arms and tombstones of its illustrious members, the point of interest here is the Treasury and its varied collection of bric-a-brac picked up during the Crusades. Among the arms and armour, there are bizarre objects such as a salt cellar made of red coral and fossilised shark's teeth, thought to be able to detect the presence of poison. Beyond the entrance on the ground floor is the tiny, beautifully painted 18th-century Sala Terrena, Vienna's earliest concert hall, where Mozart reputedly played, located at the foot of the staircase to the treasury. Here a door opens onto two recently renovated cobbled inner courtyards that eventually lead back into Stephansplatz via a shady terrace bar, an oasis in the summer heat.

In & around Kärntner Strasse

Pedestrianised since the 1970s, Kärntner Strasse connects Stephansplatz with one of Vienna's great institutions, the Staatsoper (Opera House, *see p183*). Luxury shops used to trade here, but the street is now a cacophony of illuminated signs announcing chain stores and takeaways. An occasional glimpse of former glories is offered by such establishments as Lobmeyer at no.26, a famous glass-maker with a museum containing some original items by the Wiener Werkstätte design firm. Near the corner of Stock-im-Eisenplatz is the Kärntnerdurchgang, with the fabulous Adolf Loos American Bar (1908) – *see p 196*. Weihburggasse leads down to one of Vienna's most pleasant squares, the Italianate Franziskanerplatz, probably better known locally for the Kleines Café (*see p140*) than for the good works of the Franciscans for whom it's named. Sit here in summer and admire the Baroque houses of Weihburggasse, the delightful Moses Fountain (1798) by JM Fischer and, of course, the **Franziskanekirche**.

The other streets to the east of Kärntner Strasse – Himmelpfortgasse, Johannesgasse and Annagasse – all have a number of splendid Baroque houses and a sprinkling of minor

Mozarthaus Wien.

Sightseeing

Neuer Markt, the medieval flour market.

sights, the most notable being the Winter Palace of Prince Eugène of Savoy in the first of the three, at no.8. Conceived by perhaps the most important architect of this era, JB Fischer von Erlach, and completed by his great rival Lukas von Hildebrandt in 1709, this fine Baroque palace is now used by the Ministry of Finance. Although the rooms are out of bounds, the most arresting features – the vestibule and the staircase propped up by four atlantes and the statue of Hercules on the landing – can be seen during office hours. On the corner of Annagasse and Seilerstätte, another fine Baroque mansion houses the multimedia music museum, **Haus der Musik**.

Franziskanerkirche

1, Franziskanerplatz (512 4578). U1, U3 Stephansplatz. **Open** 6.30am-6pm daily. **Map** p251 E/F7.

The Habsburgs had a penchant for austere monastic orders such as the Franciscans and Capuchins, a tradition that goes back to Rudolf of Habsburg, the founder of the dynasty. The present Church of the Franciscans dates from 1611, but some 20 years earlier the order had been given possession of the neighbouring house, itself an establishment for the reform of the city's prostitutes, where townsmen were encouraged to take them as wives. Today, in

the same vein, the church feeds the homeless. The façade is an odd mixture of Gothic and German Renaissance, dotted with curious roundels that used to contain portraits of saints. The interior is rather more luxurious than you might expect from the Franciscans, particularly the trompe-l'oeil executed by Jesuit lay brother and painter-architect Andrea Pozzo (1707), surrounded by an arched high altar.

Haus der Musik

1, Seilerstätte 30 (516 48/www.hdm.at). U1, U2, U4 Karlsplatz. **Open** 10am-10pm daily. **Admission** €10; €8.50 concessions; €5.50 children. **Credit** AmEx, DC, MC, V. **Map** p251 E7.

Housed in the former residence of Otto Nicolai, founder of the Wiener Philharmoniker, this 'modern interactive sound museum' is a bold attempt to illustrate the listening experience. Appropriately, the show begins with an instructive history of Vienna's most celebrated orchestra and a large screen showing the previous year's New Year's concert. The Sonosphere floor traces elementary aural experiences: the prenatal listening room (sounds of the womb), the Polyphonium (the perfect surround sound experience) and various natural and environmental sounds that can be combined at will and burned on to a CD to take away. Interactivity also abounds in Futuresphere, where you can tinkle on 'hyperinstruments' and sensors, but the best simulation is the 'virtual conductor' on the great composers floor where you can wield an electronic baton and conduct the Philharmoniker yourself. When it's full the place is a veritable cacophony, so make use of the daily late opening hours.

West of Kärntner Strasse

Directly west of Kärntner Strasse lies Neuer Markt, a congested rectangular square that used to be the medieval flour market. Architecturally, the square is a dreadful hotch-potch of styles that don't so much contrast as clash; however, amid the parked cars is a copy of Donner's splendid Providentia Fountain (1739). The naked figures of the original – allegories of Austria's four main rivers – proved too much for Maria Theresia's Chastity Commission and were removed in 1773, but returned intact in 1801. Among the shops, hotels and cafés, the Baroque façade of former court jewellers Koechert is the square's most notable feature. To the south, behind an unassuming but decidedly grim façade is the **Kaisergruft & Kapuzinerkirche**, the crypt containing the spectacular tombs of the Habsburgs.

Kaisergruft & Kapuzinerkirche

1, Tegetthoffstraße 2 (512 6853-16/www. kaisergruft.at). U1, U2, U4 Karlsplatz or U1, U3 Stephansdom/tram 1, 2, D, J/bus 3a. **Open** 10am-6pm daily. **Admission** €4; €3 concessions; €1.50 children. **No credit cards. Map** p250 E7.

From 1633 onwards, the Habsburgs were laid to rest in the crypt of the Church of the Capuchins. Each funeral was preceded by a belittling ritual consisting of the reigning emperor announcing his various titles to the waiting prior, who then proceeded to deny knowledge of his person and refuse him entry. Finally, the emperor was forced to identify himself as 'a humble sinner who begs God's mercy' and the cortège would be granted permission to enter. Today, an admission fee and silence ('Silentium!' reads the inscription over the entrance) are all they ask. Many of these early tombs are decorated with skull and crossbones, weapons and bats' wings, that progressively increase in size until you reach the gigantic iron double tomb of Empress Maria Theresia and her husband, Franz Stephan. For sheer size and representational extravagance – above the tomb the couple appear to be sitting up in bed embroiled in a marital tiff – this has to be the highlight of the show. In stark contrast, their son Joseph II, whose reforms tried and failed to popularise the drop-bottom reusable coffin, lies in a simple copper casket.

Further along is the New Vault, with its bizarre, diagonal concrete beams where Maximilian I of Mexico and Napoleon's second wife, Marie Louise, are to be found. Their son, the Duc de Reichstadt, was moved from here to Paris in 1940 by the Nazis in an attempt to ingratiate themselves with the French. People tend to dwell a little longer in the Franz-Josef Vault as here lie the Habsburgs who still touch hearts: Franz Josef I, the last emperor, his wife, the eternally popular Empress Elisabeth, and their son, the unhappy Prince Rudolph, of the Mayerling suicide pact. Sisi's tomb is invariably covered in flowers and small wreaths with ribbons in the colours of the Hungarian flag commemorating her sympathy for that country's national aspirations. The last room contains the remains of Empress Zita, who was buried with full pomp and ceremony in 1989, and a bust of her husband, Emperor Karl I, who died in exile in Madeira.

West of Neuermarkt

The area bounded by Neuermarkt to the east, Graben to the north and Kohlmarkt to the west consists of a network of narrow streets ideal for strolling and replete with restaurants, antique shops and galleries, unmissable Kaffeehäuser such as the Bräunerhof (*see p136*) and Hawelka (*see p137*), plus the **Jüdisches Museum** and the **Dorotheum** auction house.

Dorotheum

1, Dorotheergasse 17 (515 60-200/www.dorotheum. com). U1, U3 Stephansplatz. **Open** 10am-6pm Mon-Fri; 9am-5pm Sat. **Admission** free. **Credit** (shop only) AmEx, DC, MC, V. **Map** p250 E7.

In the past, a 'visit to Auntie Dorothy's' was a popular euphemism for falling into hard times. Set up in 1707 by Emperor Joseph I as a pawn shop for the wealthy, the Dorotheum is now Vienna's foremost

Pestäule (Plague Monument). *See p63.*

auction house and the oldest institution of its kind in the world. The celebration of its 200th anniversary in 2007 has, however, thrown some unsavoury light on its role in the dispossession of Vienna's Jews after 1938. The present building is a bit of neo-Baroque bombast from the 1890s that provides a thoroughfare between Dorotheergasse and Habsburgergasse. If you are looking to buy, auctions are held daily, with regular specialised sales. Otherwise, the Glashof on the ground floor has an ever-changing selection of reasonably affordable bric-a-brac. The more affluent should peruse the modernist furniture on the second floor.

Jüdisches Museum

1, Dorotheergasse 11 (535 0431/www.jmw.at). U1, U3 Stephansplatz. **Open** 10am-6pm Mon-Wed, Fri, Sun; 10am-8pm Thur. **Admission** €5; €2.90 concessions. **No credit cards. Map** p250 E7.

The world's first Jewish museum was opened in Vienna in 1895 and closed in 1938, its exhibits confiscated by the Nazis. The present museum has been in the Palais Eskeles since 1993 and the building remodelled in 1995 by far-out architects Eichinger oder Knechtl. It now serves as a study centre, archive and library, with three floors of exhibition space. The ground floor has an important collection of Judaica, displayed amid striking fragmented frescoes by Nancy Spero who reworked images such as those of a medieval matzo bakery, Gustav Mahler

conducting, and the smoking remains of a razed synagogue. The first and second floors hold highly recommendable temporary exhibitions that link Vienna's historical, political and artistic history with the role of Jews and their interaction with the Gentile community. On the second floor a permanent exhibition uses 21 holograms to depict aspects of Jewish culture in Vienna. A combined ticket for the museum, the synagogue and the Museum Judenplatz (*see p72*) costs €7 (€4 concessions).

Graben & Kohlmarkt

Graben and Kohlmarkt are Vienna's most majestic thoroughfares, entirely composed of Baroque, 19th-century and belle époque buildings. Graben ('ditch') today is a broad pedestrian causeway built along what was the southern moat that defended the Roman camp established on Hoher Markt a few streets to the north. Commerce harks back to imperial times with innumerable shops bearing the 'k.u.k.' (*kaiserlich und königlich*) royal warrant, among them a former gentlemen's outfitters announcing branches in Prague and Karlsbad, now sadly a branch of H&M.

Graben's most exuberant flourish is the resoundingly Baroque **Pestsäule** (Plague Monument), a feature common to all Austrian cities. Nearby on Petersplatz is **Peterskirche**, while on the corner of Tuchlauben, is the fine neo-classical Erste Österreichisches Sparkasse (First Austrian Savings Bank – built in 1836), emblazoned with an enormous gilded bee symbolising thrift and hard work. At nos.14-15 is the monumental Grabenhof (1876) built by Otto Wagner to another architect's plans. This early Wagner work has hints of the Jugendstil he would later champion – a style more clearly visible in the Ankerhaus at no.10, which Wagner designed, built and for a time used as his studio. The only remaining Baroque building is the Bartolotti-Partenfeld Palace (1720) at no.11. Where Habsburgergasse crosses Graben there are some delightful (and useful) Jugendstil public conveniences, and between the two flights of steps leading to the ladies and the gents, you'll find the fine Josef Fountain built by JM Fischer.

Graben grinds to an abrupt halt with the imposing façade of the Meinl am Graben store (*see p150*), all that remains of the chain of coffee roasters and grocery stores that once fed the bourgeoisie of much of Central and Eastern Europe. This flagship store, run by a doting staff of 250, is Vienna's Fortnum and Mason and well worth a visit. Looking south along Kohlmarkt, the city's former coal and charcoal market, the view is dominated by the sight of the magnificent copper dome that signals the

Top five Minor sights

Heeresgeschichtliches Museum
An engrossing view of Habsburg military might and more in a stupendous setting. See p93.

Karl-Marx-Hof
When the Viennese led the world in social experimentation. See p112.

Kirche am Steinhof
Otto Wagner goes ecclesiastic with astonishing results. See p104.

Museum Liechtenstein
Baroque frivolity magnificently restored. See p102.

Zentralfriedhof
The old Jewish cemetery here is a haunting reminder of the destruction of a whole community. See p110.

Michaelertor entrance to Hofburg, the Imperial Palace. This is Vienna's most glitzy shopping mile, a veritable maelstrom of designer names, with Diesel and D&G last to join the fray in 2007. Siberian billionaire Roman Abramovich owns a €27-million penthouse here and a working knowledge of Russian is a prerequisite for employment in the shops below. Among the few indigenous establishments still rejecting the roubles, many have façades of real beauty such as Adolf Loos' Manz bookshop at no.16 and Hans Hollein's keyhole entrance at no.8-10.

Pestsäule/Dreifältigkeitssäule
1, Graben. U1, U3 Stephansplatz/bus 1a, 2a, 3a. **Map** p250 E6.
Between the Josef Fountain and the other fountain that JM Fischer designed to commemorate Leopold III soars Graben's centrepiece, the Pestsäule or Plague Monument (it is also known as the Trinity Column or Dreifältigkeitssäule). Newly renovated, this fine example dating from 1692 is one of many that were erected throughout the Empire to mark the end of the 1679 plague and also to celebrate deliverance from the spiritual 'plagues' of the Turks and the Reformation. The Baroque stone carving, primarily by Fischer von Erlach, depicts a gorgeous mass of cherubs and saints swathed in clouds. **Photo** *p61*.

Peterskirche
1, Petersplatz (533 6433/www.peterskirche.at).
U1, U3 Stephansplatz/bus 1a, 3a. **Open** 7am-7pm Mon-Fri; 9am-7pm Sat, Sun. **Map** p250 E6.
Erected on the site of what was probably Vienna's oldest Christian church (dating from the late fourth

century), Peterskirche was built by Lukas von Hildebrandt and completed in 1733. Undoubtedly the finest Baroque church of the Innere Stadt, Peterskirche has a green copper dome that echoes the nearby Michaelertor entrance to Hofburg. The dome's fresco has faded but the interior remains spectacular due to a wealth of trompe-l'oeil effects around the choir and the altar. Today, the church is the stronghold of Opus Dei in Vienna – *Da Vinci Code* junkies can pick up the rather fetching multilingual prayer cards featuring the order's founder.

Michaelerplatz & Herrengasse

Kohlmarkt discharges the crowds into the circular Michaelerplatz, a carousel of ministerial limos, *Fiakers*, cyclists and jay-walking tourists circumventing some nondescript Roman ruins. Lying in a nifty recess designed by architect Hans Hollein, this is all that remains of the Roman *canabae*, the residential and whoring district. Although dwarfed by the entrance to Hofburg, the Kohlmarkt side of the square is the site of one of modernism's seminal edifices: the so-called **Loos House**, now a bank. Across the street is the **Michaelerkirche** whose neoclassical façade hides the church's early Gothic origins. These can be seen from a pretty courtyard by entering Kohlmarkt 11. Notice here too the well-conserved Baroque carriage houses. To the west, on the ground floor of a text-book 19th-century apartment building, is Café Griensteidl (*see p137*). Closed at the start of the 20th century, this plush reconstruction of what was once Vienna's most famous literary café and second home to Arthur Schnitzler, Hugo von Hofmannsthal and others, reopened in 1990.

West of Michaelerplatz runs Herrengasse – Lords' Lane – lined with innumerable palaces that today house government agencies, newspapers and corporate galleries. The Landhaus at no.13 was the seat of the Lower Austrian government until a new administrative centre was built in the regional capital St Pölten. The building witnessed the outbreak of the 1848 Revolution when troops fired on a crowd demanding the resignation of Prince Metternich. Opposite the Landhaus is the neo-Renaissance Palais Ferstel, home of Café Central (*see p136*), built by and named after architect Heinrich Ferstel. It has an elegant, if rather moribund Italian-style shopping arcade that leads into Freyung (*see p71*). Further along Herrengasse are two other fine, accessible aristocratic mansions: Palais Harrach, which was rebuilt in 1690 after it burnt down during the Turkish siege, and the high Baroque Palais Kinski, built by von Hildebrandt (1713-19). Both

have airy courtyards and shops and galleries that are on the exclusive side.

The streets heading south off Herrengasse lead to the impressive but lifeless ministerial quarter around Minoritenplatz. The cobbled square is dominated by the brooding Gothic Minoritenkirche and its striking octagonal tower. Inside is a curious copy (in elaborate, minute mosaic) of Leonardo's *Last Supper*, commissioned by Napoleon in 1806. From here it's a short walk to the lawns and benches of the Volksgarten (*see p85*), one of Vienna's historic inner city parks.

Loos Haus
1, Michaelerplatz 3. U3 Herrengasse/bus 2a.
Map p250 E6/7.
Built between 1909 and 1911 for the tailors Goldmann and Salatsch, the Loos House was soon baptised 'the house without eyebrows' in reference to the absence of window cornices. Work was even stopped at one point until Loos agreed to add ten window boxes. The tale is told that Emperor Franz-Josef was so appalled by the façade's unseemly nakedness that he ordered the curtains to be drawn on all palace windows overlooking the new neighbour. Art critic Robert Hughes sees in Loos' abandoning of ornamentation the seeds of German architect Mies van der Rohe's now-popular dictum 'less is more'. In the words of the architect himself: 'The evolution of culture is synonymous with the removal of ornamentation from utilitarian objects.' In 1938, the building was adorned with swastikas and became the property of the Opel company who also vandalised its original entrance. Today, the building is a bank, with exhibition space on the upper floors and it serves as the venue for the prestigious Adolf Loos design prize.

Michaelerkirche
1, Michaelerplatz . U3 Herrengasse/bus 2a. **Open** 7am-10pm daily. **Tours** *crypt* 11am, 2pm, 3pm, 4pm Mon-Fri; 3pm, 4pm Sat. **Tickets** €5; €3 concessions. **No credit cards. Map** p250 E7.
With its origins in the late Romanesque, the Church of St Michael mutated via the Baroque to the neoclassical look that it sports today. Recitals played on Vienna's largest Baroque organ, with a backdrop of a Rococo fastasy of falling angels above the main altar, can move even the most sceptical. However, the crypt and its collection of decrepit coffins, many of which reveal dessicated corpses still clothed, offer more macabre thrills.

Hofburg

The vast area of the Imperial Palace and its adjoining parks and gardens occupies most of the south-eastern part of the Innere Stadt, from the Burgtheater round to the Staatsoper. Within its confines are two of Vienna's universally known institutions: the **Spanische**

Hofburg.

Reitschule (Spanish Riding School) and its famous Lipizzaner horses, and the **Burgkapelle** where the Vienna Boys' Choir sings Sunday Mass. Rewarding museums are the **Weltliche und Geistliche Schatzkammer** (the Secular and Sacred Treasuries) and the collections of the **Kunsthistorisches Museum** in the Neue Burg. The Baroque splendour of the National Library's **Prunksaal** should also be seen.

An important public thoroughfare runs straight through Hofburg, connecting the Ringstrasse to Kohlmarkt and Graben, so the whole ensemble is open 24 hours a day and is particularly atmospheric after dark. Built over a period of seven centuries up until the fall of the Empire after World War I, Hofburg owes its size to the reluctance of successive royal families to occupy their predecessors' quarters.

Whereas the Habsburgs' ancestors, the Babenbergs, had their court on Am Hof, the new rulers set up shop in 1275 in the Burg, a fortress originally built by King Ottokar II of Bohemia on the site of what is today the Schweizerhof. Under Ferdinand III (1521-64) two separate entities, Stallburg and Amalienburg, were added; they were eventually joined together in the 1660s by the Leopoldischer Trakt during the reign of Leopold I (1657-1705). The name Schweizerhof comes from the time of Maria Theresia (1740-80) when Swiss guards were billeted here. However, it was under her father Karl IV (1711-40) that two of Hofburg's greatest Baroque edifices was built, namely the Hofbibliothek and the Winterreitschule by Fischer von Erlach, father and son.

The sprawling seat of the Habsburgs can be divided into four parts – the Alte Burg, the oldest section containing the **Schatzkammer** (treasury) and the **Burgkapelle** (chapel); In der Burg, where Franz Josef and Elisabeth's apartments are located; Josefsplatz, access point to the Spanish Riding School, the National Library and numerous minor museums; and finally the Neue Burg on Heldenplatz.

Alte Burg

The core of the palace is the Alte Burg, built around the original fortress (1275). The oldest part is the portion of moat running beside the Schweizertor, the entrance to this section.

Burgkapelle

1, Schweizerhof (533 9927). U3 Herrengasse, Volkstheater/tram 1, 2, D, J. **Open** 11am-3pm Mon-Thur; 11am-1pm Fri; and by appointment (groups only). Closed July, Aug, 1st half Sept. **Mass with Boys' Choir** *Mid Sept-June* 9.15am Sun; 9.15am Christmas Day. **Admission** €1.50. **No credit cards. Map** p250 E7.

Dating from the late 1440s, the original Gothic features of the Palace Chapel have been considerably tampered with over the years, but the vaulting and wooden statuary are still intact and visible. Unfortunately, you can only visit the chapel as part of a guided tour or by attending the 9.15am Sunday morning Mass in the company of the Vienna Boys' Choir and the Hofmusikkapelle. Tickets for Mass cannot be reserved by telephone, only by fax 533 9927-75, email whmk@chello.at or in person at the Palace Chapel's box office (open 11am-1pm, 3-5pm Friday and before Mass 8.15-8.45am Sunday).

Weltliche und Geistliche Schatzkammer

1, Schweizerhof (525 24-0/www.khm.at). U3 Herrengasse, Volkstheater/tram 1, 2, D, J. **Open** 10am-6pm Wed-Mon. **Admission** €10; €7.50 concessions; €3.50 children. **No credit cards. Map** p250 E7.

Undoubtedly the most important of Hofburg's museums, the Secular and Sacred Treasury contains wonders of the Holy Roman Empire, gold and precious stones aplenty, and a number of fascinating totemic artefacts. The entrance is beneath the steps to the Burgkapelle and best reached through the Schweizertor. Most of the exhibits were amassed by Ferdinand I (1521-64) but assembled in Hofburg under the reign of Karl VI in 1712. There are 20 smallish rooms with extremely subdued lighting and labelling in German; however, the entrance price includes the use of a device that gives an English commentary. In the secular section, top exhibits include the crown of Rudolph II (room 2) made in 1602 and festooned with diamonds, rubies, pearls and topped with a huge sapphire; the ornate silver cot of Napoleon's son, the Duc de Reichstadt (room 5); an amazing agate bowl once thought to be the Holy Grail, though more likely stolen from Constantinople in 1204; and opposite, the 'horn of the unicorn', a 2.4m- (8ft-) long narwhal's horn. In the twilight and confusing layout of the rooms, don't miss the star attraction: the Byzantine octagonal crown of the Holy Roman Empire. Finally, room 12 contains a number of relics – Karl VI was an inveterate collector of these – including splinters of wood that supposedly came from the True Cross, a shred of the tablecloth from the Last Supper and one of the teeth of John the Baptist.

In der Burg

This section comprises the buildings around the large square of the same name, opposite the Schweizertor. It is probably the busiest part of the Hofburg, with buses, taxis and *Fiakers* all allowed through and tourists swarming near the entrance to the Schatzkammer. The buildings are uniformly Baroque; the square is empty but for the lone statue of Emperor Franz, the first Austrian emperor and the last of the Holy Roman Empire.

To the south is the Leopoldinischer Trakt, where Maria Theresia and Joseph II resided, now the offices of the Austrian President. Opposite is the Reichskanzleitrakt, the section housing Franz Josef and Sisi's apartments. The passageway beside the Leopoldinischer Trakt takes you into Ballhausplatz and the Austrian chancellor's offices.

Kaiserappartements/ Silberkammer/Sisi Museum

1, Innerer Burghof Kaisertor (533 7570/www. hofburg-wien.at). U3 Herrengasse, Volkstheater/ tram 1, 2, D, J. **Open** *Sept-June* 9am-5pm daily. *July, Aug* 9am-5.30pm daily. **Admission** €9.90; €8.90 concessions; €4.90 6-18s; free under-6s. **Credit** AmEx, DC, MC, V. **Map** p250 E7.

To see how the Habsburgs liked to entertain, the Silver and Porcelain Collection, with its 290-piece Sèvres dinner service given to Maria Theresia by Louis XV, says it all. By contrast, the Imperial Rooms are surprisingly austere but then again, Franz Josef was a frugal old dog whose daily routine consisted of a cold wash at 4am, a spartan breakfast of a bread roll and coffee, and then down to affairs of state while 'his cities snored from the Swiss to the Turkish border', in author Frederic Morton's memorable phrase.

Empress Elisabeth was a different kettle of fish altogether. Born into the eccentric Wittelsbach dynasty (like her cousin 'mad' Ludwig II of Bavaria), she married Franz Josef at the age of 16 after a lightning courtship. Once she produced a male heir in 1860, their marriage was effectively over and she set off on numerous travels, culminating in her violent death at the hands of an Italian anarchist in Geneva in 1898. Added in 2004, the Sisi Museum is now the prelude to the Imperial Rooms and, with its portraits, photos of her various foreign residences, personal railway carriage and the stiletto used in her assassination, it's not a bad show, albeit a little mawkish. Occasionally, there are themed displays that use German collector Manfred Klauda's collection of Sisi memorabilia, acquired in 2006.

The museum leads directly to the Imperial Apartments – the first of which is the waiting room for petitioners, with a new, rather pitiful display of wooden dummies dressed in the national costumes of the Habsburgs' subject nations. The Audience Chamber has the raised desk where Franz Josef stood to receive petitions, one of his favourite pastimes. His readiness to award titles to the middle classes, especially to Jews, galled the traditional aristocracy. In his study hangs a portrait of Sisi by Franz Winterhalter. In the Grand Salon there are pictures and a bust of Field Marshal Radetzky, and Winterhalter's larger, oft-reproduced portrait of Sisi, exuding a glamour that is difficult to detect in her chambers, which come next. Here, despite the superficial common ground of marital difficulties, an obsession with the body beautiful and a violent death, any parallel with Princess Diana evaporates.

In Sisi's bedroom and boudoir the fittings are just as spartan as Franz Josef's – simple iron bed, copper bathtub. A quirky note is struck by a set of wooden exercise bars and the newly revealed toilet equipped with a glass door. After her toilet and the bathroom, visitors can now see two chambers known as the Bergl rooms after the painter who created these lavish, exotic murals of tropical fauna and flora. Beyond four rooms form the Alexander apartments, where Alexander I, Czar of Russia, stayed during the Congress of Vienna in 1815, but they are sadly bereft of a memento of his passing. The last room is the dining room with a lavishly decorated banquet table.

Neue Burg

The monumental Neue Burg overlooks the vast Heldenplatz (Heroes' Square), laid out at the end of the Napoleonic Wars. Its original features include Anton Fernkorn's two fine equestrian statues: Prince Eugène of Savoy, nearest the Neue Burg; and Karl IV, who vanquished Napoleon at Aspern in 1809. Beneath the square is a network of tunnels that once served as the emperor's larder and wine cellar. Today, they contain the moulds of all the sculptures and reliefs that adorn the Ringstrasse, covered with nylon drapes. Sadly, there is no public access to this ghostly labyrinth. Not completed until 1926, eight years after the demise of the Habsburgs, the Neue Burg's monumental neoclassicism gives Vienna a Washington DC-style 'seat of power' look; one can only wonder how it would have looked had Gottfried Semper's plans for a 'Kaiserforum', with an identical edifice on the opposite side of the square, come to fruition. Today, the Neue Burg houses the main reading room of the National Library and four museums. There is no access to the balcony where Hitler stood, but a reasonable view can be had from inside. The whole panorama can be viewed in comfort from the gorgeous Volksgarten Pavillon (*see p85*).

Some mutations have taken place in the Neue Burg's short history. In 1934, the triumphal Burgtor on the Ringstrasse side (incorporated within the city walls in 1820) was transformed into a monument to the Austrian dead of World War I by the Austro-Fascists. The latter also built two entrances to the square on either side of the Burgtor, whose stylised eagles represent one of Vienna's rare examples of truly fascistic architecture. However, Heldenplatz is inseparable from the memory of Hitler's triumphal declaration of the Anschluss, Austria's incorporation into the Third Reich. It is instructive that Thomas Bernhard, the greatest dramatist and enfant terrible of post-war Austria, should have entitled his most scathing attack on his country's past

Albertina.

Heldenplatz. The flags fluttering on the north side of the square mark the headquarters of the Organisation for Security and Cooperation in Europe (OSCE).

Sammlungen des Kunsthistorisches Museums in der Hofburg

1, Neue Burg, Heldenplatz (52 524-4602/52 524-4699/www.khm.at). U1, U2, U4 Karlsplatz/tram 1, 2, D, J. **Open** 10am-6pm Mon, Wed-Sun. **Admission** €8; €6 concessions; €2 children. **No credit cards. Map** p250 D7.

The three collections of the fine arts museums in the Hofburg are an excuse to enter the imposing edifice of the Neue Burg, from the central balcony of which Hitler announced the *Anschluss*. The museums are located on either side of the Neue Burg's monumental central staircase.

The **Ephesus Museum** displays the spoils from 19th-century Austrian archaeological digs in Ephesus and Samothrace.

The **Collection of Arms and Armour** was originally made up of ceremonial weapons acquired by two Habsburgs (Archdukes Ernst of Styria and Ferdinand of Tyrol); this is now one of the world's most extensive displays of arms and armour from the 15th to the 17th centuries.

Another collection started by Ferdinand of Tyrol is that of **Ancient Musical Instruments**. This is a chronologically arranged exhibition containing the world's greatest assembly of Renaissance instruments. Together with the initiative of Austrian conductor Nikolaus Harnoncourt, it has helped rekindle a worldwide interest in early music played on the original instruments.

Völkerkundemuseum

1, Neue Burg, Heldenplatz (525 24-0/www.ethno-museum.ac.at). U2 ;Museumsquartier/tram 1, 2, D, J/bus 2a. **Open** 10am-6pm Mon, Wed-Sun. **Admission** €10; €7.50 concessions. **No credit cards. Map** p250 D7.

The Völkerkundemuseum (Ethnological Museum) partially reopened in May 2007 and marked the occasion with an exhibition of Benin bronzes on the first floor. But to really get an idea of what the Habsburgs picked up on their travels around the world, you'll have to wait until the main collection is ready in late 2008. Apart from Emperor Maximilian's disastrous and ultimately fatal (for him) Mexican adventure, the Austro-Hungarian Empire generally preferred to colonise nearer home. Housed on the Ringstrasse side of Neue Burg, the musuem's highlights include the 'Mexican treasures', a series of Quetzal feather mosaics and most notably a magnificent Aztec crown, erroneously thought to belong to Montezuma. This unique and extremely fragile feathered headdress is the most valuable specimen on display in the Central America section. How it actually reached Europe is a somewhat contentious issue but it was apparently a gift by Cortés to Karl V. Other worthwhile sections are those on Polynesia and the Americas sections, containing artefacts collected by Captain Cook and bought at auction by Franz I.

Albertina & Josefsplatz

Directly behind the Neue Burg lies the Burggarten (*see p85*), the smallest and most bucolic of the Ringstrasse parks. From the old Hofburg ramparts directly behind the park's magnificent Palmenhaus (a Jugendstil hothouse), the Albertina comes into view. These former imperial apartments take their name from their former residents – Maria Theresia's favourite daughter Maria Christina and her husband, Duke Albert of Sachsen-Teschen. Childless, the couple poured their energies into founding one of the world's greatest collections of graphic art in 1768. Access to the present museum is via the triangular Albertinaplatz, a space formerly occupied by the Philliphof apartment building, in whose cellar 400 people were buried alive during a 1945 bombing raid. The site is now commemorated by Alfred Hrdlickla's controversial *Monument against War and Fascism*. The Austrian sculptor created four separate elements – two marble blocks symbolising the Gate of Violence; a representation of Orpheus entering Hades; the Stone of the Republic engraved with fragments of an Austrian Declaration of Independence published in 1945; and in the middle, the origin of the outrage, a small bronze statue of a kneeling Jew scrubbing the street clean.

Skirting the eastern limits of Hofburg, Augustinergasse leads to Josefsplatz, named after Joseph II, a notably progressive Habsburg, who in 1783 ordered the demolition of the wall that encased the square within Hofburg, thus converting it into a public thoroughfare. A large equestrian statue of the iconoclastic Josef (1807) stands in the middle of the square, where there is access to the **Augustinerkirche**, the **Nationalbibliothek**, the **Spanish Riding School** and the attractions of the Alte Burg. The square is used in *The Third Man* as a setting for where Harry Lime had staged his death in a motor accident in front of the Palais Pallavicini – his sumptuous place of residence. The Pallavicini (1784) and the nearby Palais Pálffy are fine examples of the Baroque aristocratic palaces that abound around Hofburg. Continuing along Augustinergasse, the road eventually opens out into Michaelerplatz.

Albertina

1, Albertinaplatz 3 (534 83-0/www.albertina.at). U1, U2, U4 Karlsplatz/tram D, J, 1, 2/bus 2a. **Open** 10am-6pm Mon, Tue, Thur-Sun; 10am-9pm Wed. **Admission** €9.50; €7-€8 concessions; €3.50 children. **No credit cards. Map** p250 E7.

Looking down on to the Burggarten and Staatsoper, the Albertina was for years the most visibly dilapidated building of the Hofburg complex. After undergoing a complete restoration of its plush state rooms and the construction of a new exhibition space (costing over €90 million) plus escalator access and an emblematic yet controversial canopy by Hans Hollein, it reopened with great fanfare in March 2003. In an effort to recoup this investment, the director opted for a policy of running up to three parallel non-permanent shows of international names, bolstered with items from the Albertina collection. This consists of some 1.5 million prints and 50,000 drawings, watercolours and etchings, including 145 Dürer drawings, 43 by Raphael, 70 by Rembrandt, a large number by Schiele and many more by Leonardo da Vinci, Michelangelo, Rubens, Cézanne, Picasso, Matisse and Klimt. The general feeling in Vienna is that the collection remains hidden in the archives while exhibition programmes adhere to the logic of the entertainment industry. The fairly steep ticket price also includes access to the state rooms, while admittance to the equally impressive Café Do&Co (see p139) and its great views of the Burggarten from the ramparts can be had for the price of a coffee. At street level, the Albertina is also home to the Filmmuseum (see p166).

Augustinerkirche

1, Augustinergasse 3 (533 7099/www.augustiner.at). U1, U2, U4 Karlsplatz, U3 Herrengasse/tram 1, 2, D, J. **Open** 8am-6pm daily. **Admission** free. **Map** p250 E7.

The Gothic church of St Augustin, dating from the early 14th century, is an important stop for those interested in Habsburg funeral rites. For here in the Herzgrüftel (Little Heart Crypt), lie (yes, you guessed it) their hearts. Sadly, for those with coronary interests, viewing is only by appointment. But free for all to see is Canova's impressive marble memorial to Maria Theresia's daughter Maria Christina and the Rococo organ on which Brückner composed his memorable *Mass No.3 in F minor*. Sunday morning Mass is celebrated with a full orchestra.

Nationalbibliothek

1, Josefsplatz 1 (53410-394/www.onb.ac.at). U1, U2, U4 Karlsplatz, U3 Herrengasse/bus 2a, 3a. **Open** 10am-6pm Tue,Wed, Fri-Sun; 10am-9pm Thur. **Admission** €5; €3 concessions. **Credit** DC, MC, V. **Map** p250 E7.

Entrance to Austria's largest library is through the western side of Josefsplatz. The main reason to go, apart from the books, is to see Fischer von Erlach's Prunksaal, 'one of the finest Baroque interiors north of the Alps'. Completed by his son in 1735, this immense space is adorned with marble pillars, an enormous frescoed dome showing the *Apotheosis of Karl IV* by Daniel Gran, and gilded wood-panelled bookcases containing over 200,000 works. These include a 15th-century Gutenberg Bible and the 15,000 volumes of Prince Eugène of Savoy's impressive collection, which his spendthrift niece sold to the Habsburgs. The library also has museums of globes, theatre and Esperanto, as well as collections of papyrus and musical scores.

Österreichisches Theatermuseum

1, Lobkowitzplatz 2 (525 24-3460/525 24-5399/ www.theatermuseum.at). U1, U2, U4 Karlsplatz/ tram 1, 2, D, J. **Open** 10am-6pm Tue-Sun. **Admission** €4.50; €3.50 concessions. **No credit cards**. **Map** p250 E7.

Housed in the Baroque Lobkowitz Palace, which lies just off Albertinaplatz, this museum has a permanent collection of costumes, stage models and theatrical memorabilia calculated to engage anyone interested in the stage. Jugendstil artist Richard Teschner designed an innovative convex mirror stage as a puppet theatre, where performances are held with his original figures and music score. Enquire about performances (which are suitable for children) at the ticket booth.

Spanische Reitschule (Spanish Riding School)

1, Michaelerplatz 1 (533 9031/www.srs.at). U1, U3 Stephansplatz, U3 Herrengasse/bus 2a, 3a. **Open** *Morning training* 10am-noon Tue-Sat. Closed Jan, July-late Aug. **Performances** check website for details. **Tickets** *Morning training* €12; €6-€9 concessions; €6 children. *Shows* €20-€165. **Credit** AmEx, DC, JCB, MC, V. **Map** p250 E7.

The world-famous Spanish Riding School, with its Lipizzaner horses, is one of Vienna's top five tourist attractions. We would say that, unless you have a serious dressage fetish, it's best to make a visit to the morning training session, which lets you see these magnificent creatures and enjoy Fischer von Erlach's Baroque winter riding hall where balls were held during the 1815 Congress of Vienna. The full tourist show is costly and the times of performance are irregular (check the website to see when it's on). These graceful grey horses are a cross between Spanish, Berber and Arab breeds and the name commemorates the imperial stud in Lipizza, near Trieste, where they have been bred since 1570. Follow your nose, the horses are stabled in the Stallburg, site of the non-essential Lipizzaner Museum.

Staatsopernmuseum

1, Hanuschgasse 3/Goethegasse 1 (514 44-2100/www.wiener-staatsoper.at). U1, U2, U4 Karlsplatz/tram 1, 2, D, J. **Open** 10am-6pm Tue-Sun. **Admission** €3; €2-€2.50 concessions; combined ticket with Opera tour €6.50; €3.50-€5.50 concessions. **No credit cards**. **Map** p250 E7.

The newly opened Vienna State Opera Museum focuses on the recent history of the world-famous opera house (see p183). It's tucked away in a corner beside the main box office and consists of an oval-shaped space arranged in the form of a chronometer. Thus laid out, you'll find one metre of exhibition space allocated to the performances of each year since it reopened in 1955. Aficionados can refresh their memories of past glories using electronic terminals as well as ogle artefacts.

Schottentor & the Mölker Bastei

To the west, Herrengasse narrows into Schottengasse, leading eventually to the Ringstrasse at Schottentor, a busy junction overlooked by the neo-Gothic **Votivkirche** (*see p83*). To the north is a network of fine, if rather lifeless, 19th-century streets, but to the south are some of the few remaining chunks of the old city walls, in the form of the minuscule but picturesque Mölker Bastei. Take the Mölkerstieg steps beside the Spar store, near the corner of Schottengasse, that lead into Schreyvogelgasse. It is here that Harry Lime makes his first shadowy appearance in *The Third Man*, in the doorway of no.8. Much has been made of the house at no.10, the Dreimäderlhaus (1803), where it was purported that Schubert had a carnal interest in all three of the daughters who lived there. Today, it is the premises of fashionable shoe maker Ludwig Reiter (*see p149*). Follow the cobbled street round and you are now on the Mölker Bastei, the old rampart. Beethoven lived for a period at no.8, the **Pasqualatihaus** (1798). The house has a small museum (535 8905, closed Mon).

Freyung

The name Schottentor (Scots' Gate) refers to the supposedly Scottish Benedictine monks invited by the Babenbergs to run the church and monastery they had founded in 1155. The monks in fact came from Scotia Major (the medieval name for Ireland). One of the many ersatz Irish pubs that flourish in Vienna now (and throughout Europe, for that matter) has led a rather absurd campaign to have the name changed. Belonging to the Benedictine order, Schottenstift (Monastery of the Scots) offered asylum to fugitives in the Middle Ages. This is the origin of the name of the broad tract that runs past the monastery, the Freyung or sanctuary. Ignore the church and pass through the adjacent entrance to the Schottenhof, a spacious neo-classical courtyard. On the opposite side is the **Museum im Schottenstift**. Freyung itself, its broad cobbled pavements flanked by the palaces Harrach and Ferstel to the south and the so-called Schubladlkastenhaus (Chest of Drawers House, 1774), is transformed on Fridays, when it hosts a market of organic farmers, apiarists, schnapps distillers and craftsmen. Further along on the north side is the BA-CA KunstForum, a corporate sponsored space hosting prestigious itinerant exhibitions of modern painting (*see p170*).

Museum im Schottenstift

1, Freyung 6 (53498-600/www.schottenstift.at). U2 Schottentor/trams 1, 2, D. **Open** 11am-5pm Thur-Sat. Closed late July-late Aug. **Admission** €5; €4 concessions. **Credit** MC, V. **Map** p250 D/E6.
Installed in the Prelacy, the museum shows off the abbey's not unimpressive collection of paintings, including some good 17th- and 18th-century Dutch, Flemish and Austrian work. Its most famed exhibit is the *Schottenaltar*, a 15th-century winged altarpiece featuring a superb painting of *The Flight to Egypt*, with a view of Vienna in the background.

Am Hof

Freyung slopes gently upwards to Am Hof, the biggest square in the Innere Stadt. Formerly the power centre of the Babenberg dynasty and the scene of jousts and executions, today it is a little windswept and lifeless, except on Fridays and Saturdays, when an antiques and antiquarian book market operates.

Am Hof's most impressive building is the **Kirche am Hof**, from the balcony of which the end of the Holy Roman Empire was effectively announced in 1806 (*see p20*). Today, it's the spiritual home of Vienna's Croatian community. Its Gothic core is only seen from the lanes at the rear, since the façade was given the habitual Baroque make-over and crowned with a host of angels in honour of the Nine Choirs of Angels to whom the church is dedicated.

Another impressive building on Am Hof is the **Bürgerliches Zeughaus** or Citizens' Armoury (1732) at no.10, topped with a double-headed eagle and gilded globe. For a time it housed Vienna's fire brigade before it moved next door to the Feuerwehr Zentrale, the slightly more modest premises at nos.7-9 that also houses the **Firefighting Museum** (9am-noon Sun, entrance free). There are a couple of fine Baroque houses at nos.12 and 13, and at no.15 in the **Palais Collalto**, Mozart made his public debut, performing at the ripe old age of six.

The Engel Apotheke chemist's shop at Bognergasse 9, just past Am Hof, is a small masterpiece of Jugendstil decoration. Naglergasse, a narrow street running parallel to Am Hof, is the natural continuation of Graben. The street was an extension of the same Roman fortifications and has some well-conserved Baroque façades hiding original Gothic houses.

Judenplatz

As you leave Am Hof to the north, an attractive network of ancient lanes and alleyways leads to what was once Vienna's medieval Jewish ghetto. Schulhof, a pretty cobbled lane beside

Take a stroll down Baroque **Kurrentgasse**.

the Kirche am Hof, is home to one of Vienna's
many small museums – the self-explanatory
Uhrenmuseum (Clock Museum). Behind the
museum, the magnificent Baroque
Kurrentgasse leads north into Judenplatz,
which was the historic centre of the ghetto,
dating back to the 12th century (*see p14*).
Surrounded by a magnificent array of Baroque
and 19th-century buildings, Judenplatz is
perhaps the most beautiful square to be found
in the Innere Stadt. Nowadays, its centrepiece
is British sculptor Rachel Whiteread's austere
monument to the Austrian victims of the Shoah.
This concrete cast of a library with the spines of
the books facing inward is set on a low plinth
engraved with the names of the concentration
camps. Although it was scheduled to be
unveiled in 1998, 60 years after the
Kristallnacht, the opening was held up until
2000 by the unexpected discovery on the site
of the remains of the medieval synagogue that
once stood here which was burnt down in the
ferocious pogrom of 1421. Virulent disputes as
to the suitability of Whiteread's design also
delayed matters. By converting the ground floor
of the nearby Torah school into the recently
opened **Museum Judenplatz**, a permanent
home was made for those parts of the unearthed
synagogue that could be salvaged.

Facing Whiteread's monument is a statue
of Gottfried Lessing (1729-81), a major figure
of the German Enlightenment whose work
Nathan the Wise was a paean to tolerance
towards the Jews. The original was destroyed
by the Nazis; the sculptor Siegfried Charoux
made a new cast after World War II but it was
not re-erected until 1982.

At no.2 is **Zum Grossen Jordan** (The
Great Jordan), the oldest house in the square.
The relief on its façade dates from the 16th
century and could not be further from the spirit
of Lessing, in that it actually celebrates the
events of 1421. Depicting the baptism of Christ,
it has a Latin inscription that reads: 'By
baptism in the River Jordan bodies are cleansed
from disease and evil, so all secret sinfulness
takes flight. Thus the flame rising furiously
through the whole city in 1421 purged the
terrible crimes of the Hebrew dogs. As the
world was once purged by the flood, so this
time it was purged by fire.'

Apart from the fine apartment buildings,
the square's most spectacular edifice is the
Böhmische Hofkanzlei (Bohemian
Chancery) from which the Habsburgs ruled
over the Czech lands for almost 300 years.
It is now the seat of the Constitutional and
Administrative Courts.

Museum Judenplatz

*1, Judenplatz 8 (535 0431/www.jmw.at). U3
Herrengasse.* **Open** 10am-6pm Mon-Thur, Sun;
10am-2pm Fri. **Admission** €3; €1.50 concessions.
No credit cards. Map p250 E6.

Opened in 2002, the Museum Judenplatz owes its
existence to the ruins of the medieval synagogue
unearthed during modifications to the square. It is
located in the Misrachi-Haus Torah school. Visitors
descend three flights of stairs (clad in the same
porous concrete as Whiteread's monument) to see
an informative audio-visual re-creation in English
of life in Vienna's medieval ghetto. Detailing living
conditions, the role of the synagogue and relations
with Gentile powers, the digital re-creation of the
ghetto's topography is marred by poor lighting and
looks rather washed out. A tunnel leads under
Judenplatz to the synagogue's foundations, which
are superbly presented in subdued lighting on a
raised plinth. The rest of the building continues to
function as a Torah school and the ground floor now
houses the Simon Wiesenthal Archive.

Uhrenmuseum

*1, Schulhof 2 (533 2265/www.wienmuseum.at).
U3 Herrengasse, U1, U3 Stephansplatz.* **Open**
10am-6pm Tue-Sun. **Admission** €4; €2 concessions;
€2 children; free admission Sun. **No credit cards.**
Map p250 E6.

Covering three floors of the Baroque Obizzi Palace,
the Clock Museum houses timepieces and chronome-
ters from the 15th to the 20th centuries, all kept to
time. The stellar exhibit is David Cajetano's finely
detailed 18th-century astronomical clock.

Maria am Gestade & around

The cobbled Jordangasse leads into
Wipplingerstrasse and the Altes Rathaus,
the Baroque Old Town Hall, home to various
municipal agencies and the interesting
Austrian Resistance Archive. Its courtyard
encloses a beautiful fountain by Donner, the
Andromeda Brunnen (1745), and the Gothic
Salvatorkapelle, the town hall chapel, with
its fine Renaissance portal located in
Salvatorgasse directly behind.

Wipplingerstrasse heads north-west
towards the Ringstrasse, past an enormous
sign showing a chimney sweep (a much-loved
figure in Viennese mythology) and over the
Jugendstil bridge spanning Tiefer Graben, once
the course of the Alserbach Danube tributary.
More atmospheric is the walk to the left of
the Altes Rathaus and along the cobbled
Salvatorgasse to where **Maria am Gestade**
(Our Lady of the Riverbank), one of Vienna's
finest Gothic churches, looks over a flight of
steps leading down into Concordiaplatz. It
used to have strong ties to the Danube
fishermen and today attracts worshippers
from Vienna's Czech community.

Archiv des Österreichischen Widerstands

*1, Wipplingerstrasse 6-8 (Altes Rathaus, stairway 3)
or Salvatorgasse 7 (22 89469-319/www.doew.at).
U1, U3 Stephansplatz, U1, U4 Schwedenplatz/tram
1, 2.* **Open** 9am-5pm Mon-Wed; 9am-7pm Thur.
Admission free. **Map** p250 E6.

The Austrian Resistance Archive was founded in
1963 by ex-resistance fighters and anti-fascist historians to chronicle the fate of the 2,700 Austrian
resistance fighters executed by the Nazis (and the
thousands more who died in the camps). The events
pre- and post-1938, leading to Austria's disastrous
pact with the Third Reich, are also portrayed.
Reopened in October 2005, this welter of fascinating
material detailing the horror – mostly photos, personal effects and propaganda – has finally been
given a more fitting setting.

Hoher Markt

Vienna's oldest square and the site of
Vindobona's Roman forum, Hoher Markt
today is an ungainly ensemble of historicist
apartment buildings and shabby post-1945
warrens. But at midday, tourists congregate
around the **Jugendstil Ankeruhr,** an
elaborate mechanical clock encrusted into a sort
of bridge between the two monumental edifices
belonging to the Anker insurance company.
The figures that trundle out on the hour include
Marcus Aurelius, Roman governor of
Vindobona, and composer Joseph Haydn. The
full list of the horological figures and a history
of the clock are given on a plaque in various
languages on the insurance building. Inside the
bridge beneath the clock, look out for the stone
brackets depicting Adam, Eve, an angel and a
devil with a pig's snout. Running below is
Bauernmarkt, a swish shopping street with a
number of designer stores and eateries. The
centrepiece of Hoher Markt is Fischer von
Erlach the Younger's flamboyant
Vermählungsbrunnen (Marriage Fountain),
currently under renovation. It dramatises
Mary's marriage to Joseph, presided over by a
high priest – undoubtedly a figment of the
sculptor's baroque imagination. In the
shopping arcade on the south side there's
access to **Roman ruins.**

Römische Ruinen Hoher Markt

*1, Hoher Markt 3 (535 5606/www.wienmuseum.at).
U1, U3 Stephansplatz.* **Open** 9am-1pm, 2-5pm
Tue-Sun. **Admission** €2; €1 concessions. Free Sun.
No credit cards. Map p251 E6.

Hoher Markt was the core of Roman Vindobona but
all that remains is this site of officers' quarters with
baths and underground heating, dating from AD 1-
4. Aficionados will enjoy the informative display on
what life was like in the Roman garrison.

Sightseeing

Judengasse & Ruprechtskirche

North of Hoher Markt further traces of medieval Jewish Vienna are visible along Judengasse and Seitenstettengasse, where the **Stadttempel**, the main synagogue, is located. Its architect Josef Kornhäusel (1782-1860) built the so-called Kornhäusel-Turm at no.2 as a studio and, according to local legend, a refuge from his nagging wife. Its sheer size can best be appreciated from behind, in Judengasse. Nineteenth-century photos of Judengasse depict it as bustling street, full of second-hand clothes dealers, and today the rag trade still operates in the form of small boutiques.

However, in the early 1980s, the area became the hub of Vienna's nightlife scene, receiving the exaggerated moniker of the 'Bermuda Triangle'. Today, it's all a bit naff, but the abundance of bars and restaurants gives the area a buzz. During the day, the streets are sleepy, often the only presence being the armed police who patrol permanently since the 1983 attack on the Stadttempel, which left three dead.

Sterngasse, home to splendid English bookshop Shakespeare & Co (*see p144*), runs off Judengasse to the west. At the end of the street a flight of steps named after Theodor Herzl, the Viennese founder of Zionism, leads down to Marc-Aurel-Strasse.

At the end of Judengasse is a railed balcony overlooking the busy Franz-Josefs-Kai and the Donaukanal. Among the high-rise buildings of the 2nd district, an area severely bombed in World War II, is the surprisingly modest headquarters of OPEC, scene in 1976 of one of terrorist Carlos the Jackal's attacks. While you're admiring the cityscape from here, don't miss the ivy-clad **Ruprechtskirche** to your right, the oldest church in the city, the existence of which is documented from 1137. Squat and Romanesque, it's a great tonic after Vienna's Baroque excesses. The steps take you down to a broad concourse leading east to Schwedenplatz. It's all 1970s cement, but the human traffic here makes it one of Vienna's few bustling zones. The ice-cream parlour at Schwedenplatz 17 is a local legend.

To the west of the steps in Morzinplatz stands the **Monument to the Victims of Fascism** (1985) on the site of the former Hotel Metropole, Gestapo headquarters during the war and bombed to bits in 1945. The monument is emblazoned with the yellow Star of David, the pink triangle and other symbols of Nazi victims. Further west the streets of the 19th-century textile quarter form an extraordinarily homogeneous network of monumental apartment buildings, the ground floor premises of which house a smattering of lively bars, restaurants and stores. If the weather is fine, the wooded parks in Rudolfsplatz and further west on Börseplatz are ideal for a rest.

Stadttempel

1, Seitenstettengasse 2-4 (535 0431-311/www.ikg-wien.at/www.jmw). U1, U4 Schwedenplatz. **Guided tours** 11.30am, 2pm Mon-Thur (except high holidays). **Admission** €2; concessions €1; free with combined ticket to Jewish Museum. **No credit cards. Map** p251 E/F6.

Built in neo-classical style by Josef Kornhäusel in 1826, the synagogue is one of the few that escaped destruction in the Nazi years, probably due to its discreet façade and because setting it on fire would have endangered neighbouring houses. On entering you are confronted by a monument to the 65,000 Austrian victims of the Shoah whose names are engraved on slate tablets that rotate around a central truncated column. The interior of the synagogue has an elegant simplicity – a blue oval dome strewn with stars and supported by classical pillars. Visitors must show photo ID.

In & around Rotenturmstrasse

Named after the red tower that stood on the city wall at today's Schwedenplatz, Rotenturmstrasse cuts through the northern section of the Innere Stadt. Lively and commercial, it is a good pointer for those unfamiliar with the city. At its most northerly end, it divides the Bermuda Triangle area from the medieval streets around Fleischmarkt, the old meat market. Among the shops and restaurants, look out for the plaque at no.7 marking film director Billy Wilder's home when he was a schoolboy in Vienna. The building is the original HQ of the Julius Meinl grocery firm and the façade is emblazoned with the coats of arms of the ports of London, Hamburg and Trieste, and symbolic reliefs showing harvesting, transport and roasting of coffee. Further east the street widens and the gilt and decorative brickwork of Theophil Hansen's Griechische Kirche (1861) comes into view. In the Middle Ages, Greek and Levantine traders made Fleischmarkt their home and this church replaced the late 18th-century Greek Orthodox church that is still visible from the narrow cobbled Griechengasse descending towards Schwedenplatz.

Hansen's Byzantine fantasy, with a carpet store on its ground floor, today seems an improbable place of worship. Sunday is the only day you can view the interior. Adjoining the church at no.11 is another of those hackneyed

Viennese institutions, the Griechenbeisl (*see p117*), one of the city's oldest restaurants, with connections to the Greek community and rooms dedicated to past patrons such as Beethoven, Brahms, Schubert and Mark Twain.

Fleischmarkt runs directly on into Postgasse and winds round into beautiful Schönlaterngasse, with its fine Baroque façades, such as the Basilikenhaus at no.7. At no.5 is the vast Heiligenkreuzerhof, a fine courtyard bounded by mid 18th-century outbuildings which were the city premises of the Cistercian monks of Heiligenkreuz. Originally an outlet for the monastery's produce, the chapel is a favourite for society weddings and the surrounding buildings are highly desirable apartments with a few ground-floor art galleries.

Schönlaterngasse, 'the street of the beautiful lanterns' (don't miss the one on no.6), comes out on Sonnenfelsgasse, which, along with the parallel Bäckerstrasse, runs from the Alte Universität (or now Dr-Ignaz-Seipel-) Platz to Lugeck, on Rotenturmstrasse.

Apart from the Renaissance portal at no.15, the most noteworthy feature of Sonnenfelsgasse is the massive Baroque Hildebrandthaus at no.3. Inside is the labyrinthine Zwölf-Apostelkeller (Twelve Apostles Cellar), Vienna's largest and best-loved Bierkeller.

Bäckerstrasse also has a handful of remarkable houses with arresting façades and courtyards, such as the marvellous Renaissance Hof at no.7, the premises of violin and piano manufacturers. Café Alt Wien (*see p197*) at no.19 has long been a Bohemian late-night drinking haunt. Note also the bizarre patch of mural that was unearthed during restoration work at no.12, showing a bespectacled cow playing backgammon with a wolf – supposedly a parody of the tension between Catholics (the cow) and Protestants (the wolf) in 17th-century Vienna.

To the east Bäckerstrasse opens out into Dr-Ignaz-Seipel-Platz and the buildings of the **Alte Universität**, the **Akademie der Wissenschaft** (Academy of Sciences) and the **Jesuitenkirche**, a gorgeously preserved establishment of the pope's vanguard. The church was built by an unknown architect in 1627, but both the façade and interior were substantially altered in 1703-05 by trompe-l'oeil master Andrea Pozzo, who introduced a painted false 'dome'. This illusion works best from the spot on the nave marked with a white stone. From here you can retreat back up Bäckerstrasse and cut through the passage way at Lügeck and stroll along Wollzeile, one of the Innere Stadt's most interesting shopping streets, towards the Ringstrasse.

Grünangergasse. *See p59.*

Sightseeing

1st District: Ringstrasse

Ring of power.

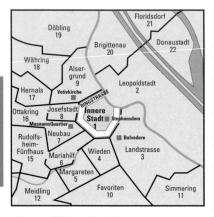

Maps p250 and p251

Unlike most cities of its size and stature, Vienna kept its city walls intact well into the 1850s. Outside lay a vast area of greenbelt known as the *Glacis*, a military parade ground which separated the old city from the suburbs.

City and suburbs became a single administrative entity in 1850, leading to huge population growth and hence an acute housing shortage. In response, in 1857 Emperor Franz Josef I initiated a building programme that helped give Vienna the face it bears today.

The broad, horseshoe-shaped Ringstrasse, and an outer ring formed by the streets running from Universitätsstrasse to the Stadtpark, were constructed along the Glacis over the following three decades. They were to become the equivalent of the Parisian *grands boulevards* – thoroughfares designed to quell revolt by ensuring the rapid movement of troops to scenes of unrest. Nevertheless the Ringstrasse's very existence is a testimony to the democratisation of public life in 19th-century Vienna, following the 1848 Revolution.

The first Ringstrasse project, the **Votivkirche**, was built to reaffirm imperial absolutism, but the military defeats of 1859 and 1866 and the advent of a constitutional monarchy in 1867 forced a reassessment of the entire programme. Gradually, emphasis was put on buildings of public utility – the city hall, the university, the parliament, the museums,

the opera house, the Burgtheater, and the numerous parks and gardens. The array of buildings takes some beating when it comes to sheer pomp and ostentation. Bill Bryson rightly observed that 'a Martian coming to earth would unhesitatingly land at Vienna, thinking it to be the capital of the planet'. Although heralding a new age, the buildings of the Ringstrasse, apart from Otto Wagner's Postsparkasse, contributed nothing particularly new. Instead, the models of the past were preferred to express the aspirations of the burgeoning Viennese middle classes, a style baptised as historicism.

Think of a day along the Ringstrasse as a way to refresh your knowledge of the principal European architectural styles. Lined with shady maples, sycamores, lime trees and horse chestnuts, each section of the road has its own name, such as the Burgring for the stretch that passes the Hofburg. As well as the civic edifices, there are innumerable palatial apartment buildings. According to dissident architect Adolf Loos, these enabled Viennese landlords to fulfil their wish to own a palace and their tenants' wish to live in one.

The vast majority of Vienna's temples to high art are located on the Ringstrasse or a stone's throw away. The world-famous **Staatsoper** (State Opera House) (*see p183*) was the first public building to be opened on the hallowed street, in May 1869. For many years, the Opera Ball, with its ostentatious show of wealth and neo-monarchist nostalgia, was the focus of virulent left-wing/anarchist demos. Spirits also run high in and around the Burgtheater (*see p207*) , possibly the most important theatre in the German-speaking world.

Down a side street off the Kärntnerring, behind the Imperial Hotel, lies Vienna's foremost concert hall, the Musikverein (*see p182*). It is Theophil Hansen's most extravagant work, for some the culminating work of historicist decoration.

Today, the Ringstrasse is no longer the address of choice it once was – traffic has put paid to that. Buildings now tend to be used as offices, with shops and restaurants on the ground floors. This commercial activity is also on the decline as high rents dissuade retailers and parking restrictions make access difficult.

The best way to get to know the Ringstrasse and form an idea of the dimensions of Vienna's inner core is a tram ride round the whole Ring. Sadly, the views from today's low-slung modern trams are not as panoramic as their predecessors. Tram 1 goes round clockwise and Tram 2 anticlockwise.

Donaukanal to Schottentor

The Schottenring ('Scots' Ring') is the most dowdy stretch of the Ringstrasse. It was named after the Benedictine monks who established a church and monastery just inside the city walls in the late 12th century. Yet there are several notable buildings along this section, including Vienna's only inner city high-rise, the Ringturm (1955), which looks over the Donaukanal, cutting quite a dash with its night time illumination.

On the opposite side of the Ringstrasse, between two apartment buildings, you get a glimpse of the Rossauer Kaserne, a bizarre red-brick barracks, one of three built in the wake of the 1848 Revolution and now occupied by the police. The finest public building along here, at Schottenring 20, is the **Börse** (stock exchange), built by one of the major Ringstrasse architects,

Museum Moderner Kunst Stiftung Ludwig Wien (MUMOK). *See p85.*

Theophil Hansen. The subdued red of the brickwork (Hansenrot, as it is often referred to) and the white stone of the cornices make this one of the Ringstrasse's most elegant edifices.

Schottentor to Oper

It's worth walking this section as the display of public buildings is awesome. Apart from a minor detour to take in the Votivkirche, it's a straight run past the **Universität**, the **Rathaus** and **Burgtheater**, before a rest in the Volksgarten. Further on come the **Parlament**, the **Kunsthistorisches Museum** and **Naturhistorisches Museum**. These last two, designed by the great German architect Gottfried Semper, were conceived as part of a grandiose plan that would link them to the Neue Burg and its planned mirror image on the other side of Heldenplatz by means of two triumphal arches across the Ringstrasse. The development of this so-called Kaiserforum was ditched after the fall of the House of Habsburg.

Kunsthistorisches Museum

1, Burgring 5 (entrance Maria Theresien-Platz) (52 524-0/www.khm.at). U2 Babenbergerstrasse, U2, U3 Volkstheater/tram 1, 2, D, J. **Open** 10am-6pm Tue, Wed, Fri-Sun; 10am-9pm Thur. Audioguides in English. **Admission** €10; €7.50 concessions; €3.50 children. **No credit cards. Map** p250 D7.

The Museum of Fine Arts is one of the finest of its kind in Europe, containing a huge collection of art treasures amassed by the Habsburgs. Indeed, more than a day is needed to appreciate these imperial galleries in full. The building's architecture and decoration – with its granites, marble and stucco interspersed with murals by Makart, Matsch, Gustav Klimt and his brother Ernst – produce an overwhelming effect upon entry. The main galleries on the first floor are arranged in a horseshoe plan with Flemish, German and Dutch paintings in the east wing and Italian work in the west.

Most visitors begin a tour in room X, the busiest in the museum, with its almost unrivalled collection of work by Pieter Bruegel the Elder, acquired by Rudolph II. The nature theme of Bruegel's work can be seen in pictures such as *Hunters in the Snow* (1565). *The Peasant Wedding Feast* (1568-69) echoes repercussions of the Reformation and was the source of inspiration for Jacob Jordaens' boisterous and bawdy *The Feast of the Bean King* (c1656) in room XI. Moving to the smaller rooms (XVI), *The Adoration of the Trinity* (1511) illustrates Albrecht Dürer's resplendent use of colour. Continuing to room XVIII, Holbein's *Jane Seymour* (1536), his first portrait executed as Henry VIII's court painter, is crisply objective in characterisation and costume. The Flemish painter Anthony van Dyck's *Portrait of a Young Man in Armour* (c1624, room XII) is a subtle psychological study contrasting hard, shiny metal with white lace and pale facial features.

Sightseeing

LEOPOLD
MUSEUM

Visit Masterpieces by

SCHIELE & KLIMT

Rooms XIII and XIV contain the museum's collection of Peter Paul Rubens; *Self Portrait* (1638-40) depicts him as a nobleman, but with tiny, tired lines around the eye. Nearby *The Little Fur* (room XIII), the name Rubens gave to the portrait of his second wife Hélène Fourment, is a sensitively painted statement of the love of an older man for a younger woman (Hélène was only 16 when she married the 53-year-old Rubens). She also stood as model for the voluptuous girl captured by a lurid satyr in the *Worship of Venus*. Some of the facets of Dutch 17th-century life are visible in Jan Steen's humorous *Topsy-Turvy World* (1663) and Jan Vermeer's reflective *Art of Painting* (1665-66) (rooms XXIII-IV). The three Rembrandt self-portraits (1652, 1656 and 1657) in room XV have withstood the critical survey of experts and de-attribution.

Crossing through the café takes you to room VII and Bernardo Bellotto. He was taught by his uncle, the Venetian Antonio Canal, better known as Canaletto. Here are several of Bellotto's views of Vienna, commissioned by Maria Theresia. Caravaggio's major work *Madonna of the Rosary Feast* (1606-67), in room V, was purchased by Rubens and his friends after the artist's death in 1610. Three large rooms (I-III) are dedicated to the Venetian school: Tintoretto, Veronese and Titian. Room II has one of the few authenticated works by Giorgione, *The Three Philosophers*. Raphael's *Madonna in the Meadow* (1505) in room IV is a serene piece, its composition influenced by Leonardo da Vinci.

On the ground floor, the Kunstkammer (the east wing) is a chamber of curiosities and exotica (rooms XIX-XXXVII), with ornaments, glassware, clocks, globes and astrolabes. However, the stellar exhibit, Benvenuto Cellini's *Saliera*, a priceless gold and enamel salt cellar (1540), was stolen in 2004, leaving the director with plenty of egg on his whiskered face. The Egyptian and Near Eastern collections (rooms I-VII) of the west wing include wall paintings, pottery, the remains of mummified bulls' heads, crocodiles and cats and examples of Books of the Dead on papyrus. The Greek and Roman collection in rooms IX-XV includes the famous *Gemma Augustea*, a two-layered onyx cameo that commemorates the military victories of the first Roman emperor.

Naturhistorisches Museum

1, Burgring 7 (52 177/www.nhm-wien.ac.at). U2 Babenbergerstrasse, U2, U3 Volkstheater/tram 1, 2, D, J. **Open** 9am-6.30pm Mon, Thur-Sun; 9am-9pm Wed. **Admission** €8; €3.50-€6 concessions. **No credit cards. Map** p250 D7.

One of the largest and most celebrated natural history museums in the world, this is the scientific counterpart to the Kunsthistorisches Museum across the square. It was opened in 1889 and not much has changed since; some of the display cases are magnificent century-old affairs, the labelling is in German and, probably because little has been done to embrace modern museum interactivity, there is still a wonderfully studious air about the place. The basis of the

collection is the work of Emperor Franz Stefan, Maria Theresia's husband, an amateur scientist who collected skulls, fossils, precious stones, meteorites and rare stuffed animals. It also includes items acquired by Rudolph II and Prince Eugène of Savoy. Displayed in a dark cubicle, the most valuable piece is the Venus of Willendorf (found in the Wachau), a curvaceous 11cm- (4in-) high limestone fertility symbol believed to be over 25,000 years old. The museum has minerals, zoological exhibits and a valuable selection of meteors. It also contains the world's largest collection of human skulls (some 43,000 – from 40,000 BC to the present). Here too is the largest single topaz known (110kg/243lb), and an ostrich given by Maria Theresia to her husband Franz Stephan studded with 761 precious stones and over 2,000 diamonds. In addition, the museum stores the oldest human sculpture, Fanny from Stratzing (dated 32,000 BC), in a vault – only photos of it are on display.

Parlament

1, Dr Karl Renner-Ring 3 (guided tours in English 40110-2665/www.parlament.gv.at). U2, U3 Volkstheater/tram 1, 2, D, J. **Admission** €4; €2 concessions. **Tours** Mid Sept-July 10am, 11am, 2pm, 3pm, 4pm Mon, Tue, Fri; 10am, 11am, 2pm, 3pm, 4pm, 5pm Wed, Thur; 10am, 11am, noon, 1pm Sat. **Tickets** €4; €2 concessions. **No credit cards. Map** p250 D7.

The neo-classical Parlament stares across the Ring at the Imperial Palace to the east. Built by the Danish architect Theophil Hansen, this wedding-cake construction bristles with Hellenistic statuary and bronze chariots. The façade of the building appears obscured by the two lateral ramps and the rather splendid statue of Athena, set in a fountain representing the Danube, Inns, Elbe and Vltava rivers. Architecturally, the edifice is as problematic as the birth of Austrian democracy itself, but restoration work in 2004-05 has given it a more accessible air by reconstructing the lateral ramps and slotting in a new media/visitors centre at street level. Now it's much easier to take a closer look at the mosaic frontal frieze of Franz Josef I granting the first, very limited democratic constitution.

Rathaus

1, Rathausplatz (52550/http://wien.at/english/cityhall). U2 Rathaus/tram 1, 2, D. **Tours** (only in German) 1pm Mon, Wed, Fri. *Meeting point* City Information Centre, Friedrich-Schmidt-Platz 1. **Admission** free. **Map** p250 D6.

Forming the centrepiece of Rathausplatz and its gardens, the town hall is undoubtedly the most imposing edifice on the Ringstrasse. Inspired by Flemish Gothic and resembling the Hôtel de Ville of Brussels, Friedrich Schmidt's building is clearly visible from the Hofburg and was a constant reminder to the court that the burghers were now running the show. Visitors are free to wander through the seven inner courtyards, but must join a guided tour to see the elaborate interior decoration and numerous frescoes illustrating scenes from Vienna's past. Open to the

Sightseeing

Waltz on Get your head around the Habsburgs

Start: MuseumsQuartier entrance
Finish: Albertina
Length: approx 4 kilometres (2.5 miles)
Time: two-and-a-half hours

This walk takes you round the major central sights associated with the dynasty that dominated central Europe for 645 years, taking in the imperial palace and the churches where their hearts, entrails and corpses are buried.

Start at the main entrance to the **MuseumsQuartier** (*see p83*), the cultural complex housed in the former imperial stables. Cross the busy Museumsstrasse into Maria-Theresien-Platz. The square's

geometric gardens centre on a statue of Maria Theresia, the only woman to rule the empire, surrounded by her ministers, generals and composers. To the left is the **Naturhistorisches Museum** (*see p79*), housing her husband Franz I's collection. To your right, the identical **Kunsthistorisches Museum** (*see p77*), contains Vienna's most important collection of paintings, a tribute to the wealth and artistic concerns of Habsburgs such as Rudolf II and Archduke Leopold Wilhelm. It was Maria Theresia's son, Josef II, who first opened the collection to the public.

Across the Ringstrasse, the 19th-century boulevard that traces the lines of Vienna's old city defences, looms **Hofburg**, the

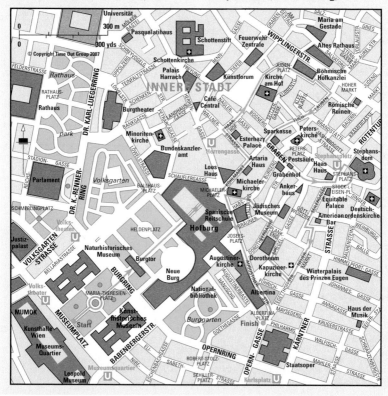

Imperial Palace. Passing beneath the **Burgtor** (1824), the triumphal arch commemorating the 11th anniversary of the victory over Napoleon at Leipzig in 1813, you enter Heldenplatz and the neo-classical **Neue Burg** (see p67), the last section of Hofburg to be completed. Follow the *Fiakers* into the midst of the palace where you can detour off into the **State Apartments** (see p67) or the **Imperial Treasury** (see p66).

From Hofburg you emerge into Michaelerplatz facing the **Loos House** (see p64), detested by Franz-Josef for its lack of ornamentation. Continue along Kohlmarkt where, among the designer shops, court bakers Demel (no.14) still sports the crucial K.u.K. (*Königlich und Kaiserlich*) royal warrant. Swing a left down Wallnerstrasse and peek into **Palais Esterházy** (no.4), one of the many aristocratic palaces that sprouted around Hofburg. Follow the alleyway on the right, via Haarhof and the narrow Baroque Naglergasse, into Am Hof. Originally the site of the Babenberger court, the Habsburg's predecessors, on the right of the square is the **Kirche am Hof** (see p71) where Napoleon forced Franz II to announce the end of the Holy Roman Empire in 1806. Continue along the right of the square and wind round into **Judenplatz** (see p72) and the Böhmische Hofkanzlei, from which the dynasty controlled the Czech lands.

When you reach Tuchlauben, centre of Vienna's medieval textile trade and now a swish shopping street, turn right until you reach the Kohlmarkt/Graben junction. At Graben no.19 is the inviting Julius Meinl store, the former imperial grocer. Along Graben take in the array of Baroque and 19th-century buildings passing the **Pestsäule** (see p63), until you hit Stephansplatz, where the entrails of the Habsburgs lie in the cathedral's crypt. To reach the **Kaisergruft** (see p60), where their corpses are interned in the elaborate tombs of the imperial crypt, take Seitergasse off Graben to reach Neuer Markt. South of Neuer Markt, take a right off Tegetthofgasse (commemorating the Empire's most illustrious admiral) and round into Spiegelgasse where you can enter the **Dorotheum** (see p61), the pawn shop and now auction house founded by Josef I in 1707. Walk straight through and exit onto Dorotheergasse and follow Habsburgergasse round into Augustinergasse. Here you'll get a whiff of the Lipizzaner horses from the Spanish Riding School, before you emerge into Josefsplatz – where it's worth entering the overwhelming Prunksaal of the **Nationalbibliothek** (see p69). On the corner of the square is the **Augustinerkirche** (see p69), where the Habsburgs' hearts are kept. The street emerges into Albertinaplatz, home to the Albertina graphic collection (see p70) and the Hotel Sacher, where Franz Josef's guests would retire for a feed after his notoriously spartan dinners. Get yourself a slice of restorative but pricey Sachertorte.

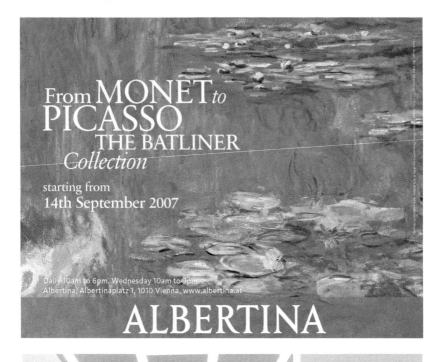
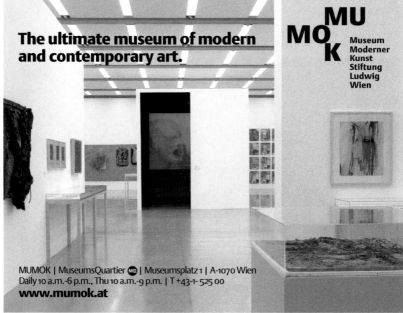

public too is the vast Rathaus Keller, a touristy but impressively grand cellar serving beer and roast pork. Now the scene of events such as the AIDS fundraising Life Ball, Rathausplatz has become something of a people's playground since the early 1990s when the mayor Helmut Zilk set about livening up the city's dreary nightlife. All summer long, the square attracts vast crowds who watch filmed operas on a giant screen and patronise the food and drink stalls run by local restaurants.

Universität

1, Dr Karl-Lueger-Ring (www.univie.ac.at). U2 Schottentor/tram 1, 2, D. **Map** p250 D6.
Due to its decisive role in the events of 1848, the university was out of favour with the forces of reaction and it was not until 1870 that this site was secured. Work began in 1873 with that master of pastiche Heinrich Ferstel given command once again. His brief was to build in Renaissance style, echoing the secular universities of Italy. It is easy to gain access to the university in term time, and a walk around the arcades of the inner courtyard is very pleasant. Try to get into the Grosser Festsaal, the main hall, to see Klimt's ceiling frescoes depicting the seven pillars of wisdom. It is clearly marked via the main entrance on the Ringstrasse, but not officially open to the public.

Votivkirche

9, Rooseveltplatz (406 1192/www.votivkirche.at). U2 Schottentor/tram 1, 2, D. **Open** 9am-1pm, 4-6.30pm Tue-Sat; 9am-1.30pm Sun. **Admission** free. **Map** p250 D5.
The Votivkirche was built opposite the spot where Franz Josef survived an assassination attempt by a Hungarian nationalist in 1853. Work began in 1854 and wasn't completed until 25 years later, owing to the exacting craftsmanship demanded by the 27-year-old architect Heinrich Ferstel. Conceived as a Viennese Westminster Abbey for the greats of Austria, the 'Ringstrassendom' never really fulfilled this function nor did it attract any real parishioners apart from soldiers billeted at the nearby barracks, the Rossauerkaserne. Despite its moribund interior, the Votivkirche's two monumental stone-carved steeples are a magnificent sight, recalling the great Gothic cathedral of Chartres.

Museumsquartier

Beyond Maria-Theresien-Platz lie the former imperial stables, designed by Fischer von Erlach and completed by his son in the 18th century. In 2001, this charmingly dilapidated network of buildings became the site for the so-called **MuseumsQuartier** (MQ), one of the most ambitious building projects undertaken in Vienna in the 20th century, costing approximately €145 million. It is now one of the ten largest cultural complexes in the world.

Like anything new in Vienna, there was considerable opposition to architects Ortner & Ortner's original design, particularly to their projected 56 metre- (184 foot-) high emblematic 'reading tower' which never came about. The resulting ensemble fits so neatly and discreetly behind the original Baroque frontage that the only clue to the wonders within is the circular orange-and-white MQ logo.

As you enter via the vaulted central portal, a broad piazza stretches out to reveal the white limestone of the **Leopold Museum** away to the left and the monolithic **Museum Moderner Kunst Stiftung Ludwig Wien (MUMOK)** lying at a slight oblique angle to the right. Between the two, the former winter riding hall has been modified to hold the Kunsthalle Wien, a concert/performance space and a restaurant. Several of the original sculpted horses' heads serve as a reminder of the building's equine past. The Viennese have taken the MQ to their hearts by storming its public areas. Thanks to a flexible seating concept consisting of geometrically shaped loungers, in summer people spend hours lying around chatting, reading and enjoying DJ sounds on these colourful beds. In winter, they can be stacked to form igloo-like constructions where mulled wine and punch are served. Far more so than the Pompidou Centre or the Tate Modern, the MQ functions as an attractive social space, a sort of multiplex of the arts where the shops and restaurants go some way to underwriting the generally loss-making galleries.

Apart from the MUMOK and Leopold museums you'll find spread over the MQ's 60,000 square metres (645,000 square feet) Vienna's most popular contemporary art gallery, Kunsthalle Wien (*see p173*), with spaces dedicated to disciplines as diverse as architecture (**Architekturzentrum Wien**) and modern dance (Tanzquartier Wien, *see p207*). Other tenants include the superbly interactive Zoom children's museum (*see p162*) and **designforumMQ**, a research and exhibition space dedicated to the cultural industries.

The frontal tract was given over to a project called quartier 21, which involved the rental of spaces to peripheral cultural initiatives such as electronic music, net activism, intercultural projects and video art, as well as some off-the-wall retailing. Six years on, quartier 21 has never really fulfilled its promise as an art-lab but its shops and bars are quite cool.

Architekturzentrum Wien

7, Museumsplatz 1 (522 3115/www.azw.at). U2 Museumsquartier, U2, U3 Volkstheater. **Open** 10am-7pm daily. **Admission** €7; €5.50 concessions. **Credit** (up to €20) AmEx, DC, JCB, MC, V. **Map** p250 D7.
Located in the vaulted section beyond the MUMOK, this is a documentation centre, archive and exhibition space that features developments in domestic

Sightseeing

and international architecture shown in two halls either side of the courtyard. In April 2007, they opened AZ West, a new exhibition space that will concentrate on the Austrian scene. Regular Sunday walking tours on architectural themes in Vienna and environs are also organised – see the website.
Other locations AZ West, 15, Flachgasse 35-37 (522 3115-32).

designforumMQ

7, Museumsplatz 1 (524 4949-0/www.design forum.at). U2, U3 Volkstheater. **Open** 10am-6pm Mon-Fri; 11am-6pm Sat, Sun. **Admission** €4; €2 concessions. **No credit cards. Map** p250 D7. Diagonally opposite AZW, the MQ's latest resident is a centre for design that features temporary exhibitions on graphics, product design and advertising.

Taking tea in the **Burggarten** by the **Palmenhaus** and **Schmetterlinghaus**.

Leopold Museum

7, Museumsplatz 1 (525 70-0/www.leopoldmuseum. org). U2 Museumsquartier, U2, U3 Volkstheater. **Open** 10am-6pm Mon, Wed, Fri-Sun; 10am-9pm Thur. **Admission** €9; €5.50-€8.10 concessions. **Credit** AmEx, DC, JCB, MC, V. **Map** p250 D7/8.

The Leopold Museum owes its existence to a Viennese ophthalmologist's lifelong obsession with the great Austrian expressionist Egon Schiele. In the 1950s, Rudolf Leopold acquired his first Schieles for a song. The museum's full catalogue now numbers over 5,000 works and embraces many other crucial figures of 19th-century and modernist Austrian painting. On the entrance floor are important works by Klimt and Richard Gerstl. The first floor is given over to the engrossing peasant art of Albin Egger-Lienz and mid century Austrians such as Maria Lassnig and Oswald Oberhuber, while the top floor houses paintings by Schiele and other expressionists, most notably Oskar Kokoschka. A panoramic window offers a superb cityscape.

Museum Moderner Kunst Stiftung Ludwig Wien (MUMOK)

7, Museumsplatz 1 (525 00/www.mumok.at). U2 Museumsquartier, U2, U3 Volkstheater. **Open** 10am-6pm Tue, Wed, Fri-Sun; 10am-9pm Thur. **Guided tours** in English by prior arrangement. Audioguides in English. **Admission** €8; €3-€7.20 concessions; €2 children. **Credit** AmEx, DC, MC, V. **Map** p250 D7.

This is Vienna's premier contemporary art collection, exhibited over five floors. In all MUMOK offers a rather dour tour through the -isms of 20th-century art. The space is claustrophobic, a feeling accentuated by the absence of natural light. On the menu is a fairly impressive collection of American pop art by Jasper Johns, Warhol, Lichtenstein, Rauschenberg and so on, plus examples of parallel European movements such as radical realism, arte povera, abstract impressionism and land art. Lurking in the depths of the bunker is a fine résumé of the local contribution: Viennese actionism, an unholy brew of animal sacrifice, action painting, and public masturbation and defecation concocted by figures such as Herman Nitsch, Arnulf Rainer and Gunther Brus. **Photo** *p77.*

The Ringstrasse parks

On the south side of the Ringstrasse there are three major parks, each offering a variety of curiosities – from statues and hothouses to classical music concerts. Some of the city's hottest nightspots are located here (out of earshot of Vienna's grumpy residents). There's also a good selection of refreshment outlets.

Burggarten

Main entrance: Burgring. U1, U2, U4 Karlsplatz/ tram 1, 2, D, J. **Open** *Apr-Oct* 6am-10pm daily. *Nov-Mar* 6am-8pm daily. **Map** p250 E7.

The Palace Gardens are leafy and informal, with expanses of lawn. Formerly the preserve of tourists who came to photograph the marble Mozart statue, the park is now a favourite with sun seekers, spliffers and frisbee enthusiasts. The statue of the musical boy-wonder, set on a plinth depicting scenes from *Don Giovanni*, was moved here in 1953 from Albertinaplatz. Far more impressive, though, is Friedrich Ohmann's 1901 Palmenhaus, restored and converted into one of Vienna's most original restaurant locations (*see p119*).

Schmetterlinghaus

1, Burggarten, beside Palmenhaus (533 8570/fax 532 2872/www.schmetterlinghaus.at). U1, U2, U4 Karlsplatz/tram 1, 2, D, J. **Open** *Apr-Oct* 10am-4.45pm Mon-Fri; 10am-6.15pm Sat, Sun. *Nov-Mar* 10am-3.45pm daily. **Admission** €5; €4-€4.50 concessions, €4 6-26s; €2.50 3-6s. **Credit** AmEx, DC, JCB, MC, V. **Map** p250 E7.

The west wing of the Palmenhaus was converted into a butterfly house after restoration in 1999. Now it's home to around 40 species acquired from butterfly farms in Thailand, Costa Rica and Brazil, none of them rare or endangered. Several hundred butterflies fly freely in 85% humidity amid a welter of tropical vegetation (the baby bananas are very tempting), tall trees and a waterfall.

Stadtpark

Main entrance: Johannesgasse (beside Stadtpark U-Bahn station). U4 Stadtpark, U3 Stubentor/ tram 1, 2. **Open** 24hrs daily. **Map** p251 F7.

The largest of the Ringstrasse parks, the Stadtpark stretches from just east of Schwarzenbergplatz to Stubentor, either side of the Wien river. Located beside Otto Wagner's Stadtpark U-Bahn station, the main entrance is flanked by superb stone-carved Jugendstil colonnades. Just to the north is the park's most emblematic building, the neo-Renaissance Kursalon, a venue for rather tacky Strauss concerts. Music is the theme here, and most visitors head for the schmaltzy but nonetheless finely executed gilt statue of Johann Strauss. Scattered around the park, you'll also find busts of Schubert, Bruckner and Lehár (he of *The Merry Widow*). Across Hermann Czech's footbridge is the riverside premises of Vienna's most prestigious restaurant, Steierereck (*see p123*).

Volksgarten

Main entrance: Heldenplatz (opposite the Neue Burg). U2, U3 Volkstheater, U3 Herrengasse/tram 1, 2, D, J/bus 2a. **Open** *Apr-Oct* 6am-10pm daily. *Nov-Mar* 6am-8pm daily. **Map** p250 D7.

Despite its egalitarian-sounding name, the People's Garden was originally a playground for Vienna's beau monde at the turn of the 19th century. It was built after Napoleon's troops demolished the southern section of the city walls, so the frenchified garden layout is somewhat ironic. The centrepiece is the Doric Theseus-Tempel, commissioned by Napoleon as a replica of the Theseion in Athens to house Canova's statue *Theseus and the Minotaur*. This statue was moved to the staircase of the Kunsthistorisches Museum in 1890. Between the

Sightseeing

temple and the Ringstrasse is a lavish rose garden. Dear to the hearts of many Austrians is the statue of Empress Elisabeth (1837-98) at the northern corner. Today, the name Volksgarten is synonymous with the large semi-open-air discotheque over the Ringstrasse from the museums, and with the superb Pavillon next door: Oswald Haerdtl's sleek 1950s construction where the tuned-in and turned-on of Vienna drink Caipirinhas (*see p197*).

Oper to the Schwarzenbergplatz

South-east of the Staatsoper, the Ringstrasse takes the name Kärntnerring, acknowledging the route south to Kärnten (Carinthia) that bisects it at this point. This is the Ringstrasse at its most bustling, with limos pulling up outside Vienna's big name hotels, shoppers and commuters scurrying on and off the trams and underground, and tourists snapping the mighty Staatsoper (*see p183*).

Where Kärntnerring turns into Schubertring, the Ringstrasse opens out into a vast rectangular concourse named after Karl von Schwarzenberg, hero of the Battle of Leipzig (1813). His equestrian statue stands amid the stream of today's iron horses that make the place a nightmare to cross on foot. Vast and windswept, the square is lined with monumental buildings such as the Kasino am Schwarzenberg (*see p207*). At the far end stands the Russen Heldendenkmal (Russian Heroes' Monument), a not universally welcomed gift from the Soviet people celebrating their liberation of Vienna. In front of this column is the Hochstrahlbrunnen, a fountain blasting water 25 metres (82 feet) into the air, built in 1873 to commemorate Vienna's first mains supply.

On the west side is the elegant art nouveau French embassy (1912), with its vaguely oriental façade. Nearby on Zaunergasse is the Arnold Schönberg Center (*see p185*).

Parkring & Stubenring

Beyond Schwarzenbergplatz, the north side of the Ringstrasse is lined with more top-of-the-range hotels overlooking the Stadtpark to the south. On foot it is more enjoyable to cut through the park, check out the Strauss memorial and walk along the river bank. At Stubentor things pick up a little and on this last stretch of the Ringstrasse there are a couple of top-class sights. If you're in need of refreshment, call in at the elegant 1950s coffee house Café Prückel (*see p138*) or Oesterreicher im MAK (*see p119*), a funky café/restaurant attached to Vienna's **Museum für Angewandte Kunst (MAK)**.

Further along, directly opposite Otto Wagner's **Postsparkasse**, is the former Kriegsministerium (Ministry of War), which today houses less bellicose sections of the civil service. This neo-Baroque monster was completed as late as 1912, demonstrating how little had changed since the start of the Ringstrasse project in the 1850s. Walk 500 metres (about 550 yards) east, and you reach the Donaukanal with its characteristic green railings. Overlooking the canal is the curious Urania, an observatory built in 1910 by Max Fabiani. Renovated in 2004, it functions as a cinema and puppet theatre and has a cool café (*see p140*) attached on the canal side.

Museum für Angewandte Kunst/ Gegenwartskunst (MAK)

1, Stubenring 5 (711 36-0/www.mak.at). U3 Stubentor/U4 Landstrasse/ tram 1, 2. **Open** 10am-midnight Tue; 10am-6pm Wed-Sun. **Guided tours** in English Sun noon (€2). **Admission** €7.90-€9.90 (with MAK-guide); €5.50-€6.30 concessions. Free Sat. **No credit cards. Map** p251 F7.

The Museum of Applied Arts is to Vienna what the Victoria & Albert Museum is to London (although rather smaller). The building dates from 1872 and is another neo-Renaissance work by Ferstel. The permanent exhibition features splendid displays of Jugendstil furniture and design as well as Klimt's *Stoclet Frieze*. In the course of a revamping completed in 1993, the director, Peter Noever, invited several artists working in Vienna to devise concepts for the various rooms. Some are excellent: Franz Graf's blue room, Gang Art's installation for the carpet collection, Barbara Bloom's presentation of the chair collection in silhouette. A visit is full of unexpected pleasures. Don't miss the excellent restaurant and what must be Vienna's sexiest museum shop.

Postsparkasse

1, Georg-Coch-Platz 2 (www.postsparkasse.at). U3 Stubentor/tram 1, 2. **Open** 8am-3pm Mon-Wed, Fri; 8am-5.30pm Thur. **Map** p251 F6.

Built from 1904 to 1912 and crammed into a narrow gap between apartment buildings, Otto Wagner's Postsparkasse (Post Office Savings Bank) is the most monumental of Vienna's modernist buildings. However, its conception as an alternative home for the savings of the middle classes rather than the powerful Jewish-dominated banking houses of the late 19th century shrouds the building in an unpleasant cloud of anti-semitism. Quite unlike anything else along the Ringstrasse, the Postsparkasse shines like a beacon of modernity with its economy of ornamentation and radical choice of materials. Clad in slabs of grey marble fastened by metal studs (17,000 in all), the façade is crowned by the institution's name rendered in unmistakable Jugendstil lettering, overseen by stylised angels of victory wielding laurel wreaths. The Postsparkasse still functions as a bank, so it can be seen during normal business hours.

2nd District

Things are looking up in Leopoldstadt.

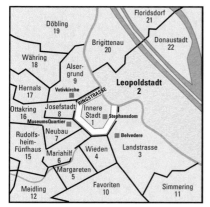

Maps p243, p244 & p245

Lying just over the bridges of the Donaukanal, the gritty and sometimes grey Leopoldstadt, the 2nd district, seems much further away from the glistening and swank inner city. Of all of Vienna's central districts, this is probably the scruffiest: full of eyesores built after wartime Allied air raids and the devastating final battle for the city fought in 1945 between the Red Army and remnants of the Wehrmacht. On the positive side, Vienna's two finest parks, the **Prater** and the **Augarten**, which contains Gustinius Ambrosi's **Atelier Augarten** and the **Augarten Porzellan Manufaktur**, are located here. Gradually its jumble of tatty shops and threadbare coffee houses is being supplemented by more Bohemian hangouts, particularly around the open-air Karmelitermarkt. Long tipped for gentrification, the district's demography will inevitably change when the U2 line and its station on Taborstrasse beside the Augarten opens in 2008. Historically, the 2nd and 20th districts make up Vienna's main Jewish quarter and since the fall of the Eastern Bloc, the community has replenished itself with immigrants from ex-Soviet republics and Iran. They now live alongside a sizeable Turkish and Yugoslav population as well as more recent arrivals from Africa. Today, Leopoldstadt offers a quirky and often interesting alternative to the Vienna that most tourists see.

Together with Brigittenau, the neighbouring 20th district, Leopoldstadt forms an elongated island between the Donaukanal and the Danube. In 1624, Ferdinand II sanctioned the creation of a walled Jewish ghetto in this isolated area. The district takes its name from Leopold I who, swayed by the anti-semitic hysteria of the post-Reformation, expelled the Jews in 1670. During the late 19th and early 20th centuries, Jews fleeing Russian and Polish pogroms flooded into the Leopoldstadt's filthy, overcrowded tenements. In the 1920s, writer Joseph Roth, himself a migrant from Galicia, could still remark that 'there is no harder lot than that of the Eastern Jew newly arrived in Vienna'. Little could he have imagined what would befall Vienna's Jews twenty years later.

In 2006, the long-overdue **Steine der Errinnerung** (Stones of Remembrance) project was launched to commemorate Jewish life in the district before the Holocaust when roughly every second resident was Jewish. It consists of laying small stone plaques to mark synagogues, cafés, theatres, schools and points from which Jews were deported to the camps. So far 17 stones have been laid on a route that runs west from the site of the main synagogue at Tempelgasse 3-5, across Prater Strasse, Taborstrasse, the Karmelitermarkt and as far as the Jewish schools in Malzstrasse. To see the present and the projected routes and an explanation in English, go to www.steinedererrinnerung.

Accessible via tram or the U1 line from Schwedenplatz, Taborstrasse and Praterstrasse are the 2nd district's main commercial arteries, and most of its more interesting sights are on and around these two streets. These include the 19th century Corn Exchange on Taborstrasse, today home of the Odeon Theatre (*see p186*), the Nestroyhof on the Praterstrasse with its Jugendstil façade, designed by Zionist architect Oskar Marmorek, a close associate of Theodor Herzl's, and the **Johann Strauss Haus** and **Kriminalmuseum**. Once the boulevard of Jewish Leopoldstadt, today's humdrum Praterstrasse eventually broadens on to Praterstern, a busy traffic junction traversed by the newly remodelled Nordbahnhof, the station that provided Vienna's eastern Jews with their first sight of the city. With constant human

Down by the river

of European history. Here there is a sumptuous view upriver towards Kahlenberg and Leopoldsberg, the two peaks skirted with vineyards that signal the end of the Vienna Woods.

After crossing the bridge, you reach the Donauinsel, a man-made island some 20 kilometres (12.5 miles) long. This was created when a new channel, the Neue Donau, was dug out on the eastern side in the 1970s. For years, the island was an inhospitable, windswept tract, but as the vegetation matured, it gradually became one of Vienna's largest amenities. Although far from an arcadia, the sheer space and relative cleanliness of the water make it ideal for cycling, bathing, in-line skating and picnicking. Nude bathing and sunbathing are also permitted. Known as Copa Cagrana after the nearby Kagran district, the environs of the Donauinsel U-Bahn station are a brash nightlife area in summer, with waterside bars, bike rentals and waterskiing. In June, the island is taken over for a weekend by the Social Democratic Party's Donauinselfest (*see p160*).

Beyond the Neue Donau to the east, a mass of glassy skyscrapers and housing complexes signals the Donau City, Vienna's carefully sequestered ghetto of modern architecture. It sprang up in the 1990s around the **Vienna International Centre** (VIC), the Vienna seat of United Nations, and includes towers by firms such as Coop Himmelb(l)au and the tiny box that is Hans Tesar's Church of Christ the Hope of the World (*pictured above*).

One tube stop after the VIC is the Alte Donau, the picturesque old Danube; lined

Maps p244 & p245

The *Blue Danube* waltz is Vienna's signature tune. But despite its ubiquity, it's perfectly possible to visit Vienna and never set eyes on Europe's longest river. This is because it lies way beyond the 2nd district to the east and it's thus easy to overlook the waterway's presence. In Vienna no fewer than four watercourses sport the name 'Danube' but the only one most visitors see is the Danube canal that snakes through the city centre. On a fine day it's worth taking the U1 to Vorgartenstrasse for a bracing walk over the Reichsbrücke to see the Danube's main course and one of the main routes with chestnuts and willows. You can stroll along these remnants of the river's side arms, rent a boat or have a few drinks or dinner at the water's edge. But remember to take insect repellent with you as mosquitoes are rampant in summer. On the southern side is the Gänsehäufel, one of the city's most popular bathing areas, comprising pools as well as the river. Many stretches of bank are the private domain of certain public workers, so you see amusing signs pointing to the Polizeibad (Police Baths) and Strassenbahner-Bad (Tram Drivers' Baths).

Opposite Gänsehäufel there is a riverside walk with several bustling restaurants among the boat houses. To the north over the Wagramer Strasse is another bathing zone, the Angelibad, facing quintessential Viennese summer schnitzel joint Birners Strandgasthaus (*see p134*). If you have children in tow, the Bundesbad (*see p206*) north of the Alte Donau U-Bahn is a great location with a safe pebble beach and a gorgeous 1950s kiosk selling ice-creams, hot dogs and, most civilised, cold beer. On this side too, adjacent to the UN, are the attractive modern gardens of the Donaupark. They surround the Donauturm (Danube Tower), for years the tallest building in Vienna, complete with revolving restaurant.

Vienna International Centre

22, Wagramer Strasse 5 (26060 3328/www.unvienna.org). U1 Vienna International Centre. **Open** *Guided tours* 11am, 2pm Mon-Fri by appointment. **Admission** €5; €4 concessions. **No credit cards. Map** p245 K2.
In the early 1970s, Austria's feisty chancellor Bruno Kreisky fought off stiff competition from Tokyo to make Vienna the third seat of the United Nations. After camping out in Hofburg for almost a decade, the present complex of grey, three-pointed cylindrical towers around a central plaza was completed in 1981. Among the agencies located here are the Nobel-Prize-winning International Atomic Energy Agency, the UN Office for Drugs and Crime and UNIDO, the threatened industrial development organisation. To join a guided tour of the complex, bring along your passport.

traffic heading to and from the nearby Prater fun fair, this is Vienna at its earthiest and most bustling, with the iconic Prater ferris wheel in the background.

Atelier Augarten

2, Scherzergasse 1a (216 8616 20/www.atelier augarten.at). Tram N, 21. **Open** 10am-6pm daily. **Admission** €5; €3.50 concessions. **No credit cards. Map** p243 F4.
Formerly the studio of Austrian sculptor Gustinius Ambrosi (1893-1975), this museum and sculpture garden is now run by the Österreichische Galerie. Contemporary art is the tonic and a same-day ticket to the Belvedere is valid here too.

Augarten

Main entrance: 2, Obere Augartenstrasse. Tram 21, N. **Open** *Nov-Mar* 6.30am-dusk daily. *Apr-Oct* 6am-dusk daily. **Admission** free. **Map** p243 F4.
Laid out in its present form in 1712 and opened to the public in 1775, the Augarten covers some 500,000 sq m (5.4 million sq ft) and is the oldest Baroque garden in Vienna. As well as housing the Augarten Porzellan Manufaktur and the Vienna Boys' Choir, the park is loved by the locals who hotly oppose current plans to build a concert hall for the choir near the Atelier Augarten to the east. Visitors sunbathe on the lawns to the south beside one of the park's two flak towers and enjoy a spritzer at the Bunkerei, a ramshackle terrace café in and around an old World War II bunker. In summer, it's home to the city's most popular open-air cinema, Kino unter Sternen (*see p168*). **Photo** *p90*.

Augarten Porzellan Manufaktur

2, Schloss Augarten, Obere Augartenstrasse 1 (21 124-0/www.augarten.at). Tram N, 21. **Open** (guided tours only) 10am Mon-Fri. **Admission** €6. **No credit cards. Map** p243 F4.
Bailed out after going into bankruptcy in 2003, the historic Wiener Porzellan Manufaktur continues to operate from Palais Augarten. Specialising in florid rococo designs, the firm also does a small line in modernist designs. Exhibitions are held in the foyer and wares are for sale on the premises or at its flagship store on Graben. Palais Augarten was originally Leopold I's summer palace but it was razed during the 1683 Turkish siege. After rebuilding, it hosted concerts by Mozart, Beethoven and Schubert. The Vienna Boys' Choir lodges here and the boys go to school in the neighbouring Kaiser Josef-Stöckl (1781).

Johann Strauss Haus

2, Praterstrasse 54 (214 012/www.wienmuseum.at). U1 Nestroyplatz. **Open** 2-6pm Tue-Thur; 10am-1pm Fri-Sun. **Admission** €2; €1 concessions. Free to all Sun. **No credit cards. Map** p251 G5.
Unlike most of Vienna's music museums, this one at least has a bash at period decor and does include exhibits belonging to the 'King of the Waltz', such as his grand piano, organ and stand-up composing desk. There's also a vast collection of ball-related memorabilia. Strauss lived here from 1863 to 1878.

Sightseeing

Kriminalmuseum

2, Grosse Sperlgasse 24 (214 4678/www.kriminal museum.at). Tram 21, N. **Open** 10am-5pm Thur-Sun. **Admission** €5; €4 concessions; €2.50 children. **No credit cards. Map** p251 F5.

Exhibits at the Criminal Museum are mostly photographs and press clippings, so a good understanding of German is needed. The show oscillates between lionising villains such as Breitwieser (Vienna's greatest safecracker) and offering interesting social background to cases such as that of Josephine Luner, who tortured her maid to death. Gruesome displays on murder *à la viennoise* feature strongly.

Prater

Prater

Formerly a royal hunting ground, the Prater covers a huge expanse of 60 square kilometres (23 square miles). The gaudy attractions of the Prater fun fair only take up a fraction of it. The chestnut-bordered central artery, the Hauptallee, has been synonymous with a Viennese Sunday stroll since it was opened to the public in 1766. May Day celebrations attract over 500,000 people, and all year round the Viennese come in droves for fresh air or a spot of jogging, cycling or in-line skating. In summer, splashes from the Olympic-size Stadionbad pool can be heard on the Hauptallee. Locals also flock in for the football at the Ernst-Happel-Stadion, trap racing

at the adjoining Krieau course and flat racing at the Freudenau course (*see p201*). More leisurely pursuits include floating through overgrown tracts of the old Danube in a rowing boat, snoozing beneath the hundreds of magnificent oaks and chestnuts, or tucking into roast pork and Budweiser at beer gardens such as the Schweizerhaus (*see p121*). The fun fair is open from mid-March to late October and entrance is free as the booths, rides and restaurants are run by different operators. Attractions range from old-fashioned merry-go-rounds, to the latest in fairground technology.

Wiener Riesenrad

2, Prater 90 (729 54 30/www.wienerriesenrad.com). U1 Praterstern, trams 5, N. **Open** *Nov-Feb* 10am-8pm daily; *Mar-Apr* 10am-10pm daily; *May-Sept* 10am-midnight daily; *Oct* 10am-10pm daily. **Admission** €8; €7 concessions; €3.20 children. **Credit** AmEx, DC, MC, V. **Map** p244 H5.

No trip to Vienna is complete without a ride on the 19th-century Riesenrad or giant ferris wheel that features in *The Third Man*. It's the only remaining work of British engineer Walter Basset who also built wheels for Blackpool, London and Paris. It was completed in 1897 to commemorate the Golden Jubilee of Franz Josef. A full circle in one of the 15 wooden gondolas takes a gentle 20 minutes; at its highest point you are 65 metres (213 feet) up but there's plenty of time to take in the views.

There's no knowing what lies at the end of the **Augarten**'s tree-lined paths. *See p89.*

3rd-9th Districts

Three, six, nine the city looks fine.

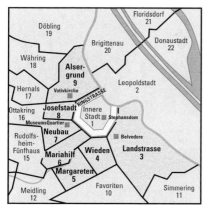

Landstrasse

Maps p244 & p245

The third is Vienna's largest inner city district, taking its name from Landstrasse-Hauptstrasse, the busy road heading south-east from the Stadtpark in the direction of Hungary. Bordered to the east by the Donaukanal with its opulent 19th-century apartment buildings, its southern reaches are markedly more working class, full of modern flats and Red Vienna housing fortresses from the 1920s such as the mighty Rabenhof.

Top of Landstrasse's varied sights is the Baroque **Belvedere Palace**, just south of Schwarzenbergplatz, followed by some quirky museums and examples of Vienna's boldest and quirkiest modern architecture, in particular the KunstHausWien and the Hundertwasser Haus of Friedensreich Hundertwasser.

Belvedere

Occupying a vast sweep of land that gently rises from Schwarzenbergplatz to the Gürtel, the palaces and gardens of the Belvedere are both a tourist hot-spot and an amenity for the locals. The Belvedere gets its name from the panoramic vista of the city and the distant Vienna Woods from the terrace of the **Oberes (Upper) Belvedere**, one of the finest secular Baroque buildings in Europe. Amazingly, it was built for Prince Eugène of Savoy (1663-1736) by architect Lukas von Hildebrandt in only one year (1721-

22). One of the master strategists of the defeat of the Turks (*see p19*), Eugène acquired the land in 1697 but had to wait until 1714 (when he'd received his share of the booty from the emperor) to start building. Beyond the statues, fountains and topiary of its terraced French gardens lies the **Unteres (Lower) Belvedere**, Eugène's summer residence and the first element to be constructed (1714-16).

Eugene, homosexual and a notorious cross-dresser with a love of the arts, used the monumental Oberes Belvedere as a palace for receptions, negotiations and feasts. He established various gardens on the eastern side of the grounds, which contained his aviary and menagerie – once home to the first giraffe to survive in captivity in Central Europe. To the south, botanists will enjoy the Alpine Garden and the University Botanical Gardens. After the Prince's death the Belvedere passed to Viktoria, Eugène's thoughtlessly extravagant niece, who sold the contents of his library to the Habsburgs and the picture collection all over Europe. In 1752, Maria Theresia bought the Belvedere itself and in 1776 Joseph II opened the gardens to the public and had the imperial picture collection moved there. Today, the Upper Belvedere houses the **Oesterreichische Galerie**, the Austrian National Gallery, famed for its collection of Klimts, Schieles and Kokoschkas.

The last Habsburg to reside in the Belvedere was Archduke Franz Ferdinand, who set up a rival court there. It returned to the political limelight in 1934, when Schuschnigg, chancellor of the Austro-Fascist government, briefly inhabited it, and again in 1955, when the Austrian State Treaty that re-established Austria as an independent neutral state was signed in the palace.

The main entrance to the Belvedere is on today's Gürtel, to the south. Visitors can also enter via Prinz-Eugen-Strasse or from Rennweg. To get the full effect use the main entrance.

Oberes Belvedere & Österreichische Galerie

3, Prinz-Eugen-Strasse 27 (79557-134/www. belvedere.at). Tram 18, D, O/bus 13a, 69a. **Open** 10am-6pm daily. **Admission** €9.50; €6-€7.50 concessions; €3 children. *Upper Belvedere, Lower Belvedere, Orangerie* €12.50 combicard; €8.50-€9.50 concessions; €5 children. Audioguides in English. **Credit** AmEx, DC, MC, V. **Map** p247 F9.

Unteres Belvedere & Orangerie. Psst, want to see my other palace?

The façade of the Upper Belvedere is one of Vienna's great sights and the contents of the Austrian Gallery no less impressive. The big draw is Vienna's modernist triumvirate of Klimt, Schiele and Kokoschka, which dwarfs the rest of the exhibits. However, in 2006, the collection was dealt a severe blow when Klimt's *Portrait of Adele Bloch-Bauer* (1906) and four of his landscapes were restored to their owner after an acrimonious legal battle. Masterpieces immediately recognisable by any visitor, such as *The Kiss* (1907-08) and *Judith* (1901), are on show and it remains the largest collection of Klimt paintings in the world. Nearby you can see the magnificent draughtsmanship of Egon Schiele's disturbingly emaciated human forms and Oskar Kokoschka's more animated, twisted Expressionist brush strokes. The highlight is his superb *Tiger-Lion* (1926), painted after being scared out of his wits in front of a lion's cage at London Zoo.

More unfamiliar works of 19th-century Austrian Realism such as Carl Moll's *Naschmarkt in Wien* (1894), *Steamer at Kaisermühlen* (1872) by Emil Jakob Schindler (Alma Mahler's father) and Hans Makart's sensual historicism are another of the gallery's strong points. Finally, there is a rather chaotic smörgåsbord of European Romanticism, Realism and Impressionism that includes works by Corot, Courbet, Daumier, Delacroix, Renoir and Van Gogh; but the one true stroke of genius among them is Caspar David Friedrich's *Sea-Shore in Mist* (1807).

Changes are underway at Austrian Gallery since the boundlessly ambitious Agnes Hüsslein was appointed director in 2006. A former director of Sotheby's Vienna and an ex-professional figure skater, she plans to make the gallery live up to its name and centre the collection on Austrian art from the Middle Ages to 1945 and move away from the Belvedere's pursuit of tourist bucks. So far she's concentrated on enlivening the Belvedere's many 'dead zones': the Orangerie and the Lower Belvedere are now temporary exhibition spaces and the next big project will be the reopening of the Zwanziger Haus.

Unteres Belvedere & Orangerie

3, Rennweg 6a (79557-134/www.belvedere.at). Tram 71. **Open** *Gardens dawn till dusk daily. Museums* 10am-6pm Tue, Wed, Fri-Sun; 10am-9pm Thur. *English highlights tour 4pm Sun.* **Admission** *Lower Belvedere, Orangerie* €7.50; €4.50-€5.50 concessions; €3 children. Audioguides in English. **Credit** AmEx, DC, MC, V. **Map** p247 F9.

Despite its modest façade, the flamboyant interiors of Prince Eugène's summer quarters make the upper palace's chambers seem pale in comparison. Although the Lower Belvedere is gradually being transformed into a temporary exhibition space and is no longer billed as the 'Baroque Museum', the idiom still dominates. The Marmorsaal in particular, rigged out with all manner of trompe l'oeil effects and illusory stucco work, is a two-floor extravaganza that celebrates Eugène's military career in a fresco by Martino Altamonte, shamelessly transforming him into the god Apollo. The Hall of Grotesques is so called because of oddball sculptor Franz Xaver Messerschmidt's (1732-83) ultra-realist busts that display a variety of facial grimaces, a form of Baroque psychology. After the Marmorgalerie, you reach the Goldkabinett – a Baroque freak-out fuelled by oriental vases, 23-carat gold panelling and a lot of mirrors. The adjacent Orangerie was renovated in 2006 and now serves as additional exhibition space.

Here it is. **Oberes Belvedere & Österreichische Galerie.** *See p91.*

Prinz-Eugen-Strasse

Running parallel to the Belvedere on the western side, Prinz-Eugen-Strasse, dividing the 3rd and 4th districts, is lined with imposing edifices, many of them now embassies. Beside the Soviet memorial on Schwarzenbergplatz is the discreet entrance to the Palais Schwarzenberg (1720), built by Fischer von Erlach and son for Adam Franz von Schwarzenberg, equerry to Emperor Karl VI. Now a hotel and currently closed for renovation, the palace backs on to a tract of woodland between the Belvedere gardens and Prinz-Eugen-Strasse. Its present owner, Karl von Schwarzenberg, appointed the Czech Republic's Minister of Foreign Affairs in 2007, reputedly thanked Elizabeth II for 'bombing my palace into a profitable hotel'. Nearby at Prinz-Eugen-Strasse nos.20-22, Adolf Eichmann ran the Central Office for Jewish Emigration from the former Rothschild residence, where in 1938 fleeing Jews (the lucky ones) were fleeced of their property in return for a passport. The building was destroyed in the war and is now the seat of the Chamber of Labour.

A few blocks further south of the entrance to the Upper Belvedere is Goldeggasse, where at no.19 you can visit, by prior appointment, the **Bestattungsmuseum** (Burial Museum). At the end of Prinz-Eugen-Strasse, across the traffic-clogged Gürtel (the inner city ring road), is the depressing sight of the post-war Südbahnhof (train station). Vienna disappoints railway enthusiasts since all its 19th-century stations

were bombed out of existence. It's somehow appropriate that the **Heeresgeschichtliches Museum** (Museum of Military History) is only a short walk from here. You can stroll through the leafy Schweizergarten, taking in its duckponds and monument to educationalist Rudolf Steiner. Karl Schwanzer's reconstructed pavilion for the 1958 Brussels Expo housed part of the Stiftung Ludwig modern art collection. In 2008, it will reopen as an exhibition space run by the Belvedere.

Bestattungsmuseum

4, Goldeggasse 19 (50 195/4227). U1 Südtirolerplatz/tram D. **Open** noon-3pm Mon-Fri by appointment. **Admission** €4.50; €1.50-€2.50 concessions; free under-10s. **No credit cards. Map** p247 F10.
The Burial Museum, the only one of its kind in the world, is a fitting testimony to the local obsession with the ceremonies and paraphernalia of death. Some exhibits are bizarre – a coffin with a bell pull for those mistakenly buried alive and a packet of undertakers' cigarettes bearing the legend *Rauchen sichert Arbeitsplätze* ('Smoking protects jobs'). The museum also displays photographs of the funerals of Emperor Franz Joseph and Archduke Franz Ferdinand, as well as touching accounts of ordinary folk, for example a photograph of a couple pushing their son's coffin on a cart in 1945.

Heeresgeschichtliches Museum

3, Hauptgebäude, Arsenal Objekt 18 (information 79 561-0/www.hgm.or.at). U1 Südtirolerplatz/tram 18, D, O/bus 13a, 69a. **Open** 9am-5pm Mon-Thur, Sat, Sun. **Admission** €5.10; €3.30 concessions; free under-10s. **No credit cards. Map** p248 G10.

Waltz on Otto Wagner & Viennese Jugendstil

Start: U4 Pilgramgasse
Finish: Postsparkasse
Length: 6 kilometres (4 miles)
Time: 2-3 hours

Art nouveau is a fixture of many European cities. In Vienna it's called Jugendstil (the youthful style) and its foremost practitioner, architect/engineer Otto Wagner (1841-1918), merged those familiar organic motifs with modern engineering and building techniques to often beautiful and startling effect.

Like many of the stations Otto Wagner designed for Vienna's district railway network (today's U4 and U6), **Pilgramgasse** has the air of a miniature temple. Upriver to the left is the **Vorwärts building** (1907), an influential socialist publisher built by Wagner students Franz and Hubert Gessner. Its façade has the undulating stucco and prominent bay windows of the period, with a metal rooftop crown adding a decorative flourish.

Following the Rechte Wienzeile down river, you approach the magnificent spectacle of Oscar Marmorek's **Rüdigerhof apartment building** (1902), with its curvaceous facing, gilded balconies and elaborate azure guttering. On the ground floor is the wonderfully improvised interior of **Café Rüdigerhof** (*see p141*), where Viennese socialist leader Viktor Adler went to chew the cud with the likes of Lenin and Trotsky.

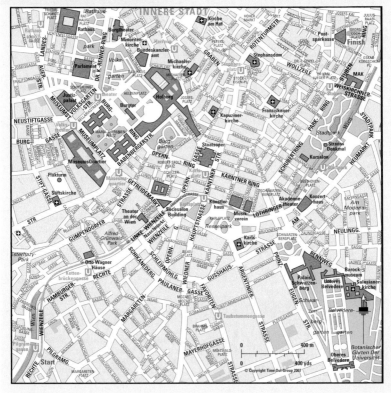

Take the new footbridge across the river to admire the neighbouring **Langer building** (1902), built by one of Wagner's most influential students, the Slovenian architect Jože Plečnik.

From here to the Naschmarkt, the river's course is covered. On Saturdays, this empty parking lot transforms into Vienna's most lively flea market. Note the Gessner brothers' monumentally rounded insurance building (1912) to the left. When you reach **Kettenbrückengasse**, another of Wagner's stations, the single-most impressive sight of Vienna's Jugendstil pantheon comes into view – Wagner's two apartment buildings at **Linke Wienzeile**, nos. 38-40 (see p99).

The Naschmarkt is a good spot to get some sustenance before taking on Karlsplatz and its cluster of Jugendstil gems. As you approach the end of the market, walk along the Linke Wienzeile and the Secession and see its gilded dome of laurel leaves rise above the passing traffic (see p99). Follow round Karlsplatz to **Café Museum** (see p138), where architect Adolf Loos' original interior was clumsily restored in 2005. Heading east across Karlsplatz, you encounter the two ornate **railway pavilions** that Wagner designed with Olbrich. One is now a small museum to Wagner, run by the nearby **Wien Museum** (see p99), our next stop. Housed in an austere 1950s building contrasting starkly with the Baroque flourish of neighbouring Karlskirche, the second floor fin-de-siècle rooms of the Wien Museum contain a handful of Klimt and Schiele paintings and a reconstruction of Loos' surprisingly cosy living room.

If you feel fit, you can walk to Otto Wagner's **Stadtpark station** or take the U4 one stop from Karlsplatz. Astride the river, this station has a remarkable setting in one of the Vienna's most attractive parks. From the station, there's a beautiful walk along the Wien river causeway lined with Wagner's signature green iron railings. Beyond the Stadtpark lies the **Museum of Applied Arts** (MAK, see p86) that has Vienna's largest collection of the Wiener Werkstätte, the legendary design firm that had its roots in Jugendstil. Five minutes walk from here along the Ringstrasse, you arrive at the **Postsparkasse** (see p86), which is Wagner's most stripped-down work of pure functional beauty.

Commissioned by Franz Josef I and completed in 1856, the Museum of Military History was Vienna's first purpose-built museum. Theophil Hansen's fantastic synthesis of Byzantine, Moorish and late-medieval Italian elements is a part of the Arsenal complex – one of four large barracks built post-1848 to quell popular unrest. Of these, only the Arsenal and the Rossauer Kaserne remain. Access to the museum is through the Feldherrenhalle (Hall of the Generals), which is lined with statues of pre-1848 Austrian military leaders.

The museum is on two floors, with courtyards given over to armoured vehicles. Upstairs there are displays on the Napoleonic Wars, the Thirty Years' War (1618-48) and the second siege of Vienna (1683). The trophies from the last of these include Turkish standards, tents and the Great Seal of Mustafa Pasha. The west wing of the ground floor assembles all the uniforms of the armies of the Crown Lands after the 1867 reform, conclusive proof that the Austro-Hungarians were the best-dressed soldiers ever. At one time, they oversaw an empire of over 54 million subjects and the military manuals on display had to be printed in 11 languages. Next comes the room covering the assassination of Archduke Franz Ferdinand in Sarajevo on 28 June 1914. It features the car in which he was shot, his blood-stained tunic and the Mayor of Sarajevo's couch on which he bled to death. This was brought to Vienna in 1997 during the siege of Sarajevo. In the east wing, there's a chillingly instructive display of Austria under the Nazis.

Rennweg & the South

'Beyond Rennweg, begins the Orient.' There must be some truth in Prince Metternich's famous adage, since the 'Coachman of Europe' lived at no. 27, in what is today the Italian embassy. Rennweg slopes up the eastern side of the Belvedere from Schwarzenbergplatz, its lower reaches lined with fine buildings such as the early Otto Wagner houses at no.3 and no.5 (where Gustav Mahler lived from 1898 to 1909). On Sundays, there's always a crowd of Polish worshippers filing in and out of the Gardekirche (1763), opposite the entrance to the Unteres Belvedere. It's worth the detour down Metternichgasse and along Jaurèsgasse, the heart of Vienna's diplomatic quarter, to see the stunningly renovated, onion-domed **Russian Orthodox** church at no.2. Beyond the railway, at Ungargasse nos.59-61 is Max Fabiani's **Portois & Fix** building (1900). Built for the fashionable design firm that created the interior of the Demel pastry shop (see p139), it has a Wagneresque tiled façade in shades of green, with Jugendstil ironwork aloft. Further north off Neulinggasse are two of Vienna's six World War II **Flaktürme** (anti-aircraft towers) in the adjacent Arenberg Park, one of which, **CAT**, in a collision of acronyms, is now used by the

Sightseeing

ESSL MUSEUM CONTEMPORARY ART

ESSL MUSEUM CONTEMPORARY ART
An der Donau-Au 1
A-3400 Klosterneuburg / Vienna, Austria, Europe
info@essl.museum / www.essl.museum

OPENING HOURS
TUE – SUN   10:00 – 18:00
WED   10:00 – 21:00
              18:00 – 21:00 FREE ADMISSION!

CONTEMPORARY ART
ESSL MUSEUM

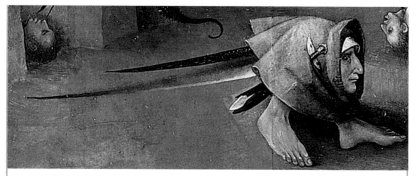

The Picture Gallery
Academy of Fine Arts Vienna
Hieronymus Bosch: The Last Judgement Triptych

Gemäldegalerie
Akademie der bildenden Künste Wien
1010 Vienna, Schillerplatz 3
www.akademiegalerie.at

]a[
akademie der
bildenden künste   GEMÄLDE
wien   GALERIE

Tues - Sun 10am - 6pm
Closed on Monday

MAK (Museum of Applied Arts). Further south along Rennweg, the landscape turns into the familiar sprawl of any modern city. At nos.97-99 Günther Domenig's extraordinarily expressive yet functional T-Mobile Centre (2004), the largest privately owned building in Austria, raises spirits briefly. One tram stop further lies **St Marxer Friedhof**, Vienna's most bucolic cemetery, hemmed in by busy roads and a motorway flyover. And for the real tram lover there is **Strassenbahnmuseum**.

CAT (Contemporary Art Tower)

3, Arenbergpark-Dannebergplatz/Bamherzigenstrasse (711 36 298/www.mak.at). U3 Rochusmarkt/bus 74a. **Open** *May-Nov* 11am-4pm Sun. **Admission** €5.50 or same-day MAK ticket. **No credit cards**. **Map** p248 G8.

Since the MAK (*see p86*) started using one of the two Arenberg flak towers as a depot for its contemporary art collection, it has been touting its Contemporary Art Tower (CAT) project as an on-site location for artists to work. Despite commissioning projects for the exterior by Jenny Holzer and James Tyrell, nothing really concrete has materialised as yet. Inside there are works by Holzer and Tyrell as well as some fine pieces by Erwin Wurm and Franz West, and it's one of the few opportunities you'll get to see the interior of these extraordinary monoliths.

Gasometer

3, Guglgasse. U3 Gasometer. **Map** p249 K10.

On your way in from the airport, you may spot four circular brick gas tanks, each 70m (230ft) high. These 19th-century behemoths briefly served as venues for raves before the council stumped up some €230 million to convert them into a housing complex to revitalise the peripheral Erdberg district. In the architectural competition, the outright winners were celebrated Viennese deconstructionists Coop Himmelb(l)au, whose prize was to build an external symbol on Gasometer B in the form of an angular glass shield that houses a student residence. It looks great but inside it's all low ceilings and cheapo materials. Gasometer A, beside the complex's purpose-built U-Bahn station, was designed by French architect Jean Nouvel who built nine towers inside his tank, knocking huge windows into the walls and cladding the exterior with a shimmery metallic finish. Gasometers C and D, designed by Austrian architects Manfred Wehdorn and Wilhelm Holzbauer respectively, both opted for communal gardens in the interior and are probably the most liveable.

St Marxer Friedhof

3, Leberstrasse 6-8 (796 3613). Tram 71. **Open** *Nov-Mar* 7am-dusk daily. *Apr, Oct* 7am-5pm daily. *May, Sept* 7am-6pm daily. *June-Aug* 7am-7pm daily. **Admission** free. **Map** p248 H10.

St Mark's was the first of Vienna's outer-limits cemeteries, built on the orders of Joseph II, who in the 1780s ordered the closure of all the Innere Stadt cemeteries for reasons of hygiene. No burials have been held

here since 1874 and from then on, nature has taken its course, leaving crumbling tombs and headstones peeping through a mass of vegetation. St Marx's most illustrious corpse was Mozart's, given a pauper's burial in a mass grave in 1791. Mozart's death coincided with Josef II's diktat making mass burial the norm. His wife Constanze's attempts to pinpoint the exact place of burial led to the erection of the so-called Mozartgrab, featuring an angel in mourning and a truncated pillar representing his early death. A plan of the graves is available at the entrance.

Strassenbahnmuseum

3, Ludwig-Koessler-Platz (786 03 03/www.tram.at). U3 Schlachthausgasse/tram 18, 73. **Open** *May-Oct* 9am-4pm Sat, Sun, public holidays. **Admission** €3. **No credit cards**. **Map** p248 J8.

Housed in three brick sheds, this museum contains all forms of carriage to have graced the rails of Vienna's vast tram network, including horse-drawn trams, a working steam tram and several buses. The ubiquitous red-and-white tram is known as the Bim, aping the sound of its bell. The newest Siemens-built, Porsche-designed ultra-low platform model is also on display.

By the Donaukanal

The area of the 3rd district bordering the Danube Canal is quiet and residential, with easy access to the lower reaches of the Prater. A steady stream of visitors heads for the **Hundertwasser Haus**, a surreal municipal housing project dreamed up by the late Friedensreich Hundertwasser (1928-2000), artist, ecologist and amateur architect. If his Gaudiesque swirls appeal, head for the nearby **Kunsthaus Wien**, a similarly extravagant gallery space housing a permanent collection of his work. The **Wittgenstein-Haus** turns a much more severe face to the world.

Hundertwasser Haus

3, corner Löwengasse/Kegelgasse (www.hundertwasserhaus.at). Tram N. **Map** p248 H7.

Hundertwasser's first of many forays into architecture, finished in 1985, was a commission to jazz up this existing council block. He added all manner of colourful facings, protruberances, onion domes, roof gardens and disconcerting undulating floors, in a distillation of his 'war on the straight line'. None of it is open to the public and residents stoically ignore the crowds of sightseers. Later he used his not inconsiderable business acumen to fashion an adjacent shopping complex in a similar idiom. Much to the chagrin of local intellectuals, the building is now on virtually every tour bus itinerary.

Kunsthaus Wien

3, Untere Weissgerberstrasse 13 (712 0491/www.kunsthauswien.com). Tram N, O. **Open** 10am-7pm daily. **Admission** €9; €7 concessions; half-price Mon. **Credit** AmEx, DC, MC, V. **Map** p248 G6.

Hundertwasser designed the former Thonet furniture factory as a repository for his dubious eco-art, applying to it his trademark spirals, splashes of mosaic and undulating brick floors. His work takes up two floors while the remaining two are given over to flagrantly commercial shows by celebrity and fashion photographers and big name artists. On the plus side, the café/terrace's exuberant vegetation makes it an agreeable spot to have a drink.

Wittgenstein-Haus

3, Kundmanngasse 19/Parkgasse 18 (713 3164/ www.haus-wittgenstein.at). U3 Rochusgasse. **Open** 10am-noon, 3-4.30pm Mon-Thur. **Admission** €3. **No credit cards. Map** p248 H7.

Tucked away in the leafy bourgeois streets between Landstrasse and the Donaukanal, the Wittgenstein house stands out as a forboding series of grey concrete cubes surrounded by high walls. Originally Ludwig Wittgenstein's sister Gretl had commissioned architect Paul Engelmann, a student of Adolf Loos, to build her a town house. When Ludwig saw the plans, he muscled in and personally designed the door handles, radiators and windows, each of which took him a year to complete. As it's lit with bare bulbs and had no carpet or curtains – instead Wittgenstein used 150-kilo metal blinds operated by an effective pulley system of his own invention – Gretl found the house suited her austere disposition. In fact she even returned there after spending the Nazi years in New York. Narrowly escaping demolition after Gretl's son sold it to a speculator, the house is now the cultural centre of the Bulgarian embassy. In 2007, the Bulgarians decided to let the public in on a regular basis, albeit with carpet on the floors.

Around Karlsplatz

Maps p250, p251 & p247

With its great concentration of sights and attractions clustered around one square, Karlsplatz should really be one of Vienna's great showpiece arenas. In reality, it's just an amorphous mass of streets, tramlines and green spaces that does no justice to the buildings that surround it. If you approach it from the bustling Ringstrasse/Kärnterstrasse junction, it's best to take the U-Bahn underpass that leads directly into the Resselpark, Karlsplatz's green heart. The underpass is also an antiquated underground mall that is home to a proportion of the city's substance abusers, who stumble around with can in hand but rarely hassle anyone but their peers.

Walking east through the park, you can take in **Otto Wagner's Stadtbahn Pavillons** (Railway Pavilions), before reaching the majestic Baroque **Karlskirche** and the **Wien Museum**. If you double back along the dual carriageway, you pass the venue of Vienna's world famous New Year's Concert, the Musikverein (*see p182*) and the neighbouring neo-Renaissance Künstlerhaus (1868) (*see p173*). Stop maybe for a coffee at over-fussily renovated Café Museum (*see p138*) before taking on the pearl of the Karlsplatz oyster, the iconic **Secession** building and the nearby **Akademie der Bildenen Künste**. For a final repose before heading on to the multi-culti

Secession.

delights of the Naschmarkt, Vienna's marvellous open market, head for the terrace of the arty Kunsthalle Project Space (*see p173*).

Akademie der Bildenden Künste

1, Schillerplatz 3 (1st floor on the right) (58816-225/www.akbild.ac.at). U1, U2, U4 Karlsplatz/tram 1, 2, D, J. **Open** 10am-6pm Tue-Sun. **Admission** €7; €3-€5 concessions; free under-10s. Audioguide in English. **No credit cards**. **Map** p250 E8.

The Academy of Fine Arts – which rejected the young Adolf Hitler on two occasions – is a short walk from the Secession. Theophil Hansen's building houses a fine, if largely forgotten, picture gallery. The star of the show is Hieronymus Bosch's *The Last Judgement* (1504-06), his only monumental triptych outside Spain. The collection also includes *Tarquin and Lucretia* by Titian, Botticelli's *Madonna Tondo* and Rembrandt's early *Unknown Young Woman*, but features mostly Flemish and Dutch paintings.

Karlskirche

4, Karlsplatz (504 6187). U1, U2, U4 Karlsplatz. **Open** 9am-12.30pm; 1-6pm Mon-Sat; noon-5.45pm Sun. **Admission** €6; €4 concessions; free under-10s. **No credit cards**. **Map** p251 E8.

Visible from all sides of the Karlsplatz, this masterpiece of Baroque architecture has more than a hint of Rome and even a touch of Byzantium about it. Emperor Karl VI commissioned Fischer von Erlach to build a church to mark the end of the 1713 plague, dedicating it to the memory of St Carlo Borromeo, himself renowned for his role in tending victims of the 1576 plague in Milan. Thus Karl could celebrate the work of his selfless namesake by having the events of his life depicted on Fischer's splendid columns and then topping them with his own imperial eagles. The church was completed in 1737 by Fischer's son. The exterior is a hard act to follow, but inside it is all light and airiness, showing off Rottmayr's immense fresco and Fischer's sunburst above the altar to great effect. See them close up and enjoy the view from the roof by taking the 47m-(154ft) glass elevator built for restoration work. In front of the church, a large ornamental pond with a Henry Moore sculpture (*Hill Arches*, 1978) reflects the building's impressive curves.

Otto Wagner's Stadtbahn Pavillons

1, Karlsplatz (505 8747). U1, U2, U4 Karlsplatz. **Open** *Apr-Oct* 9am-6pm Tue-Sun. Closed Nov-Mar. **Admission** €2; €1 concessions. **No credit cards**. **Map** p250 E8.

Had it not been for a protest by students from the Technische Universität, these splendid pavilions might have been demolished during U-Bahn construction in the 1960s. Originally located either side of the Akademiestrasse, they were reconstructed here with only a few slabs of discoloured Carrara marble being replaced. One now houses a small exhibition dedicated to his work run by the Wien Museum. The other is a café with a fine terrace that hosts Club U (*see p197*) in the evenings

Secession

1, Friedrichstrasse 12 (587 5307/www.secession.at). U1, U2, U4 Karlsplatz. **Open** 10am-6pm Tue, Wed, Fri-Sun; 10am-8pm Thur. **Admission** €6; €3.50 concessions. **No credit cards**. **Map** p250 E8.

The temple-like home of the Viennese Secession is the one building you shouldn't leave Vienna without seeing. Bank-rolled by Karl Wittgenstein, father of Ludwig, and completed in 1898 to a design by architect Josef Olbrich, the building was the focal point of the Secession movement, a group of artists who rejected the stultifying historicism of Vienna's leading artists' association, the Künstlerhaus. It was intended as a gallery and a meeting space, and the legend above the entrance clarified their aims: 'To the age its art, to art its freedom'. Crowned with a gilded globe of laurel leaves, the building's delicate stucco work is interspersed with sculpted salamanders, ceramic turtles and door handles in the form of snakes. The building was severely damaged in World War II and only restored to its present form in the mid 1980s. Inside space is at a premium. There are usually two or three parallel exhibitions, divided between the main space, the dismal little graphics cabinet upstairs and the cellar, which houses Klimt's baffling but beautiful *Beethoven Friese* and photographs documenting the building's history. In 2006, the Secession elected its first woman president, artist Barbara Holub. Instead of competing with the other public galleries of contemporary art, she aims to restore the Secession's role as an artists' association and make its presence felt throughout the city.

Wien Museum

4, Karlsplatz (505 8747/www.wienmuseum.at). U1, U2, U4 Karlsplatz/tram 1, 2, D, J/bus 3a. **Open** 9am-6pm Tue-Sun. **Admission** €6; €3-€4 concessions; free to all Sun. **No credit cards**. **Map** p251 E8.

As well as scale models of the city, artefacts from the Turkish siege and worthwhile temporary exhibitions on Vienna themes, the second floor of the Wien Museum has some unmissable fin-de-siècle treasures. These include four paintings by Klimt, household objects designed by Josef Hoffmann and Kolo Moser for the Wiener Werkstätte firm, and a reconstruction of Adolf Loos' surprisingly cosy living room. It also runs numerous smaller museums throughout the city, so check the website.

Wienzeile

Maps p250 & p247

No stay in Vienna would be complete without a Saturday morning stroll along the bustling concourse of Vienna's principal food market, the Naschmarkt (*see p151*). The market operates through the week, but Saturday has the added attraction of a large flea market. Here, beside **Otto Wagner's** Kettenbrückengasse U-Bahn station, are his two magnificent apartment buildings on the Linke

Sightseeing

Wienzeile. Either side of the market, there are several sights worth taking in. At Linke Wienzeile 6 is the Theater an der Wien (*see p185*), dating back to 1801 when the venue first opened under the directorship of Emanuel Schikaneder, author of the libretto for Mozart's *Magic Flute*. He is depicted as Papageno, the bird-catcher in the opera, in a statue above the main portico. More interesting than the modern façade is the backstage area down the adjacent side street, which eventually leads west to Café Sperl (*see p141*) on Gumpendorfer Strasse, one of Vienna's most atmospheric coffee houses. Off the Rechte Wienzeile, Schleifmühlgasse (*see p172* **Let's stick together – Vienna's gallery clusters**) and its adjoining streets are fast filling up with galleries, hip shops and restaurants. Cinephiles visiting on Saturday afternoon might like to look in on the **Third Man Private Collection**.

Otto Wagner Houses

6, Linke Wienzeile 38, 40. U4 Kettenbrückengasse. **Map** p247 D8.
These houses are the culmination of Otto Wagner's welding of Secessionist decorative vernacular with his own belief in the use of modern materials. At no.38 the gorgeous floral designs of the façade's majolica tiles (it's known as the Majolika Haus) and the clear distinction between commercial premises and dwelling make the buildings the antithesis of the Ringstrasse palace. The gilded embossing of the exterior of no.40 is by Secessionist Kolo Moser.

Third Man Private Collection

4, Pressgasse 25 (586 4872/www.3mpc.net). U4 Kettenbrückengasse. **Open** 2-6pm Sat; also by appointment. **Admission** €6; €4 under-16s. **No credit cards. Map** p247 D9.
This excellent private museum houses one aficionado's extensive collection of *Third Man* marginalia and documentation on the aftermath of the war in Vienna. Posters, lobby cards and star portraits from around the world chronicle the movie's marketing and its unforgettable rogues' gallery of secondaries. You can see one of Anton Karas' original zithers and hear the haunting theme tune on a 78, or access via computer over 300 often bizarre versions (the original sheet music for which adorns the walls). Also on show are numerous *Third Man* spin-offs such as board games, clocks and lighters. A visit also includes the showing of an excerpt from the film on a 1936 German Ernemann VIIb 35mm projector, the model in use when post-war Viennese audiences shivered through the première in 1949.

Mariahilf & Neubau

Maps p250 & p246

Vienna's 6th district, **Mariahilf**, rises from the hollow of the Wien river valley via various steep lanes and flights of steps to **Mariahilfer Strasse**, the city's prime shopping mile and former home of Joseph Haydn. On the way you cross Gumpendorfer Strasse, whose lower reaches house numerous switched-on bars and restaurants. Sights are thin on the ground, but the uneven geography, human bustle and varied architecture make it pleasant to stroll. Over the Mariahilfer Strasse, you're in Neubau (district 7). On the corner of Kirchengasse, take the high-speed lift to the top floor of the Gerngross shopping centre for an excellent view north to the hills of the Wienerwald and, to the south, the onion domes of the **Mariahilferkirche** with one of this district's two monolithic **Flaktürme** behind. This one can be seen from inside as it's been turned into an aquarium.

Neubau is one of Vienna's most happening areas in terms of nightlife, shops and alternative lifestyles. This bastion of the Green Party is full of handsome buildings housing firms of architects and designers, and small quirky clothing and jewellery operations. It's worth investigating the streets either side of Siebensterngasse and its continuation, Westbahnstrasse. The latter heads west to the Gürtel, where you can climb to the top of the new public library for beautiful views towards the south. Neubau is at its most picturesque east of the pleasant, commercial Neubaugasse. Known as **Spittelberg**, this atmospheric network of cobbled streets and heterogeneous Biedermeier architecture is lovely for strolling. The area was once a red-light district, where Hitler reputedly had his first sight of the prostitutes that serviced the adjacent barracks, the Stiftskaserne. Today, homes in its narrow streets are among the most desirable in Vienna and its numerous restaurants and antiques dealers are evidence of the area's gentrification. Before Christmas the whole area is transformed into an Advent market, although you won't find the Habsurg furniture on show at **Hofmobiliendepot** for sale. Futher east, there is access to the MuseumsQuartier (*see p83*). Along Siebensterngasse the terraces of Shultz (*see p200*) and Siebenstern (a swish bar owned by the Communist Party), on the corner of Kirchengasse, are great hangouts. Don't miss the splendid apartment building round the corner in Mondscheingasse, with three lions' heads and a stucco tree.

Down Kirchengasse beyond Burggasse is the fine Baroque church of St Ulrich, in a gorgeous square sloping down to Neustiftgasse. At no.40 is one of Otto Wagner's most beautiful, austere apartment buildings; round the corner at Döblergasse 4 is the house where the architect himself lived and worked until his death in 1918.

Haydnhaus

6, Haydngasse 19 (596 1307). U3 Zieglergasse.
Open 10am-1pm, 2-6pm Wed, Thur; 10am-1pm
Fri-Sun. **Admission** €2; concessions €1. **No
credit cards**. **Map** p246 C9.

Composer Joseph Haydn spent his last 12 years in
this small house just off Mariahilfer Strasse, writing
his great oratorios. Opened as a museum in 1899, it
displays letters, two pianos and Haydn's death
mask. A separate room is dedicated to Johannes
Brahms, who lionised Haydn and did much to maintain the memory of his idol. Here Brahms' clavicord
(possibly a gift from Haydn) is exhibited. Another
admirer was Napoleon who placed a guard of honour outside the house as Haydn lay dying in 1809.

Hofmobiliendepot

*7, Andreasgasse 7 (524 3357-0/www.hofmobilien
depot.at). U3 Zieglergasse/bus 13a.* **Open** 10am-6pm
Tue-Sun. **Admission** €6.90; €4.50 concessions;
€3.50 children. **Credit** AmEx, DC, MC, V.
Map p246 C8.

Founded by Maria Theresia in 1747, this gigantic
lock-up for the monarchy's unwanted furniture and
fittings is a splendidly laid-out museum guaranteed
to interest anyone with a weakness for interior decoration. Entire rooms have been reconstructed, such
as a bedroom from the Laxenburg palace, Crown
Prince Rudolph's opium den and numerous modernist pieces by Hoffmann, Loos and Wagner.

Josefstadt

Maps p246 & p242

The genteel 8th district of Vienna takes its
name from Joseph I (1678-1711), during whose
reign (1705-11) this residential area was laid
out. It borders on Landesgerichtsstrasse
directly behind the Rathaus (*see p79*) and in
the cobbled streets around Lenaugasse there
are many fine examples of Biedermeier
architecture. Although in 2006 the Josefstadt
became the second district to be run by the
Greens, it has yet to acquire Neubau's
fashionable buzz. Its well-heeled residents
patronise the historic Theater in der Josefstadt
and Vienna's English Theatre (*see p210*), read
the papers in period coffee houses such as the
Florianihof (*see p142*) or hang out with their
children in the lovely local parks.

Throughout the neighbourhood plaques
commemorate the district's distinguished
former residents and today actor Klaus-Maria
Brandauer and the Austrian president Heinz
Fischer both live locally. Sights include the
Museum für Volkskunde (Folklore Museum),
the Church of the Holy Trinity at Alserstrasse
no.17, where Beethoven's funeral was held in
1827, and best of all, the wedding cake Baroque
of the **Piaristenkirche**. Otherwise, a spot of
window shopping in the antique and second-

Spittelberg.

hand shops in the streets off the Josefstädter
Strasse is a pleasure in itself.

The section of the Gürtel that traces the
northern boundary of Josefstadt is one of the
city's hippest nightlife zones, with several DJ
bars and live venues built into the arches of
Otto Wagner's Stadtbahn, today the route of the
U6. The Gürtel is also home to numerous peep
shows, sex shops and concommitant prostitution
but is not threatening. During the day, it's worth
crossing the Gürtel into the 16th for the vibrant
Brunnenmarkt (*see p151*), in the heart of the
Turkish and Yugoslav communities.

Museum für Volkskunde

*8, Laudongasse 15-19 (406 8905/www.volkskunde
museum.at). U2 Rathaus/tram 5, 33, 43, 44/bus
13a.* **Open** 9am-5pm Tue-Sun. **Admission** €5;
€3.50 concessions. **No credit cards**. **Map** p246 C6.

Backing on to the park of the same name, Von
Hildebrandt's early 17th-century Palais Schönborn
houses the Museum for Folklore. It deals with the
customs, religious rites and secular celebrations of
the Austrians and puts on excellent exhibitions.

Piaristenkirche

*8, Jodok-Fink-Platz (www.mariatreu.at). U2
Rathaus/tram J/bus 13a.* **Open** 8am-noon, 6-8pm
Sun; or call at parish office (Piaristengasse 43-45, 405
0425) between 9am-noon Mon-Fri for key. Photo ID
needed. **Admission** free. **Map** p246 C6.

Joseph I included in his plans land to be set aside for the Order of the Piarists to found a monastery. The Maria Treu or Piaristenkirche (1753) stands between the monastery outbuildings, its convex façade flanked by two elegant towers. The original design was traced by Von Hildebrandt in 1716, but it was not completed until the 19th century. The interior is notable for Franz Maulbertsch's ceiling frescoes and for its organ, on which Anton Brückner took his examination for the Academy. As he played, an examiner commented, 'He should be examining us!'

Alsergrund

Maps p242, p243 & p250

Occupying a large area stretching from Alserstrasse down to the Danube canal, Alsergrund, Vienna's 9th district, is the city's medical and university district and contains the largest concentration of sights outside the Innere Stadt. Directly opposite the Church of the Holy Trinity on Alserstrasse is the **University Campus**, housed in the former Altes Allgemeines Krankenhaus, one of Europe's oldest hospitals. It is home to some curious sights, such as the **Narrenturm**, an 18th-century lunatic asylum that has been converted into the fascinating **Pathologisch-anatomische Bundesmuseum**. To the north a couple of monolithic towers denote the presence of the AKH (Allgemeines Krankenhaus), the largest hospital in Europe.

Nearby on Währinger Strasse is the **Josephinum**, Joseph II's academy for military surgeons – now a medical museum. However, the district is probably most famous for Berggasse 19, now the **Sigmund Freud Museum**, where Freud lived and did most of his pioneering work on psychoanalysis.

West of Berggasse, the Servitenviertel is a lovely villagey quarter with the only church outside the city walls to survive the Turkish siege, the late 17th-century **Servitenkirche**. Nearby too is the small Jewish cemetery of Seegasse. Access is through the old people's home at Seegasse 9-11, built on the site of the old Jewish hospital. Like all such cemeteries in Vienna, this one bears the scars of rabid anti-semitism, with virtually every tomb desecrated. Look out for the curious mound of stones with a carved fish on top – it's not clear whether it's actually a gravestone.

Further along Seegasse you come to the congested Rossauer Lände which follows the canal embankment where various ramps and flights of steps lead to the waterside. It's worth following the path to get a fantastic view of one of Vienna's most singular buildings, the **Fernwärme**, a municipal rubbish incinerator embellished by artist Hundertwasser. The 9th district's most exuberant edifice is Palais Liechtenstein, a wonderful Baroque garden palace built to a design by Domenico Martinelli. It remains the property of the Princes of Liechtenstein, and in 2004, they opened the **Liechtenstein Museum** of Baroque art. Classical music buffs may want to venture to the district's less scenic end to take in the **Schuberthaus**, the birthplace of Franz Schubert on Nussdorfer Strasse. The alternative is to cross Liechtenstein Strasse and climb the magnificent Jugendstil ensemble of the Strudelhof Steps leading to Währinger Strasse, where you can return to the centre by tram.

Fernwärme

9, Spittelauer Lände 45 (313 26 20 30). U4, U6 Spittelau/tram D. **Open** Tours by appointment. **Admission** free. **Map** p243 D2.

Few cities can boast a municipal rubbish incinerator that features in sightseeing guides, but Friedensreich Hundertwasser's 1989 remodelling of a hideous industrial building is now one of Vienna's great visual surprises. This is mainly due to the enormous smoke stack, wrapped in vitro-ceramic tiles and crowned with a large golden mosaic bulb.

Josephinum

9, Währinger Strasse 25 (4277 63401). Tram 37, 38, 40, 41, 42. **Open** 9am-3pm Mon-Fri; 10am-2pm 1st Sat of mth. **Admission** €2; €1 concessions. **No credit cards. Map** p243 D5.

The Josephinum museum of medical history is a Canevale building dating from 1775. Fronted by impressive wrought ironwork, the institution was intended as a school for military surgeons. The exhibits include a through-the-ages look at surgical instruments, but the main draw is a collection of life-size wax anatomical models made by Florentine craftsmen in 1780.

Liechtenstein Museum

9, Fürstengasse 1 (319 57 67 252/www. liechtensteinmuseum.at). Tram D. **Open** 10am-5pm Mon, Fri-Sun. **Admission** €10; €5-€8 concessions. Guided tours in English by appointment. **Credit** AmEx, JCB, MC, V. **Map** p243 D4.

The Princes of Liechtenstein have been patrons of the the arts for centuries. In the 1960s, faced with (relatively) dire straits, they sold a real Leonardo, used the spoils to start a bank and resumed their collecting. Their stupendous collection of Baroque painting, including a large number of important works by Rubens, now hangs in this expensively, but discreetly, renovated Baroque garden palace (built 1691-1711). Although the unenlightened may find the experience akin to having two chocolate puddings, the superb lighting and lack of labelling (it's all explained in a handy booklet) make it a triumph of museum presentation. The work on Andrea Pozzo's monumental ceiling fresco in the Hercules Hall is probably the highlight. The gardens have been restored to their original Baroque layout.

Sometimes a cigar is just a cigar. **Sigmund Freud Museum**.

Pathologisch-anatomische Bundesmuseum

9, Spitalgasse 2 (Courtyard 13, entrance Van-Swieten Gasse) (406 8672/www.pathomus.or.at).
Tram 5, 33, 43, 44. **Open** 3-6pm Wed; 8-11am
Thur; 10am-1pm 1st Sat of mth. **Admission** €2.
No credit cards. **Map** p242 C5.
The so-called Narrenturm (Fool's Tower) is hidden in
a courtyard of the University Campus. Commissioned
by the emperor, this house of internment for the mentally ill was built by Canevale in 1784 and was used
as such until 1866. The present museum is a medical
house of horrors – not for the faint-hearted.

Schuberthaus

9, Nussdorfer Strasse 54 (317 3601/www.wien
museum.at). Tram 37, 38. **Open** 10am-1pm, 2-6pm
Tue-Sun. **Admission** €2; €1 concessions. **No credit**
cards. **Map** p242 C3.
Schubert was born in the kitchen of this two-room
home and lived here, sharing with 12 other family
members, till the age of four. The collection of memorabilia – contemporary portraits of the composer
and his original trademark spectacles – also includes
audio sound bites of his most important pieces.

Servitenkirche

9, Servitenplatz. U4 Rossauer Lände/tram D.
Map p243 D4/5.
Servitenviertel is a charming villagey network of
streets. This church belongs to the Serviten Order
and was designed by Canevale. It's Baroque to the
marrow, with a fine interior, impressive stucco, a

pulpit by Moll (1739) and a relief showing the mar-
tyrdom of Czech saint, John Nepomuk. Apart from
Mass, the church must be seen through iron railings.

Sigmund Freud Museum

9, Berggasse 19 (319 1596/www.freud-museum.at).
U2 Schottentor/tram 37, 38, 40, 41, 42, D. **Open**
Oct-June 9am-5pm daily. *July-Sept* 9am-6pm daily.
Archive, library by appointment. **Admission** €7;
€4.50-€5.50 concessions; free under-12s. Guided tours
by appointment. **Credit** DC, MC, V. **Map** p250 D5.
Opened in 1971, the museum is located in the apartment where Sigmund lived and worked from 1898
to 1938, when he was forced into exile by the Nazis.
On arrival, the visitor is offered a guide to the
exhibits in a choice of languages and then let loose
in the various rooms. Throughout the apartment,
photos, letters, first editions and the ethnic bric-a-
brac Freud so assiduously collected are displayed in
glass cases. Some items, such as a photo of the house
daubed with swastikas, are chilling. One room has
a video set-up showing 8mm films of Freud and family. Staff are aficionados and extremely helpful.

University Campus

9, Alser Strasse/Spitalgasse. Tram 5, 33, 43, 44.
Map p242 C5.
This labyrinth of 15 or so inner courtyards opened
in 1784 as the Allgemeines Krankenhaus (General
Hospital), but in the mid 1990s it was converted into
a university campus. In the summer months, it's a
delightful place to hang out, as it's dotted with book-
shops, terrace bars, and a great playground.

Further Afield

Among vineyards and woodland, Vienna's verdant fringes house some of the city's greatest attractions.

Sightseeing

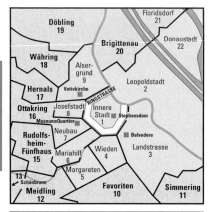

West of Vienna

The main draw on the western side of Vienna is the city's most popular tourist attraction: the Habsburgs' summer palace, **Schönbrunn**, and its gardens and parkland. Locals also flock here to jog around the park and visit the **Tiergarten** (zoo) and **Botanical Gardens**. Combine the trip with a look at the neighbouring district of Hietzing. A treat for architecture freaks – Otto Wagner, Adolf Loos and later Viennese Modernists built in this prosperous suburb. You could also call in at the **Technisches Museum Wien**, Vienna's impressive science museum, a couple of tram stops from Schönbrunn. However, for those with a particular interest in Otto Wagner and Jugendstil, a trip to the far-flung 14th district in the west of the city is a must. In reasonable proximity there are two of his villas and the outstanding **Kirche am Steinhof** – Wagner's only stab at ecclesiastical architecture.

Kirche am Steinhof

14, Baumgartner Höhe 1 (91060 11204). U2, U3 Volkstheater/U3 Ottakring/bus 48a. **Open** 4-5pm Sat. **Tours** (German only) 3-4pm Sat or by appointment. **Admission** free. *Tours* €4. **No credit cards.**
Otto Wagner's church is located within the grounds of Steinhof, originally a pioneering experiment in the care of the mentally ill but later scene of some of the greatest horrors of Nazi 'psychiatry'. Set in hectares of beautiful parkland, the church was built for use

by patients and staff. Wagner designed Steinhof's layout (built 1902), and many of the 61 pavilions that make up the centre. In 2000, Steinhof was renamed the Otto Wagner Hospital and in 2007 the church celebrates its centenary. Take the path up the hill to the left of the admin buildings and slowly the immense (32m-/105ft-high), splendidly renovated copper cupola comes into view.

Set on a huge stone plinth and clad in white marble with four Jugendstil angels, the Kirche am Steinhof is one of the world's first examples of ecclesiastical functionalism. Inside it is all light and clean surfaces. With the altar to the north, sunlight pours in through Kolo Moser's magnificent stained-glass windows depicting a procession of saints. Moser started the work on the mosaic of the altar fresco (which features St Peter with Franz Josef's head), but conversion to Protestantism led to his being dropped from the team (despite Wagner's intervention).

In fact, Wagner imagined that his church would be a shrine for all religions, particularly for Steinhof patients. To that end he oversaw all the details, even designing special robes for the priests. The church was opened by Archduke Franz Ferdinand, who could barely hide his contempt, saying in his inaugural address that the architecture of Maria Theresia's time was far superior. Since the 1980s Steinhof has been an open centre, with patients free to leave of their own accord. With the constant stream of visitors to the church and to performances at the Jugendstiltheater (*see p186*) on the grounds, Steinhof breathes an apparent air of normality.

However, its history is haunted by its part in the Nazis' euthanasia policy. An exhibition in Pavillion V (to the left after the admin building), entitled 'War Against the Inferior: the History of Nazi Medicine in Vienna', documents the two-fold atrocity that involved Steinhof. First, its patients were murdered in their thousands between August 1940 and August 1941, when they were transported to the gas chambers of the infamous Hartheim Castle in Upper Austria. Secondly, at the reformatory and children's clinic called Spiegelgrund set up in 1940 in thirteen of Steinhof's pavilions, outrageous experiments were carried out on children, in particular those suffering from rickets, hydrocephalus and tuberculosis. In all 789 children died. Although the director was sentenced to death in 1946, his assistant Heinrich Gross received a two-year manslaughter sentence, later rescinded. He went on to have a prestigious academic career and received numerous awards. In 1976, in his capacity as court psychologist, Gross was handed the case of Friedrich Zawrel,

Sightseeing

Who takes away the sins of the world? **Kirche am Steinhof**.

one of his Spiegelgrund victims who had managed to escape with the aid of a nurse. Zawrel contacted the press and in 1979 an association of doctors exposed Gross's role in the killing of children. He was not charged with murder until 2000 and the case was finally dropped as the 84-year-old Gross was adjudged to be suffering from senile dementia. The exhibition and its excellent website in English (www.gedenkstaettesteinhof.at) document these tragic events in heart-rending detail.

Otto Wagner Villas

14, Hüttelbergstrasse 26, 28 (914 8575/www.ernst fuchs-zentrum.com). Tram 49. **Open** 10am-5pm Mon-Fri. Weekend guided tours in English for groups by appointment. **Admission** €11; €4-€6 concessions. **Credit** AmEx, DC, MC, V.

The villa at no.26 is the only one of the two open to the public, since it is home to the Ernst-Fuchs Museum, a lamentable piece of egomania by the magical realist painter of the same name, who filled the house and garden with his gaudy oeuvre. Some credit must be given to Fuchs and his contemporary and soulmate Hundertwasser, who, in 1968, squatted the house in order to save it from a council demolition order. Fuchs purchased no.26 in 1972 and set about its restoration and transformation. An early work of Wagner's, completed in 1888, it is reminiscent of his Ringstrasse work, with Ionic pillars and a touch of the Palladian. The cube-like villa at no.28, however, is more rooted in his familiar functionalist tradition: a simple steel-and-concrete structure, completed in 1913. Sparsely adorned with characteristic blue tiles and aluminium rivets, it also features some Kolo Moser glasswork over the two entrances.

Technisches Museum Wien

14, Mariahilferstrasse 212 (899 98-0/www.tmw.at). U4 Schloss Schönbrunn/tram 10, 52, 58. **Open** 9am-6pm Mon-Fri; 10am-6pm Sat, Sun. **Admission** €8.50; €5-€7 concessions. **Credit** AmEx, DC, MC, V.

Housed to great effect in an elegant 19th-century edifice with hints of Jugendstil, the Technical Museum documents the not-inconsiderable Austrian contribution to the history of technology. Exhibits include luxurious Habsburg imperial railway carriages, the full range of early Puch Steyr motorbikes, steam engines, power turbines and flying machines. The TMW also does a fine line in temporary exhibitions, and the children's play area is tremendous.

Schönbrunn

Schönbrunn is easily accessible from the city centre via the U4 to Schloss Schönbrunn, where you should take the exit marked Grünbergstrasse and enter through the Meidlinger Tor. If you want to head directly for the main entrance and access to the state rooms, leave via the other new exit. Alternatively you could travel a stop further to Hietzing and enter the park through the Hietzinger Tor, near the zoo and botanical gardens. The latter enables you to take a quick look at Otto Wagner's **Hofpavilion Hietzing**, Franz Josef's private U-Bahn station, before embarking on Schönbrunn.

ORIGINS

One feature of the Baroque era in Vienna was an enthusiasm for building obscenely large summer residences. Following the defeat of

Technisches Museum Wien.

the Turks in 1683, the Belvedere, Palais Liechtenstein and Schönbrunn were all built. Schönbrunn's connection to the Habsburgs dates back to 1569, when Maximilian II acquired the land, then known as Katterburg, to build a hunting lodge. It stood near what is today the Meidlinger Tor, where at this time the natural spring that gives Schönbrunn ('beautiful spring') its name was discovered.

After the siege of 1683, Leopold I commissioned Fischer von Erlach to build a summer palace for his son, the future Joseph I. Envisaging a palace on the scale of Versailles on the hill where the Gloriette stands today, his original plans are thought to be among the great unrealised works of Baroque architecture. Due to financial constraints, however, work on the present site did not start until 1696 and was delayed throughout the War of the Spanish Succession (1701-14).

The present form of the palace owes much to Empress Maria Theresia's passion for the place. In order to accommodate her ever-expanding brood (she had 16 children, ten of whom lived to adulthood), her architect Nikolaus Pacassi added another floor to the two wings. She also supervised the work on the Rococo interiors and the layout of the gardens. Her son Joseph II inherited rather more of Maria Theresia's thrift than her love for Schönbrunn and had vast uninhabited sections of the palace boarded up.

GARDENS

While earlier Habsburgs had opposed the pernicious rationalist influence of France, Maria Theresia became the first monarch to speak French and the Baroque gardens of Schönbrunn are a sign that Paris fashions were finally reaching Vienna. From Maria Theresia's time on, the language spoken at court was Schönbrunner Deutsch, a nasal upper-class twang, peppered with French expressions. Today, the Viennese still call their milky coffee a *mélange*, refer to the pavement as the *trottoir* and take a leak in a *pissoir*.

The gardens originally traced out in the early 18th century by Jean Trehet following Fischer von Erlach's plans were greatly extended under the joint monarchy of Maria Theresia and Joseph II. A keen gardener, Joseph oversaw the completion of the classical layout of the gardens, resulting in the network of avenues that intersect at two central points either side of the broad parterre that runs from the palace to the Neptunbrunnen (Fountain of Neptune), built in 1781. In the distance, on the brow of the hill, rises the majestic form of the Gloriette, commissioned by Joseph II to commemorate the 1775 victory over the Prussians at Kolin, which returned Prague to Habsburg rule. Today it's a

rather snooty café but has the best view of the palace and gardens. To the east of the fountain lie most of the park's follies amid encroaching woodland: Von Hohenberg's superb *Roman Ruins* (1778) and his *Obelisk Fountain* (1777), as well as the original *Schöner Brunnen*. This was later set in a grotto by Canevale, with the statue of a nymph pouring its waters into an enormous scallop basin. To the west lies Schönbrunn zoo.

Like the Prater and the Augarten, the gardens of Schönbrunn were opened to the public during the reign of Joseph II (in 1779). He reputedly countered objections at court by remarking that if he wanted to spend all his time among equals, he would have to dwell in the Kaisergruft among the tombs of the dead Habsburgs.

RESIDENTS AND VISITORS

Napoleon occupied Schönbrunn in 1805 and 1809, and his son, the Duc de Reichstadt, spent most of his short life within the confines of the palace. The reign of Franz Josef is intimately connected to the palace as the emperor was born and died in Schönbrunn (1830 and 1916 respectively), but his wife Elisabeth had no fondness for the place, probably because she spent her wedding night there, reputedly staving off her husband's advances for all of two nights.

What was actually consummated in the Blue Chinese Salon at Schönbrunn was the dissolution of the Austro-Hungarian Empire in November 1918, when Karl I signed away any chance of the monarchy's survival. During the four-power occupation of Vienna after 1945, Schönbrunn was first HQ to the Russians and then to the British before it returned to the Austrian state in 1947. In 1961, it briefly assumed centre stage when Kennedy and Khrushchev met for the first time at the palace and put the word 'détente' on everyone's lips.

Schloss Schönbrunn

13, Schönbrunner Schlossstrasse (811 13-239/www. schoenbrunn.at). U4 Schönbrunn, Hietzing/tram 10, 58/bus 15a. **Open** *Palace* Apr-June, Sept-Oct 8.30am-5pm daily. July, Aug 8.30am-6pm daily. Nov-Mar 8.30am-4.30pm daily. *Gardens* Apr-Oct 6am-dusk daily. Nov-Mar 6.30am-dusk daily. **Admission** *Grand Tour* €12.90; €6.90-€11.40 concessions. *Imperial Tour* €9.50; €4.90-€8.50 concessions. *Parks and gardens* free. **Credit** AmEx, DC, MC, V. Painted in the ubiquitous but slightly nauseating tone of yellow known as *Schönbrunnergelb*, the gigantic palace is the focal point of a gorgeous expanse of parkland which is larger than the Principality of Monaco. Nowadays, the palace is run by a semi-private company that likes to use the Great Court for rock concerts and advent markets and holds corporate events in the state rooms.

Architecturally, Schönbrunn is not particularly distinguished, but the Great Court, with its impressive iron gates and obelisks topped with imperial

Sightseeing

eagles, is a sight in itself. Entrance to the state rooms is by way of the Blaue Stiege (Blue Staircase) on the west wing, but tickets are sold at the front of the east wing. For those determined to go inside, the Grand Tour covering 40 rooms (of a total of 1,441) is the best option as the Imperial Tour of 22 rooms does not include access to Maria Theresia's west wing, undoubtedly the most impressive section. The ticket includes the use of a hand-held device with a commentary in English; note that you are given an exact entrance time.

The circuit begins at the west wing. At the top of the Blue Staircase are Elisabeth and Franz Josef's nine private rooms, as dowdy as those of the Hofburg. From the billiard room, which served as a waiting room for petitioners, you pass into the actual audience chamber, the Nussbaumzimmer (Walnut Chamber). Next come the Emperor's study and the bedroom containing the simple iron bed on which he died, complete with a painting by Makart recreating the sombre scene of his demise. After the joyless shared bedroom, things pick up a little with the Maria Antoinette room and the nursery, which have the original decor from Maria Theresia's time, and the breakfast room with lovely views over the park.

Here the state apartments begin with the Spiegelsaal (Hall of Mirrors), where the child Mozart played a duet with his sister Nannerl in 1792 for Maria Theresia and her daughters. This leads into the largest of the three rooms dedicated to the landscapes of the Polish court painter Josef Rosa, and then out into the highly impressive Grosse Galerie, aflame with the lights of chandeliers and wall appliqués illuminating three huge ceiling frescoes by Guglielmo Guglielmi celebrating the glory of the House of Habsburg. The most easterly of the three, *The Glories of War*, is a copy, the original ironically destroyed by a bomb in 1945. Used as a ballroom during the nine-month long Congress of Vienna in 1815 (the Congress danced but didn't advance, it was observed at the time), the Grosse Galerie was also where Kennedy and Khrushchev met in 1961. Off the Great Gallery on the park side is the Small Gallery, which also contains a fresco by Guglielmi and access to the two chinoiserie rooms. In one of these, the Round Chinese room to the west, Maria Theresia held secret meetings with her foremost adviser Prince Kaunitz. Beyond the Great Gallery you pass through the Carousel room, with a painting of an Amazonian Maria Theresia mounted on a Lipizzaner in a ladies' tournament held at the Winter Riding School in 1743, to the Ceremonial Hall, with Van Metyens paintings of Joseph II's wedding to Isabella of Parma in 1760. Here the cheapskates who opted for the Imperial Tour are ushered out.

Only included in the Grand Tour, the audience rooms are undoubtedly the most worthwhile. Starting with the airy chinoiserie of the Blue Chinese room, where Karl I abdicated in 1918, visitors pass into the rather stultifying Vieux-Lacque-Zimmer where the black lacquered panelling adorned with Japanese landscapes was designed by Canevale

around 1770. Here too is Batoni's portrait of Maria Theresia's husband Franz I. The walnut-panelled Napoleon room is where the diminutive Corsican is thought to have slept. The elaborate Porcelain room, the work of Isabella of Parma, with its trompe l'oeil criss-cross parasol motifs, has more painted woodwork than Meissen porcelain. However, no expense was spared in the subsequent Millionenzimmer, where Maria Theresia reputedly spent a million silver florins on its rosewood panelling and priceless Persian and Indian miniatures.

After the Gobelinsalon, with its 18th-century Brussels tapestries, you arrive at the Memorial room dedicated to 'L'Aiglon' (the Little Eagle), the Duc de Reichstadt, Napoleon's son by Archduchess Marie Louise, who was virtually kept prisoner in Schönbrunn after his father's fall from grace in 1815 until his untimely death at the age of 21. After Maria Theresia's bedroom, the remaining rooms were formally the domain of Franz Josef's father Archduke Franz Karl and contain innumerable portraits of sundry Habsburgs. The Bergl rooms, decorated by Dutch botanist Jacquin with magnificent colourful frescoes depicting tropical birds and plantlife against idealised classical backgrounds, have been opened to the public after years of neglect. Outside you have the opportunity to visit two sets of outbuildings, the Orangerie and the Wagenburg, for which there is an extra charge.

Tiergarten und Palmenhaus

13, Hietzinger Tor (Zoo 877 9294/www.zoovienna. at/Palm house 877 5087 406/www.bundesgaerten. at). U4 Hietzing. **Open** *Zoo* Nov-Jan 9am-4.30pm daily. Feb 9am-5pm daily. Mar, Oct 9am-5.30pm daily. Apr-Sept 9am-6.30pm daily. *Palm House* Oct-Apr 9.30am-5pm daily. May-Sept 9.30am-6pm daily. **Admission** *Zoo* €12; €5 children; €4 3-6s; free under-3s. *Palm House* €4; €2-€3.50 concessions. **Credit** AmEx, DC, MC, V.

A large section of the western side of the gardens is taken up by the Tiergarten (zoo). It's built on the site of Franz Stephan's royal menagerie (1752), making it the world's oldest zoo. The first animals came from Prince Eugène's menagerie at the Belvedere. Many of the original Baroque buildings and cages are still in use, but most of the zoo's 750 or so species now have more modern quarters. In recent years, elephants and leopards have both bred in captivity, and killed two keepers. The cages are laid out radially in 12 units around the central octagonal pavilion (1759), all the work of Jean Nicholas Jadot. Originally used as a breakfast room by the imperial family, the pavilion is now an unappealing restaurant.

The Palmenhaus (Palm House) is situated near the Hietzinger Tor entrance, beside the botanical gardens (1754). Maria Theresia's husband, Emperor Franz, was a keen botanist and gardener, financing expeditions to Africa and the West Indies to collect rare species and bring them back to Vienna. The magnificent iron-and-glass construction of the Palmenhaus, a replica of the one in London's Kew Gardens with three separate climatic zones, dates from 1882.

Wagenburg Imperial Coach Collection Schönbrunn

*13, Schönbrunner Schlossstrasse (525 24-0/
www.khm.at). U4 Hietzing, Schloss Schönbrunn/
tram 10, 58, 60/bus 10a.* **Open** *Apr-Oct* 9am-6pm
daily. *Nov-Mar* 10am-4pm Tue-Sun. **Admission**
€4.50; €3 concessions; €2.50 schoolchildren.
No credit cards.

This breathtaking collection of imperial coaches has
been housed in the former winter riding school of
Schönbrunn Palace since the demise of the Habsburgs
after World War I. The wealth of the Empire is amply
illustrated by the variety of horse-drawn carriages
and sleighs the family had at their disposal, the most
extravagant being Emperor Franz Stephan's gold-
plated coronation carriage with Venetian glass windows, weighing over 4,000kg.

Hietzing

With the presence of the imperial family at
nearby Schönbrunn, it's no surprise that the
process of gentrification started early in the
neighbouring village of Hietzing. The process
didn't end with the Habsburgs and today, along
with the 19th district around Grinzing, it is one
of the city's poshest areas. Hietzing's rapid rail
link to the city centre, and the lure of a vast area
of the Wienerwald on its doorstep, attracted
the 19th-century business elite and successful
bohemians such as Egon Schiele. From 1912, he
had his studio at Hietzinger Hauptstrasse 101,
the area's main drag. Today, the street is not
particularly charming, but once you wander
into the side streets and see some of the
magnificent Modernist and Biedermeier villas,
a leafy gentility reminiscent of London's
Hampstead is revealed.

Hietzing institutions include Café Dommayer
(*see p142*), where Johann Strauss gave his first
public concert in 1844. More recommendable for
food, drinks and atmosphere is the slightly
shabby Jugendstil Café Wunderer on
Hadikgasse. Round the corner from the
Dommayer is the imposing edifice of the
Parkhotel Schönbrunn (1907), where the
emperor's guests were accommodated.

Hofpavillon Hietzing

*13, Schönbrunner Schlossstrasse (505 8747-0/
www.wienmuseum.at). U4 Hietzing.* **Open** 10.30am-
12.30pm Sun. **Admission** free. **No credit cards**.
Built in 1899 by Otto Wagner on his own initiative,
this private train station for the imperial family was
used by Franz Josef on precisely two occasions.
Although it features Wagner's classic lattice ironwork, the Hofpavillon's copper dome suggests a certain deference to imperial taste for a greater degree
of decorativeness. The interior, designed by Wagner
and Josef Olbrich, is more rewarding. It includes
mahogany panelling, silk wall hangings and a
bird's-eye view of the city painted by Carl Moll.

HIETZING'S VILLAS

Architecture fanatics will have a field day
wandering through Hietzing's residential
streets. There are houses by Josef Hoffmann,
Friedrich Ohmann and Adolf Loos, but
unfortunately none are open to the public.
The individual villas are widely dispersed, but
many are concentrated along Gloriettegasse,
west of the Schlosspark. Here, at no.9,
Katharina Schratt, Franz Josef's lover, was
installed in a rather modest Biedermeier villa.
Further west along the street, at no.21, is the
Villa Schopp, Friedrich Ohmann's fine
Jugendstil house built in 1902 with floral
motifs and superb decorative ironwork. At
no.18 is Josef Hoffmann's monumental Skywa-
Primavesi Villa (1913-15), a rather neo-classical
reading of Modernism, with four imposing
central pillars on a symmetrical frontage with
two large triangular pediments each housing a
relief of a male and female figure.

Walk further west up the Gloriettegasse and
on the brow of the hill you get a stupendous view
of the Kirche am Steinhof with the woods behind.
There are five Adolf Loos villas in Hietzing.
Three of them are located in the area bounded
by Lainzer Strasse and Hietzinger Hauptstrasse
(bus 58 and 60): Villa Scheu at Larochegasse 3;
Villa Strasser at Kupelwiesergasse 28; and the
famous barrel-roofed Villa Steiner at St-Veit-
Gasse 10. Beyond Hietzinger Hauptstrasse and
close to the Kai is Villa Rufer at
Schliessmanngasse 11 and a great deal further
west is the Villa Horner at Nothartgasse 7.

A kilometre up on the Veitingergasse is the
Werkbundsiedlung, a wedge-shaped housing
project of 70 individual homes built between
1930 and 1932 by a group of Modernist
architects including Loos, Hoffmann and Richard
Neutra under the direction of Josef Frank. These
small geometric Bauhaus-style homes were
originally intended for sale, but despite strict
economic criteria for their construction, they
proved too expensive for purchasers and were
bought by the city council in 1934 and let. Four
were destroyed in World War II, but today, after
renovation in the early 1980s, there is something
almost idyllic about the whole estate. In the
house Frank designed, at Woinovichgasse 32,
is a small documentation centre on the project
(www.werkbundsiedlung.at).

Hietzinger Friedhof (Hietzing Cemetery)

*13, Maxingstrasse 15 (no phone). U4 Hietzing, then
10-minute walk. Bus 56b, 58b, 156b.* **Open** *Mar,
Apr, Sept, Oct* 8am-5pm daily. *May-Aug* 8am-6pm
daily. *Nov-Feb* 9am-4pm daily. **Admission** free.
The graves of many illustrious Viennese reside in this
picturesque cemetery, a testimony to Hietzing's popularity among both the wealthy and the artistically

Sightseeing

inclined. Top tombs include those of Gustav Klimt and Otto Wagner, though the latter's is regrettably pompous. Also buried here are the composer Alban Berg, the dramatist Franz Grillparzer, the leader of the Austro-Fascists Engelbert Dollfuss, and Klimt and Wagner's friend and collaborator Kolo Moser.

Lainzer Tiergarten & Hermesvilla

13, Lainzer Tiergarten (entrance on Lainzertor) (804 1324/www.wienmuseum.at). U4 Hietzing, then tram 60 Hermesstrasse, then bus 60b Lainzer Tor. **Open** *Apr-Oct* 10am-6pm Tue-Sun. *Nov-Mar* 10am-4.30pm Fri-Sun. **Admission** *Lainzer Tiergarten* free. *Hermesvilla* €5; €3.50 concessions; €2.50 children. Free to all Sun. **No credit cards.**

To the west of Hietzing lies a vast tract of country-side bordering the Wienerwald known as the Lainzer Tiergarten, literally 'zoo', but referring more than anything to the large number of deer and wild boar that roam freely throughout its woods and meadows. It's a bit of a trek from the city centre, but for those seeking peace and quiet and a walk in the woods it can't be bettered. Apart from the wildlife and the forest, the only major sight is Hermesvilla, a brick-built mansion commissioned by Franz Josef as a gift to his wife in an attempt to save their marriage. It was named by Sisi herself after her favourite Greek god, but despite interiors by Klimt and Makart and a purpose-built gymnasium she never developed any great fondness for the place. Now a branch of the Wien Museum, it hosts a variety of exhibitions and is signposted from the Lainzer Tor, a gentle ten-minute walk.

Wotruba Kirche

23, Georgsgasse/Rysergasse (888 6147/www. georgenberg.at). U4 Hietzing then tram 60 Maurer Hauptplatz and then bus 60a. **Open** 2-8pm Sat; 9am-5pm Sun. **Guided tours** by appointment. **Admission** *Church and tours* free.

To the south of Lainzer Tiergarten, near the village of Mauer, lies another of Vienna's ecclesiastical eccentricities – the Church of the Holy Trinity by Austrian sculptor Fritz Wotruba (1907-75), a rather curious conjunction of rectangular slabs of concrete illuminated by narrow, vertical glass panels. The general effect is of a voluminous brutalist sculpted mass. Its attempt to create the atmosphere of a sanctuary within these threatening forms has been unanimously applauded by the Viennese.

Southern Vienna

The southern districts of Vienna hold little of specific interest for the visitor, but for anyone wishing to get off the beaten track and see something of the city's main working-class districts there are a handful of minor sights. The main reason people head south is to visit the vast **Zentralfriedhof**, Vienna's main cemetery, where tombs outnumber the city's present population.

Vienna's 10th district, Favoriten, is the city's largest, with a population of around 170,000. It

was the focus of emigration for Czechs in the 19th century, and a Favoritner today is something like the Viennese equivalent of a cockney Londoner, with Reumannplatz as the Bow Bells of Vienna. Named after labour leader and Socialist politician Jacob Reumann, it is a lively square with a market on the nearby pedestrian Favoritenstrasse and Vienna's best-loved ice-cream salon Tichy. There's a fast connection to the city centre via the U1. Right on the square is the imposing **Amalienbad** (*see p206*), built in 1926 and Vienna's largest public baths, with room for 1,300 bathers. The main pool has an arched glass roof that can be opened, and the facilities are decorated throughout with fine colourful mosaics in Jugendstil designs. From Reumannplatz you can take bus 68a to Urselbrunnengasse to visit the Böhmischer Prater (Bohemian Prater), a curiously old-fashioned mini-version of Vienna's premier fairground with antiquated rides, beer gardens and sausage stands.

Zentralfriedhof

11, Simmeringer Hauptstrasse 234 (760 410). Tram 71 direct or U3 Enkplatz, then tram 71. **Open** *May-Aug* 7am-7pm daily. *Mar, Apr, Sept, Oct* 7am-6pm daily. *Nov-Feb* 8am-5pm daily. **Admission** free (€1.80 for cars). **No credit cards.**

The Central Cemetery ranks alongside Paris's Père-Lachaise and London's Highgate on the European graveyard itinerary. Opened by the city council in 1870, its 2.5 million tombs, pantheons and memorials cover an area larger than the Innere Stadt. As you see from the tram, one side of the Simmeringer Hauptstrasse is taken up with undertakers and stonemasons (there are none on the city's high streets), as well as occasional cafés and restaurants. Of these, try the bizarre, candlelit Schloss Concordia, opposite the first entrance to the cemetery where the old Jewish section is located. The next tram stop is at the main entrance, followed by a third by the entrance to the Protestant and new Jewish sections.

From the main entrance the path heads straight for the Ehrengräber (the tombs of honour). Follow the main avenue past the semicircular line of tombs encrusted into arches – don't miss the memorial to mining baron August Zwang, resembling the entrance to a mine guarded by lamp-wielding dwarfs – and in sector 32A you will see the tombs and memorials to Austria's most famous composers. The centrepiece is a monument to Mozart, although his remains are lost in St Marxer Friedhof. Beethoven and Schubert were moved here from the Währing cemetery in 1899, but among those originally laid to rest in Zentralfriedhof are Brahms, Hugo Wolf and most of the Strauss clan. Across the avenue are the tombs of influential Viennese such as Ringstrasse architect Hansen and the painter Makart, and towards the main church, in a circular recess, is the Präsidentsgruft, the graves of the Second Republic presidents. Nearby, in section 33C,

Amalienbad.

are some curious headstones, such as those of Bruno Kreisky and Arnold Schönberg, who lies under an extraordinary cube-like form crafted by sculptor Fritz Wotruba, himself buried in the same area.

The central monument of the cemetery is the Dr-Karl-Lueger-Kirche (1910), dedicated to Vienna's populist mayor, 'der schöne Karl', anti-semite extraordinaire Karl Lueger. Built by Otto Wagner's pupil Max Hegele, it bears a resemblance to his mentor's Kirche am Steinhof. Behind the church there are fascinating sections given over to the Soviet soldiers who died during the 1945 liberation of Vienna, a monument to the victims of World War I, the graves of 7,000 Austrians who died fighting the Nazis (sector 97) and those of Austrian International Brigade members from the Spanish Civil War (section 28). Non-Catholics also lie in the Zentralfriedhof: south of the main gate, near the outer wall, is the Russian Orthodox sector arranged around an appropriately onion-domed church, and sectors 26 and 36 contain Muslim graves. But it is the old Jewish section to the north near the first gate that is the most moving. Overgrown and desecrated, the sheer size of it (over 60,000 graves) and the virulence of the vandalism that overwhelmed it emphasise the tragic destiny of Vienna's pre-war Jewish community. Among those buried here are members of the Austrian branch of the Rothschild family and the novelist and playwright Arthur Schnitzler.

Northern Vienna

The hills of the northern part of the Wienerwald are visible from various points along the western side of the Ringstrasse. This range, ending abruptly at the Danube, is in fact the continuation of the foothills of the Alps away to the south-west. Half an hour by tram from Schottentor you can explore the four wine-growing villages that nestle below the Vienna Woods on the city's urban edge. Formerly separate entities, Nussdorf (tram D), Grinzing (tram 38), Sievering (bus 39a) and Neustift am Walde (bus 35a) became wealthy by supplying the city with the tart white wine the Viennese drink with so much relish. With olde worlde architecture surrounded by vines and forests and impressive views over the whole city, they rapidly became home to the city's wealthier residents.

Despite a peppering of significant architectural and historical sites – the Beethoven memorials, the **Karl-Marx-Hof** housing complex, the Jugendstil villas of Hohe Warte – the chief attraction here are the many Heurigen (*see p131*). While any self-respecting *echte Wiener* (real Viennese) would dismiss the establishments that you'll find in the area as tourist schmaltz, there are still plenty of attractive settings offering an unforgettable combination of wine and views.

Monolithic city

Vienna's varied architectural inventory includes two phenomena of extreme dimensions: its inter-war public housing and the flak towers built by the Nazis during World War II. The former is a monument to the socialist fantasies of the inter-war years; the others an unshakeable reminder of the disasters of fascism.

Built by forced labour in 1943-44 to defend the city from aerial bombardment, store munitions and provide shelter for the population, Vienna's six flak towers are each about the size of the Arc du Triomphe. Their central location, arranged in a triangle around Stephansdom, was apparently chosen by Hitler himself. The first pair to go up were those in Arenbergpark in the 3rd district. The two in the 6th and 7th districts are separated by a couple of streets and those of the Augarten in the 2nd are a few hundred metres apart. Surprisingly for a city that prides itself on festooning its historic buildings with flags and plaques, there is nothing to explain the purpose of these awesome structures. Sixty years on, Hitler's claim that they would stand for 4,000 years seems perfectly reasonable. Plans for their demolition have long been deemed impractical and despite an endless stream of proposals for alternative uses, only two of them currently serve a practical purpose: one is now an aquarium and another an art project (*see p97*).

Some 20 years before the flak towers, Vienna was a much more optimistic place. The victory of the Social Democratic Workers' Party (SDAP), led by Freud's friend Viktor Adler, in the municipal elections of 1919 heralded a 12-year programme of far-reaching reforms, known today as Rotes Wien, or Red Vienna. By increasing taxation on private building, luxury goods and unearned income, the municipality financed some 400 housing projects (63,736 apartments) between 1923 and 1934, many of them on an enormous scale.

You encounter these vast, impressively solid tenements throughout the city – even in the wealthy periphery of the 18th and 19th districts. Emblazoned with the dates of their construction, and earnest murals and statuary symbolising social progress, many are dedicated to international labour leaders such as Rosa Luxemburg or Karl Liebknecht. The best-known is probably the kilometre-long Karl-Marx-Hof (*see p112*) in the lower reaches of the 19th district. Bearing the name of its bearded namesake in huge red capitals, it is not however the largest – both Sandleiten-Hof in Ottakring and Friedrich-Engels-Hof in Brigittenau are bigger. To see the most architecturally innovative examples, take the U4 to Margaretengürtel in the 5th district. This section of the Gürtel used to be known as the 'Ringstrasse der Proletariat'. Here a dense cluster of projects includes the Reumann-Hof and Matteotti-Hof, and together they form Red Vienna's most impressive ensemble. Further east in the third district, the Rabenhof (U3 Kardinal-Nagl-Platz) is another immense complex dating from 1927, remarkable for its self-contained 'town within a town' layout.

Walking tours in English of the principal Red Vienna housing complexes are run by the Architekturzentrum Wien (www.azw.at) and www.dasroteswien.at has some fine photos.

Karl-Marx-Hof

19, Heiligenstädter Strasse 82-92. U4 Heiligenstadt/ tram D.

This imposing salmon-pink kilometre-long housing complex is the flagship of the so-called Rotes Wien (Red Vienna) period of municipal Socialism between 1919 and 1934. Built between 1926 and 1930 by Karl Ehm, a pupil of Otto Wagner, Karl-Marx-Hof originally consisted of 1,325 flats, some as small as 26sq m (280sq ft), as well as a laundry, kindergarten, library, post office, clinic, shop premises, public baths and gardens. Not ground-breaking in an architectural sense, it and hundreds of similar projects nevertheless provided hundreds of decent dwellings and facilities at a time of poverty and destitution when Vienna was the world's fifth largest city.

During the 1934 Civil War that brought the Austro-Fascists to power, the building and many of its residents were the victims of heavy artillery fire. Renamed the Heiligenstädter-Hof during the Nazi era, it was patched up and given its original name after World War II. A full restoration programme involving the modernisation of the flats and a connection to the Fernwärme district heating system was completed in 1989.

Nussdorf & Leopoldsberg

The nearest of the wine villages to the Danube, Nussdorf lies in the shadow of Leopoldsberg (425m/1,395ft), the second-highest point of the Wienerwald, overlooking the Danube valley.

Leopold of Babenberg had built a fortress on top of the hill in the 11th century. The summit can be reached by bus 38a from Heiligenstadt U-Bahn along the impressive cobbled Höhenstrasse. Walkers can choose between an uphill trek from Nussdorf or the shorter, more intense zigzag footpath that begins in Kahlenbergerdorf. Next to Leopoldskirche (1693) and the ramparts there is a shady courtyard where you can have a drink and enjoy the views. Inside the church there is a display detailing the Turkish siege, and the main lookout point has a memorial to Austrian PoWs imprisoned in the USSR until the 1950s.

Nussdorf's reputation is built around its vineyards and numerous Heurigen, especially along the narrow picturesque Kahlenberger Strasse. The Eroicagasse on the south side of the Kahlenberger Strasse takes you to the popular Mayer am Pfarrplatz, more a restaurant than a Heuriger, located in a fine Biedermeier house where Beethoven lived for a time. Almost next door is Heiligenstädter-Testament-Haus. The area bristles with Ludwig memorabilia, with street names such as Eroicagasse and Beethovengang, as well as a Beethoven monument (1910) by Robert Weigl in the Heiligenstädter Park on the south side of Grinzinger Strasse. On this street too, at no.64, is the house that Beethoven shared in 1808 with the dramatist Franz Grillparzer. If you head back towards the city with tram 37, along Döblinger Hauptstrasse you can visit the Eroicahaus (no.92) where Beethoven composed his *Third Symphony*, the *Eroica*. This is one of three Beethoven Museums, all with identical opening times.

In the opposite direction, tram 37 takes you to Hohe Warte, where the block comprising Wollergasse, Steinfeldgasse and Geweygasse has a number of fine villas by Josef Hoffmann that formed a Secessionist colony in the early 1900s. Sadly none of them is open to the public. From here it's a gentle walk down Armbrustergasse to Nussdorf.

Those who have the energy could walk to the end of Eroicagasse then up through the vineyards for about a kilometre to Sirbu (*see p133*), a Heuriger with magnificent views of the Danube and an excellent buffet. If you fancy further exertions, you could attempt the Kahlenberg, the highest point of this section of the Wienerwald at 484m (1,588ft), or the more gentle option of walking downhill to Kahlenbergerdorf beside the Danube where there are buses back to the city.

Heiligenstädter-Testament-Haus

19, Probusgasse 6 (370 54 08). Tram 37, D/ bus 38a. **Open** 10am-1pm, 2-6pm Tue-Sun. **Admission** €2; €1 concessions. **No credit cards.**

The so-called Heiligenstädter-Testament-Haus is one of Beethoven's many residences in this area. Here in 1802, he wrote his famous 'testament' to his brothers, in which he bequeathed them his fortune, apologised for his misanthropy, and spoke frankly of his oncoming deafness. Here too he wrote his *Second Symphony*. The house is now one of Vienna's three museums dedicated to the composer, and exhibits include a copy of the testament, Beethoven's death mask and a lock of his hair. Across the courtyard is the rival Beethoven Ausstellung, belonging to the Beethoven Society, but it has little to recommend it.

Grinzing & Kahlenberg

The village of Grinzing, the most famous of Vienna's wine villages, is the quintessence of Viennese rural kitsch, ably manipulated by inn-keepers and restaurateurs to keep the cash registers ringing. Tour groups are bussed into Grinzing for a night of white wine and *Schrammelmusik* at any one of the establishments along the picturesque main drag. The combination of villagey atmosphere and countryside makes Grinzing, like the other lesser-known nearby villages, a popular choice of the diplomatic community and the wealthy.

Mahler fans may well consider a visit to Grinzinger Friedhof to visit his austere Jugendstil tomb by Josef Hoffmann. Other famous residents include Ringstrasse architect Ferstel and art groupie Alma Mahler. The daughter she had by Walter Gropius, Manon, is also buried here. The cemetery is located on Mannagettagasse, off Strassergasse.

If you tire of quaint Grinzing, a trip on the 38a follows one of the most spectacular routes in the city, along Höhenstrasse, taking in fine views of the forest and the city. The first possible stop is Am Cobenzl, a lookout point with bar and restaurant with views of Grinzing's vineyards. From there it's a 10-minute walk west to the Bellevuewiese, a gorgeous rolling meadow with the best panorama of the city and a plaque marking the spot where the 'secret of dreams was revealed to Sigmund Freud'. Further along the 38a route, get off at Krapfenwaldgasse for a swim at the Krapfenwaldbad (*see p206*), the city's poshest but nevertheless municipal swimming baths. Although the pools are fairly small, the parkland is magnificent, with some of the most northerly Mediterranean pines in Europe and, of course, superb views. The 38a chugs on up to the highest point on the range, Kahlenberg. Back down in Grinzing, Heurigen to try are Weingut Reisenberg (for the food and the views), or better still Zawodsky (for the beautiful garden, good simple food and drinkable wine). For both, *see p133*.

Sisi Ticket

Schönbrunn Palace	**Imperial Furniture Collection**	**Imperial Apartments Sisi Museum Imperial Silver Collection**

Schloss Schönbrunn · 1130 Wien	**Andreasgasse 7 · 1070 Wien**	**Hofburg · 1010 Wien**
daily from 8.30 am	Tue - Sun 10 am - 6 pm	daily from 9 am to 5 pm (July and August to 5.30 pm)
U4 Schönbrunn	U3 Zieglergasse	U3 Herrengasse

Your advantage:

You save up to 25% compared with 3 individual tickets; immediate admission to the tour of Schönbrunn Palace

Valid 1 year from date of issue for single admission to each attraction

Tickets:

Adults	€ 22,50
Children	€ 11,50
Students 19-25 Vienna Card	€ 20,00

Eat, Drink, Shop

Hollmann Salon. *See p118.*

Restaurants

The Beisl, the Heuriger and the coffee house – Vienna's singular trio.

The Viennese love to tell you that *Wiener Küche*, or Viennese cooking, is the only cuisine named after a city rather than a country or region. Less debatable is the fact that most of its signature dishes did not originate in the city but in various corners of the empire: the thick, paprika-laden goulash originated in Hungary, the world-famous Wiener Schnitzel in (Habsburg) Milan, the *Knödel* (dumplings) and *Palatschinken* (pancakes) in Bohemia and the *Apfelstrudel* from the Ottoman lands.

All these delights feature on the menu of any *Beisl*, the traditional Viennese eating house that, along with the coffee house and the wine tavern or *Heuriger*, make up the city's peculiar gastronomic trinity. Deriving from a Yiddish word meaning 'little house', the Beisl is generally a wood-panelled beer house, where all ages and social classes congregate around period Formica tables, with warmth from a ceramic stove, for a few drinks or a meal. Authentic establishments such as **Reinthaler** and **Gasthaus Quell** continue the tradition today. Pork features prominently: the pleasure of a crisp, caraway-studded *Schweinsbraten* complemented with the tang of sauerkraut and the velvety smoothness of bread dumplings is an experience not be missed. The setting and atmosphere of an old-fashioned Beisl will charm even the most reluctant.

Long considered an endangered species, the late 1990s witnessed a Beisl revival with young chefs taking over old establishments. The so-called *neo-Beisl* added some cool styling to traditional interiors, conserving the tone but bolstering the menu with more modern dishes. Entirely new spots such as **Skopik & Lohn** or reruns like the **Gmoa Keller** now offer great, atmospheric dining at knock-down prices. Similar bargains are available at the wine taverns that pepper Vienna's green periphery. A trip out to a Heuriger (*see p131* **Heurigen**) is as much a part of experiencing the city as an afternoon with the Klimt's in the Belvedere.

If you're aiming higher, Vienna isn't short of gourmet dining. The long-established **Steierereck** and **Meinl am Graben** have been joined by newcomers such as the **Coburg** and in 2005 the first edition of a *Michelin Guide* to Austria was published. The only drawback with these establishments is the rather stiff service and overly traditional interiors.

All in all, the joys of eating out in Vienna remain basically twofold: the locations are often overwhelmingly atmospheric and the food intensely seasonal. Spring sees restaurants preparing juicy local asparagus or dishes flavoured with *Bärlauch*, the aromatic wild garlic leaves that grow in the Vienna Woods. Summer desserts feature strawberries from Burgenland and Wachau apricots, while in early autumn chanterelles, *Steinpilze* (ceps), pumpkin and *Sturm* – the cloudy semi-fermented new wine – are treated as objects of devotion. Around St Martin's Day in early November, there's hardly a Beisl in the city that doesn't offer *Martinigansl* – succulent roast goose, served with spiced red cabbage and potato dumplings. For all these reasons, this guide concentrates on establishments that provide an unforgettable Viennese experience, with the odd accomplished sushi temple or trattoria providing variation.

Austrian eating times are on the early side, so it's common to see diners tucking into a roast before midday or wolfing down a pizza at six in the evening. Apart from exclusive establishments, most Viennese restaurants offer meals throughout the day and double as cafés or

The best Restaurants

For great Beisl food with a twist
Immervoll. *See p118.*

For hungry hikers
Hirt. *See p133.*

For a major splurge
Steierereck im Stadtpark. *See p123.*

For the culture crowd
Öesterreicher im MAK. *See p119.*

For a Wiener Schnitzel
Zu den Zwei Lieseln. *See p130.*

> ❶ Purple numbers given in this chapter correspond to the restaurant locations in the street maps. See pp242-251.

bars. A ten per cent tip is commonplace in all cafés and restaurants: it's usually done by rounding up the price when the bill comes. Bear in mind that credit card payment is by no means the norm here. Generally speaking, it's advisable to reserve a table, particularly in the evenings.

1st district

Do&Co Restaurant

1, Stephansplatz 12 (535 3969/www.doco.com). U1, U3 Stephansplatz. **Open** noon-3pm, 6pm-midnight daily. **Main courses** €19-€26. **Credit** V. **Map** p251 E6/7 **❶**
There's no finer location for a splurge than Do&Co's elegant premises overlooking Stephansdom. Here there's something for all tastes – Mediterranean, pan-Asian and Austrian classics, all equally reliable. Choose from the superb ingredients at the open kitchen for a wok feast or go for Vienna's most expensive doner kebab (€21!). Otherwise there's sensational sushi, Uruguayan beef and desserts that look as good as they taste. Booking is essential.

Esterházykeller

1, Haarhof 1, near Naglergasse (533 3482/www. esterhazykeller.at). U3 Herrengasse. **Open** 11am-11pm Mon-Fri; 4-11pm Sat, Sun. **Main courses** *Buffet menus* €9.50-€14. **Credit** AmEx, V (from €50). **Map** p250 E6 **❷**
Located in the bowels of the Palais owned by the Hungarian nobles of the same name, this conspiratorial cellar became the first outlet for Hungarian wine and food in Vienna in the late 18th century. Apart from a few refrigerated cabinets for the cold cuts and dips, little has changed since. (Descend the steep stone steps with care.) Today, the reasonably priced *Heurigen*-style food and rough-and-ready wines attract mostly local custom.

Expedit

1, Wiesingerstrasse 6 (512 3313-0/www.expedit.net). U3 Stubentor/tram 1, 2. **Open** noon-midnight Mon-Fri; 6pm-midnight Sat. **Main courses** €9-€15. **No credit cards. Map** p251 F6 **❸**
This former textile warehouse now contains one of Vienna's most original restaurants. Instead of rolls of crimplene, the metallic shelving is replete with the joys of Liguria – jars of tiny olives, artichokes in oil and pesto, cases of oil and wine. A no-nonsense communal cantina, complete with blaring TV, Expedit serves a young clubby clientele with exquisitely prepared, if a touch pricey, antipasti and a choice of five main courses, all with a distinctive Ligurian touch. Wines are reliable and fairly priced.

Fabios

1, Tuchlauben 6 (532 2222/www.fabios.at). U1, U3 Stephansplatz, U3 Herrengasse. **Open** *Bar* 10am-1am Mon-Sat; *Restaurant* 10am-1am (meals served from noon-11.30pm) Mon-Sat & holidays. **Main courses** €17.50-€29.50. **Credit** AmEx, DC, JCB, MC, V. **Map** p250 E6 **❹**

Fabios is an elegantissimo designer Italian, clad in acres of dark wood and black leather. Local *Promis* (as they call celebs in the German-speaking world) adore the theatrical summer terrace on pedestrian Tuchlauben, where they don their shades and pick at the superb fish-dominated cuisine. However, recouping a sizeable investment means they pack in some 140 diners. That and the waiters' hard-sell are Fabios main downers. Otherwise, if you have the cash, you can eat the best tuna in land-locked Vienna.

Figlmüller

1, Wollzeile 5 (512 6177/www.figlmueller.at). U1, U3 Stephansplatz/bus 1a. **Open** *Jan-July, Sept-Dec* 11am-10.30pm daily. **Main courses** *Schnitzel* €15.40. **Credit** AmEx, DC, JCB, MC, V. **Map** p251 F6 **❺**
Ask a hotel porter where to eat Wiener Schnitzel and chances are you'll be directed to Figlmüller. Tucked into a lane between Wollzeile and Bäckerstrasse, this cramped and slightly expensive restaurant certainly fries up excellent Schnitzels of alarming dimensions, but the combination of the tourist trade and pseudo-rustic bonhomie is a bit irritating. All wines come from the owner's vineyards in Grinzing.
Other locations: 1, Bäckerstrasse 6 (512 1760); 19, Grinzinger Strasse 55 (320 4257).

Griechenbeisl

1, Fleischmarkt 11 (533 1977/www.griechenbeisl.at). U1, U4 Schwedenplatz/tram 1, 2, 21, N. **Open** 11.30am-11.30pm daily. **Main courses** €12-€24. **Credit** AmEx, DC, JCB, MC, V. **Map** p251 F6 **❻**

Hollmann Salon.
See p118.

Originally an inn patronised by Greek and Levantine merchants (hence the name) visiting Vienna to trade, and mentioned in chronicles under a variety of names as far back as 1500, the quaint Griechenbeisl suffers from an excess of historical connections. Due to its association with illustrious regulars such as Beethoven, Schubert and (briefly) Mark Twain, as well as its role in the Viennese legend of street musician Liebe Augustin, its maze of panelled rooms is generally occupied by residents of Omaha or Osaka. All the traditional Austrian dishes are on the menu, but you pay a supplement for the history. As you go under the arched entrance, peer down through the iron grill to see a figure of Augustin at the bottom of a well.

Hansen

1, Wipplingerstrasse 34 (532 0542/www.hansen. co.at). U2 Schottentor/tram 1, 2, D/bus 1a, 3a. **Open** 9am-9pm Mon-Fri; 9am-5pm Sat. **Main courses** €9-€19. **Credit** AmEx, DC, MC, V. **Map** p250 E5 **7**

Housed beneath the stock exchange yet bathed in natural light, Hansen takes its name from the building's architect. It's a sensual combination of restaurant and florist's (Lederleitner, *see p153*). Hansen trades exclusively in delicious breakfasts, light lunches and early dinners.

Hollmann Salon

1, Grashof 3 (961 19 6040). U2, U4 Schwedenplatz, U3 Stubentor. **Open** 11am-10pm Mon-Sat. **Main courses** €12.90-€24. **Credit** AmEx, DC, MC, V. **Map** p251 F6 **8**

Owned by the folks behind the chic Hollmann Beletage (*see p41*), the Salon displays more of the witty decorative touches that make the hotel so charming. The two vaulted rooms either side of a sleek central bar have nothing but a single pair of chamois horns and a black metal cuckoo clock. On the food front, both kitchen and service are still teething, with one Vienna daily describing it as 'Very Slow Food!' Dishes change daily and always feature meat, fish and veggie options (best to stay clear of the tasteless steamed pike though) and are gorgeously presented. The Hollmann is 100% no smoking and summer puffers can enjoy the terrace on Heiligenkreuzerhof. **Photo** *p117*.

Hotel Riviera

1, Schönlaterngasse 13 (907 6149/www.lametta. com). U2, U4 Schwedenplatz, U3 Stubentor. **Open** 11am-midnight Mon-Sat. **Main courses** €8.90-€15.90. **No credit cards. Map** p251 F6 **9**

Hotel Rivieran is run by Harry and Julia Lametta, whose Notte Italiana nights in the 1990s managed to convince Vienna's clubbers and nighthawks that Italian pop/lounge music could be hip and enjoyable. With its dark wood and cream panelling, and an expansive summer terrace, Hotel Riviera has a distinct touch of *Roman Holiday* about it. A winning combination of very reasonably priced Italo-Adriatic dishes in a gorgeous setting.

Immervoll

1, Weihburggasse 17 (513 5288). U1, U3 Stephansplatz. **Open** noon-midnight daily. **Meals served** noon-10.45pm daily. **Main courses** €7.40-€14.90. **No credit cards. Map** p251 E7 **10**

Adapted by architect Hermann Czech with a wink at the Loos Bar (*see p196*), this small vaulted establishment is great for city-centre dining. Immervoll's exuberant owner, actor Hanno Pöschl, rightly believes that Viennese classics, cooked with care, can and do compare proudly with more feted cuisines. The lightly fried *Saibling* (lake trout) and chanterelles on thyme polenta are both to die for. The menu changes daily, offering a choice of seven starters and main courses. In summer, there's seating nearby on the glorious Fransiskanerplatz.

Indochine 21

1, Stubenring 18 (513 7660/www.indochine.at). U3 Stubentor. **Open** 11.30am-2am daily. **Meals served** noon-3pm, 6pm-midnight daily. **Main courses** €15-€38. **Credit** AmEx, DC, JCB, MC, V. **Map** p251 F7 **11**

Indochine 21's French/Vietnamese fusion food has been wowing well-heeled locals for five years. The neo-colonial decor – all whirling fans, potted palms and red lacquered sunshades – is looking a bit scuffed but chef Wini Brugger's subtly spiced and beautifully presented seafood, fish, meat and noodle dishes are great for a special occasion.

Limes

1, Hoher Markt 10 (905 800/www.restaurant-limes.at). U1, U3 Stephansplatz. **Open** 10am-10.30pm Mon-Sat. **Main courses** €8.50-€23. **Credit** DC, MC, V. **Map** p251 E6 **12**

Think the Roman Empire's eastern defence line, not the citrus fruit. Located on the site of Roman Vienna in the imposing Anker insurance building, Limes serves a metropolitan selection of bagels, burgers, fresh fish and salads. Uncommonly chic by Viennese standards, it's hard to get in at lunchtime as it has a deal with Anker's employees – but by 2pm, they're generally back at their work stations.

Markt-Restaurant Rosenberger

1, Mayserdergasse 2 (512 3458). U1, U2, U4 Karlsplatz/tram 1, 2, D, J. **Open** 7.30am-11.30pm daily. **Main courses** €5-€12. **Credit** AmEx, DC, JCB, MC, V. **Map** p250 E7 **13**

If foreign-language menus bring you out in a rash, this low-priced self-service restaurant is a godsend. Arranged like a subterranean market place, the various stalls offer Argentinian steaks and grilled fish, grilled and boiled vegetables, salads and soups – all at the point of a finger. Pour your own wine and beer or mix a cocktail from the excellent selection of freshly squeezed juices. Desserts are generously sized portions of apple strudel or *Sachertorte* (Viennese chocolate cake). At lunchtimes, it's jam-packed.

Meinl am Graben

1, Graben 19 (from 7pm entrance around the corner on Naglergasse) (532 33 34-6000/www. meinlamgraben.at). U1, U3 Stephansplatz, U3

The spectacular **Österreicher im MAK**, Vienna's latest must-visit restaurant.

Herrengasse. **Open** 8.30am-midnight Mon-Wed; 8am-midnight Thur, Fri; 9am-midnight Sat. **Main courses** €22-€35. **Credit** AmEx, DC, JCB, MC, V. **Map** p250 E6 ⓮

Located above the city's premier food store (*see p150*), Meinl am Graben is one of Vienna's best and most elegant venues. Chef Joachim Gradwohl promotes lighter, more nuanced fare favouring herbs and essences over salt. The wine cellar is famous, the cheese perfectly ripe, the staff hyper-informed and, if you angle a window booth, the view down Graben alone justifies the hefty price of the meal.

Österreicher im MAK

1, Stubenring 5 (714 0121/www.oesterreicher immak.at). U3 Stubentor/tram 1, 2. **Open** 10am-1am daily. **Main courses** €8.50-€17.80. **Credit** AmEx, DC, JCB, MC, V. **Map** p251 F7 ⓯

The reopening of the old MAK café was one of the gastronomic events of 2006. Now named after Helmut Österreicher, the chef that turned the Steirereck into Vienna's top restaurant, it's been given a spectacular makeover by celebrated architect duo Eichinger oder Knechtl. Diners can choose between the airy main room with a wine-bottle chandelier over the central bar or the pastel booths of the winter garden. And in the summer, there's a nice alfresco bar in the garden. The menu is divided between Viennese classic and modern dishes, and Österreicher's craft (and the reduced portions) make it an affordable and enjoyable experience.

Palmenhaus

1, Burggarten (entrance Goethegasse) (533 1033/ www.palmenhaus.at). U1, U2, U4 Karlsplatz/tram 1, 2, D, J. **Open** 10am-2am daily. **Meals served** 10am-midnight daily. **Main courses** €12-€22. **Credit** DC, MC, V. **Map** p250 E7 ⓰

The Burggarten's Jugendstil hothouse is one of Vienna's most spectacular bar/restaurants. Full of tall palms and succulents with a fine view over the gardens, the Palmenhaus is optimally oriented for winter sunshine. That said, the grilled fish and pasta can be spoiled by the proximity of boozy groups of chain smokers and the appalling acoustics of this cavernous space. In the afternoons, Vienna's beau monde shows up for cakes and pastries on the terrace.

Plachutta

1, Wollzeile 38 (512 1577/www.plachutta.at). U3 Stubentor/tram 1, 2/bus 1a. **Open** 11.30am-11.15pm daily. **Main courses** €16-€23. **Credit** AmEx, DC, JCB, MC, V. **Map** p251 F7 ⓱

The stately Plachutta is the Viennese temple of beef eating, and rightly famed for one dish, *Tafelspitz*. The boiled beef tenderloin, Emperor Franz Josef's favourite Sunday lunch, is served with rösti, puréed spinach and an apple and horseradish sauce. *Tafelspitz*'s elaborate preparation (the meal begins with bowls of the tremendous beef broth left over after cooking the meat) has probably prevented it from becoming well known internationally, so a meal here should be a priority for carnivorous visitors.

Eat, Drink, Shop

Endangered species

Although Trzesniewski's gorgeous eggy canapés are the highlight of Viennese snack food (*see p120*), late-night grazing is traditionally dominated by the *Würstelstand*. As well as functioning as the cradle of Viennese slang, these ramshackle sausage stands serve up countless varieties – from the spicy *Bosna* to the cheese-pumped *Käsekrainer*, fondly referred to as an *Eitriger*, or pus-stick. That meatloaf sweltering in the glass oven is *Leberkäs* (literally, liver cheese), a challenging local delicacy made of horse meat. The uninitiated should stick with the thinner, meatier *Bratwurst*.

However, in recent times, the *Würstelstand* have been fairing badly: many have closed and the council threatens to demolish the stands that lie empty. And, to add insult to injury, many more have been converted into pizza/kebab outlets. This and the city-wide outbreak of dodgy pan-Asian grills are the two current curses on Vienna's culinary horizon.

The decline of the *Würstelstand* has a lot to do with the poor quality, crack-in-the-mouth tubes of reconstituted meat slurry that so many of them serve. Nevertheless, most of the Innere Stadt stands are a cut above: **Deninger** on Hohemarkt (7am-5am daily) is one of the best, serving all the faves plus a bewildering choice of Austrian ales. So do your bit to save this great Viennese institution, preferably after a few beers.

Other locations Grünspan 16, Ottakringer Strasse 266 (480 5730); 13, Auhofstrasse 1 (877 7087-0); 19, Heiligenstädter Strasse 179 (370 4125).

Reinthaler

1, Gluckgasse 5 (512 3366). U1, U2, U4 Karlsplatz. **Open** 9am-11pm Mon-Fri. **Main courses** €5.70-€10.50. **No credit cards. Map** p250 E7 ⑱

A rare example of an authentic, low-priced Innere Stadt Beisl. Its wood-panelled rooms and green Formica tables are nearly always packed with pensioners, students, workers in overalls and suits – all hunched together at companionable tables over beers and newspapers. You'll find the usual dishes, including great *Schweinsbraten* (roast pork), a stinging goulash and much offal.
Other locations 1, Dorotheergasse 2-4 (513 1249).

Restaurant Coburg

1, Coburgbastei 4 (518 18800/www.coburg.at). U3 Stubentor/tram 1, 2. **Open** 6.30pm-midnight Tue-Sat. **Main courses** €22-€39. **Credit** AmEx, DC, JCB, MC, V. **Map** p251 F7 ⑲

With former Meinl am Graben (*see p118*) chef Christian Petz at the helm, the restaurant of the Palais Coburg is considered by many cognoscenti to be the city's top luxury destination. Contrasting with the fine table settings and expensive but uninspired decor, Petz favours pigeon, parsnip and other earthy ingredients over wild sea bass, langoustines and the like. These pervade the four- and six-course menus (€68 and €98), which feature signature dishes such as tripe ravioli with clams or crayfish. The more intrepid can opt for the five-course surprise menu (€92) with a €50 wine accompaniment.

Soho

1, Am Josefsplatz 1 (entrance via Burggarten) (0676 309 5161). U1, U2, U4 Karlsplatz/tram 1, 2, D, J. **Open** 9am-4pm Mon-Fri. **Main courses** €4.40-€4.90. **No credit cards. Map** p250 E7 ⑳

The National Library canteen beside the Palmenhaus is a pleasantly designed spacious bar/restaurant offering excellent food at true canteen prices. It is located in the basement of the imposing Neue Burg. The two lunch menus consist of Italian-inspired food with the odd wink at the Far East.

Trzesniewski

1, Dorotheergasse 1 (512 3291/www.speckmitei.at). U1, U3 Stephansplatz/bus 3a. **Open** 8.30am-7.30pm Mon-Fri; 9am-5pm Sat. **No credit cards. Map** p250 E7 ㉑

The only splash of colour in this austere period open-sandwich bar comes from the display of striped egg-based canapés on rye bread. Diners queue at a counter (overseen by a troupe of rather severe matrons), point to what they want, pay, then find a seat. Twenty-one varieties include speck, spicy green pepper, sardine, and herring and onion – all at ¢90 a pop; there are also gorgeous little spinach or meat pasties at €1.50. Drinks (wine or beer) are ordered from the cashier, who hands you the corresponding colour-coded counter that you exchange at the other end of the bar. Go for a mid afternoon snack, as the lunchtime rush detracts from its wonderfully gloomy Mitteleuropa feel. A must visit.
Other locations 3, Landstrasser Hauptstrasse 97 (712 9964); 6, Mariahilfer Strasse 95 (596 4291); 7, Kirchengasse 6-8 (523 8462).

Weibel 3

1, Riemergasse 1-3 (513 3110/www.weibel.at). U3 Stubentor/tram 1, 2. **Open** 5pm-midnight Tue-Sat. **Main courses** €17.50-€24. **Credit** AmEx, MC, V. **Map** p251 F7 ㉒

Of the three restaurants owned by the canny Weibel clan, the intimate, naffly named Weibel 3 is the most experimental. After the departure of (Ramsay and Arzak alumnus) Konstantin Filippou, chef Günther Maier was brought in and the place has been given

Eat, Drink, Shop

a Spanish contemporary spin. Expect crispy sea bass on a porcini paella, salt cod and a modest but highly informed range of Spanish wines and cavas.

Ein Wiener Salon

1, Stubenbastei 10/1 (0660 654 2785/www.ein wienersalon.com). U3 Stubentor/tram 1, 2. **Open** 6pm-midnight Tue-Sat. **Menus** *4 courses €33; 5 courses €40; 6 courses €47.* **Credit** MC, V. **Map** p251 F7 ㉓
The motto of this two-man operation (Sven cooks and Felix serves) is *'de gustibus non est disputandum'* ('there's no accounting for taste'). And there's no doubting the high camp of the small but lofty interior, papered in royal blue and silver flock and hung with huge portraits of Maria Theresia and husband (with Felix and Sven's eyes scanned in). The two run the place like an intimate drawing room, serving rather exquisite if petite (apart from the desserts) dishes that can be eaten as part of four-, five- or six-course menus. Strict vegetarians will have trouble with the main courses and the shy may feel rather too much in the limelight. Nevertheless, one of the most curious restaurants in Vienna.

Zum Finsteren Stern

1, Schulhof 8 (535 2100). U3 Herrengasse. **Open** 5pm-1am Mon-Sat. **Main courses** *€12-€20.* **Credit** MC, V. **Map** p250 E6 ㉔
Ella da Silva's creative Italian-inspired dishes feature plenty of juicy, slow-cooked meats and vegetables served up in chilled, unpretentious surroundings. The fairly priced wines are mostly Austrian and excellent and the summer terrace, in one of the Innere Stadt's most charming corners, is simply gorgeous.

Zum Schwarzen Kameel

1, Bognergasse 5 (533 81 25/www.kameel.at). U1, U3 Stephansplatz/bus 1a, 2a, 3a. **Open** *Restaurant* noon-3pm, 6-11pm Mon-Sat. *Delicatessen buffet* 8.30am-10pm Mon-Sat. **Main courses** *€16-€25.* **Credit** AmEx, DC, MC, V. **Map** p250 E6 ㉕
This classic Viennese address opened as a grocer's in 1618 and was reputedly patronised by Beethoven. Today, it still sells wine and cold cuts but most of the expensively dressed clientele come for the vast assortment of delicate open sandwiches and canapés served in the wood-panelled main bar. The restaurant itself has possibly the most beautiful dining room in Vienna, full of gorgeous Jugendstil ceramic reliefs and lamps (avoid the sterile-looking inner sanctum, though). New chef Christian Domschitz does good things in and around the Viennese pantheon, but you can't beat the cooked ham with freshly grated horseradish on brown bread from the bar.

Zwölf Apostelkeller

1, Sonnenfelsgasse 3 (512 6777/www.zwoelf-apostelkeller.at). U1, U3 Stephansplatz. **Open** 4.30pm-midnight daily. **Main courses** *€5.45-€9.60.* **Credit** AmEx, DC, MC, V. **Map** p251 F6 ㉖
Stacked beneath one of von Hildebrandt's most spectacular Baroque houses, this cellar on three subterranean levels is touristy but good fun. A vast quantity

of typical Austrian grub, beer and wine, to the accompaniment of traditional music (7-11pm Wed-Fri), is the tonic. Nevertheless, the labyrinth of vaulted Gothic and early Baroque cellars have a Harry Potter-esque charm. Ordering is made easier by a choice of buffets. Note that there's a long walk up to the toilets from the lower ground floor.

2nd district

Gasthaus am Nordpol 3

2, Nordpolgasse 3 (333 5854). Tram 5. **Open** 5pm-midnight Mon-Sat; noon-midnight Sun. **Main courses** *€6.80-€11.* **No credit cards.** **Map** p243 F3/4 ㉗
On the northern side of the Augarten, the 'North Pole' is a minimally renovated Beisl specialising in everything Bohemian – from dishes, beer and absinthe to attitude. In its gorgeous ageing interior you can work your way through hearty dishes such as tripe soup, cured pork with horseradish and Würst (made in-house), as well as the typical Bohemian poppy-seed desserts. The owners bake their own bread, welcome children with open arms and there's a great summer terrace.

Schöne Perle

2, corner Leopoldsgasse & Grosse Pfarrgasse (0664 243 3593/www.schoene-perle.at). Tram 21, N. **Open** noon-midnight daily. **Main courses** *€6.50-€15.* **No credit cards.** **Map** p243 F5 ㉘
Conserving the name of its predecessor, a Chinese restaurant, the 'beautiful pearl' is a typical example of a neo-Beisl. Besides the Schnitzel and *Tafelspitz*, there's always fresh grilled fish and a couple of meat-free dishes, served in an environment that's informal, well designed and wearing well over the years. The larder is stocked exclusively with organic produce. Note that the restaurant has an intransigent 'no dogs' policy in contrast to other local eateries.

Schuppich

2, Rotensterngasse 18 (212 4340/www.schuppich.at). U1 Nestroyplatz/tram 21, N. **Open** *Sept-June* 6pm-midnight Wed-Sat; noon-4pm Sun. **Main courses** *€7-€19.* **Credit** AmEx, DC, MC, V. **Map** p251 F5 ㉙
Lurking in the backstreets off Taborstrasse, this is the address for the hybrid Austro-Italian food of Friuli and Trieste. Try the €25 four-course set menu or the seasonal specialities for a good introduction to a cuisine rarely seen outside Italy. The Beisl-style interior oscillates between gloomy emptiness and packed-to-the-gills chaos, but the food and wines are reliable and children are welcome.

Schweizerhaus   Closed for winter

2, Strasse des 1 Mai 116 (728 0152/www.schweizer haus.at). U1 Praterstern, then tram 21. **Open** *Mid Mar-Oct* 11am-11pm Mon-Fri; 10am-11pm Sat, Sun. **Main courses** *€5.60-€11.70.* **No credit cards.** **Map** p244 H5 ㉚
Every flesh eater in Vienna makes it here once a year. The bustling establishment is loud, sweaty and beery

Skopik & Lohn.

and housed in and around what was the Swiss Pavilion at the 1870 Expo, on the edge of the Prater fun fair. Run since 1920 by the Kolarik family, the Schweizerhaus is famous for serving huge portions of specialities such as *gegrillte Steltzen* (grilled pork knuckle studded with caraway seeds – 600 consumed every day), tripe soup and rivers of Budweiser.

Skopik & Lohn
2, Leopoldsgasse 17 (219 8977/www.skopikund lohn.at). U1 Nestroyplatz. **Open** 5pm-1am daily. **Main courses** €8.90-€21. **Credit** MC, V. **Map** p243 F5 ③
A beautiful Beisl update in the Leopoldstadt. Skopik & Lohn's traditional caramel wood panelling is off-set with the impressive black maze that artist Otto Zivko scrawled over its white vaulted celings. Owner Horst Scheuer learned his trade at numerous Viennese addresses before widening his experience with a sojourn in Paris. He now serves reworked Beisl classics, with a hint of the Med. There's a large summer terrace seating 80.

3rd district

Gasthaus Wild
3, Radetzkyplatz 1 (920 9477). Tram N. **Open** 9am-1am daily. **Meals served** 11.30am-11pm Mon-Sat; 11.30am-10pm Sun. **Main courses** €9-€20.50. **Credit** V. **Map** p251 G6 ③
Weinhaus Wild was once one of Vienna's most charming *Gasthäuser* (guesthouses) despite appalling food and service. Now, these spacious premises have been given a new lease of life. By conserving original features such as the beautiful wooden *Schank* (the 'bar') and ditching the net curtains, Wild has become an atmospheric neo-Beisl without scaring away its original clientele. The menu always has an authentic Viennese meat or offal dish, but the more ambitious dishes are often a bit of a lottery. Service is excellent, as are the wines and beers.

Gmoa Keller
3, Heumarkt 25 (712 5310/www.gmoakeller.at). U4 Stadtpark/tram D. **Open** 11am-midnight Mon-Sat. **Main courses** €6.90-€12.50. **Credit** AmEx, DC, MC, V. **Map** p251 F8 ③
Evening reservations are advisable at this tremen-dous old vaulted Beisl, as it's often stormed by crowds from the nearby Akademietheater and Konzerthaus. Previously ruled by two cantankerous matrons who allegedly kept the evening's takings in a plastic shop-ping bag, the new owners offer perfectly executed, totally affordable Viennese classics. Apart from hang-ing a large Hermann Nitsch 'blood painting' in the beautiful main room, the Gmoa Keller's splendid inte-rior remains intact. Highly recommendable.

Stadtwirt
3, Untere Viaduktgasse 45 (713 3828/www. stadtwirt.at). U3, U4 Wien Mitte. **Open** 10am-11pm Mon-Fri; 5-11pm Sat. **Main courses** €5.50-€16. **Credit** AmEx, DC, MC, V. **Map** p251 G7 ③

It's essential to book in advance at this spacious, cut-above Viennese Beisl. The speciality at Stadtwirt is seasonal cooking with influences from Upper Austria and Bürgenland. The house red is so good that you can easily dispense with the more expensive wines. The only down side is the presence of all the shiny suited bureaucrats from the nearby ministries.

Steierereck im Stadtpark

3, Am Heumarkt 2 (Stadtpark) (713 3168/www. steirereck.at). U4 Stadtpark. **Open** noon-4pm; 7pm-1am Mon-Fri. **Main courses** €10.90-€36. **Credit** AmEx, DC, JCB, MC, V. **Map** p251 F7 ㉟
Soon after the Steierereck moved into these impressive new premises, chef Helmut Oesterreicher – fundamentally responsible for its status as Austria's leading restaurant – announced he was leaving. The kitchen is now steered by Reitbauer Jnr (the owner's son) who has managed to hang on to his Michelin star while promoting the restaurant's new policy of offering lighter, value-for-money lunch options (in the hallowed upper-floor main restaurant). Dinner there remains a six-course affair (€98) with an optional course of wines (€57). Perhaps the most interesting aspect of the new location is the riverfront Meierei, which operates as a designer milk bar, serving superb desserts and light lunches.

Taverna Lefteris

3, Hörnesgasse 17 (713 7451/www.taverna-lefteris.at). U3 Rochusmarkt/bus 4a. **Open** 6pm-midnight Mon-Sat. **Main courses** €8.90-€14.50. **Credit** AmEx, DC, MC, V. **Map** p248 H7 ㊱
Employees of the Greek Embassy declare this the best Greek restaurant in town. The menu has a Cretan slant, plus several Turkish-influenced dishes. Lefteris

is also pretty, with beautiful wooden floors, and walls painted light blue. In summer, you can eat under the trees. Greek musicians play on Tuesdays.

4th district

Amacord

4, Rechte Wienzeile 15 (587 4709). U4 Kettenbrückengasse. **Open** 10am-2am daily (meals till midnight). **Main courses** €7.20-€12.90. **No credit cards. Map** p247 D8 ㊲
Amacord's vaulted confines are full of Naschmarkt overspill and arty types, enjoying a beer or a coffee while browsing through the excellent selection of international newspapers. In the tiny restaurant area, gratifying Italian-inspired cooking is served. Drawbacks are the smoke and dearth of space.

Artner

4, Floragasse 6 (503 5033/www.artner.co.at). U1 Taubstummengasse/tram 56. **Open** 11am-midnight Mon-Fri; 6pm-midnight Sat, Sun. **Main courses** €11.80-€22.80. **Credit** DC, MC, V. **Map** p247 E9 ㊳
Wine and cheese-maker Markus Artner has a chic yet relaxed restaurant hidden in a network of small streets not far from Karlsplatz. His wonderful unpasteurised goat's cheese crops up in various starters but there's also great lamb and stupendous locally reared Galloway beef to follow. Cool interior, great crocks and friendly attentive service. **Photo** *p125.*

Beograd

4, Schikanedergasse 7 (587 7444). U4 Kettenbrückengasse/bus 57a. **Open** 5pm-2am Mon, Tue; 11.30am-2am Thur-Sun. **Main courses** €5.70-€16.80. **Credit** MC, V. **Map** p247 D8 ㊴

Gmoa Keller.

Canteen scene

Vienna, as befits a town that was once the centre of a polyglot empire, is a city of bureaucrats and students, all of whom have to be fed and watered. Inside the city's hulking ministries and cultural institutions, canteens are open from Monday to Friday and access to these subsidised salons is generally unrestricted. If you're on a shoestring budget or merely fancy a peek at the innards of the Austrian state machinery, here are some of the more inviting options.

Bear in mind that in Austria the acronym MENSA indicates a student refectory, not an organisation for people with high IQs. Near the Schottentor U-Bahn you can ride a hop-on-hop-off paternoster lift to the top floor of the **NIG** (1, Universitätsstrasse 7, 406 4594) to a penthouse MENSA with striking views of the Rathaus, Votivkirche and the Josefstadt prison where revisionist historian David Irving spent the summer of 2005. The food, however, is fairly pedestrian. In the Innere Stadt, the MENSA of the **Musikakademie** (1, Johannesgasse 8, 512 9470) combines a historic building, decent main courses at around €4 and the strains of classical music. Nearby on the Ringstrasse, another MENSA at the **Akademie für Angewandte Kunst** (Oscar Kokoschka Platz, 2) is a dirt-cheap pre-fab full of art school objects.

For good basic Austrian dishes the canteen of the state-run **Akademietheater** (51444-4740, see p207) is pretty faultless. Enjoy a €5 Schnitzel and sautéd potatoes (with a €1 spritzer) on period Formica tables in the company of stage hands, actors and chin-tugging academics. However, for the finest in institutional dining, join the legal eagles at the **Kantine im Justizpalast** (Schmerlingplatz 10, 52152-3828). This Ringstrasse monolith was burned down by rioters in 1927 and later served as the headquarters for Allied Command during the ten years of the four-power occupation. To get in, you have to negotiate some fairly stringent security at the entrance then take the lifts from the splendid vestibule to the top floor. For those panoramic snaps of Vienna, it's a great location, with a fish tank, a summer terrace and great food at those wonderful subsidised prices.

Sampled and immortalised by Dr Rockit aka Matthew Herbert on one of his numerous visits to Vienna, the late-night sound of the Beograd is clinking glasses, raucous laughter and a gypsy violin. This popular Balkan tunnel pulls in a varied clientele attracted by its excellent grilled meats and lengthy opening hours (2am is only in theory). If you're in a group, try the 'burning sword of the Hun' – a massive mixed grill for four served with chips and *letschko* (the Balkan ratatouille) – a snip at €34.

Kiosk – Der Stand der Wurst

4, *Schleifmühlgasse 7 (585 4077). Bus 57a.* **Open** 11am-2am Mon-Wed, Sun; 11am-4am Thur-Sat. **Main courses** €3-€5.50. **No credit cards**. **Map** p247 E8 ⑩
'The State of the Wurst' is doing its bit to protect Vienna's threatened sausage culture. In its bustling canteen/bar atmosphere you can try classic bangers from all over the German-speaking world, plus the odd exotica, such as Spanish *morcillas*. There's potato salad and vegetable stews for those who disdain the noble swine. Much loved by the art dollies and hipsters of the Schleifmühlgasse, its turntables are deftly operated by local music journalists.

Tancredi

4, *Grosse Neugasse 5 (941 0048/www.tancredi.at).* *Tram 62, 65.* **Open** 11.30am-2.30pm, 6pm-midnight Tue-Fri; 6pm-midnight Sat. **Main courses** €10.80-€18.80. **No credit cards**. **Map** p247 E9 ⑪
Tancredi is a refined Beisl that changes with the seasons. Expect game and fungi in the autumn and some great asparagus creations in spring. The large dining room has lovely high arched windows and outside there's a florid covered summer terrace. Its menu of eight starters and eight or nine mains changes monthly, with a couple of purely vegetarian options. Wines are Austrian and fairly priced, with some potent Bürgenland reds.

Ubl

4, *Pressgasse 26 (587 64 37). U4 Kettenbrückengasse.* **Open** noon-2.30pm, 6pm-midnight daily. **Main courses** €8-€15. **No credit cards**. **Map** p247 D8 ⑫
With its ancient panelling, wood-burning stove and atmospheric sedateness, Ubl is an outstandingly conserved specimen of the Viennese Beisl. The usual staples, such as fine *Schwiebelrostbraten*, are augmented with Italian-influenced cooking, like side orders of braised fennel and other vegetables. The service has improved vastly in recent times and the shady summer terrace is a restorative spot after a trip to the Naschmarkt.

Umar

4, *Naschmarkt Stand 76-79 (587 0456). U1, U2, U4 Karlsplatz.* **Open** 11.30am-11pm Mon-Sat. **Main courses** €10.90-€19. **Credit** AmEx, DC, MC, V. **Map** p250 E8 ⑬
The Naschmarkt's best fishmonger has expanded into the restaurant business. As it's located next door to the stall, diners can pop out and point at the

fish of their choice. For lunch there are three good-value set menus for €9.90, €11.90 and €12.90. The cooking is little more than the application of hot coals, salt and lemon juice with a levantine garnish, but the fish is fresh and the place fun and lively.

Urbanek

4, Naschmarkt, Stand 46 (587-2080). U1, U2, U4 Karlsplatz. **Open** 9am-6.30pm Mon-Thur; 8am-6.30pm Fri; 7.30am-4pm Sat. **No credit cards.** **Map** p250 D8 ㊹

Chefs and celebrities are often seen necking far too much white wine and braying loudly at the high tables outside Urbanek. This tiny deli has the Naschmarkt's finest selection of international cold cuts and some great cheeses too.

5th district

Gergely's

5, Schlossgasse 21 (544 0767/www.schlossquadr.at). Bus 13a, 59a. **Open** 6pm-2am Mon-Sat. **Main courses** €6.90-€19.50. **Credit** V. **Map** p247 D9 ㊺

Two restaurants share one of Vienna's best conserved Biedermeier-era inner courtyards shaded by horse chestnuts. For this alone it's worth visiting either Gergely's or the neighbouring Silberwirt. The former serves good steaks and fish grilled on lava stone as well as some pan-Oriental dishes; the latter focuses on traditional Viennese cooking. Late dining, good beers and the curious surroundings are the best reasons to pop in.

Motto

5, Schönbrunner Strasse 30 (entrance Rüdigergasse) (587 0672/www.motto.at). U4 Pilgramgasse/bus 59a. **Open** 6pm-2am Mon-Thur, Sun; 6pm-4am Fri, Sat. **Main courses** €8-€21. **Credit** MC, V. **Map** p247 D9 ㊻

At Motto they camp it up well into the early hours. With low lights, beautiful vaulting and a funky soundtrack, Motto is a magnet for models and media folk, since it's one of the few places that offers a reasonable meal at 3am, with a free ego massage thrown in. Despite a preponderance of beef – in the form of carpaccios, tartare and steaks – the menu's increasingly Far Eastern bent at least offers vegetarians a fair choice. The gorgeous garden, swish bar and fine-looking waiters (Helmut Lang was once among them) chatting in a variety of languages more than compensate for the lack of culinary coherence.

6th district

Dots Experimental Sushi

7, Mariahilfer Strasse 103 (920 9980/www.dots-lounge.com). U3 Zieglergasse. **Open** 11am-midnight Mon; 11am-2am Tue-Sat; 5pm-midnight Sun. **Main courses** €9.90-€19.90. **Credit** DC, MC, V. **Map** p246 B8 ㊼

Hidden in a rather moribund mall just off Vienna's main shopping street, Dots is one of the swishest, most active lounge/restaurants to land in town in recent times. Bereft of natural light, owner Martin Ho commissioned a superb lighting concept from a team of architects that gives the all white dining area an agreeable warmth while highlighting the beauty of his twisted Japanese dishes. The nigiri and sashimi are among Vienna's best. In the darkened entrance lounge, some of Vienna's best DJs are at work.

Gastwirtschaft Steman

6, Otto-Bauergasse 7 (597 8509). U3 Zieglergasse. **Open** 11am-midnight Mon-Fri. **Main courses** €5.50-€13.50. **No credit cards.** **Map** p246 C9 ㊸

The young crew that runs Steman zealously reject any contemporary touches to the original dark wood interior of this historic Beisl. Divided from the bar

Artner. *See p123.*

area by a clouded glass partition, the large spacious dining room offers well-priced local classics such as offal, game, wild mushrooms and the humble hog in all its manifestations.

Lutz – Die Bar

6, Mariahilfer Strasse 3 (585 3646/www.lutz-bar.at). U2 Museumsquartier. **Open** 8am-4am Mon-Fri; 9am-4am Sat; 10am-4am Sun. **Main courses** €6-€14. **Credit** AmEx, DC, MC, V. **Map** p250 D8
This first-floor lounge opposite the MQ has a big-city vibe of leather seating in chocolate tones, where you can get a late breakfast (till 4pm), sip cocktails or enjoy good brasserie food until the early hours. No DJs, no gimmicks, just a splendidly designed interior that glows nicely (discreet lighting is hidden behind the polished wood panels running along the walls). Pretty damn cosmopolitan for Vienna.

Ra'mien

6, Gumpendorfer Strasse 9 (585 4798/www. ramien.at). U2 Museumsquartier. **Open** 11am-midnight Tue-Sun. **Main courses** €6-€14.50. **Credit** AmEx, DC, MC, V. **Map** p250 D8 ⑤⓪
Vienna's hippest noodle temple, Ra'mien has a sparse, airy designer interior that attracts a young, fashionable bunch. Come here at lunch or early evening, when the menu features vast bowls of tasty, reasonably priced ramen and Vietnamese pho noodles, along with rice dishes and *gyoza* dumplings. Dinner is a costlier affair, with great pan-Asian fish, seafood and tofu dishes – but it can get crowded. The downstairs lounge, all *Hong Kong Phooey* chintz, is a popular pre-club venue with good DJs spinning until 4am. For dinner, booking is essential.

Vinissimo

6, Windmühlgasse 20 (586 4888/www.vinissimo. at). Bus 57a. **Open** 11am-11pm Mon-Sat. **Main courses** €7-€17. **Credit** AmEx, DC, MC, V. **Map** p250 D8 ⑤①
This high vaulted wine bar/bistro hybrid offers a weekly selection of 15-20 wines that are available to try by the glass. The full list includes some 400 labels (of which at least half are Austrian), which can be sampled either in situ or taken away to linger over later. The restaurant offers solid Italian cuisine in starters such as *Weinbeisserteller* ('wine nibble platter' – antipasti and cheeses) and homemade pastas like basil and cream cheese ravioli with tomato butter. There's alfresco seating on Raimundhof.

Zum Roten Elefanten

6, Gumpendorferstrasse 3 (966 8008/www. zumrotenelefanten.at). U1, U2, U4 Karlsplatz/ trams 1, 2, D. **Open** 11am-midnight Mon-Fri; 6pm-midnight Sat. **Main courses** €12.50-€16.50. **No credit cards**. **Map** p250 D8 ⑤②
The dimly lit and sparsely decorated 'Red Elephant' is currently a darling of the city's arty set. And quite properly so. This is the latest addition to the lower Gumpendorfer Strasse's attractive cluster of bars, shops and restaurants, offering excellent set lunch menus (€6.90) and more elaborate evening fare – all cooked by Melanie Branschädl, who was formerly the personal chef to art collector and socialite Francesca von Habsburg (*see p171* **My Vienna**). Another major factor in Zum Roten Elefanten's current popularity is the short wine list that offers no less than eight drinkable bottles for under €20.

Whether at a new, design-influenced venue like **Zum Roten Elefanten** or...

7th district

Amerlingbeisl

7, Stiftgasse 8 (526 1660/www.amerlingbeisl.at).
U2, U3 Volkstheater/tram 49. **Open** 9am-2am daily.
Main courses €5-€8. **Credit** DC, MC, V.
Map p250 C7 ⑤

The Amerlingbeisl is Spittelberg's most iconic
address. Squatted in the 1980s as part of a campaign
against plans to redevelop this picturesque quarter,
the building remains a focal point of political radi-
calism. And although the restaurant serves some
fairly pedestrian brasserie grub, an hour or two in
its gorgeous leafy inner courtyard is a delight.

Gastwirtschaft Schilling

7, Burggasse 103 (524 1775/www.schilling-wirt.at).
U6 Burggasse/bus 48a. **Open** 11am-1am daily.
Main courses €6.60-€14.70. **No credit cards**.
Map p246 B7 ⑤

The cosy, antiquated Schilling is Beisl heaven on a
cold, winter's evening. Its vintage wood-panelled
and milk glass interior, tremendous roasts and liver
dishes, foxy waitresses and powerful puds (the
Mohr im Hemd is Vienna's greatest) all induce the
most divine sense of well-being.

Glacis Beisl

7, Museumsquartier (access from Breitegasse 4)
(526 5660/www.glacisbeisl.at). U2, U3 Volkstheater.
Open 11am-2am daily. **Meals served** 11am-11pm
daily. **Main courses** €6.60-€21.50. **Credit** DC, MC,
V. **Map** p250 D7 ⑤

The Glacis Beisl was around long before the MQ was
a twinkling in a politician's eye. After the museums

opened, it returned in a stylish, contemporary form
but with its gorgeously unkempt garden trimmed and
tamed. Since then, its repertoire of Viennese classics
with a twist has been a resounding success. So much
so that communication breakdowns between kitchen
and staff are frequent on busy days, leading to irk-
some waits. Avoid weekends and public holidays.

Halle

7, Museumsplatz 1 (523 70 01). U2
Museumsquartier, U2, U3 Volkstheater. **Open**
10am-2am (meals till midnight) daily. **Main courses**
€7.60-€16. **Credit** MC, V. **Map** p250 D7 ⑤

Operated by the folk behind Motto (*see p125*), Halle
is incorporated into the west wing of the Old Winter
Riding School, the Baroque stucco of which occasionally peeks out amid the establishment's signature cool steel and wood. The menu caters for an
all-day clientele of museum-goers and poseurs, and
runs from breakfast to cocktails. Food is typical
museum-gastro – Italian with hints of the Orient –
beautifully presented but rather dear.

Hidori

7, Burggasse 89 (523 3900). Bus 48a. **Open** 6pm-
midnight Tue-Sun. **Main courses** €9-24. **Credit**
AmEx, DC, MC, JCB, V. **Map** p246 B7 ⑤

Hidori is a great no-frills *yakitori* grill. Unlike most
of Vienna's noodle and sushi joints, it isn't operated
by indeterminate Asians but bona fide Japanese.
Named after a manga character 'fire bird', Hidori
offers western seating as well as a neat, raised *tata-
mi* area. On the menu there's great skewered chick-
en, a pungent miso soup and fine sushi, that all come
to the table beautifully presented.

... a traditional Beisl like **Gastwirtschaft Schilling** one thing you can be sure of: the beer.

Menu glossary

Useful phrases

Do you have a table for (number) people?
Haben Sie einen Tisch für... Personen?
I want to book a table for (time) o'clock
Ich möchte einen Tisch für... Uhr bestellen
I'll have (name of food)
Ich nehme...
I'll have (name of food) with/
without (ingredient)
Ich nehme... mit/ohne...
I'm a vegetarian
Ich bin Vegetarier
Can I/we have an ashtray, please
Einen Aschenbecher, bitte
The bill, please
Zahlen, bitte
Waitress/waiter
Fräulein/Herr Ober

Basics

Couvert/Gedeck Cover charge
Das Menü Fixed-price menu
Die Speisekarte Menu
Die Tageskarte Menu of the day
Die Weinkarte Wine list
Das Glas Glass
Das Messer Knife
Die Gabel Fork
Der Löffel Spoon
Die Hauptspeise Main course
Das Frühstück Breakfast
Die Vorspeise Starter
Das Mittagessen Lunch
Das Abendessen Dinner
Die Nachspeise Dessert

Menu

Almdudler Herbal lemonade
Apfelsaft (-gespritzt) Apple juice (mixed with
soda water)
Bärlauch Wild garlic
Basilikum Basil
Bohnen Haricot beans
Brot Bread
Durch Well done (as in steak)
**Ei (Spiegelei; Rührei; pochiertes/verlorenes
Ei; weiches Ei; hartgekochtes Ei)** Egg (fried;
scrambled; poached; boiled, hard-boiled)
Eierschwammerln Chanterelle mushrooms
Eis Ice-cream
Eiswürfel Ice cube

Englisch Rare (as in steak)
Ente Duck
Erbsen Peas
Erdbeer Strawberry
Essig Vinegar
Fisch Fish
Fisolen Green beans
Fleisch Meat
Forelle Trout
Gans Goose
Garnelen Prawns
Gebacken Fried
Gebraten Roast
Gekocht Boiled
Gemüse Vegetables
Gurke Cucumber
Hecht Pike
Hendl/Hahn/Huhn Chicken
Himbeer Raspberry
Honig Honey
Kabeljau Cod
Karfiol Cauliflower
Kartoffel/Erdäpfel Potatoes
Käse Cheese
Kichererbsen Chickpeas
Knoblauch Garlic
Knödel Dumplings
Kotelett Chop
Kümmel Caraway seed
Kürbis Pumpkin
Lachs Salmon
Lamm Lamb
Lauch Leek
Leber Liver
Leitungswasser Tap water
Linsen Lentils
Lungenbraten Fillet steak
Marillen Apricots
Medium Medium-rare (as in steak)
Meeresfrüchte Seafood
Mehlspeise Pâtisserie
Milch Milk
Mineralwasser Mineral water
Obst Fruit
Öl Oil
Oliven Olives
Orangensaft/Frischgepresster Orangensaft
Orange juice/Freshly squeezed orange juice
Paprika Peppers
Paradeiser Tomatoes
Petersilie Parsley
Pfeffer Pepper
Pommes frites Chips
Reis Rice

Eat, Drink, Shop

Rind Beef
Rosmarin Rosemary
Rostbraten Steak
Rotwein Red wine
Saibling Lake trout
Salz Salt
Sauce/Saft Sauce/Gravy
Schinken/Speck Ham
Schittlauch Chives
Schlag Whipped cream
Schokolade Chocolate
Schwein Pork
Semmel White roll
Senf Mustard
Serviettenknödel Sliced dumplings
Spargel Asparagus
Steinpilze Porcini mushrooms
Sulz Brawn
Suppe Soup
Tee Tea
Thymian Thyme
Topfen Curd cheese
Torte Cake
Trauben Grapes
Vollkorn Wholemeal
Wasser Water
Weisswein White wine
Wels Catfish
Wurst Sausage
Zitrone Lemon
Zucker Sugar
Zwetschke Plum
Zwiebel Onion

Gemischter Salat Tomatoes, potato salad, green beans, lettuce and lots of onions, covered in tart wine or cider vinegar
Griessnockerlsuppe Clear beef broth with floating semolina dumplings
Heringsalat Pickled herring salad; traditionally served on Ash Wednesday
Käsekrainer Sausage filled with melted cheese
Käsespätzle Baby dumplings, covered in a powerful cheese sauce
Kraut/Schinkenfleckerl Pappardelle-type pasta with cabbage or ham
Leberknödelsuppe Clear beef broth made with liver; includes small dumplings
Rindsgulasch Beef stew spiced with paprika and served with dumplings (originally a Hungarian recipe)
Schweinsbraten Roast pork, usually served with sauerkraut and sliced dumplings
Tafelspitz mit g'röste Boiled beef served with fried, grated potatoes, covered in an apple and horseradish sauce (Emperor Franz Joseph used to eat this every Sunday lunchtime, apparently)
Tiroler g'röstl Potato and sausage hash served in a blackened skillet
Wiener Eintopf Vienna stew (vegetables, potatoes and sausage in a clear beef broth)
Wiener Schnitzel Veal or pork escalope fried in breadcrumbs
Zwiebelrostbraten Tenderloin steak in onion sauce

Typical savoury dishes

Bauernschmaus 'Peasants' treat': a plate of hot meats including roast and smoked pork, or pork cutlet, frankfurters and a selection of ham; usually served with dumplings
Beuschel Chopped offal in sauce
Blunzn Black pudding
Brathendl/Backhendl Fried/roast chicken
Eierspeise Scrambled omelette served in a pan, sometimes with ham
Erdäpfelgulasch Potato stew; often includes pieces of frankfurter sausage
Frittatensuppe Clear beef broth with floating slivers of pancake
Gebratene Bachforelle mit Petersilerdäpfel Fried brook trout with potatoes in parsley sauce
Gefüllte Kalbsbrust Veal breast filled with several types of meat or vegetable

Dessert

Birne Helene Pear Helene
Germknödel Sweet dumplings, filled with jam
Griessschmarrn Semolina pancake, chopped into small pieces, served with a plum compôte
Kaiserschmarrn Thick fluffy pancake, chopped into small pieces and covered in icing sugar; usually served with a plum compôte
Mohr im Hemd Rich steamed chocolate pudding, served with a hot chocolate sauce and whipped cream
Palatschinken Thicker than the French crêpe; served sweet or savoury
Reisauflauf Rice pudding
Topfen/Marillenknödel Curd cheese or apricot dumplings, breadcrumbed and fried in butter; served with hot fruit purée

Eat, Drink, Shop

St Josef

*7, Mondscheingasse 10 (526 6818). U3
Neubaugasse/tram 49.* **Open** 8am-7.30pm Mon-Fri;
8am-4pm Sat. **Main courses** €5.70-€6.80. **Credit**
AmEx, DC, MC, V. **Map** p246 C8 ❸
Located in the charming Mondscheingasse, this
bustling vegetarian restaurant and organic food-
store is adored by the 7th district's media bods and
fashionistas. It serves good salads and a variety of
oriental-influenced dishes from an open kitchen. The
shop stocks organic fruit and vegetables, excellent
bread and the finest grazing food.

Siebensternbräu

*7, Siebensterngasse 19 (523 8697/www.7stern.at).
Tram 49.* **Open** 10am-midnight (meals till 11pm)
daily. **Main courses** €6-€14.90. **Credit** DC, MC, V.
Map p250 C8 ❺❾
A large, gregarious beer hall/microbrewery that
appeals to all ages, the Siebensternbräu has an indifferent interior plagued by cooking smells. However,
the garden – shaded by two large horse chestnut trees
– is a lovely spot to enjoy the brewery's trademark
cloudy beer and robust Austrian dishes. The hemp
and chilli beers should be approached with caution.

Una

*7, Museumsplatz 1 (523 6566). U2
Museumsquartier, U2, U3 Volkstheater.* **Open** 9am-
midnight Mon-Fri; 10am-midnight Sat; 10am-6pm
Sun. **Main courses** €9-€16.50. **No credit cards**.
Map p250 D7 ❻❶
Una occupies one of the original vaulted wings of
the MuseumsQuartier, beneath a ceiling clad in magnificent Turkish tiles. The bistro-style menu can feature straightforward pasta dishes, grilled fish and
seasonal specialities such as game and wild mushrooms. House wines, particularly the Zweigelt, is
good value, and the desserts likewise. The only
drawback can be the stressed out staff.

Winetime

*7, Zollergasse 5 (522 3508/www.winetime.at). U3
Neubaugasse.* **Open** 4pm-late Mon-Sat. **Main
courses** €4.20-€10.50. **Credit** V. **Map** p246 C8 ❻❶
A stylish yet totally laid-back wine bar, Winetime
serves organic cheeses and cold cuts, plus the odd
warm dish, to accompany some 25 wines by the
glass (from a cellar housing 250 varieties). Prices are
very reasonable and the accent is firmly on local produce, although the odd foreign tipple crops up. The
tiny interior is cleverly enhanced by a relaxing blend
of bare brick, unusual ironwork and natural light
from the glassed-off patio. Surprisingly for a
vinothèque, a great varied soundtrack is always
bubbling in the background.

Zu den Zwei Lieseln

7, Burggasse 63 (523 3282). Bus 48a. **Open** 11am-
10pm daily. **Main courses** €4.90-€10.90. **No credit
cards. Map** p246 C7 ❻❷
The Zwei Lieseln are a duo of imposing Viennese
matrons who fry up vast Schnitzels for everyone
from brickies to the Bürgermeister. The interior of

this Viennese institution is authentic Beisl-style spit
'n' sawdust with lovely old Formica. In summer, the
courtyard and its spreading chestnut tree are a joy.

8th district

Café Pars

*8, Lerchenfelder Strasse 148 (405 8245). U6
Thaliastrasse/tram 46.* **Open** 11am-midnight
Mon-Sat. **Main courses** €5.40-€16.90. **Credit** V.
Map p246 B6/7 ❻❸
Headquarters of Vienna's Persian community, Café
Pars cooks rice the way only Persians know – maximum fluffiness, with a wonderful crispy base.
Served with butter, egg yolk and mixed fresh herbs,
this is a meal in itself, but it comes with superbly
spiced chicken kebabs or char-grilled beef fillet in
thin strips. There's a choice of vegetable and bean-
based appetisers and dips. The heavy-handed decoration – elaborate tiling and illustrations of
questionable artistic merit – is alleviated by the
chance to ogle the handsome customers.

Hold

8, Josefstädter Strasse 50 (405 1198). Tram J. **Open**
8am-11pm Mon-Fri; 9am-11pm Sat. **Meals served**
11.30am-2.30pm, 6-10.30pm Mon-Sat. **Main courses**
€6.80-€12. **No credit cards. Map** p246 C6 ❻❹
A small café-cum-trattoria oozing northern Italian
authenticity, Hold makes a useful pitstop if you're
exploring Vienna's noble 8th district. As well as
being great for a revitalising cappuccino and almond
pastry, or a quick glass of house Chianti, it also
serves reasonably priced lunches and dinners featuring substantial soups, fresh antipasti and good
pasta dishes. Space is at a premium, which makes
communal dining de rigueur.

Konoba

*8, Lerchenfelder Strasse 66-68 (929 4111/www.
konoba.at). Tram 46.* **Open** 11am-2pm, 6pm-
midnight Mon-Fri, Sun; 6pm-midnight Sat. **Main
courses** €5.90-€25. **Credit** MC, V. **Map** p246 C7 ❻❺
Once again it's down to the Croats to supply Vienna
with affordable fish and seafood. In a pleasant setting of stripped wood and (rather inefficent) po-mo
ventilation ducts, Konoba imports a refreshing taste
of the Dalmatian coast with dishes such as the hefty
Buzara – mussels in a potent wine, garlic, olive oil
and parsley sauce. Garlic sometimes overpowers
superbly grilled sea bass and bream, but the edge
can be removed by downing plenty of fruity
Dalmatian whites, such as Laski Rizling and Dingac.

Il Sestante

8, Piaristengasse 50 (402 9894). U2 Rathaus/tram J.
Open 11.30am-11.30pm daily. **Main courses**
€7-€16. **No credit cards. Map** p246 C6 ❻❻
The arrival of this Sicilian outfit on the gorgeous
Maria-Treu-Platz made it one of Vienna's most spectacular alfresco locations. Enjoy the surroundings
while munching no-nonsense Italian food. This
means crispy pizzas oozing buffalo mozzarella and

Eat, Drink, Shop

fresh herbs, a fiery *suppa di povero*, and (not quite as reliable) pastas and risottos. The wine list features potent southern reds such as Ciró and Nero d'Avola. The brisk service is very friendly by local standards.

Die Wäscherei

8, Albertgasse 49 (409 2375-11/www.die-waescherei.at). U6 Josefstädter Strasse/tram 43, 44, J. **Open** 5pm-2am Mon-Fri; 10am-2am Sat; 10am-midnight Sun. **Main courses** €5.60-€18.50. **Credit** AmEx, DC, MC, V. **Map** p246 B6 ⑥⑦
Besieged by a boisterous, good-looking young crowd, the 'Laundromat' does a roaring trade in competitively priced, substantial Austro-ethnic dishes, with a better-than-average choice for vegetarians. Saturdays and Sundays are particularly popular, and there are great brunches for €14 (10am-4pm). The beer is another big draw, especially the bone-dry Trumer Pils and Die Weisse, a Salzburg wheat beer rare in these parts. Call by early in the evening; as later on, both the pleasant interior and chilled sounds are blocked out by the crowds. A great summer terrace and some of Vienna's prettiest waitresses add to the allure.

Weinstube Josefstadt

8, Piaristengasse 27 (406 4628). Tram J/bus 13a. **Open** Apr-Dec 4pm-midnight daily. **No credit cards. Map** p246 C6 ⑥⑧
The entrance to this city Heuriger is so discreet that even many Josefstadt residents are completely unaware of its existence. It's best enjoyed during high summer, when the ivy-clad garden becomes a shady oasis. The kitchen serves a limited selection

of good-value dishes such as roast pork, black pudding, salads and dips and, unlike in most Heurigen, you can even get an ice-cold Budweiser.

9th district

Flein

9, Boltzmanngasse 2 (319 7689). Tram 37, 38, 40, 41, 42. **Open** 11.30am-3pm, 5.30pm-midnight Mon-Fri. **Main courses** €8-€15. **No credit cards. Map** p243 D4/5 ⑥⑨
Located in the gardens of the new-defunct Alliance Française, Flein is a slightly cramped Beisl-style attraction with some fine old fittings (a magnificent iron-and-ceramic stove, for example). It really comes into its own when the good weather kicks in and you can sit outside. Chef Hubert Beaumont offers great seasonal cooking that includes plenty of meat-free options. In addition, Flein serves good Austrian wines and superb Schremser beer.

Gasthaus Wickerl

9, Porzellangasse 24a (317 7489). Tram D. **Open** 9am-midnight Mon-Fri; 10am-midnight Sat. **Main courses** €4.90-€14. **Credit** AmEx, DC, MC, V. **Map** p243 D4 ⑦⑩
Wickerl is a classic wood-panelled Vienna Beisl, popular with students. The city's top chefs can be spotted here wolfing down dumplings. Food consists of the usual Beisl repertoire, but carefully elaborated with high-quality materials. Football fans will appreciate both the big screen TV in the back room and the three beers on tap (including Budweiser).

Heurigen/wine taverns

The seven square kilometres (2.7 square miles) of vineyards that lie within its boundaries make Vienna the world's largest wine-growing city. The most extensive area is on the northern fringe in districts 16-19, but the highest quality is found in the Transdanubian 21st district. On balmy summer evenings, join the Viennese for an evening in a *Heuriger*, one of the scores of rustic wine taverns dotted among the vineyards in the shadow of the Vienna Woods. Like *Beisln*, Heurigen are a splendid Viennese foible, named after the tart new wine they serve. Strictly speaking, Heurigen owners only sell their own wines, along with a limited selection of food such as cuts of roast pork, various cheesy dips and the odd vegetable or salad. The wine is served at tables; the food comes via a self-service buffet. Hard to find these days, the real McCoy even allows customers to bring along picnics. From May to September, a pine branch is hung outside to

show that a Heuriger is open, but as a rule, it's best to phone ahead as places operate a rotation system in some areas. The website www.heurigenkalender.at is a useful resource in English that provides up-to-date opening hours for establishments in Vienna and beyond.

The Heuriger has, of course, been corrupted over the years – the wine villages of Neustift, Nussdorf and particularly Grinzing are now awash with places serving full meals and full rural kitsch. And as the city grows, more and more Heurigen, such as **10er Marie** (*see p133*), are to be found in urban areas. However, the rural spots are still within easy reach of the city centre. The further you go, the higher the chances of encountering the authenticity and breathtaking views that make a real Heuriger so memorable. The following are recommended: **Heuriger Göbel** (*see p134*), **Hirt**, **Sirbu** and **Zawodsky** (for all three, *see p133*).

Noi.

Kim Kocht

9, Lustkandlgasse 6 (319 0242/www.kimkocht.at).
U6 Volksoper. **Open** 6pm-midnight Wed-Fri. **Main**
courses 3, 4 & 5 course menus €42, €51, €59.
Credit AmEx, DC, JCB, MC, V. **Map** p242 C4
This diminutive pan-Asian restaurant is famous for
its long waiting list. Kim, a former designer, cooks
tuna in a myriad styles and her exquisite eye is evident in the presentation. Now that the cookbooks,
magazine articles and the rest of the hype surrounding it have subsided, getting a table is a little easier.

Stomach

9, Seegasse 26 (310 2099). Tram D. **Open** 4pm-
midnight Wed-Sat; 10am-10pm Sun. **Main courses**
€10-€18. **No credit cards. Map** p243 E4 ⓲
Stomach has long supplied one of Vienna's most sat-
isfying eating experiences. Don't be put off by its
dilapidated façade; it hides a cosy, kitsch-free old
world interior and a splendidly bedraggled inner
courtyard for summer evenings. Much frequented by
theatre folk, Stomach is gradually abandoning its
vegetarian slant to concentrate on Styrian beef dishes such as the divine marinated Tafelspitz with boiled
egg, chives and drizzled pumpkin seed oil. Game
abounds in winter in the form of wild boar and veni-
son; there's wonderful lake trout too. Reliable wines,
Murauer beer and great schnapps are also to be had.

15th district

Gasthaus Quell

15, Reindorfgasse 19 (893 2407/www.quell.cc). U6
Gumpendorfer Strasse. **Open** 11am-midnight Mon-
Fri; 5pm-midnight Sat. **Main courses** €4.50-€12.80.
No credit cards. Map p246 A10 ⓳
A good ten-minute walk from the U-Bahn station,
this classic Beisl has an atmospheric wood-panelled
interior, a cracked old ceramic stove and an affable
landlord. The menu offers the run of meaty Viennese
staples, supplemented by seasonal specials. A further attraction is the pleasant summer terrace on the
traffic-free Reindorfgasse.

Happy Buddha

15, Mariahilfer Gürtel 9 (893 4217/www.happy
buddha.at). U6 Gumpendorfer Strasse. **Open**
11.30am-2.30pm, 5.30-11.30pm daily. **Main courses**
€7.50-€13.90. *Dim sum* €3.80-€4.50. **Credit** AmEx,
DC, MC, V. **Map** p246 B9 ⓴
The 15th district has some of Vienna's best Chinese
restaurants. When it comes to who serves the top dim
sum, opinions are divided between here and Tsing
Tao, in nearby Gerstnerstrasse. Both offer excellent
Cantonese food, but Happy Buddha is chintz-free.

16th district

Café Kent

16, Brunnengasse 67 (405 9173/www.kent
restaurant.at). U6 Josefstädter Strasse. **Open** 6am-
2am daily. **Main courses** €6-€10. **Credit** AmEx,
DC, MC, V. **Map** p246 A6 ⓯

Summer at Vienna's best-loved kebab house means
long evenings in its wonderful garden. Its popularity with locals is unsurprising: excellent meze plat-
ters and grilled meats retail at knock-down prices,
with plenty of aubergine and courgette concoctions
too. Located in the Brunnenmarkt, a step from the
Gürtel night scene, Kent attracts shoppers, slackers
and stallholders with its long hours. **Photo** *p134.*

Etap

16, Neulerchenfelder Strasse 13 (406 0478/www.
etap-restaurant.at). U6 Josefstädter Strasse/tram J.
Open 8am-midnight Mon-Thur, Sun; 8am-4am Fri,
Sat. **Main courses** €4-€15. **No credit cards.**
Map p246 B6 ⓰
The elegant version of the Kent (*see p132*), Etap
attracts a more well-heeled Turkish clientele who
like to relax in its comfy lounge after dinner. On the
menu there's plenty of grilled meat, fish and veg as
well as a substantial weekend buffet (from 6pm) that
features a large selection of appetisers (€8.90). A
small summer garden and live Turkish music on
Fridays and Saturdays are further draws.

Noi

16, Payergasse 12 (403 1347/www.noi.at.vu). U6
Josefstädter Strasse/tram 44. **Open** 11am-midnight
Tue-Fri; 9am-midnight Sat. **Main courses** €8.90-
€17. **No credit cards. Map** p246 A/B6 ⓱
Tiny Noi is an organic foodstore/restaurant beside
the Brunnenmarkt on Yppenplatz. As it barely seats
ten diners, it's best to come when the weather is fine
and eat outside. The accent is on earthy Italian dishes made with seasonal, 100% organic fare. The midday specials and evening menus always have
meat-free options and in summer there are some sensational ice-creams – beetroot and lime anyone?

10er Marie

16, Ottakringer Strasse 222-224 (489 4647/www. fuhrgassl-huber.at). Tram 46, J. **Open** 3pm-midnight Mon-Sat. **Main courses** €5-€9.60. **Credit** MC, V.
Dating back to 1740, 10er Marie is reputedly Vienna's oldest Heuriger. Located on the northern limits of the Ottakring district, this rural idyll was overtaken by the urban sprawl, but its two courtyards, full of horse chestnuts, walnut trees and oleander, retain a taste of the past. The place serves all the Heuriger staples, with excellent vegetable bakes and noodle dishes, and attracts a colourful clientele of all ages.

18th district

Trattoria L'Ambasciata della Puglia

18, Währinger Strasse 170a (479 9592). Tram 40, 41. **Open** noon-3pm, 6-11pm Mon-Sat. **Main courses** €8-€20. **Credit** MC, DC, V. **Map** p242 A3 ⑦
The informal 'embassy' trades in a great selection of hearty southern Italian wines and fresh pastas. Apulian specialities such as broad bean purée and *braciola* (a horse-meat roulade) feature, and pasta for children is free. It's a favourite of well-heeled members of the city's DJ clique, whose compilations provide the funky soundtrack.

Wirtshaus Steiererstöckl

18, Pötzleinsdorfer Strasse 127 (440 4943). Tram 41. **Open** 11.30am-midnight (meals till 10pm) Wed-Sun. **Main courses** €7.50-€17.50. **No credit cards.**
After a walk round Pötzleinsdorfer Park, this rustic tavern is ideal for snacks, salads and more substantial meat dishes – all genuinely Styrian. Don't leave without sampling a glass of the Schilcher Most, the restorative juice of Styria's most idiosyncratic grape variety. Booking is advisable.

19th district

Bamkraxler

19, Kahlenberger Strasse 17 (318 8800/www. bamkraxler.at). Tram D. **Open** 4pm-midnight Tue-Sat; 11am-midnight Sun. **Main courses** €5.20-€13.20. **Credit** MC.
Located on Nussdorf's main Heuriger drag, Bamkraxler is one of Vienna's most child-friendly locations. Shaded by large chestnut trees, its pretty garden has a well-equipped playground, plus toys and drawing materials for rainy days. They serve children's portions decorated with cartoon characters. For adults, there's an acceptable choice of Austrian dishes and the excellent Augustiner, a cloudy beer from Salzburg.

Hirt

19, Eisernenhandgasse 165 (318 9641). S-Bahn from Franz-Josefsbahnhof to Kahlenberger Dorf. **Open** *Apr-Oct* 3-11pm Wed-Fri; noon-11pm Sat, Sun. *Nov-Mar* noon-11pm Fri-Sun. **No credit cards.**
Probably the best way to reach this superb little out-of-the-way Heuriger is via a visit to Sirbu (*see below*).

After a couple of spritzers there, take the path beside Sirbu and head on downhill towards the flowing river. Hirt has two terraces – one overlooking the Danube and another with views of Leopoldsberg – where you can feast on the usual Heuriger grub. The interior is appropriately rustic and cosy.

Schreiberhaus

19, Rathstrasse 54 (440 3844/www.dasschreiber haus.at). Bus 35a. **Open** 11am-1am daily. **Credit** AmEx, DC, JCB, MC, V.
A Heuriger offering great food and above-average wines in a spot well known for catering to friendly family parties and various corporate events. The big terraced garden is pretty, and the interior comfortable, stylish and low on the usual Heuriger kitsch. Have a post-prandial walk along the path that runs through the vineyards behind the garden.

Sirbu

19, Kahlenberger Strasse 210 (320 5928). Bus 38a, then 15min walk. **Open** *Apr-mid Oct* 3pm-midnight Mon-Sat. **Credit** MC, V.
Sirbu has outstanding views of the Danube from a sunny terrace surrounded by vineyards. Like all Heurigen, it has the statutory self-service buffet consisting of various cuts of pork – try the superlative *Kümmelbraten*, a fatty roast belly-pork dotted with caraway seeds, plus various salads and cold cuts.

Weingut Reisenberg

19, Oberer Reisenbergweg 15 (320 9393). Tram 38, then bus 38a. **Open** *Apr-Oct* 5pm-midnight Mon-Fri; 1pm-midnight Sat, Sun; *Nov-Dec* 6pm-midnight. **Credit** MC, V.
The steep walk from the edge of Grinzing up to this Heuriger-style attraction will earn you some of the best views of Vienna. Also spectacular is the tart white wine served here – make like the locals and douse with liberal quantities of mineral water. The food is a cut above that of the average Heuriger.

Zawodsky

19, Reinischgasse 3 (320 7978/www.zawodsky.at). Tram 38. **Open** *Feb-Dec* 5pm-midnight Mon, Wed-Fri; 2pm-midnight Sat, Sun. **Credit** AmEx, DC, MC, V.
One of the best-kept secrets of Vienna's Heuriger culture, Zawodsky offers a tremendous view of the city and a gorgeously unkempt garden full of apple trees. There's no decor to speak of, just picnic tables and benches, and the selection of cold meats and cheeses is less extensive than at most places. Opening times vary, so phone ahead.

Zimmermann

19, Mitterwurzergasse 20 (440 1207/www.weinhof-zimmermann.at). Bus 35a. **Open** *Mid March-mid Dec* 3pm-midnight Mon-Sat. **Credit** DC, MC, V.
A Heuriger with a reputation for attracting upper-class custom. It has beautiful outdoor seating under fruit trees, and a pet zoo with rabbits and guinea pigs. The classic Viennese dishes served here are a notch above the usual buffet fare, but pricier.

Eat, Drink, Shop

21st district

Birners Strandgasthaus

21, An der Oberen Alten Donau 47 (271 5336/www. noessi.at/birner). U6 Neue Donau. **Open** *Summer* 9am-11.30pm Mon, Tue, Thur-Sun. *Winter* 9am-9pm Mon, Tue, Thur-Sun. **Main courses** €5.70-€12.70. **No credit cards**.

This spit 'n' sawdust chop house comes into its own in the summer months, when sun-groggy Viennese fresh from the nearby Angeli baths cross the narrow bridge to Birners' delightful riverside terrace.

Heuriger Göbel

21, Stammersdorfer Kellergasse 151 (294 8420/ 0664 2439835). Tram 31, then bus 125. **Open** 4-10pm Mon; 11am-10pm Sat, Sun 1 wk each mth; phone for details. **No credit cards**.

Architect Hans-Peter Göbel is a prize-winning vintner whose cabernet sauvignon and Zweigelt (particularly the 1993) are possibly the best red wines produced in the Vienna area. He designed this chic Heuriger himself. Göbel's innovative approach involves classic Heuriger roast pork specialities plus exquisite salads and antipasti. Limited opening times, so be sure to ring in advance.

Heuriger Wieninger

21, Stammersdorfer Strasse 78 (292 4106/www. heuriger-wieninger.at). Tram 31. **Open** *End Feb-Dec* 3pm-midnight Wed-Fri; noon-midnight Sat, Sun. **No credit cards**.

Stammersdorf is Vienna's biggest wine-producing district. This tavern features wines from Fritz Wieninger, considered one of Austria's top wine makers. The chardonnay and cabernet-merlot it produces come recommended. The establishment is run by Fritz's mother and brother and has a good menu.

Weingut-Heuriger Schilling

21, Langenzersdorferstrasse 54 (292 4189/www. weingut-schilling.at). Tram 32. **Open** 4-11pm Mon-Fri; 3-midnight Sat, Sun. **Credit** DC, MC, V.

This large Heuriger has a friendly atmosphere and extensive gardens at the foot of the Bisamberg Hill. Weingut Schilling also has a good reputation for its wines – try the Cuvée Camilla. There's a copious buffet, offering such Austrian specialities as blood sausage (*Blutwurst*) and grilled pork knuckle (*Stelze*).

22nd district

Strandcafé

22, Florian-Berndl-Gasse 20 (203 6747/www. strandcafe-wien.at). U1 Alte Donau. **Open** 10am-midnight daily. **Main courses** €5.50-€14.30. **No credit cards. Map** p245 M2 ⑲

On a fine summer afternoon, the Strandcafé is a great antidote to the rigours of the city. It is situated among huge poplars and weeping willows on the banks of the old arm of the river. The big draw here is racks of barbecued pork ribs served with divine roast potatoes. Tables are laid out on a floating pontoon; note that dinner may require lashings of insect repellent.

Vienna's best-loved kebab house: the inappropriately named **Café Kent**. *See p132.*

Cafés & Coffee Houses

Vienna state of mind.

There's nowhere quite like a Vienna *Kaffeehaus*. Once the brass-handled door creaks open, you step into a world of extravagant impracticality, dogged resistance to change and often scant regard for profit. These spacious interiors are bathed in sedate silence; the tinkling of teaspoons and rustle of newspapers is dampened by thickly upholstered booths, ageing parquet floors and the disdainful glance of liveried waiters. Often likened to London's gentlemen's clubs, coffee houses in Vienna are tailored to suit one's profession, pocket or political persuasion. Nevertheless, they share a common iconography of marble-topped tables, booths and Thonet bentwood chairs in varying degrees of disrepair, a bewildering selection of periodicals and a large omnipresent clock. The price of a cup of coffee is the only entrance fee to these archaic theme parks, often described as more a state of mind than actual geographic locations. Long waits to order and to pay are de rigueur, but the waiter's haughtiness should never be read as 'order another or move along': *Herr Ober* (as he should be addressed) is more than likely tutting at the sound of your mobile phone.

In a country known for prizing legend over historical fact, the coffee house phenomenon is shrouded in mythology. The story goes that it originated after the 1683 Turkish siege, when two of the Habsburgs' most effective spies received compensation in the form of what they had first taken to be camel fodder: sacks of coffee beans. One of the two (his identity is subject to varying degrees of polemic) also earned a concession to open an establishment for the consumption of the 'Turkish drink' at Rotenturmstrasse 14, though, unusually for Vienna, no plaque commemorates this seemingly momentous occurrence.

Most of the grand coffee houses still operating today date from either end of the 19th century, when, in times of overcrowding and poor heating, they became a refuge for penniless men of ambition who often used their café of choice as a postal address and the waiters as sources of cash loans. Many such patrons were part of fin-de-siècle Vienna's extraordinary outpouring of intellectual, artistic and political activity. Thus cafés **Griensteidl** and **Central** are associated with the comings and goings of literati and revolutionaries, the **Museum** with the shenanigans surrounding the Secessionist movement and **Sperl** with musical giants such as Gustav Mahler. The tradition continued into the post-World War II era when newer cafés such as **Hawelka** and **Bräunerhof** became second homes to bourgeois baiters such as Thomas Bernhard and the Viennese Actionists.

So what of the coffee? Anyone conditioned to Italian varieties will not be greatly impressed. Viennese roasts from firms such as Santora, Café do Brasil and Meinl simply don't compare to the Illys and Lavazzas of this world. That said, Vienna's coffee houses do offer a kaleidoscopic range of versions on the theme – but for a frothy, milky coffee, order a *melange* (*see p141* **Ein Melange, bitte**).

Competing with traditional coffee houses are a variety of establishments ranging from the dirt-cheap Eduscho stores to the kitsch Aida chain; coffee from either is an acquired taste. In 2002, Starbucks reached Vienna, but five years on, only a modest ten branches operate.

1st district

Café Aida

1, Stock-im-Eisen-Platz 2 (512 2977/www.aida.at). U1, U3 Stephansplatz. **Open** 7am-8pm Mon-Sat; 9am-8pm Sun. **Melange** €2.60. **Credit** AmEx, DC, MC, V. **Map** p251 E7 ❶

Aida's iconic pink neon sign burns brightly at 26 branches throughout the city, making it by far Vienna's biggest café chain, with the widest selection of cakes and pastries, and an idiosyncratic blend of coffee that is enduringly popular. Although Aida's clientele hails from diverse age groups and social classes, the extraordinary interiors from the 1950s, '60s and '70s have earned the chain a cult status. Curious colour schemes where browns and pinks appear to mirror the cakes, chrome railings, plastic bucket chairs and acres of people-watching plate glass give many Aidas an air of post-modernity that contrasts vividly with their practical function. This city centre branch has all its trademark *Schnitten* (slices) and *Schüsserln* (cup cakes), as well as a splendid first-floor cake bar lined with comfortable fake-leather stools and views over the square. **Other locations** throughout the city.

❶ Pink numbers given in this chapter correspond to the café locations in the street maps. *See pp242-251.*

Cake as far as the eye can see at **Café Central** and...

Café Bräunerhof

*1, Stallburggasse 2 (512 3893). U3 Herrengasse/bus
2a, 3a.* **Open** 8am-8.30pm Mon-Fri; 8am-6pm Sat;
10am-6pm Sun. **Melange** €3.10. **No credit cards.**
Map p250 E7 ❷
The ironically named Café Sans Souci was one of
many cafés to be 'aryanised' – its Jewish owners
expropriated – during the Nazi era, and renamed
Café Bräunerhof. Its reputation as a literary café
owes much to the patronage of former regular
Thomas Bernhard, the irascible novelist and playwright, and philosopher Paul Wittgenstein,
Ludwig's nephew, who lived in the same building
(*see p98*). More austerely decorated than other classic Viennese coffee houses, the Bräunerhof still
attracts colourful characters; blood 'n' guts performance artist Hermann Nitsch is often seen sketch-
ing in a corner. The Bräunerhof has one of the best
selections of international newspapers of any
Kaffeehaus in the city, as well as a great array of
cakes and strudels, all served with a generous dol-
lop of *Schlagobers* (whipped cream). A string trio
plays on Saturday and Sunday afternoons.

Café Central

*1, Herrengasse 14 (533 37 63-24/www.ferstel.at). U3
Herrengasse/bus 1a, 2a, 3a.* **Open** 7.30am-midnight
daily. **Melange** €3.50. **Credit** AmEx, DC, MC, V.
Map p250 E6 ❸
When the original Café Griensteidl was demolished
at the turn of the 19th century, the literary set moved
to the Central, making it Vienna's principal intellectual hangout. Trotsky, or Bronstein, as he was

known in his clandestine years before World War I,
was such an assiduous regular at the Central that an
Austrian minister, on being informed of imminent
revolution in Russia, supposedly remarked, 'And
who on earth is going to make a revolution in Russia?
I suppose you're going to tell me it's that Bronstein
who sits all day at the Café Central!' These days the
clientele is almost exclusively tourist. Pop in, though,
to admire the decorated pseudo-Gothic vaulting and
pay your respects to the dummy of the penniless poet
Peter Altenberg that sits just inside the door reading
the paper. Across the road is the pâtisserie branch
Café Central Konditorei (*see p152*).

Café Excelsior

*1, Opernring 1 (585 7184). U1, U2, U4
Karlsplatz/tram 1, 2, D, J.* **Open** 7.30am-midnight
daily. **Melange** €2.90. **Credit** AmEx, DC, MC, V.
Map p250 E7 ❹
This Turin-based coffee roaster operates internationally. In its comfortable but somewhat soulless
premises (teak, steel and glass à la 21st century) opposite the Staatsoper, it makes some of the best coffee
in Vienna. You can also snack on bruschetta,
tramezzini, ciabatta et al while observing the human
traffic around Vienna's most transited junction.
Other locations 1, Stephansplatz 7 (512 1444).

Café Frauenhuber

*1, Himmelpfortgasse 6 (512 83 83). U1, U3
Stephansplatz/tram 1, 2.* **Open** 8am-11.30pm
Mon-Sat; 10am-10pm Sun. **Melange** €3.20.
Credit V. **Map** p251 E7 ❺

...even more at **Café Weinwurm**. See p139.

The Baroque façade of Vienna's oldest café and the neighbouring Winter Palace of Prince Eugène are both the work of Johann Lukas von Hildebrandt. Operating since 1824, Frauenhuber is steeped in musical mythology and history of the highest order, since Mozart lived in the building for a time and Beethoven occasionally performed his piano sonatas in the café itself. Today, despite its plush vaulted interior, it's a more mundane establishment, filled with shoppers and tourists from the nearby Kärntner Strasse, but one that thankfully still retains the essential coffee house attributes.

Café Griensteidl

1, Michaelerplatz 2 (535 2693). U3 Herrengasse/ bus 2a, 3a. **Open** 8am-11.30pm daily. **Melange** €3.20. **Credit** AmEx, DC, V. **Map** p250 E7 ⑥

The present Café Griensteidl remains in the shadow of Hofburg, on the site of the original café – a veritable battleground of such late 19th-century literary giants as Karl Kraus, Arthur Schnitzler, Hermann Bahr and Hugo von Hofmannsthal, who all decamped to Café Central (*see p136*) after the building was demolished in 1897. Here too, Theodor Herzl is also said to have drafted *The Jewish State*, his blueprint for Zionism. The café reopened in 1990 and now attracts a mixture of civil servants and tourists recovering from a visit to the Hofburg. Its spacious interior and numerous windows looking out on to the bustle of Michaelerplatz are the principal attractions for visitors. Unusually for a Viennese Kaffeehaus, it's child-friendly and even has several high chairs.

Café Hawelka

1, Dorotheergasse 6 (512 8230/www.hawelka.com). U1, U3 Stephansplatz/bus 3a. **Open** 8am-2am Mon, Wed-Sat; 4pm-2am Sun. **Melange** €2. **No credit cards. Map** p250 E7 ⑦

Immortalised in Kraftwerk's 'Transeurope Express' video, Hawelka is dark, smoky and charmingly threadbare, but no longer the intellectual hangout it was between the 1950s and the 1970s, when it was a favourite of the Viennese Actionists, and Canetti, Warhol and Millers Henry and Arthur all used to drop by. Part of its ongoing charm lay in the husband and wife duo of Leopold and Josefine Hawelka; since Josefine's death in 2005, there's been nobody to seat single clients next to lonely members of the opposite sex. Leopold still bakes the house's trademark pastries for the succession of German tourists.

Café Korb

1, Brandstätte 9 (5337215). U3 Herrengasse. **Open** 8am-midnight Mon-Sat; 10am-11pm Sun. **Melange** €3.20. **Credit** AmEx, MC, V. **Map** p251 E6 ⑧

This city centre coffee house frequented by writers and journalists has international newspapers, contemporary art (Arnulf Rainer), stylish designer toilets and a basement bowling alley. The summer terrace is a great place for spying on passers-by.

Café Landtmann

1, Dr-Karl-Lueger-Ring 4 (24100-120/www. landtmann.at). U2 Schottentor/tram 1, 2, D. **Open** 7.30am-midnight daily. **Melange** €4.20. **Credit** AmEx, DC, MC, V. **Map** p250 D6 ⑨

Café Goldegg. *See p140.*

This elegant café was a favourite of Sigmund Freud, where the old man regularly enjoyed a slice of *Guglhupf*, the sponge cake with a hole. It's a traditional Kaffeehaus where hats and coats are surrendered to a frowning cloakroom dame and liveried waiters refuse to smile. Subjected to over €500,000 of grandiose renovation, Café Landtmann has lost much of its authenticity but remains popular with academics, Burgtheater regulars and powerbrokers from Austrian business and politics. To combat the incipient anti-smoking measures, an expansive new winter garden was tagged on to the entrance in 2007.

Café Markusplatz

1, Tuchlauben 16 (533 4136). U3 Herrengasse.
Open 7.30am-7pm Mon-Fri; 8.30am-7pm Sat.
Melange €2.50. **No credit cards. Map** p251 E6 ⑩
The former Café Tuchlauben was a 1950s gem that new owner Markus Muliar (hence the name) has lovingly conserved. Having improved the coffee, kept all the classic pâtisserie and brought in some good midday menus, Muliar has attracted a markedly Bohemian clientele.

Café Mozart

1, Albertinaplatz 2 (24 10 00-2/www.cafe-wien.at).
U1, U2, U4 Karlsplatz/tram 1, 2, D, J/bus 3a. **Open** 8am-midnight daily. **Melange** €3.80. **Credit** AmEx, DC, JCB, MC, V. **Map** p250 E7 ⑪
Located behind the Staatsoper, the Mozart has become another victim of the tourist trade. Its splendid 19th-century interior made a big impression on Graham Greene during the shooting of *The Third Man* and it became the film's Café Alt Wien. Anton Karas, composer of the immortal 'Harry Lime Theme', even wrote a Café Mozart waltz in its hon-our. Probably unbeknown to Greene, the Mozart was confiscated from its Jewish proprietors after the *Anschluss* and handed over to one Fritz Quester, a card-carrying Nazi and chimney sweep by trade.

Café Museum

1, Friedrichstrasse 6 (586 5202). U1, U2, U4 Karlsplatz/tram 1, 2, D, J. **Open** 8am-midnight Mon-Sat; 10am-midnight Sun. **Melange** €3.20.
Credit AmEx, DC, MC, V. **Map** p250 E8 ⑫
The best way to experience the original Adolf Loos-designed interior of Café Museum (1899) is to visit the Hofmobiliendepot (*see p100*). What was a charmingly scuffed modernist coffee house was given such a zealous bout of renovation in 2003 that many regulars abandoned it for good. Although it restored the café's original layout, the bright red Thonet chairs and some other mindless decorative touches spoil the effect. To recall the days when Klimt and co used to drop in from the nearby Secession requires a titanic leap of the imagination.

Café Prückel

1, Stubenring 24 (512 61 15/www.prueckel.at). U3 Stubentor/tram 1, 2. **Open** 8.30am-10pm daily.
Melange €3.10. **No credit cards. Map** p251 F7 ⑬
Originally a classic Ringstrasse café that opened in 1903, this place was given its present 1950s-style look in 1989 by Viennese architect Oswald Haerdtel. Comfortable yet functional, the Prückel's understated furnishings and high ceilings adorned with magnificent Venetian chandeliers form a spacious, airy interior loved by everyone from bridge players and elderly ladies to students and Bohemians. It hit the headlines in 2005 when waiters ejected a couple of women for over-enthusiastic kissing – an act that

led to a mass gay snog-in. Anecdotes aside, this is one of Vienna's great coffee house experiences and ideal after a visit to the nearby MAK (*see p86*).

Café Sacher Wien

1, Philharmonikerstrasse 4 (512 1487/www.sacher. com). U1, U4 Karlsplatz/tram 1, 2, 62, 65, D, J/ bus 3a. **Open** 8am-midnight daily. **Melange** €4. **Credit** AmEx, DC, MC, V. **Map** p250 E7 ㉔
The café of the starry Sacher hotel is starchy, conservative and full of monarchic clutter – Thomas Bernhard used to take refuge here from literary hoi polloi. A visit to Café Sacher today usually involves a lengthy queue (although the winter months are less busy). The café's world famous *Sachertorte* is available in a variety of formats from the hotel shop.

Café Schwarzenberg

1, Kärntner Ring 17 (512 89 98). Tram 1, 2, D. **Open** 7am-midnight Mon-Fri, Sun; 9am-midnight Sat. **Melange** €3.40. **Credit** AmEx, DC, MC, V. **Map** p251 E8 ㉕
Another victim of excessive coffee house renovation. The pompous pseudo-belle époque interior, with mirrors gleaming from every wall, is certainly very eye-catching, but once you're inside, the tuxedoed waiters who condescendingly serve your coffee and appear to assume generous tips soon remove the shine.

Café Weinwurm

1, Stephansplatz 11 (533 9531/www.cafe-weinwurm.com). U1, U3 Stephansplatz. **Open** 7am-midnight Mon-Fri; 8am-midnight Sat, Sun. **Melange** €3. **No credit cards**. **Map** p251 E6 ㉖
Undoubtedly the most fashionable locale on Stephansplatz, Weinwurm is great for both daytime coffee and snacks, and a late, restorative goulash or Schnitzel. Clad in a glinting pastel swimming pool mosaic with comfy leather seating, it has one of the city's longest bars. **Photo** *p137*.

Demel

1, Kohlmarkt 14 (535 1717-1/www.demel.at). U3 Herrengasse/bus 2a. **Open** 10am-7pm daily. **Melange** €3.80. **Credit** AmEx, DC, MC, V. **Map** p250 E6 ⑰
This 200-year-old former k.u.k. (*kaiserlich und königlich* – imperial and royal) bakery has a magnificent choice of cakes and biscuits, and steep prices to match. More a *Konditorei* (pâtisserie) than a Kaffeehaus, its grandiose interior is sickly sweet, with a more modern glassed-over patio at the back. A hot chocolate here is a must, as is the *Sachertorte*. Demel and Sacher (*see below* **Cake wars**) claim to be the only bakeries in possession of the real recipe. A great place to buy trad Viennese confectionery in gorgeous period-piece boxes, many with Jugendstil designs, Demel also has the most wonderful window displays.

Diglas

1, Wollzeile 10 (512 57 65/www.diglas.at). U1, U3 Stephansplatz/bus 1a. **Open** 7am-midnight daily. **Melange** €3.30. **Credit** AmEx, DC, MC, V. **Map** p250 F6/7 ⑱

Plush red velvet booths give this Biedermeier café an air of intimacy. No surprise, then, that Viennese grandes dames reputedly come here to discuss their infidelities. Renowned for its coffee menu and good selection of teas served in bird-bath cups, Diglas offers some of the best cakes in town and possibly the best *Apfelstrudel* going. German speakers may be able to fathom the *Wiener Schmäh* (Viennese ironic, occasionally biting, always charming humour); the waiters here ooze it.

Do&Co Albertina

1, Albertinaplatz 1 (532 96 69/www.doco.com). U1, U2, U4 Karlsplatz/tram 1, 2, D, J. **Open** 9am-midnight daily. **Melange** €3.20. **Credit** AmEx, DC, MC, V. **Map** p250 E7 ⑲
The principal attraction of this new café-restaurant on the ramparts of the Albertina is the view of the Burggarten and Neue Burg. Inside, the styling is sleek and the onyx opulent, but the excellent breakfasts and lunches are nevertheless affordable.

Kleines Café

1, Franziskanerplatz 3 (no phone). U1, U3 Stephansplatz. **Open** 10am-2am daily. **Melange** €2.90. **No credit cards**. **Map** p251 E7 ⑳
As the name suggests, this place is tiny, though architect Hermann Czech's design makes great use

Cake wars

In 2007, Vienna's most universal sponge cake celebrates its 175th birthday. This heavy-duty chocolate cake with an apricot jam filling was first concocted in 1832 by Franz Sacher, a 16-year-old pastry cook apprenticed to Count Metternich. His son Eduard went on to open the illustrious Sacher Hotel, and patent the cake's secret recipe. The intrigue began in 1930 after the demise of Anna Sacher, the charismatic owner of the hotel, when her son defected to former royal pâtissiers Demel and negotiated the concession of the cake's exclusive rights to Demel. Decades of legal action ensued in which Vienna's lawyers grew fat debating whether the real *Sachertorte* had one or two layers of apricot jam or whether the use of margarine was permissible or not. In 1965, an agreement was reached whereby the hotel would retain the 'Original *Sachertorte*' brand and the baker's trade under the name 'Demel's *Sachertorte*' that persists until this very day. The essential difference between the two is that the Demel version has the jam directly beneath the chocolate glaze instead of in the middle.

Eat, Drink, Shop

of mirrors. Customers, and indeed staff, are an eccentric mix of arty-intellectual, proto-Bohemian types. More a boozer than a coffee house, in truth.

Operncafé Hartauer Zum Peter'

1, Riemergasse 9 (512 8981). U3 Stubentor/tram 1, 2. **Open** 8am-5pm Mon-Fri; 5pm-2am Sat. **Melange** €2.80. **No credit cards. Map** p251 F7 ㉑
A camp spot for opera lovers. Photos of opera stars, immortal and up-and-coming, adorn this quirky late-night Jugendstil café.

Urania

1, Uraniastrasse 1 (713 3066/www.barurania.com). Trams 1, 2, N. **Open** 9am-2am Mon-Sat; 9am-midnight Sun. **Melange** €2.90. **Credit** AmEx, DC, MC, V. **Map** p251 F6 ㉒
Following the renovation of the old Urania observatory in 2003, this sleek, modern café was discreetly slotted into the canal-facing side of the building. It mutates between breakfast club, lunch spot and boozer; the big plus is the raised terrace overlooking the Danube canal, with the Prater ferris wheel in the distance.

2nd district

Café Sperlhof

2, Grosse Sperlgasse 41 (2145864). Tram N, 21. **Open** midday-1am Mon-Fri; 10am-1am Sat, Sun. **Melange** €2.60. **No credit cards. Map** p243 F5 ㉓

The Sperlhof is a mix of fading coffee house and an Aladdin's Cave piled high with board games, books, an aquarium and a display cabinet full of sweets and chocs. Regulars of all ages play billiards on the three fine tables in the alcove or hunch up over their chessboards. It's so authentically retro that you can even pay for your drinks with Austrian shillings.

4th district

Café Do-An

4, Naschmarkt, Stand 412 (586 4715). U4 Kettenbrückengasse. **Open** 7am-midnight Mon-Sat. **Melange** €2.20. **No credit cards. Map** p247 D8 ㉔
Adored by Vienna's bourgeois Bohemians, the Do-An does wicked Illy coffee, great salads and sandwiches and superb Kremser beer, all in a fishtank location in the Naschmarkt. Getting a table, inside or out, is a matter of luck.

Café Goldegg

4, Argentinierstrasse, 49 (505 9162). Tram D. **Open** 8am-9pm Mon-Thur; 8am-8pm Fri; 8am-midday Sat. **Melange** €2.60. **No credit cards. Map** p247 F10 ㉕
This tranquil period café is your best bet after a visit to the Belvedere. Located in a sleepy corner of the 4th district, the Goldegg is a classic Viennese establishment, complete with plush seating, marble tables, lines of potted sansevieria, billiards and mirrors aplenty. It does a fine *Goulaschsuppe* too. **Photo** *p138.*

All that a proper Viennese coffee house should be. **Café Westend**.

Eine Melange, bitte

Ordering a coffee in Vienna is a potential minefield. These are some of the many varieties on offer:

Biedermeier *Grosser Brauner* with a shot of Biedermeier liqueur (an apricot flavoured eggnog).

Café Maria Theresia with orange liqueur and a dash of whipped cream.

Cappuccino confusing. Unlike the Italian version, Viennese cappuccino has whipped cream on top.

Einspänner a *Schwarzer* (black coffee) served in a long glass with whipped cream.

Fiaker Austrian-German for the horse and carriage you can take around town. The coffee is a *Verlängerter* with rum and whipped cream.

Franziskaner made with hot milk and a topping of whipped cream.

Grosser Brauner a coffee with a dash of milk.

Kleiner Brauner comes in a smaller cup.

Grosser/Kleiner Mocca/Schwarzer a large or small espresso.

Kaffee verkehrt more milk than coffee.

Kaisermelange with an egg yolk and brandy.

Kapuziner a *Schwarzer* with a shot of cream.

Mazagran cold coffee with rum and ice. To be downed in one go.

Melange most people's favourite; a milky coffee served with milk foam on top (like an Italian cappuccino).

Milchkaffee milkier than a *Melange*.

Pharisäer strong black coffee with whipped cream on top, served with a glass of rum.

Türkischer Kaffee served with grounds and sugar in a copper pouring pot.

Verlängerter Brauner like the *Brauner*, but with a little more water in the coffee.

Verlängerter Schwarzer a watered-down *Schwarzer* (black coffee).

5th district

Café Rüdigerhof

5, Hamburgerstrasse 20 (586 3138). U4 Pilgramgasse/bus 13a, 14a. **Open** 9am-2am daily. Melange €2.50. **No credit cards. Map** p247 D9 ㉖
Located in a magnificently restored Jugendstil building, this café features in Nic Roeg's disturbing 1970s movie *Bad Timing*. Inside it's a veritable museum of retro fittings, including some especially wacky 1950s fluorescent lamps and furnishings that previously adorned King Hussein of Jordan's Vienna home. In summer, there's a pleasant ramshackle terrace. Small eats are available, but most people come for a draught Budweiser or a coffee.

6th district

Café Jelinek

6, Otto-Bauer-Gasse 5 (597 4113). U3 Zieglergasse. **Open** 9am-9pm daily. **Melange** €2.80. **No credit cards. Map** p246 C9 ㉗
With its ramshackle furniture and open fire, this quiet coffee house is perfect for intense conversations or solitary musing. Now run by the folk from the neighbouring Steman restaurant, it has been mercifully left just as it was – slow, a bit tatty and atmospheric.

Café Kafka

6, Capistrangasse 8 (586 1317). U2 Museumsquartier. **Open** 8am-midnight Mon-Sat; 2-9pm Sun. **Melange** €2.50. **No credit cards. Map** p250 D8 ㉘
The forebodingly named Café Kafka is in fact a cosy, nicotine-aged nook just off Mariahilfer Strasse.

Dishevelled yet authentically Viennese (the requisite chandelier, large tarnished mirror and woodburning stove are all present and correct) this café offers Asian vegetable dishes at lunch, as well as great coffee and select Austrian wines. Labyrinth, Vienna's English language poetry group, holds its regular open-mic sessions here.

Café Sperl

6, Gumpendorfer Strasse 11 (586 4158). Bus 57a. **Open** 7am-11pm Mon-Sat; 11am-8pm Sun. **Melange** €3.20. **Credit** AmEx, DC, MC, V. **Map** p250 D8 ㉙
The apotheosis of the Viennese Kaffeehaus, the Sperl's faded grandeur is today surprisingly cosy despite its awesome dimensions. The Sperl plays the role of Kaffeehaus in more films than any other. It has managed to retain an atmosphere of stately silence, in part due to a ban on mobile phones. Most Viennese have a soft spot for the Sperl, with its tuxedoed grumpy waiters and mousy waitresses, velvet booths and expansive windows. It also has two billiard tables. Approach the own-made cake display with care: it's uncovered.

7th district

Café Westend

7, Mariahilfer Strasse 128 (523 3183). U3, U6 Westbahnhof. **Open** 7am-midnight daily. **Melange** €2.90. **Credit** DC, MC, V. **Map** p246 B9 ㉚
Conveniently located opposite the Westbahnhof, this café provides new arrivals in town with everything that is authentic in a proper Viennese coffee house – somewhat grubby-looking stucco, marble-topped

Eat, Drink, Shop

marble-topped tables, and generous portions of strudel and chocolate cake from ancient display cabinets all await the customer. And to cap it all, the coffee is very good and, in one departure from the traditional coffee house we wholeheartedly welcome, the waiters are uncommonly friendly.

Espresso

7, Burggasse 57 (526 89 51). Bus 13a, 48a. **Open** 7.30am-1am Mon-Fri; 10pm-1am Sat, Sun. **Melange** €2.50. **No credit cards. Map** p246 C7 ③

This lovingly renovated 1950s espresso bar is a big favourite both for coffees and cocktails. From the espresso machine to the wall hangings, the place exudes an eye for detail; the red leather benches are both comfortable to park one's posterior on and a joy to behold. There's always great music playing and the evenings feature the odd DJ night such as Espresso Sabroso, a great Latin soul session (second and last Thursday of the month).

8th district

Café Eiles

8, Josefstädter Strasse 2 (405 3410). U2 Rathaus/tram J. **Open** 8am-10pm daily. **Melange** €2.80. **Credit** AmEx, MC, V. **Map** p250 C6 ③

A favourite haunt for lawyers and politicians because of its proximity to the Parliament and Rathaus, Eiles is also a practical stop for tourists before taking on the delights of Vienna's 8th district. It has booths and high tables and serves a hearty Viennese breakfast from 8am to 11.30am.

Café Florianihof

8, Florianigasse 45 (402 4842/www.florianihof.at). Tram 5, 43, J. **Open** 8am-midnight Mon-Fri; 10am-8pm Sat, Sun. **Melange** €2.70. **Credit** DC, MC, V. **Map** p246 C6 ③

You won't find a more lovingly preserved turn-of-the-century café in all Vienna. With its Jugendstil cream panelling, aged parquet floor and long curved bar, the Florianihof is nevertheless one of the few Viennese coffee houses with a contemporary feel. All right, they occasionally mess it up by hanging gaudy, suspect art, but all in all, the drinks are great, the breakfasts divine, the clientele attractive and the service attentive. What more could you want?

Café-Restaurant Hummel

8, Josefstädter Strasse 66 (405 5314/www.cafe hummel.at). Tram 5, 33, J. **Open** 7am-midnight Mon-Fri; 8am-midnight Sat, Sun. **Melange** €2.70. **Credit** AmEx, DC, MC, V. **Map** p246 B6 ③

This bustling bar/restaurant/coffee house is the life and soul of the Josefstadt district. Despite its undistinguished decor and really rather pedestrian menu, children with their fathers, students and scribblers, Powerbook posers and octogenarian card players all seem to adore the place and treat it as a second home. The suited waiters are a gruff yet diplomatic bunch and the interior and summer terrace make great locations for an afternoon of people-watching.

13th district

Café Dommayer

13, Auhofstrasse 2 (877 5465/www.dommayer.at). U4 Hietzing. **Open** 7am-10pm daily. **Melange** €3.50. **Credit** AmEx, DC, MC, V.

Café Dommayer is one of the city's best-known traditional Kaffeehäuser, and is just a stone's throw from the Palace of Schönbrunn. Johann Strauss Junior made his debut here in 1844. The restaurant has a huge garden where different theatre companies perform on the third Sunday of the month, from May through to September. Strauss concerts by the Vienna Strauss Ensemble are held all year (2-4pm Sat). The café holds a Christmas market in its garden in December.

Café Gloriette

13, Gloriette, Schönbrunn Schlosspark (879 1311/ www.gloriette-cafe.at). U4 Schloss Schönbrunn. **Open** *Summer* 9am-8pm daily. *Winter* 9am-5pm daily. **Melange** €3.30. **Credit** AmEx, DC, MC, V.

Although beautifully situated high up on the hill overlooking Schönbrunn, this café is little more than an unimaginative slice of wedding cake housed in the Gloriette, an impressive neo-classical arcade erected in 1775 during the reign of Maria Theresia. The view is the café's redeeming feature, so book ahead to make sure you secure a window table.

16th district

Café Club International

16, Payergasse 14 (403 1827). U6 Josefstädter Strasse. **Open** 8am-2pm Mon-Sat; 10am-2am Sun. **Melange** €2. **No credit cards. Map** p246 A6 ③

Part of a local initiative to better integrate the Ottakring district's various immigrant communities into Austrian society through housing advice and language courses, Club International runs a cheerful little café with the sunniest terrace on Yppenplatz. It's particularly worth a visit here on Saturdays, when the nearby Turkish/Balkan-flavoured Brunnenmarkt (*see p151*) is accompanied by an excellent farmers' market selling flowers, vegetables, wine and other country produce.

Café Weidinger

16, Lerchenfelder Gürtel 1 (492 0906). U6 Burggasse. **Open** 7am-1am Mon-Fri; 7.30am-12.30am Sat, Sun. **Melange** €2. **No credit cards. Map** p246 A7 ③

With its threadbare upholstery and nicotine-stained ceilings, the roomy L-shaped Café Weidinger is one of those Viennese establishments that used to occupy every major junction in the city. Today, the majority have been turned into betting shops, so it's worth doing your bit to preserve them. Here the clientele is a pleasant mixture of switched-on slackers and tubby early-retired males who drop in for a coffee or a beer and a game of cards or billiards. The green baize and ageing wood-panelling are magnificently lit by a line of suspended white globes.

Shops & Services

Big designer names, bespoke establishments, kooky independent boutiques and bric-a-brac galore: shopping in Vienna is a serendipitous experience.

Ten years ago, shopping in Vienna was a very low-key affair, confined to the Innere Stadt and one or two outer streets such as Mariahilfer Strasse. Once the big Swedish, Italian and Spanish clothing chains arrived in the 1990s, the city got a taste of international retailing and it wasn't long before the high-end designer names followed. These cluster on Kohlmarkt and other 1st district streets, edging out the traditional establishments, many of which dated from the days of the empire. You still occasionally spot the royal 'k.u.k.' (*kaiserlich und königlich*) warrant on the odd jeweller or pâtisserie, and small stores specialising in gloves, brushes, hats and bench-made shoes, but franchise fever is gradually signing their death warrant.

Nevertheless Vienna hasn't been swamped by global uniformity. Part of the attraction is the city's magnificently appointed shop premises that make the most banal goods look inspiring. This is also the case outside the centre, particularly in districts 6 and 7, where a new generation of shopkeepers is putting Vienna's historic retail infrastructure to great use.

What's more, if you enjoy a junk shop, Vienna is an absolute paradise. When you're done with the exuberant Saturday flea market, you'll find bric-a-brac emporia throughout the city, particularly around the **Naschmarkt**. Much of the stuff they sell is the legacy of the fine craft tradition that flourished here under the patronage of Vienna's enlightened fin de siècle bourgeoisie. If lady luck is smiling, you may unearth a lamp or ceramics by the Wiener Werkstätte (*see p94* **Waltz on**) – but it's much easier to pick up a repro from shops such as **Woka** or **Backhausen**.

Another thing to bear in mind is that Austria's reputation for being on the pricey side is a bit of a myth. As capital cities go, Vienna is a bargain, especially for eating, drinking and buying clothes. Opening hours, once very restricted with half-day Saturdays, have loosened up a lot: several supermarkets and, increasingly, small bakers open on Sundays and public holidays. More widespread Sunday opening can't be far off. Most shops are open 9am to 6pm or 7pm on weekdays, and 9am to 5pm or 6pm on Saturday – with busy streets staying open later.

The best Shops

For crocks, pots and vases with a sense of humour
no nonsens. *See p156.*

For sensualists looking for something different
Saint Charles Apothecary. *See p154.*

For retro rats
Eselmist. *See p147.*

For keeping your conscience clear
gabarage_upcycling design. *See p155.*

For dressing up like a proper Austrian
Trachten Tostmann. *See p147.*

For a quiet browse
Phil. *See p155.*

General

Malls

Generali Center
6, Mariahilfer Strasse 77 (586 30 24/www.generali center.at). U3 Neubaugasse. **Open** 10am-7pm Mon-Fri; 10am-6pm Sat. **Credit** varies. **Map** p246 C8.
A two-storey shopping centre with a big supermarket in the basement, Generali is home to a Nike store, fashion outlets and oddities such as a kite shop.

Gerngross
7, Mariahilfer Strasse 42-48 (52180-0). U3 Neubaugasse/bus 13a. **Open** 9.30am-7pm Mon-Wed; 9am-8pm Thur; 9am-7pm Fri; 9.30am-6pm Sat. **Credit** varies. **Map** p246 C8.
A five-floor complex of various franchises, including a massive branch of electrical goods and CD/DVD retailer Saturn, a two-storey Zara and an excellent Merkur supermarket (in the basement) with direct access to the U3 Neubaugasse station. The rooftop terrace has various gastronomic options and tremendous views over the city.

Mühlbauer. *See p146.*

Ringstrassen Galerien

1, Kärntner Ring 5-7, 9-13 (512 51 81/www.
ringstrassen-galerien.at). U1, U2, U4 Karlsplatz/
tram 1, 2, D, J/bus 3a. **Open** 10am-7pm Mon-Fri;
10am-6pm Sat. **Credit** varies. **Map** p251 E8.
A squeaky-clean, central shopping and office complex on three floors. Fashion outlets dominate, but
the basements hold the best Billa supermarket in
town and a large Interio, Vienna's Habitat.

Steffl

1, Kärntner Strasse 19 (514 31-0/www.kaufhaus-
steffl.at). U1, U3 Stephansplatz. **Open** 9.30am-7pm
Mon-Fri; 9.30am-6pm Sat. **Credit** AmEx, DC, MC, V.
Map p251 E7.
This franchise forum has cosmetics, bags and pre-
dictable designer names for men and women; the
basement is taken up with young fashion labels. On
the top floor is the Skybar, a classy watering hole
with a great view of the Stephansdom.

Markets

See p155 for flea markets and p151 for
food markets.

Specialist

Books & magazines

English-language

British Bookshop

1, Weihburggasse 24 (512 1945/www.britishbook
shop.at). U3 Stubentor/tram 1, 2. **Open** 9.30am-
6.30pm Mon-Fri; 9.30am-6pm Sat. **Credit** AmEx,
DC, MC, V. **Map** p251 E/F7.
British Bookshop, as you might in part guess, is an
English-language shop associated with Blackwell's,
with stacks of novels, history and Viennesia. It's also
the best EFL shop – teachers ply their trade on the
noticeboard at the back.
Other locations 6, Mariahilfer Strasse 4 (522 6730).

Shakespeare & Co

1, Sterngasse 2 (535 5053/www.shakespeare-
company.biz). U1, U4 Schwedenplatz. **Open**
9am-7pm Mon-Sat. **Credit** AmEx, DC, MC, V.
Map p251 E6.
This tiny shop is Vienna's most reliable for literature and academic titles in English. Shakespeare is
great on contemporary and classic literature, with a
good selection of fine arts and music, sociology and
Vienna-related themes on ceiling-high shelves.

General

Babette's

4, Schleifmühlgasse 17 (585 5165/www.babettes.at).
U1, U2, U4 Karlsplatz. **Open** 10am-7pm Mon-Fri;
10am-5pm Sat. **Credit** MC, V. **Map** p247 D/E8.

Babette's has recipe books from all over the world (a large number of them in English), as well as a cosy little café at the back, where you can sit and enjoy the dish of the day or a speciality coffee while watching more dishes being prepared and cakes being baked. The staff also sell a huge range of herbs and spices and organise cookery courses.

Freytag & Berndt

1, Kohlmarkt 9 (533 8685/www.freytagberndt.at). *U3 Herrengasse.* **Open** 9am-7pm Mon-Fri; 9am-6pm Sat. **Credit** AmEx, DC, MC, V. **Map** p250 E6/7.
If your bag is large, don't miss the chance to visit this fine store located in Max Fabiani's Jugendstil Artariahaus. There are excellent maps of the Wienerwald, plus travel and cookery books.

Prachner im MQ

7, Museumsplatz 1 (512 85880/www.prachner.at). *U2, U3 Volkstheater.* **Open** 10am-7pm Mon-Sat; 1-7pm Sun. **Credit** MC, V. **Map** p250 D7.
'We read our books' is Prachner's motto. In the expansive, circular space, tables are loaded with sexy art and design titles, the mainstay of this branch. It also stocks plenty of books on Vienna.

Specialist

Comic-Treff Steiner

6, Barnabitengasse 12 (586 7627). U3 Neubaugasse. **Open** 10am-7pm Mon-Fri; 10am-2pm Sat. **Credit** V. **Map** p246 C8.
The best comic book emporium in Vienna, run by helpful, clued-up English speakers. It has a decent line in quirky American productions, and is good on peripheral items, from the Simpsons and manga merchandising to *Hello Kitty*.

Children

Fashion

Herr & Frau Klein

7, Kirchengasse 22 (990 4394/www.herrundfrau klein.com). U3 Neubaugasse/bus 13a. **Open** 11am-6pm Tue-Fri; 11am-4pm Sat. **Credit** MC, V. **Map** p250 C8.
Typical of the chic new stores mushrooming in the 7th district, Mr and Mrs Klein has lovely children's clothes, baby accessories and a good selection of toys. It is also guaranteed 'teddy bear-free'.

Toys

Imaginarium

1, Neuer Markt 8a (513 1342/www.imaginarium. *info). U1, U2, U4 Karlsplatz.* **Open** 10am-7pm Mon-Fri; 10am-6pm Sat. **Credit** MC, V. **Map** p250 E7.
The excellent Spanish toy chain has opened its first Vienna shop stocking interesting, robust toys with an educational angle. Showing the store's usual attention to detail, there's a tiny separate entrance for children that the little mites adore.

Kindergalerie Sonnenschein

7, Neubaugasse 53 (524 1766). U3 Neubaugasse. **Open** 10am-6.30pm Mon-Fri; 10am-5pm Sat. **Credit** AmEx, DC, MC, V. **Map** p246 C8.
Kindergalerie Sonnenschein sells stuffed toys, puppets and cushions for babies and children of all ages, and some lovely wooden toys.

Spielzeugschachtel

1, Rauhensteingasse 5 (512 44 94/www. *spielzeugschachtel.com). U1 Stephansplatz.* **Open** 10am-6.30pm Mon-Fri; 10am-5pm Sat. **Credit** AmEx, DC, MC, V. **Map** p251 E7.
A toy shop for demanding parents and those children not willing to settle for computer world. You won't find much plastic here, but a wide range of creative and educational toys for children of all ages.

Electronics & photography

Cameras

Leica Shop

7, Westbahnstrasse 40 (523 5659/www.leicashop. *com). Tram 49.* **Open** 10am-6pm Mon-Fri. **Credit** AmEx, DC, JCB, MC, V. **Map** p246 B/C8
The only independent company authorised to use the hallowed brand name, Vienna's Leica Shop has an astounding selection of this and other makes, and exports worldwide. It is also associated with the Westlicht gallery in the courtyard that has a permanent exhibition of classic Leicas and regular photography shows (www.westlicht.com).

Photobörse

8, Lerchenfelder Strasse 62-64 (961 0964/ *www.photoboerse.at). Tram 46.* **Open** 10am-7pm Mon-Fri; 10am-2pm Sat. **Credit** AmEx, DC, MC, V. **Map** p246 B/C7.
Vast selection of new and second-hand cameras as well as trade-in possibilities. It also provides developing and other photo-related services.

Computers

Der Computer Doktor

18, Gentzgasse 9 (470 7005/0650-946 2121/ *www.computerdoktor.at). U6 Volksoper/tram 40,41/* *bus 40a.* **Open** 9.30am-11.45pm, 2.30-6pm Mon-Fri. **No credit cards**. **Map** p242 C3/4.
The good computer doctor will repair your PC, Notebook or flatscreen monitor, but call in advance to book a slot. You can also phone the technical hotline on 0900 56 0201 during the same opening hours, but beware of the high call charges if you use this service. English is spoken.

McShark Multimedia

5, Schönbrunner Strasse 71 (587 87 80/www. *mcshark.at). U4 Pilgramgasse.* **Open** 10am-6pm Mon-Fri; 10am-3pm Sat. **Credit** MC (not for Apple machines). **Map** p246 B/C10.
The place to call for Apple queries.

Eat, Drink, Shop

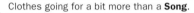
Clothes going for a bit more than a **Song**.

Fashion

Mainstream and big-name designer fashion is available on the Mariahilfer Strasse and the Innere Stadt. For more innovative clothes and accessories, head for the boutiques of districts 6 and 7, where the work of up-and-coming local designers such as Wendy & Jim (www.wujsympathisant.com) and fabrics interseason (www.fabrics.at) occasionally surface. One foible seen in few other European countries is a fondness for traditional peasant garb, or *Trachten*. Even in Vienna lots of people wear the traditional round-collared woollen jackets, and a few even appear in lederhosen or dirndl pinafores (*see p147* Trachten Tostmann).

General

Chegini Check-Out

1, Kohlmarkt 4 (courtyard) (535 6091). U3 Herrengasse. **Open** 10am-6.15pm Mon-Fri; 10am-5pm Sat. **Credit** AmEx, DC, MC, V. **Map** p250 E6.
Hidden in a courtyard off Kohlmarkt, this is the discount outlet of Vienna's historic snooty designer boutique Chegini.
Other locations 1, Plankengasse 4 (512 2231); 1, Kohlmarkt 7 (533 2058).

Frontline

6, Mariahilfer Strasse 77 (Generali Center) (586 3068/www.frontline.at). U3 Neubaugasse. **Open** 10am-7pm Mon-Fri; 10am-6pm Sat. **Credit** AmEx, DC, MC, V. **Map** p246 C8.
Vienna's best address for hoodies, Hawaiian shirts and the full Carhartt range. Frontline also stocks T-shirts with great prints by London firm Grade.

2006FEB01

1, Plankengasse 6 (513 4222). U1, U3 Stephansplatz. **Open** 10am-6.30pm Mon-Fri; 10am-5pm Sat. **Credit** AmEx, DC, MC, V. **Map** p250 E7.
The firm that took over Helmut Lang's old Vienna store at nearby Seilergasse no.6 moved into these chic new premises last year (hence the silly name). 2006 trade in pricey men and women's designer ware that ranges from sturdy Aquascutum and Burberry to more challenging garments by the likes of Alexander McQueen, Veronique Branquinho and Viktor&Rolf.

Modus Vivendi

6, Schadekgasse 4 (587 2823/www.modus-vivendi.at). U3 Neubaugasse. **Open** 11am-7pm Mon-Fri; noon-5pm Sat. **Credit** DC, MC, V. **Map** p246 C8.
Gorgeous, elegant knitwear and tailoring for men and women, both off the peg and made to measure.

Nachbarin

6, Gumpendorfer Strasse 17 (587 2169/www.nachbarin.co.at). Bus 57a. **Open** noon-6.30pm Mon; 11am-6.30pm Tue-Fri; 11am-4pm Sat. **Credit** AmEx, DC, MC, V. **Map** p250 D8
This über-cool clothing and accessories store lies at the trendy end of the Gumpendorfer Strasse and stocks what they call 'European fashion design'. The roster currently includes Londoners PREEN, Belgian designer Veronique Leroy and Austrians such as the Flor de Ilusion label. It is also one of the few places in Vienna where you'll find Florian Ladstätter's globally acclaimed jewellery.

Mühlbauer

1, Seilergasse 10 (512 2241/www.muehlbauer.at). U1, U3 Stephansplatz. **Open** 10am-6.30pm Mon-Fri; 10am-6pm Sat. **Credit** AmEx, DC, MC, V. **Map** p250 E7.

The playthings of an emperor: **Tiberius**.

Klaus Mühlbauer is the latest figure in a long line of Viennese milliners. In late 2005, he opened this showcase for the pillboxes and felt pork pies in stunning colours that put him on an international footing. The firm has now branched out into street wear with another sleek outlet opposite that stocks Smedley and Japanese jeans from Edwin. **Photo** *p144*.

Park

7, Mondscheingasse 20 (526 4414/www.park.co.at). *U3 Neubaugasse.* **Open** 10am-7pm Mon-Fri; 10am-6pm Sat. **Credit** AmEx, DC, MC, V. **Map** p246 C8.
Park mashes up off-the-wall designer wear from established Belgians such as Ann Demeulmeester and Raf Simons with classic Fred Perry and T-shirts by 2K Park. They now also feature local heroes such as Wendy&Jim and Fabrics Interseason, previously unavailable in Vienna. Laid out on two vast gleaming white floors, Park operates as a semi-concept store with shoes, scents, repro Eames chairs and a rotating selection of art books also on sale. A bit ambitious for Vienna, but it's now in its third year.

Song

2, Praterstrasse 11-13 (532 2858/www.song.at). *U1 Nestroyplatz.* **Open** 10am-7pm Mon-Fri; 10am-6pm Sat. **Credit** AmEx, DC, MC, V. **Map** p245 F6.
Daringly located in the distinctly unfashionable 2nd district, this former warehouse shows off all manner of desirable garb by Antwerp's and Tokyo's finest. Of the former, Martin Margiela for men and women features prominently, as does Comme des Garcons and its Play and TAO lines.

Tiberius

7, Lindengasse 2 (522 0474/www.tiberius.at). *U3 Neubaugasse/tram 49.* **Open** noon-7pm Mon-Fri; 11am-6pm Sat. **Credit** AmEx, DC, MC, V. **Map** p246 C8.

Vienna's foremost address for leather, rubber and S&M requisites offers a huge selection of accessories. The shop has had a superb facelift from the design team behind Fabios, BEHF.

Trachten Tostmann

1, Schottengasse 3a (533 5331/www.tostmann.at). *U3 Herrengasse.* **Open** 10am-6pm Mon-Fri; 9.30am-6pm Sat. **Credit** AmEx, DC, MC, V. **Map** p250 E7.
Gerti Tostmann is Vienna's *tracht* guru. Author of numerous books on the origins and varieties of trad Austrian clothing, her shop near Schottentor stocks the best of Loden and other fine cloths. In the building's cellar she has assembled a museum on the genre, which she gladly opens to interested parties, and she will regale you with a variety of anecdotes in thickly accented English.

Used & vintage

Districts 6 and 7 are best for second-hand clothing; try Neubaugasse in the 7th district.

Eselmist

7, Burggasse 89 (524 1523). U6 Burggasse/bus 49a. **Open** 10.30am-7pm Mon-Fri; 10.30am-5pm Sat. **Credit** MC, V. **Map** p246 B7
For over two years, local cool hunters have patronised this treasure trove of vintage clothing from all over Europe. Bizarre headgear, boots and shoes, Eastern-bloc chic T-shirts and lots of leathers from owner Josef's Hungarian homeland are among the wares. Why he decided to call his shop 'donkey shit' is anyone's guess.

Flo Nostalgische Mode

4, Schleifmühlgasse 15a (586 0773). U1, U2, U4 Karlsplatz/bus 59a. **Open** 10am-6.30pm Mon-Fri; 10am-3pm Sat. **Credit** DC, MC, V. **Map** p247 D8.

Ingrid Raab has been selling vintage clothes in Vienna for 25 years and claims she introduced the expression to Austria. As well as catering to retro-fashion fans, she kits out actors in television, film and stage shows in clothes from 1880 to 1980.

Polyklamott

6, Hofmühlgasse 6 (969 0337/www.polyklamott.at). U4 Pilgramgasse/bus 13a, 14a. **Open** 11am-7.30pm Mon-Fri; 11am-5pm Sat. **Credit** AmEx, DC, MC, V. **Map** p246 C9.

Visitors will find here lots of 1970s clothing neatly displayed in a cool, laid-back atmosphere, plus a smattering of vintage Warsaw Pact items and the shop's own-brand stripy holdalls.

Fashion accessories & services

Jewellery

Galerie Slavik

1, Himmelpfortgasse 17 (513 4812/www.galerie-slavik.com). U1, U3 Stephansplatz. **Open** 10am-1pm, 2-6pm Tue-Fri; 10am-5pm Sat. **Credit** AmEx, DC, MC, V. **Map** p251 E7.

Galerie Slavik shows off the work of international jewellery designers in bizarre glass vitrines that hang from the ceiling. Prices range from around €100 for young designers up to stratospheric sums.

Kaufhaus Schiepek

1, Teinfaltstrasse 3 (533 1575). U2 Schottentor/tram 1, 2, D. **Open** 10.30am-6.30pm Mon-Fri; 10am-5pm Sat. **Credit** AmEx, DC, MC, V. **Map** p250 D6.

Kaufhaus Schiepek sells brightly coloured jewellery, gorgeous little bags and purses, plus lots of cheap and cheerful kitsch items, much of which originally came from Mexico. It's also worth crossing the road to the sister store, Shipping, at no.4 which has an array of brightly coloured Far Eastern melamine plates, bowls and ashtrays.

Lila Pix

7, Lindengasse 5 (990 4351/www.lilapix.net). U3 Neubaugasse/tram 49. **Open** noon-7pm Wed-Fri; 11am-5pm Sat. **Credit** AmEx, DC, MC, V. **Map** p246 C8.

Bulgarians Nik and Lili make memorable jewellery and accessories from fine materials in very limited editions, then sell them from this stylish little store. Scarves, bags and belts, informed by the same design sense, are also all available.

Swarovski

1, Kärntner Strasse 8 (512 903233/www.swarovski. com). U1, U3 Stephansplatz. **Open** 10am-7pm Mon-Fri; 10am-6pm Sat. **Credit** AmEx, DC, MC, V. **Map** p251 E7.

Tyrolean glass-animal maker Swarovski is one of Austria's biggest exporters. The Vienna flagship store also stocks the crystal jewellery and bags that Madonna et al have made fashionable.

Wiener Interieur

1, Dorotheergasse 14 (512 2898). U1, U3 Stephansplatz. **Open** 10am-1pm, 2.30-6pm Mon-Fri; 10am-1pm Sat. **Credit** AmEx, DC, MC, V. **Map** p250 E7.

Dorotheergasse and environs are full of antique jewellers. This small establishment deals in art nouveau, art deco and 1950s costume jewellery.

Agent Provocateur.

Laundry & dry cleaning

Bendix Laundrette

7, Siebensterngasse 52 (523 2553). Tram 49/bus 13a. **Open** 8am-5pm Mon, Tue, Thur. **No credit cards. Map** p250 C8.
Self-service or service wash – a load costs €15.

Hartmann

1, Jasimirogottstrasse 6 (533 1584/www.textilpflege-hartmann.at). U1, U3 Stephansplatz. **Open** 9am-6pm Mon-Fri. **Credit** DC, MC, V. **Map** p251 E6.
A reliable, centrally located dry cleaners.
Other locations 6, Linke Wienzeile 164 (597 0208).

Lingerie

Agent Provocateur

1, Tuchlauben 14 (890 4192). U1, U3 Stephansplatz. **Open** 10am-6.30pm Mon-Fri; 10am-6pm Sat. **Credit** DC, MC, V. **Map** p239 E6
The arrival of AP in 2006 was good news for local lingerie buffs. Its gorgeous interior, fetching sales staff and natty window dressing also show the city's retailers what a shop should look like.

Palmers

1, Kärntner Strasse 53-55 (512 5772/www. palmers.at). U1, U3 Stephansplatz. **Open** 9.30am-6.30pm Mon-Fri; 9.30am-5pm Sat. **Credit** AmEx, DC, MC, V. **Map** p251 E7.
Palmers, Austria's number one underwear manufacturer and retailer, runs a high-profile billboard advertising campaigns and its images of scantily clad models are everywhere. The Palmers shops sell everything from thermals to basques.
Other locations throughout the city.

Rositta

1, Kärntner Strasse 17 (512 4604/www.rositta.at). U1, U3 Stephansplatz. **Open** 10am-6.30pm Mon-Fri; 10am-5.30pm Sat. **Credit** AmEx, DC, MC, V. **Map** p251 E7.
Vienna is full of little designer lingerie boutiques, and Rositta is one of the nicest, selling nighties and slips as well as bras and knickers. The staff are a bit starchy, but it's worth it for the La Perla undies.

Wolford

1, Gonzagagasse 11 (535 99000/www.wolford.at). U2, U4 Schottenring. **Open** 9am-6pm Mon-Fri. **Credit** AmEx, DC, MC, V. **Map** p243 E5.
Its tights and stockings have a worldwide reputation, but Wolford also carries a range of underwear and some tops, dresses and skirts.
Other locations throughout the city.

Shoes

Humanic

1, Kärntner Strasse 1 (513 8922/www.humanic.at). U1, U3 Stephansplatz. **Open** 10am-7pm Mon-Wed; 10am-8pm Thur, Fri; 10am-6pm Sat. **Credit** AmEx, DC, MC, V. **Map** p251 E7.

The flagship store of Austria's leading shoe chain stocks a wide range of international brands.
Other locations throughout the city.

Ludwig Reiter

1, Mölkersteig 1 (533 420 422/www.ludwig-reiter.com). U2 Schottentor. **Open** 10am-6.30pm Mon-Fri; 10am-5pm Sat. **Credit** AmEx, DC, MC, V. **Map** p250 D6.
There are many bespoke shoemakers in Vienna, but Ludwig Reiter has made an international name for himself, especially in the US. A pair of Reiter's superbly finished trainers (based on regulation Austrian army issue) make a great souvenir.
Other locations 1, Führichgasse 6 (512 6146); 4, Wiedner Hauptstrasse 41 (505 8258).

Shu!

7, Neubaugasse 34 (523 1449/www.shu.at). U3 Neubaugasse/bus 13a. **Open** noon-7pm Tue-Fri; noon-5pm Sat. **Credit** AmEx, DC, MC, V. **Map** p246 C8.
Viennese women go all misty-eyed when they talk about this shop, which has Patrick Cox, Camper and other trendy labels laid out in a spacious, airy store.

Terra Plana

7, Neubaugasse 12-14 (526 3727/www.terra plana.com). U3 Neubaugasse/bus 13a. **Open** 11am-7pm Mon-Thur; 10am-7pm Fri; 10am-6pm Sat. **Credit** AmEx, DC, MC, V. **Map** p246 C8.
This new 7th district emporium has great looking shoes made with recycled materials by Galahad Clark's eco-friendly Terra Plana label. The shop also stocks the firm's two sub-labels Viva Barefoot – with ultra-thin Kevlar soles – and Worn Again, 99% recycled out of parachute cloth, tweed jackets and rubber. Also check out Keen, a quality local design store that has just moved in upstairs.

Food & drink

Delicatessens

Georg Ruziczka

4, Naschmarkt 57-59a (0699-18 204 709/www. uhudler.com). U1, U2, U4 Karlsplatz. **Open** 10am-8pm Tue-Fri; 9.30am-8pm Sat. **No credit cards. Map** p247 D8.
This small stand is great for Austrian staples such as pumpkin seed oil, jams and preserves, fine schnapps and good-value dessert wines such as Gerdenits's superb Ausbruch. It also stocks the curious Bürgenland Uhudler, a cult local red wine.

Grimm

1, Kurrentgasse 10a (533 13840/www.grimm.at). U1, U3 Stephansplatz. **Open** 6.30am-6.30pm Mon-Fri; 6.30am-noon Sat. **Credit** AmEx, DC, V. **Map** p250 E6.
Bread is invariably excellent in Austria, and a quite bewildering range of cereals, seeds and spices is employed in its manufacture. Most of the city's bakeries are good; Grimm is one of the best.

Eat, Drink, Shop

Piccini

6, Linke Wienzeile 4 (587 5254/www.piccini.at). U1, U2, U4 Karlsplatz. **Open** 9am-6.30pm Mon-Thur; 8.30am-6.30pm Fri; 8.30am-2pm Sat. **Credit** MC, V. **Map** p250 D8.

Vienna's historic Italian deli stocks all the varieties of pancetta and pecorino any self-respecting foodie could possibly desire. Italian down to the 'take the chit to the cashier' mode of payment, Piccini now has a smart bar area serving delicious nibbles and choice wines and aperitivi that stays open an hour later from Mondays to Thursdays.

Staud's

16, Yppenmarkt 93 (406 880 521/www.stauds.com). U6 Josefstädter Strasse. **Open** 8am-12.30pm Tue-Sat; 3.30-6pm Fri. **Credit** AmEx, DC, MC, V. **Map** p246 A6.

From their store in the 16th district's earthy Brunnenmarkt, Hans Staud and his family have been dealing in fine preserves and pickled vegetables since the days of the empire. The clientele includes the Japanese royal family.

Drinks

Jeroboam

4, Schleifmühlgasse 1 (585 6773/www.jeroboam.at). U1, U2, U4 Karlsplatz. **Open** 10am-3pm Tue, Sat; 3-8pm Wed-Fri. **No credit cards. Map** p247 E8.

A specialist shop dealing exclusively in sekt, spumante and all things sparkling. More than 80 different types of champagne are stocked.

Unger und Klein

1, Gölsdorfgasse 2 (532 1323/www.ungerundklein. at). U2, U4 Schottenring. **Open** 3pm-midnight Mon-Fri; 5pm-midnight Sat. **Credit** MC, V. **Map** p251 E6.

A magnificent 'theatre of drinking' designed by Eichinger oder Knechtl in 1992. Wine bar and store under one roof, Unger und Klein is a favourite of media bods, but don't let that put you off. Wines by the glass or bottle change from day to day.

Wein & Co

6, Getreidemarkt 1 (585 7257-13/www.weinco.at). U1, U2, U4 Karlsplatz. **Open** 10am-midnight Mon-Fri; 9am-midnight Sat; 11am-midnight Sun. **Credit** AmEx, DC, MC, V. **Map** p250 E8.

Wein & Co cheekily circumvented Austria's restrictive retail legislation by opening wine bars and shops in one store, so you can buy bottles here until midnight. As well as wines from all over the world and gourmet conserves, there is a smart bar serving drinks and tasty meals.

Other locations 1, Jasomirgottstrasse 3-5 (535 0916-12); 1, Dr Karl-Lueger-Ring 12 (533 85 30 12).

General

By the standards of Britain, the United States or France, Vienna's supermarkets are really rather pokey affairs. The most ubiquitous is Billa, which is gradually revamping its city centre stores to include delicatessen counters and a better selection of wines. Merkur, the bigger version of Billa, can be found under Gerngross (*see p143*) on Mariahilfer Strasse. Billa's main competitor is Spar, which took over the old Julius Meinl shops (*see p150*), and generally offers superior wares. Another good option is the expanding Hofer. This dirt cheap, pile 'em high chain has excellent fruit and vegetables and some bargain wines.

Billa Corso

1, Kärntner Ring 9-13, Ringstrassen Galerien (512 6625). U1, U2, U4 Karlsplatz/tram 1, 2, D, J/bus 3a. **Open** 8am-7pm Mon-Thur; 8am-7.30pm Fri; 7.30am-6pm Sat. **No credit cards. Map** p250 E8.

The Billa Corso is the best thing about the Ringstrassen Galerien. This branch has a huge delicatessen area with a butcher's and fish counter (something not to be taken for granted in Austrian supermarkets), as well as a pretty extensive drinks selection. Again, not to be taken for granted, most Billa supermarkets have a deli counter where you can at least buy good fresh sausage or cheese rolls.

Bobby's Foodstore

4, Schleifmühlgasse 8 (586 7534/www.bobbys.at). U1, U2, U4 Karlsplatz/bus 59a. **Open** 10am-6.30pm Mon-Fri; 10am-5pm Sat. **Credit** MC, V. **Map** p247 E8.

For homesick expats, Bobby's imports all the food you miss from England, the US and Australia, and the welcoming English-speaking staff will give you a taste of home.

Meinl am Graben

1, Graben 19 (532 3334/www.meinl.com). U3 Herrengasse/bus 2a, 3a. **Open** 8am-7.30pm Mon-Wed; 8.30am-8pm Thur, Fri; 9am-6pm Sat. **Credit** AmEx, DC, MC, V. **Map** p250 E6.

Meinl am Graben, Vienna's finest and most elegant grocery, sells excellent food from all over the world, from simple ready meals to exotic condiments as well as fresh meat, fish and an enticing range of cheeses. Apart from stocking up on groceries, Vienna's great and good also patronise the wine bar, sushi stand and coffee shop, and feast in the first-floor restaurant (*see p118*).

Weltladen

9, Schwarzspanier Strasse 15 (405 4434/www. suedwind.at). Trams 43, 44. **Open** 9am-6pm Mon-Fri. **Credit** AmEx, DC, MC, V. **Map** p250 D5.

The Weltladen (world shop) chain of fair trade stores is present throughout Vienna and its green, blue and black fair-trade seal is visible on many of the products that you'll find for sale in Viennese supermarkets. This branch specialises in books and CDs but also carries coffee, tea and cocoa. Pop in next door to the pleasant Weltcafé, a popular spot with students and activists, open daily from 9am to 2am. **Other locations** throughout the city.

Eat, Drink, Shop

Brunnenmarkt.

Markets

Brunnenmarkt
16, Brunnengasse. U6 Josefstädter Strasse. **Open** 6am-6.30pm Mon-Fri; 6am-3pm Sat. **Map** p246 A6.
Not as spectacular a sight as the Naschmarkt (*see below*) and more limited in its range of wares, the Brunnenmarkt is nevertheless a bustling, colourful market with a distinctly Balkan/Turkish flavour. Stretched out along Brunnengasse are stalls and shops offering fruit and vegetables, halal meat, kitsch decorative stuff and sticky Turkish pâtisserie. Saturday, when a farmers' market sets up on the neighbouring Yppenplatz, is the best day to go.

Naschmarkt
4, Linke und Rechte Wienzeile. U1, U2, U4 Karlsplatz. **Open** 6am-6.30pm Mon-Fri; 6am-5pm Sat. **Map** p250 E6.
A visit to Vienna's premier open-air food market should be on everyone's itinerary. Located on a long esplanade covering the course of the Wien river, this superb market will satisfy the most demanding foodie. It's also an ideal spot to eat, drink and hang out, particularly on Saturdays. Approaching from Karlsplatz, the first section is taken up with fishmongers, pork butchers and the market's priciest and most exotic greengrocers. Other highlights here include a number of excellent juice bars and the famous Sauerkraut stall. Further along are several Chinese and Indian shops, and behind them runs a line of stalls selling excellent Thai, Japanese and Italian food. After the market is bisected by Schleifmühlgasse, the stalls are of the more workaday fruit and veg variety, but prices are more reasonable than on the first stretch. This last section opens out on to a broad tract where, on Saturdays, there's a thriving flea market. **Photo** *p152*.

Organic Market Freyung
1, Freyung. U2 Schottentor. **Open** 8am-7.30pm Fri, Sat. **Map** p250 E6.
This market sells exclusively organic products directly from the growers. Some stalls also display non-edible wares – such as candles and wooden toys.

Organic produce & health food

Austria is the European Union leader in organic farming, and so-called 'bio' products can be found everywhere. Both leading supermarket chains carry their own organic label: Billa/Merkur's is called *Ja! Natürlich* and Spar's is *Natur Pur*. Outside the big chains, St Josef is a colourful organic deli with good lunch menus (*see p130*).

Maran
7, Kaiserstrasse 57-59 (526 58860-18/www.bio markt.co.at). U6 Burggasse/tram 5. **Open** 7.30am-7pm Mon-Fri; 8am-5pm Sat. **Credit** AmEx, DC, MC, V. **Map** p246 B7.
Vienna's largest organic supermarket has the best and most reasonably priced fruit, veg and meat in the city. Plenty of organic beers and wines as well.

Reformhaus Buchmüller
7, Neubaugasse 17-19 (523 7297/www.reformhaus-buchmueller.at). U3 Neubaugasse/bus 13a. **Open** 9am-6.30pm Mon-Fri; 9am-5pm Sat. **Credit** DC, MC, V. **Map** p246 C8.
A small shop selling everything from organic vegetables and vegan products to health-conscious cosmetics and homeopathic remedies. There is a little café in the back that serves freshly squeezed fruit juices and cheap meals, but be warned that it gets pretty packed at lunchtimes.

Reformhaus Verde
8, Josefstädter Strasse 27 (405 1329). Tram J. **Open** 10am-6.30pm Mon-Fri; 10am-1pm Sat. **No credit cards. Map** p246 B6.
Reformhaus Verde is a well-stocked health-food store with organic vegetables, bread, beers and wines, and over 200 varieties of tea.

Pâtisserie & chocolate

Look out for the magic word *Konditorei* (pâtisserie) for the largest selection of cakes, but most bakers have the basic strudels and *Golatschen* (like Danish pastries).

Eat, Drink, Shop

Café Central Konditorei

*1, Herrengasse 17 (533 3764 24/www.palais
events.at). U3 Herrengasse.* **Open** 7.30am-10pm
Mon-Sat; 10am-6pm Sun. **Credit** AmEx, DC, MC, V.
Map p250 E6.
The pâtisserie division of the famous Café Central
(*see p136*) is a rather stuffy establishment. But it's
worth a visit to taste the chocolate truffles.

Kurkonditorei Oberlaa

*1, Neuer Markt 16 (513 2936-0/www.oberlaa-
wien.at). U1, U2, U4 Karlsplatz.* **Open** 8am-8pm
daily. **Credit** AmEx, DC, MC, V. **Map** p250 E7.
Ignore the provincial interiors – when it comes to
tortes, sponge cakes and chocolates, Oberlaa takes
the proverbial biscuit.
Other locations throughout the city

Manner

*1, Rotenturmstrasse 2/Stephansplatz 7 (513 7018/
www.manner.at). U1, U3 Stephansplatz.* **Open** 10am-
9pm daily. **Credit** AmEx, DC, MC, V. **Map** p251 E6.
Austria's most popular chocolate snack is Manner
Neapolitaner Schnitten, hazelnut-flavoured wafer
biscuits in a distinctive pink wrapper bearing the
outline of Stephansdom. This historic Viennese firm
has been raising its profile by patenting its trademark pink, getting the products on to *Friends* and
opening this flagship store. Here they sell the full
range of wafers, the gorgeous Schokobananen and
rum coconuts and T-shirts, toy cars and trams, and
other corporate souvenirs. A true slice of Vienna.

Xocolat

*1, Freyung 2 (Palais Ferstel) (535 4363/www.
xocolat.at). U3 Herrengasse.* **Open** 10am-6pm
Mon-Fri; 10am-5pm Sat. Closed 27 May-2 Sept.
Credit AmEx, DC, MC, V. **Map** p250 E6.
The city's best-stocked chocolate emporium, in the
stone arches of the Ferstel passage. Come here for
the fabulous creations of Catalan chocolatier Enric
Rovira and aromatic Californian Scharffen Berger.

Gifts & souvenirs

Flowers

Vienna has excellent florists. Seasonal
specialities such as sunflowers, sticky buds
and berries inundate the stands. There are
shops and stalls all over the city, but don't
miss the Saturday stands at the Flohmarkt
end of the Naschmarkt with their fabulous
choice of meadow flowers.

Bloom The Flower Shop

*1, Kärntnerstrasse 55 (513 4720). U1, U2, U4
Karlsplatz/tram 1, 2, D, J.* **Open** 10am-7.30pm Mon-
Fri; 10am-6pm Sat. **Credit** MC, V. **Map** p250 E7.
Lederleitner (*see p153*) runs the delightful Bloom
chain of mini florists, which sell lovely seasonal stuff
as well as single flowers such as water lilies.
Other locations 7, Mariahilfer Strasse 100
(526 5537).

Naschmarkt. *See p151.*

Blumenkraft

4, Schleifmühlgasse 4 (585 7727/www.
blumenkraft.at). U1, U2, U4 Karlsplatz/bus 59a.
Open 10am-7pm Mon-Fri; 9am-2pm Sat. **Credit**
AmEx, DC, MC, V. **Map** p247 E8.
Blumenkraft's display looks more like a design concept than a florist. Christine Fink decorates homes and offices with her fantastic selection of plants, flowers and trees. It is worth a visit just to see the building, designed by prominent Austrian architects Eichinger oder Knechtl. **Photo** *p154.*

Lederleitner

1, Römische Markthalle im Börsegebäude,
Schottenring 16 (532 0677/www.lederleitner.at). U4
Schottenring/tram D. **Open** 10am-8pm Mon-Fri;
9am-5pm Sat. **Credit** DC, MC, V. **Map** p250 E5.
A huge emporium under the Börse, Vienna's stock exchange, where paths are lined with plants, flowers and seasonal decorations, as well as cookery books from all over the world.

Health & beauty

Complementary medicine

Die Kräuterdrogerie

8, Kochgasse 34 (405 4522/www.kraeuterdrogerie.
at). Tram 43, 44/bus 13a. **Open** 8.30am-6pm Mon-
Fri; 8.30am-12.30pm Sat. **Credit** AmEx, DC, MC, V.
Map p242 C5.

Healing herbs and oils (Birgit is a trained pharmacist), as well as ayurvedic products. The food section gets regular deliveries of organic veg.

Mag. Kottas

1, Freyung 7 (533 9532/www.mag-kottas.at). U2
Schottenring. **Open** 8.30am-6pm Mon-Fri; 9am-
12.30pm Sat. **Credit** MC, V. **Map** p250 E6.
Kottas has been the most reliable herbalist in the city since 1795. Its trademark infusions are available at all Viennese chemists, but for the full range of over 600 herbs, and to admire the magnificent Baroque premises, call in at this branch.

Pharmacies

Bipa

1, Kärntner Strasse 1-3 (512 2210/www.bipa.at).
U1, U3 Stephansplatz. **Open** 8am-7.30pm Mon-Fri;
8am-5pm Sat. **No credit cards**. **Map** p251 E7.
Bipa, Billa's cosmetics and cleaning products outlet, is present in every shopping street. It also has cheap photo developing. Rival DM is very similar (you'll find it throughout Vienna; a central branch is at 1, Rotenturmstrasse 12, 512 39 60).
Other locations throughout the city.

Karin Van Vliet

1, Köllnerhofgasse 2 (513 1155/www.makeup-studio.
com). U1, U4 Schwedenplatz. **Open** 10am-6pm Mon-
Fri; 10am-5pm Sat. **Credit** DC, MC, V. **Map** p251 F6.
A beautiful frontage behind which lies Karin Van Vliet's own-brand non-animal-tested make-up products. Treat yourself to a make-up session (€37) or a one-hour course (€100).

Hairdressers

Be a Good Girl

7, Westbahnstrasse 5a (524 4728-11/www.bea
goodgirl.com). Tram 49. **Open** noon-6pm Mon;
10am-7pm Tue, Wed; 10am-8pm Thur, Fri; 10am-
5pm Sat. **Credit** AmEx, DC, MC, V. **Map** p246 B8.
Have your hair cut by friendly staff in a relaxed atmosphere. Be a Good Girl also sells Freitag bags and cool leisureware by other Swiss labels.

GmbHaar

7, Siebensterngasse 40 (523 3763/www.gmbhaar.at).
Tram 49. **Open** 9am-9pm Mon-Fri; 9am-4pm Sat.
No credit cards. **Map** p250 C8.
Brothers Reini and Roland and the rest of the staff are Toni & Guy trained and have been tending to Vienna's clubbers for over 17 years. Their 7th district salon resounds with trippy beats.
Other locations 4, Margaretenstrasse 20 (585 6644).

London Underground

8, Josefstädter Strasse 29 (407
1607/www.underground.at). Tram J. **Open** 1-6pm
Mon; 9am-6pm Tue, Wed; 9am-8pm Thur, Fri; 8am-
1pm Sat. **No credit cards**. **Map** p246 B6.
Run by a talkative, expatriate Brit, Kurt, this salon – and its English-speaking staff – caters for all ages.

Eat, Drink, Shop

Opticians

Brillen.manufaktur

7, Neubaugasse 18 (523 8200/www.brillen manufaktur.at). U3 Neubaugasse/bus 13a. **Open** 10am-6.30pm Mon-Fri; 10am-5pm Sat. **Credit** AmEx, DC, MC, V. **Map** p246 C8.
Vienna's hippest eyewear address seems to turn its nose up at Gucci, Armani et al to concentrate on designer frame specialists such as LA Eyeworks, Booth & Bruce, Eye DC and the oh so cool IC! Berlin.

Optiker Maurer (See Me)

8, Josefstädter Strasse 8 (405 0788). U2 Rathaus/ tram J. **Open** 9.30am-1.30pm, 3-6pm Mon-Fri; 9.30am-12.30pm Sat. **Credit** AmEx, DC, MC, V. **Map** p246 C6.
An optician with a good mix of friendly service and reasonable prices. Top frames too.
Other locations 7, Siebensterngasse 40 (523 6494).

Schau Schau Brillen

1, Rotenturmstrasse 11 (533 4584/www.schau- schau.at). U1, U3 Stephansplatz. **Open** 10am-6pm Mon-Fri; 10am-5pm Sat. **Credit** AmEx, DC, MC, V. **Map** p251 E6.
If horn rims are your bag, this bespoke establishment makes them out of the real (buffalo) thing. If not, there's a wide range of handmade frames, and they will even reconstruct broken favourites.

Pharmacies

Saint Charles Apothecary

6, Gumpendorfer Strasse 33 (0676 586 1366/ www.saint.info). Bus 57a. **Open** 10am-6.30pm Mon-Fri; 10am-5pm Sat. **Credit** AmEx, DC, MC, V. **Map** p250 D8
Consisting of a chemist's, a food store and this skin care shop, the Saint Charles chain forms a chic little cluster either side of Gumpendorfer Strasse. The Apothecary sells top brands such as Ren and Korres as well as their own potions.

House & home

Antiques & modern classics

Austrians have a fondness for all things old and a corresponding reluctance to throw stuff away. This, naturally, makes Vienna a happy hunting ground for the antiques' collector. The city is full of junk shops (*Altwaren* or *Trödler*), upmarket antiques shops (*Antiquitäten*) and stamp, coin and postcard emporia. In the 1st district the streets around the Dorotheum are dotted with noble purveyors of antique furniture and fine art. Jugendstil emporia are located in the 7th district around Siebensterngasse. For modern classics and kitsch, the Naschmarkt area is best, particularly Schleifmühlgasse and Kettenbrückengasse.

Bananas

5, Kettenbrückengasse 15 (0664 312 9449/www. bananas.at). U4 Kettenbrückengasse. **Open** 1-6pm Mon-Fri; 11am-4pm Sat. **No credit cards.** **Map** p247 D9.
If you draw a blank at the Saturday flea market, head for the neighbouring Kettenbrückengasse. Fast rivalling Schleifmühlgasse for original shops and cafés, the street features attractive establishments such as Bananas which stocks a variety of modern design classics and bric-a-brac from the 1950s to the 1970s at very affordable prices.

Das Kunstwerk

4, Operngasse 20 (0650 230 9994/www.das kunstwerk.at). U1, U2, U4 Karlsplatz/bus 59a. **Open** 11am-6pm Mon-Fri; 10am-2pm Sat. **Credit** DC, MC, V. **Map** p250 E7.
Das Kunstwerk specialises in Murano and Lötz glass as well as art deco and art nouveau furniture, and design up to 1980, including Thonet and Kohn. The shop also carries big names in Austrian design such as Otto Wagner and Adolf Loos.

Blumenkraft. *See p153.*

Lichterloh

*6, Gumpendorfer Strasse 15-17 (586 0520/www.
lichterloh.com). Bus 57a.* **Open** 11am-6.30pm
Mon-Fri; 11am-4pm Sat. **Credit** AmEx, DC, MC, V.
Map p250 D8.
Lichterloh has two sections: on one side of its big
new store are spacious rooms full of classic design
from the 1950s to the 1970s, including a basement
with some wild rugs, and on the other a smaller room
with art deco furniture and jewellery on display.
Other locations Glasfabrik 16, Lorenz-Mandl-
Gasse 25 (494 3490/www.glasfabrik.at).

Phil

*6, Gumpendorfer Strasse 10-12 (581 0489/www.
phil.info). U2 Museumsquartier.* **Open** 5pm-1am
Mon; 10am-1am Tue-Sun. **No credit cards.**
Map p250 D8.
Phil feels like someone's living room transformed
into an informal concept store. Decked out in mix 'n'
match junk-store furniture, including the odd
Jacobsen chair and other modern classics, it's a
chilled spot to have a drink and leaf through its
choice of books in English and German or listen in
to good sounds. Phil also sells lamps and objects
from the 1950s to the 1970s.

Rauminhalt

*4, Schleifmühlgasse 13 (409 9892/www.rauminhalt.
com). U1, U2, U4 Karlsplatz.* **Open** noon-7pm Tue-
Fri; 10am-3pm Sat. **Credit** AmEx, DC, MC, V.
Map p250 E8.
Offering modern design from the 1950s to the 1980s,
Rauminhalt specialises in Scandinavian stuff and its
friendly staff are always ready to help the uninitiated. Rauminhalt now has an interesting collection
of Berber rugs and ceramics that sits nicely among
the Eames chairs.

Flea markets

Flea market burrowers can have the time of
their lives in Vienna. And don't hesitate,
bargaining with the stall holders is de rigueur.
Check out posters advertising other small
markets all over town.

Flohmarkt

5, Kettenbrückengasse. U4 Kettenbrückengasse.
Open dawn-5pm Sat. **Map** p247 D8.
This market has something for everyone, with the
bargain-basement stalls located beside the U-Bahn
and the more specialised dealers further towards the
Linke Wienzeile. There are stands selling furs,
leathers and Loden stuff, lamps and light fittings, tin
toys and dolls, antique watches and jewellery, and
loads of crocks. Look out for the attractive pastel-
coloured Austrian Lilien Porzelan from the 1950s.
The atmosphere is quite unlike the flea markets of
most European cities. The babble of languages is
extraordinary – Russians flogging icons and Soviet
memorabilia, Romanian gypsies plying (possibly
fake) Roman coins and figures, and others from the
Balkans selling more or less anything.

Flohmarkt im Auto-Kino

*Autokinostrasse 2, 2301 Gross Enzersdorf (02249
2260/www.autokino.at). U1 Kagran, bus 26a.*
Open 5.30am-1pm Sun.
You have to be a really rather dedicated bargain
hunter to trek out to this trans-Danubian flea market at a drive-in cinema – it's a half-hour bus ride
from Kagran. However, in spring and summer, over
10,000 eager rummagers show up every week for
this car boot-sale type event.

General

Backhausen

*1, Schwarzenbergstrasse 10 (514 040/www.
backhausen.com). Tram 1, 2.* **Open** 9.30am-6.30pm
Mon-Fri; 9.30am-5pm Sat. **Credit** AmEx, DC, MC, V.
Map p247 E8.
K.u.k. textile manufacturers Backhausen and Sons
worked closely with the Wiener Werkstätte and maintain an archive of over 3,000 of their Japanese-
influenced fabric designs that can be seen in a small
museum in the shop's basement. Today, you can get
home furnishings, glassware, miniature WW chairs,
rugs and cheaper related knick-knacks.

Boudoir

*9, Berggasse 14 (319 1079/www.boudoir.at). Tram
D.* **Open** 2-6pm Tue-Fri. **Credit** AmEx, DC, MC, V.
Map p250 D5.
Sheets and pillowcases decorated with winged
phalli, subtitled 'The subconscious custom-made',
are sold in this little boutique. As well as home fur-
nishings, it also stocks corsets, negligées and seduc-
tively frilly undies. All this was dreamed up by
Renate Christian, who is an ex-pupil of Vivienne
Westwood (and it shows).

gabarage_upcycling design

*4, Schleifmühlgasse 6 (585 7632/www.gabarage.at).
Tram 52/bus 59a.* **Open** 10am-6pm Mon-Fri; 10am-
3pm Sat. **No credit cards. Map** p247 E8
The latest arrival on chic Scheifmühlgasse transforms bowling balls and sheet metal into lamps, skis
into hat stands and tetra pak into flower pots. This
eco-design collective also turns out highly original
jewellery, bags and furniture at competitive prices.

Interio

*1, Ringstrassen-Galerien, Kärntner Ring 5-7 (513
9936/www.interio.at). U1, U2, U4 Karlsplatz.* **Open**
9am-7.30pm Mon-Wed; 9am-9pm Thur, Fri; 9am-6pm
Sat. **Credit** MC, V. **Map** p251 E8.
Interio stocks attractive, well-designed, reasonably
priced home furnishings, crocks, picture frames,
bedlinen, candles and more.
Other locations 6, Mariahilfer Strasse 19-21 (585
1730).

Lobmeyr

*1, Kärntnerstrasse 26 (512 0508/www.lobmeyr.at).
U1, U2, U4 Karlsplatz.* **Open** 10am-7pm Mon-Fri;
10am-6pm Sat. **Credit** AmEx, DC, MC, V.
Map p247 E7.

Eat, Drink, Shop

Standing amid the Benettons and H&Ms of Kärntner Strasse, Lobmeyr is a class act that has produced chandeliers for such lofty interiors as the Hall of the Supreme Soviet and the Metropolitan Opera. It also reproduces Josef Hoffmann's iconic 'Serie B' drinks set. The second floor houses a small museum.

no nonsens
16, Grundsteingasse 36 (924 7824/www.nono.at). U6 Josefstädter Strasse/tram J. **Open** noon-6pm Tue-Fri or by appointment. **Credit** AmEx, DC, MC, V. **Map** p246 A6.
Hedwig Rotter's witty yet functional ceramics and glassware are sold from her store/workshop on the street that provided Kruder & Dorfmeister with the name for their G-Stone label. Bowls and plates with comic screen-printed motifs, wall lights and pockets and vases based on sick bags from vintage airlines are among the products of her fertile imagination.

Woka
1, Singerstrasse 16 (513 2912/www.woka.com). U1, U3 Stephansplatz. **Open** 10am-6pm Mon-Fri; 10am-1pm Sat. **Credit** AmEx, DC, MC, V. **Map** p251 E7.
Since 1978, Wolfgang Karolinsky and his firm Woka have been making superb reproductions of lamps and light fittings designed by members of the Wiener Werkstätte set, including Adolf Loos. As Karolinsky has acquired many of the original tools, moulds and presses, these lamps are as close to the real thing as you are likely to get. He also sells some fetching standard lamps of his own design.

Music & entertainment

Vienna is not badly off for music emporia. If classical is your bag, note that prices are high in 1st district shops such as EMI Austria at Kärntner Strasse 30. Teuchtler Alt&Neu (*see below*) has a good selection of classical music.

Audio Center
1, Judenplatz 9 (533 6849). U1, U3 Stephansplatz, U3 Herrengasse. **Open** 10am-7pm Mon-Fri; 10am-5pm Sat. **Credit** AmEx, DC, MC, V. **Map** p251 E6.
An excellent jazz store offering both CDs and vinyl. It has a good selection of world music too, and is not afraid to stock crazier improv and crossover jazz. There's a comfy listening area, plenty of knowledgeable advice and flyers.

Black Market
1, Gonzagagasse 9 (533 2458/www.blackmarket.at). U2, U4 Schottenring. **Open** noon-7pm Mon-Fri; 11am-6pm Sat. **Credit** AmEx, DC, MC, V. **Map** p243 E5.
The best hip hop/funk/dance store in town, Black Market is run by Alexander Hirschenhauser, one of the original movers behind the Vienna scene, and London DJ Alan Brown does its distribution. You can listen to CDs and vinyl on headphones and get tips from the knowledgeable and helpful staff. There's a café, and a small selection of T-shirts too.

Rave Up
6, Hofmühlgasse 1 (596 9650/www.rave-up.at). U4 Pilgramgasse/bus 13a, 14a. **Open** 10am-6.30pm Mon-Fri; 10am-5pm Sat. **Credit** AmEx, DC, MC, V. **Map** p242 B4.
Popular with local DJs on the hunt for beats, reggae, electronica and hip hop, Rave Up is also good for Viennese labels like Mego, Klein, Cheap and Couch.

Record Shack
5, Reinprechtsdorfer Strasse 60 (545 77 57/www.recordshack.org). Bus 14a. **Open** 12am-7pm Mon-Fri; noon-5pm Sat. **Credit** AmEx, DC, MC, V. **Map** p246 C10.
Lapsed architecture student Jörg is a 1960s and '70s soul fanatic whose Sound of Soul club nights are among Vienna's best. He started the business as a mail-order service before branching into retailing with a small, funky store. Treat yourself to some classic northern soul and vintage reggae on vinyl and CD.

Substance
7, Westbahnstrasse 16 (523 6757/www.substance-store.com). U3 Neubaugasse/tram 49. **Open** noon-7.30pm Mon-Fri; 10am-6pm Sat. **Credit** AmEx, DC, MC, V. **Map** p246 C8.
Substance is run by serious aficionados – fans of everything from John Zorn to West Coast hip hop à la Quannum. CDs predominate, but there's also vinyl some music books and DVDs.

Teuchtler Alt&Neu
6, Windmühlgasse 10 (586 2133). U2 Babenbergergasse. **Open** 1-6pm Mon-Fri; 10am-1pm Sat (10am-5pm 1st Sat in month). **Credit** AmEx, DC, MC, V. **Map** p250 D8.
A long-standing Aladdin's cave selling used and new CDs and vinyl. Jazz and classical are its strong points. Prices are the best in Vienna, although the categorising is slightly chaotic. Staff are approachable.

Travellers' needs

Contracting services, especially repairs, can prove expensive. Always ask for an estimate.

Key cutting

Mister Minit
1, Führichgasse 4 (512 4865). U1, U3 Stephansplatz. **Open** 9.30am-1.30pm, 2-6pm Mon-Fri. **No credit cards. Map** p250 E7.
Key cutting and shoe repairs. For service on a Saturday until 1pm, visit the branch in Gerngross. **Other locations** 7, Mariahilfer Strasse 48 (524 5654).

Travel

Die Restplatzbörse
1, Kärntner Ring 18 (505 01 70-0/505 850). U1, U2, U4 Karlsplatz/tram 1, 2, J. **Open** 9am-6pm Mon-Fri; 9am-noon Sat. **Credit** DC, MC, V. **Map** p251 E8.
The best place to pick up last-minute deals. **Other locations** throughout the city.

Arts & Entertainment

Features

Gartenbaukino. *See p166*.

Festivals & Events

A city for all seasons.

Wiener Festwochen. *See p160.*

In contrast to its usual dour, middle-European reputation, Vienna knows how to party. No matter what the time of year, there's always something exciting to look forward to. With its central European climate, the seasonal swings from the heat of summer to the winter freeze are celebrated with a vibrant and varied calender of events and activities. Festival fun is to be had all year round, so check out the newspapers, especially local listings weekly *Falter*, or visit the websites listed on *p233*. Here are some of the highlights.

Spring

After winter's rigours, the city's cultural life bursts into spring bud.

Easter Market

1, Freyung. U2 Schottentor. **Date** two weeks up to Easter. **Map** p250 E6.
A traditional Easter market, selling hand-painted eggs and other Easter knick-knacks, plus food and drink. Open 9.30am-7.30pm daily.

OsterKlang

Information & tickets: Theater an der Wien, 6, Linke Wienzeile 6 (58830-661/www.osterklang.at). U1, U2, U4 Karlsplatz/tram 1, 2, D, J. **Date** Easter. **Map** p250 D8.

The OsterKlang (Sound of Easter) festival is dedicated to devotional works from Baroque to the late 20th century in the city's most prestigious venues. It is always opened by the Wiener Philharmoniker.

Frühlingsfestival

Konzerthaus, 3, Lothringerstrasse 20 (242 002/info 242 00 100/www.konzerthaus.at). U4 Stadtpark/ tram D. **Map** p251 F8.
Musikverein, 1, Bösendorferstrasse 12 (505 8190/ info 505 1363/www.musikverein.at). U4 Stadtpark/ tram D. **Map** p251 E8.
Date Mar/Apr-May.
This famous spring festival is held alternately in the Konzerthaus and the Musikverein. It features concerts by leading ensembles and soloists from around the world. Each year has a different motto, with 'Youth' picked as the theme for 2007, focusing on young artists and a young audience.

ViennAfair

2, Messe Platz 1 (72720-0/www.viennafair.at). U1 Praterstern. **Date** late Apr. **Map** p244 J5.
Held at the city's revamped trade-fair grounds, Vienna's international contemporary art fair was relaunched in 2005 with a focus on young artists and galleries from Central and Eastern Europe.

Donaufestival

Information & tickets: (02732 908033/ www.donaufestival.at). **Date** late Apr-May.

This festival in the Danube Valley town of Krems has ditched its jazzy/world music angle in favour of a cutting-edge programme focusing on performance art and music. To give you an idea of what to expect, the 2007 Danube festival, under the heading 'Unprotected Games', featured artists such as Throbbing Gristle and Bonnie Prince Billy. Shuttle buses run from Vienna.

Balkan Fever

913 1411/www.balkanfever.at. **Date** Apr/May.
This relatively new addition to the festival calender reflects Vienna's role as a gateway to the new easterly territories of the European Union and beyond. There's cinema, in addition to some vivid musical performances spanning a lively spectrum of genres, with Balkan roots in the Konzerthaus as well as at jazz and club venues.

Vienna City Marathon

(606 9510/www.vienna-marathon.com).
Date Apr or May.
The marathon starts on the Reichsbrücke (the bridge over the Danube before the UNO City) in the 22nd

district and ends at the central Heldenplatz. Early online registration costs €50, rising to €70 for late-comers. Also a half marathon and children's events.

International Music Festival

Konzerthaus, 3, Lothringerstrasse 20 (242 002/ fax 242 00 110/info 242 00 100/www.konzert haus.at). U4 Stadtpark/tram D. **Date** May-June. **Map** p251 F8.
In odd-numbered years, when it's not hosting the Frühlingsfestival, the Konzerthaus runs the theme-based International Music Festival, which also includes jazz and world music performances.

Soho in Ottakring

16, Brunnengasse. (524 0909/www.sohoin ottakring.at). **Date** May-June. **Map** p246 A/B6.
This public art project was initiated to revitalise a shabby area in the 16th district and promote communication between the Austrian and (mainly Turkish) immigrant populations. Exhibitions, gigs and films are put on in bars, restaurants and shops in and around the Brunnenmarkt, one of Vienna's last true street markets.

Conspicuous consumption

It's a Thursday night in late winter, the Ringstrasse is closed to traffic, trams and buses have been cancelled and security forces are patrolling the cordoned-off streets around the State Opera House. The scenario might suggest world leaders and state visits but this is no political summit. It's the climax of the Vienna ball season – the Opernball.

Every year on the last Thursday before Ash Wednesday, high art makes way for high society and the opera house's balance sheet racks up over a million euros. It's rumoured to be the only night in the year when the (heavily subsidised) State Opera actually rings a profit. Hardly surprising, when a box will set you back a mere €16,000 and a bottle of champagne upwards of €250. In the past, tight security was needed because the display of extravagance sparked large protests which often turned violent. Today, the demonstrations only attract a handful of anarchist rabble-rousers.

Dating back to 1935, the Opernball remains a monument to tradition, complete with debutantes in virginal white and insignia-decorated politicians, and it still commands an entire evening of live coverage on state television, laden with saccharine smiles and inane interviews. To the amusement of many, the tone is regularly taken down a brow or two by the exploits of one-time construction

tycoon Richard Lugner, whose admission to the ball elite owes more to the size of his wallet than to his family tree. He has managed over the years to scoop media attention by inviting female celebrities of Hollywood stature to be his guest for the evening. The list includes Sophia Loren, Joan Collins, Sarah Ferguson, Pamela Anderson, Carmen Electra and, in 2007, Paris Hilton. But the imported glamour tends to look ill-at-ease, and does little more than raise the cringe factor. At the 2007 ball, the director of the State Opera, Ioan Holender, stole back the show, personally chauffeuring star soprano Anna Netrebko into the ballroom in a carriage drawn by real horses.

Those more concerned with social conscience than social status will be glad to know that there are alternatives: the Opferball (Victims' Ball) was initiated as a deliberate counterweight to the Opernball, and the Flüchtlingsball (Refugee Ball) raises money to help asylum seekers. Of all the events on the waltzing calendar, the shrillest is the Life Ball, Europe's biggest HIV/AIDS fundraising event. Far more so than the Opernball, it's 100 per cent celebrity powered. So 2007 kicked off with a fashion show by NY cowboys Heatherette; the Scissor Sisters played a couple of numbers and Sharon Stone blew kisses.

Arts & Entertainment

Stadtfest

(www.stadtfestwien.at). **Date** May.
A Saturday of music, circus-style acts and children's activities staged throughout the first district as the People's Party's answer to the Donauinselfest (*see below*). It's not quite the same extravaganza, but nonetheless it is entertaining.

Wiener Festwochen

Main festival office: 6, Lehárgasse 11 (589 2222/info 0800 664 020 from late Apr/www.festwochen.at). U1, U2, U4 Karlsplatz/bus 57a. **Date** May-June.
The Vienna Festival is the city's premier performance arts showdown and a permanent thorn in the side of the establishment due to the controversial themed productions programmed by maverick director Luc Bondy. Every year, internationally acclaimed theatre and dance companies and orchestras descend on Vienna for six weeks of performance madness. The Festwochen begins with a free musical extravaganza on Rathausplatz (the 2007 show featured Bobby McFerrin alongside Joe Zawinul and other established and up-and-coming Austrian artists). **Photo** *p158.*

Summer

In July and August, the city has two highly popular open-air cinemas – the Kino unter Sternen and Freiluftkino Krieau, *see p168*. For the out-of-town Wiesen and Konfrontationen music festivals, *see p194*. For the Rainbow Parade, *see p179*.

Donauinselfest

22, Donauinsel (www.donauinselfest.at). U1 Donauinsel, U6 Neue Donau. **Date** June.
Map p244 J3.
Organised by the Social Democrats, this three-day festival is one of the largest free events in Europe. The Danube island is invaded by nearly three million revellers of all ages and from all walks of life. Different stages spread along the island feature a whole spectrum of orchestras, bands and acts, local as well as international. The FM4 stage generally has some interesting indie/dance action. There's a special section of activities for children, and food and drink from all corners of the globe.

JazzFest Wien

8, Lammgasse 12/8 (712 4224/www.viennajazz.org). **Date** June-July.
Vienna's largest jazz festival offers many of the most famous names of jazz, soul and blues in different settings, ranging from the daftly inappropriate (Staatsoper) and the bizarrely fitting (the grounds of the Spittelau power station) to the downright enchanting (Rathaus courtyard). The highlights of the 2007 festival included names like Juliette Greco, Gata Barbieri, Archie Shepp and world music fusion group Dobrek Bistro, and it was all kicked off in fine style with a free concert by the Taj Mahal Trio and Doretta Carter in the MuseumsQuartier. Tickets are available from the festival's website.

ImPulsTanz

7, Museumstrasse 5/21 (info/tickets 523 5558/ www.impulstanz.com). U2 Volkstheater/bus 48a. **Date** July-Aug.
Staged around the city, the Vienna International Festival for Contemporary Dance and Performance attracts companies and artists from all over the world. ImPulsTanz also includes a series of workshops for all levels on ballet, hip hop, children's dance and yoga, among others.

Rathausplatz Music Film Festival

1, Rathausplatz. U2 Rathaus/tram 1, 2, D, J. **Date** July, Aug. **Map** p250 D6.
Every evening at twilight, opera and classical music films are shown for free on a giant screen in front of the city hall. Films and music pull culture buffs; food stands bring everyone else. Get there early for a seat.

Autumn

After summer the ripening months of autumn bring with them *Sturm* (young half-fermented wine that tastes as sweet as lemonade, but with an unmeasured alcohol content), as well as game, pumpkin and *Eierschwammerl* (chanterelle mushrooms), specialities in Austrian restaurants.

Viennale

7, Siebensterngasse 2 (526 5947/www.viennale.at). U3 Neubaugasse. **Date** Oct.
Austria's biggest international film festival has been running since 1960 and features Austrian and international premières. *See p165.*

Wien Modern

Konzerthaus, 3, Lothringerstrasse 20 (242 002/ www.wienmodern.at). U4 Stadtpark/tram D.
Date Nov. **Map** p251 F8.
Founded by Claudio Abbado in 1988, Wien Modern is devoted to contemporary composition, fearlessly combining reruns of pioneering work by the likes of Gyorgy Ligeti or Luigi Nono, with excursions into electronica and the constant presence of Vienna's leading new music ensemble, Klangforum Wien.

Winter

Winter is the most quintessentially Austrian time of year: snow (sometimes) blankets the city, the Christmas markets appear and the ball season starts (*see p159* **Conspicuous consumption**). *Fasching*, the German-speaking world's version of Carnival, runs until Ash Wednesday.

Christkindlmärkte

These advent markets appear in mid November. Christmas for the Viennese is a social affair, where people meet up at the markets for *Punsch* or *Glühwein* (the local mulled wine), chestnuts and spicy Christmas cookies. These are the principal hotspots:

From Africa to Austria: Malia at **JazzFest Wien**.

Rathausplatz market Map p250 D6.
Its stalls are tacky but it's still worth a visit for a glimpse of the Advent windows on the Town Hall, decorated by local artists, and the enchanting tree illuminations in the park.

Schönbrunn Palace market
Another spectacular backdrop with slightly more upmarket stalls can be found at the Schönbrunn Palace market.

Altwiener Christkindlmarkt Map p250 E6.
For a cosier, more arty feel and stalls selling hand-made wares, visit the Altwiener Christkindlmarkt at the Freyung.

Spittelberg market Map p246 C7.
Set in the cobbled streets between Burggasse and Siebensterngasse in the 7th district, the Spittelberg market is one of the loveliest and offers goods not found elsewhere.

Finally there are the three '**Christmas Villages**' – on Maria-Theresien-Platz between the Art History Museum and the Natural History Museum, in the grounds of the Belvedere and at the Altes AKH/Vienna University Campus in the 9th district.

New Year's Eve
www.wien.info.

The city centre transforms into a giant party for Silvester. Children's events start on Rathausplatz around 2pm, the streets of the old town are lined with stalls offering food and punch, and musical events take place in the squares. The festivities end in Stephansplatz for the cathedral chimes and fireworks.

New Year's Day Concert
1, Rathausplatz. U2 Rathaus/tram 1, 2, D, J.
Date 1 Jan, 10.45am. **Map** p250 D6.
Those without the money or political clout to secure a ticket for the famous concert by the Wiener Philharmoniker can watch it live on a huge screen in front of the Rathaus

Wiener Eistraum
1, Rathausplatz. **Date** Jan-Mar. **Map** p250 D6.
Ice-skating outside City Hall, to the accompaniment of disco lighting and hackneyed tunes.

Vienna International Accordion Festival
www.akkordeonfestival.at. **Date** Feb-Mar.
This month-long squeezebox celebration features the finest international accordion practitioners from the Balkans to the Basque countries, at various unusual venues throughout the city.

Children

How a city masters the art of cultivating youngsters.

The coming of age of a new generation of youthful, cultivated parents in Vienna has gone hand in hand with a boom in cultural activities on offer for children. The city also boasts an impressive range and quality of services and facilities. It's easy to get around on public transport, even with a pram. On underground trains, buses (middle door) and the newer trams you just roll on and park in the space allocated. The older models of tram still have steps, but usually another passenger or the driver will help, but remember to use the front entrance. Many cafés and restaurants provide baby facilities and there's a relaxed attitude towards breastfeeding. There are plenty of clean, well-equipped playgrounds dotted around the city: try the park in front of the Rathaus (*see p79*), the Stadtpark (*see p85*) and the Resselpark in front of the Karlskirche (*see p99*), and at the University Campus (*see p103*) children play right beside a couple of beer gardens. The best of Vienna's museums offer wonderful guided tours for children, but usually only in German. However, there are plenty of other activities and with a bit of planning, families can enjoy outings which offer something for everyone.

Innere Stadt

A stroll around the first district could include a visit to the Haus der Musik (*see p60*), or 'Sound Museum', which is full of interactive sound and music displays, including the opportunity to (virtually) conduct the Vienna Philharmonic Orchestra. The Baroque Lobkowitz Palace houses the Österreichisches Theatermuseum (*see p70*) which has a small collection for children accessible by a steep slide from the main museum. Here you can see magical stage sets and marionettes up close and play in a mini-theatre. You must ring ahead to book. The Schmetterlinghaus (Butterfly House) in the Burggarten (*see p85*) is a steamy jungle populated by a variety of colourful tropical butterflies and a troop of dwarf quails. Outside, the Burggarten is one of several parks where you can stretch out on the grass, and the sumptuous Palmenhaus café and brasserie (*see p85*) next door is bright and airy, equipped with nappy-changing facilities and provides coloured pencils for children to doodle with. For budding classical music buffs the Wiener

Staatsoper (*see p183*) is doing its bit to captivate a young audience, putting on performances of operas for children in a tent on the roof terrace of the opera house. There are two seasons in spring/early summer and autumn/winter. And for weary feet consider the ultimate in Viennese tourist kitsch: a ride in a *fiaker* (horse-drawn carriage) is a great way to keep the kids entertained while enjoying a tour of the sights. Just hop on at one of the *fiaker* stands on Stephansplatz, on Heldenplatz or on Albertinaplatz behind the Staatsoper.

MuseumsQuartier

Touting itself as a spectacular blend of Baroque buildings, modern architecture and cultural institutions of all shapes and sizes, as well as recreational facilities, the MuseumsQuartier (*see p83*) can hardly fail to please. It's also a relaxed place to hang out, with seating outside in summer and space for children to run around.

On the other side of the main road in front of the MuseumsQuartier you will find the Naturhistorisches Museum (*see p79*). Many of the exhibits are old-fashioned and lacking in imagination, but some of the newer displays are more interesting and the dinosaur section is a favourite. There is also a collection of living creatures including fish, insects and reptiles.

Dschungel Wien

7, Museumsplatz 1(522 0720-20/www.dschungel wien.at). U2 Museumsquartier. **Open** *Ticket office* 4.30-6.30pm daily and one hour before and after performance starts. **Admission** daytime performance €7.50; evenings €12. **No credit cards. Map** p250 D7.
Professional theatre, dance, music and workshops for children and teenagers with local and international performers.

WienXtra-kinderinfo

7, Museumsquartier, Museumsplatz 1 (4000-84 400/ www.kinderinfowien.at). U2 Museumsquartier, U2, U3 Volkstheater/tram 46, 49/bus 2a. **Open** 2-7pm Tue-Thur; 10am-5pm Fri-Sun. **Map** p250 D7.
Provides information on what's going on in Vienna for children of all ages. There's an indoor play area and nappy changing facilities.

Zoom Kindermuseum

7, Museumsquartier, Museumsplatz 1 (522 6748/ www.kindermuseum.at). U2 Museumsquartier, U2, U3 Volkstheater/tram 46, 49/bus 2a. **Open**

The playground of the **Technisches Museum**.

Ticket office 8am-5.30pm Mon-Fri; 10am-6pm Sat, Sun, but entrance to exhibitions closes earlier.
Admission free-€5; €5 children; €12 family.
Credit AmEx, DC, MC, V. **Map** p250 D7.
Zoom is the place to get stuck in to the serious business of play as a learning experience. The Ozean for children aged up to six is a great touchy-feely permanent exhibition on the theme of the sea. The Atelier, for three- to 12-year-olds, focuses on creative activities. There are guided, interactive exhibitions for children from the age of six upwards and the Zoom Lab introduces eight- to 14-year-olds to the world of multimedia technology. The guides and instructors can speak English. Participation is for a limited number only and there are fixed starting times, so you'll need to book in advance. Check the schedule on the website.

Prater

The Prater (*see p90*) is a must with its famous funfair. Behind the child-friendly Schweizerhaus beer garden (*see p121*), there's an array of rides suitable for younger children. The best are truly retro; we recommend in particular the 1950s racing-car rides, a 19th-century carousel pulled by real ponies and pony rides. For the less nostalgic, there's the Kinderparadies, where you pay once for all the rides and games. Or take a ride on the Liliput Bahn mini railway. In the woodland of the Prater you'll find a large number of playgrounds, including the fenced-in baby one near the child-friendly Café Restaurant Meierei at Hauptallee 3, and two big ones on the Jesuitenwiese. At the Hochschaubahn, Prater 113 behind the Schweizerhaus you can hire bikes of all shapes and sizes by the day or hour. The Original Praterkasperl (789 0301, www.praterkasperl.at), on the Wurstelplatz near the Schweizerhaus, is the Austrian equivalent of Punch and Judy.

Schönbrunn

Just because it's one of the biggest tourist magnets in Vienna doesn't mean Schönbrunn (*see p106*) hasn't got plenty to offer for children. The obvious starting point is the Tiergarten (*see p108*). It may be the oldest zoo in the world, but has been extensively modernised in recent years with a number of new enclosures. Highlights include the Rhino Park, the giant pandas, the Aquarium and Terrarium House, the Rainforest House (complete with tropical storms) and the Insect House. There is also an alpine farmhouse from Tyrol as well as a large children's playground, and the sea lions' feeding time is guaranteed to entertain. In the palace grounds outside, the maze will provide innocent fun for everybody. The Schönbrunner Bad (*see p206*) on the eastern side of the park i s one of Vienna's chicest open-air baths, but is also popular with families because mums and dads can lounge next to the children's pool which has a shallow end for babies and toddlers and a deeper half for swimming practice

Just up the road from Schönbrunn is the Technisches Museum (*see p106*), which has lots of levers to pull and buttons to push, and for two- to six-year-olds there's a play area featuring specially designed games and models.

Marionettentheater Schloss Schönbrunn

13, Hofratstrakt, Schloss Schönbrunn (817 32 47/www.marionettentheater.at). U4 Schönbrunn.
Admission €7-28 adults; €5-€19 children.
Credit AmEx, DC, MC, V.
These exquisite but pricey puppet performances of *The Magic Flute*, *Aladdin* and *Eine Kleine Nachtmusik*, or new stories such as *Ritter Kamenbert*, rely on music and costume rather than language to keep children's attention. Most performances last

about an hour, but *The Magic Flute* is over two hours. Tickets can be booked online or by phone and picked up half an hour before the performance.

Seasonal activities

In summer try the city's excellent open-air swimming pools like the Schönbrunner Bad (*see p206*), or head up to the Viennese Woods and enjoy pools such as the Krapfenwaldbad, with its beautiful views. If you hate chlorine, visit the beaches on the Old Danube (Gänsehäufl, Angelibad or Bundesbad Alte Donau, *see p206*), or take a trip to the Danube island, a favourite destination for Vienna's nudists, youngsters and families. You can also head for the lively Copa Cagrana (U1 Donauinsel), where you can rent in-line-skates or bicycles, and go boating. The Rathausplatz in front of the City Hall is a year-round hive of activity, usually of interest to children. In January and February there's an outdoor ice-skating rink and on summer evenings, operas and classical concerts are shown on a large screen, with food from around the world. The Christmas market in December has tacky stalls, but the trees are beautifully decorated and there are pony and train rides plus a baking/modelling workshop for three-to 16-year-olds inside the city hall.

The fun of the fair at the **Prater**. See *p163*.

For a rainy day

It's pouring down and the children are behaving like caged animals? There are two cinemas, English Cinema Haydn (*see p167*) and Artis (*see p166*), which show English-language films, or try one of the following:

Bogi Park

23, Gutheil-Schoder-Gasse 17 (230 0000/www.bogi park.at). Badner Bahn Gutheil-Schoder-Gasse. **Open** 10am-7pm daily. **Admission** €3.50; €7.50 3-16s; €2.50 1-3s. **Credit** AmEx, DC, MC, V.
A huge indoor playground, where kids can climb, bounce, slide and run riot to their hearts' content.

Diana-Erlebnisbad

2, Lilienbrunngasse 7-9 (219 8181/www.dianabad-wien.at). U1, U4 Schwedenplatz/tram N, 1, 2, 21 then 5min walk over the Marienbrücke. **Open** 10am-10pm Mon-Sat and holidays; 9am-8pm Sun. **Admission** €14; €11 concessions; €8 6-14s; €2.50 2-5s; free under-2s. **Credit** MC, V. **Map** p251 F5/6.
An indoor adventure pool featuring a fun slide, waves, pirate ship, and a baby pool.

Haus des Meeres

6, Esterhazypark, Fritz-Grünbaumplatz 1 (587 14 17/www haus-des-meeres.at). U3 Neubaugasse/bus 13a, 14a, 57a. **Open** 9am-9pm Mon-Wed, Fri-Sun. **Admission** €10.30; €4.80 6-15s; €3.30 3-5s; free under-3s. **No credit cards. Map** p246 C8.
A fascinatingly colourful array of tropical fish and other sea creatures, as well as reptiles, amphibians, insects, birds and monkeys housed in a flak tower.

Lilarum

3, Göllnergasse 8 (710 2666/www.lilarum.at). U3 Kardinal-Nagl-Platz (exit Keinergasse). **Open** *Mid June-mid Sept* 3pm Wed, Fri; 2.30pm, 4.30pm Sat, Sun. **Admission** €7.60 (children on your lap pay €3.80). **Credit** MC, V. **Map** p248 H8.
This excellent puppet theatre makes its own figures, composes and plays great backing music and uses several Burgtheater actors as story readers. All the productions are in German but small children will definitely find it enchanting.

Minopolis

22, Cineplexx Reichsbrücke, Wagramerstrasse 2 (0810 970 270/www.minopolis.at). U1 Donauinsel exit Hubertusdamm. **Open** 2-7pm Thur, Fri; 10am-7pm Sat, Sun, holidays. *Summer holidays* 2-7pm daily. **Admission** *Thur, Fri, summer holidays* €4; €8 children. *Sat, Sun, other holidays* €6; €12 children. **No credit cards. Map** p245 K2.
A mini city where children can earn and spend 'eurolinos' just like in real life. Plenty of activities are self-explanatory and parents can help.

Smalltalk Kids Café

6, Mariahilferstrasse 47 (0664 854 6482/www.kids cafe.at). U3 Neubaugasse/bus 2a. **Open** 9am-7pm Mon-Sat. **No credit cards. Map** p250 C/D8.
A haven for parents with young children.

Film

It's not all feel-bad films and dark documentaries. Unless you want it to be.

The city of Vienna, it's sometimes said, looks like an enormous film set. Those who find themselves wandering through the impossibly picturesque streets of the Innere Stadt, or contemplating the enormity of the great buildings on the Ringstrasse, will have no problem in concurring. Catching just the right note of expressionist bewilderment, Carol Reed's *The Third Man* (1949) is a perfect evocation of the city's faded post-war glamour, and is now the subject of books, walking tours and exhibitions (*see p100*). More recently, Richard Linklater's *Before Sunrise* (1995) is a gorgeous love story, ravishingly filmed in locations all over the city.

Meanwhile, the Austrian contribution to film history is undisputed: Fritz Lang, Erich von Stroheim, Josef von Sternberg, Fred Zinnemann, Edgar G Ulmer, Billy Wilder and Otto Preminger were all linked to Vienna. And while these figures may not constitute an identifiable Viennese school, they do share a non-judgemental, ironic detachment that rejects the use of facile sentimentality and soothing clichés to manipulate the audience's emotions. Such approaches are also discernible in a number of films from the last decade or so, including those of Michael Haneke, probably the most famous living Austrian director. Haneke's adaptation of Elfriede Jelinek's novel *The Piano Teacher* won the Grand Jury Prize at Cannes in 2001, and his later *Hidden* (2005) is a masterpiece of clammy urban paranoia. Elsewhere, Viennese filmmaker Ulrich Seidl made the tense, affectless *Dog Days* in 2001, and traced a bleakly honest narrative of migration in his acclaimed second feature *Import/Export* (2006). Female directors have secured a reputation as well, with accomplished features such as Jessica Hausner's *Hotel* (2004) and Barbara Albert's *Fallen* (2006). The annual festival of Austrian film, the **Diagonale** in Graz, has nurtured the work of many of these film-makers, and can take much of the credit for the revival in the fortunes of Austrian film-making.

LISTINGS AND TICKETS

Films are listed in all newspapers, but for the best coverage of foreign-language movies try *Der Standard* (daily) or, best of all, the weekly *Falter*, with an A-Z listing by film title. Film details are abbreviated as follows: *OF* is original version; *OmU* is original version with

Plaque commemorating Fritz Lang.

German subtitles; and *OmenglU* or *OmeU* is original version with English subtitles. When booking by phone or in person, specify the row – the first three are usually cheaper. On *Kino-Montag* (Mondays) all tickets are reduced.

FESTIVALS

In July and August, most arthouse cinemas drop regular programming to screen classic and cult films in the Sommer-Kino season. Listings appear on flyers and in the newspapers. In the summer, Vienna also has two open-air cinemas, complete with food stalls – *see p168*. The Viennale two-week international film festival starts in mid October and features Austrian premières, retrospectives and international feature, documentary and short films. Although there's no competition as such, there is the Vienna Film Award – 2006's winner was *Kurz Davor ist es Passiert*, a film on human trafficking in Austria by Viennese director Anja Salomonowitz. The FIPRESCI (the International Film Critics' Federation) awards a prize too – in 2006 it went to Albert Serra's *Honor de*

Cavalleria. Book in advance, as the festival is extremely popular (90,000 tickets sold in 2006). Following recent tributes to Lauren Bacall and Jane Birkin, 2007 is dedicated to Jane Fonda, who will grace the opening.

Cinemas

Admiral
7, Burggasse 119 (523 3759). U6 Burggasse/ tram 5/bus 48a. **Tickets** €6. **No credit cards**. **Map** p246 B/C7.
An old neighbourhood cinema, whose only drawback is that the cosy elongated interior is marred by the drone of passing traffic. The Admiral's programming features less commercial films – and they are always shown in the original version with subtitles.

Artis
1, Schultergasse 5 (535 6570). U1, U3 Stephansplatz/ U3 Herrengasse. **Tickets** €5.50 Mon-Wed; €8.50-€9.20 Thur-Sun. **No credit cards**. **Map** p251 E6.
An inner-city cinema that only shows mainstream Hollywood films without subtitles in English. The Artis has six rooms and so offers a large selection, but the screens are rather small (there are 848 seats altogether, but the biggest screen has 316).

Bellaria
7, Museumstrasse 3 (523 7591). U2, U3 Volkstheater/tram 46, 49/bus 48a. **Tickets** €4.50-€5.50 matinées; €6 in the evening. **No credit cards**. **Map** p250 D7.
Those with a weakness for time travel will adore the original 1950s interior at the Bellaria. The foyer's shabby but evocative decor features the original bar and box office, as well as fading portraits of the stars of *Heimat* and German films. The afternoon and early evening sessions here invariably include films from this epoch, whereas later in the day, the showings tend to be reruns of recent arthouse productions.

Breitenseer Lichtspiele
14, Breitenseerstrasse 21 (982 2173/www.bsl.at.tf). U3 Hütteldorfer Strasse/tram 10, 49. **Tickets** €7. **No credit cards**.
Nostalgics will also love the far-flung Breitenseer Lichspiele, Vienna's oldest operational cinema since the Erika closed in 1999. Dating from 1905, it has occupied its Jugendstil premises since 1909. On the occasion of the theatre's 100th anniversary in 2005, the 186 original wooden seats, appliqué wall lighting and neon sign were all renovated and a new piano installed to accompany silent films. It normally screens retrospectives, with films in original versions.

Burgkino
1, Opernring 19 (587 8406/www.burgkino.at). U1, U2, U4 Karlsplatz/tram 1, 2, D, J/bus 57a. **Tickets** €7-8. **No credit cards**. **Map** p250 E7.
The Burg has been screening *The Third Man* on Friday and Saturday nights since the early 1980s. Centrally located, it has two screening rooms (292

and 73 seats): the larger is a poorly conceived affair that generally shows the latest in thinking man's Hollywood, in plain original versions; the smaller room is for reruns and classics – Stanley Kubrick's *Dr Strangelove* is another perennial favourite.

De France
1, Hessgasse 7 (317 5236). U2 Schottentor/ tram 1, 2, D. **Tickets** €6.50-€7.50. **No credit cards**. **Map** p250 D5/6.
Now run and programmed by the generally reliable Votiv Kino team, this cinema shows original versions with subtitles in two small but very comfortable screening rooms.

Filmcasino
5, Margaretenstrasse 78 (587 9062/www.film casino.at). U4 Pilgramgasse/bus 13a, 14a. **Tickets** €5.50-€7.50. **No credit cards**. **Map** p247 D9.
It's worth a trip just to see the Filmcasino's magnificent neon sign and well-preserved 1950s decor. This unusually spacious 254-seat auditorium – ask for row five – premières the best in European and American cinema as well as new Asian films.

Filmhaus am Spittelberg
7, Spittelberggasse 3 (522 4816). U2, U3 Volkstheater/tram 49/bus 48a. Closed Aug. **Tickets** €5.80-€6.50. **No credit cards**. **Map** p250 C7.
This 100-seater arthouse cinema in Spittelberg is surrounded by bars and restaurants. Municipally owned, like the Stadtkino (*see right*), it has a similar schedule of original versions.

Filmmuseum
1, Augustinerstrasse 1 (533 7054/www.filmmuseum. at). U1, U2, U4 Karlsplatz/tram 1, 2, D/bus 3a. **Tickets** €5.50 members; €9.50 non-members; €12 annual membership. **No credit cards**. **Map** p250 E7.
After years of neglect, the Filmmuseum was refurbished in 2005 – probably something to do with legendary filmmaker Martin Scorsese being made honorary president in the same year. Founded in 1964 to preserve film as a medium and make it publicly accessible, it does a great job of exhuming forgotten classics and showcasing new talent from the world over. Recent retrospectives included the French film maker Chris Marker and Austrian performance artist Valie Export. The chic bar is a great for post-film drinks.

Gartenbaukino
1, Parkring 12 (512 2354/www.gartenbaukino.at). U3 Stubentor, U4 Stadtpark/tram 1, 2. **Tickets** €6-€7. **No credit cards**. **Map** p251 F7.
Saved from becoming a multiplex by the Viennale (*see p160*), the city's largest cinema (seating 750) is great for glamorous festival premières but a tad too large to turn much of a profit. Quite how long film fans will continue to enjoy the best of international film on its magnificent concave screen will depend on municipal largesse and the proceeds of club nights held in Gartenbau's elegant 1960s-style foyer.

Arts & Entertainment

Gartenbaukino.

Haydn English Cinema

6, Mariahilfer Strasse 57 (587 2262/www.
haydnkino.at). U3 Neubaugasse/bus 13a, 14a.
Tickets €5.90 Mon; €6.60 Tues, Wed; €6.60-€8.40
Thur-Sun. **Credit** AmEx, DC, MC, V. **Map** p246 C8.
Three screens of mainstream English-language fare.

Lugner Kino City

15, Gablenzgasse 1-3 (0810 584 637 www.lugner
kinocity.at). U6 Burggasse, 48a. **Tickets** €16.
Credit MC, V. **Map** p246 A7.
This ultra-modern multiplex in the grim Lugner
shopping centre shows Hollywood fodder, mostly in
German but occasionally in English. Apart from the
extra-spacious seats, the main draw here is the daily
'arthouse' session, albeit in a mere 20-seater room.
The whopping ticket price includes a drink and
unlimited nachos and popcorn in the 'Lugner Lounge'.

Metro Kino

1, Johannesgasse 4 (512 1803/www.filmarchiv.at).
Tram 1, 2. **Tickets** €5.50-€7.50. **No credit cards**.
Map p251 F7.
A gorgeous belle époque cinema, Metro Kino
shows retrospectives of Austrian and related films
selected by Film Archiv, the body that polices the
country's film heritage. With a stock of over 60,000
films, Film Archiv also hold summer screenings in
a marquee beside their offices in the Augarten
(see *p89*). Film buffs are hoping that plans to build
a modern cinema in the Augarten will get preference
over the projected Vienna Boys' Choir auditorium.
We can but live in hope.

Schikaneder

4, Margaretenstrasse 24 (585 2867/www.
schikaneder.at). U1, U2, U4 Karlsplatz/
bus 59a. **Tickets** €6. **No credit cards**.
Map p247 D9.
A hip, alternative cinema that shows about ten films
a week, most original subtitled versions. Their
80-seater screening room regularly puts on student
films and shorts. The popular bar pulls in the arty
crowd and hosts regular DJs plus poetry slams.

Stadtkino

3, Schwarzenbergplatz 7 (712 62 76/www.
stadtkinowien.at). U2 Stadtpark/tram 71, D. Closed
Aug. **Tickets** €6.50; €50 10-film card. **No credit
cards**. **Map** p251 E/F8.
This austere, 172-seat municipally funded cinema
screens original versions. It's run by film buffs who
publish detailed leaflets on each film shown.

Topkino

6, Rahlgasse 1 (208 3000/www.topkino.at). U2
Museumsquartier. **Tickets** €5.50-€8. **No credit
cards**. **Map** p250 D8.
Run by the the Schikaneder (*see above*) team, Topkino
repeats the winning formula of rerun films plus cool
bar/restaurant. The largest of the two screens seats 109
and hosts the Identities – Queer Film Festival (*see p179*).

Votiv-Kino

9, Währinger Strasse 12 (317 3571/www.votivkino.
at). U2 Schottentor/tram 1, 2, 37, 38, 40, 41, 42, D.
Tickets €6-€8; €6 Mon. **No credit cards**.
Map p250 D5.

This is one of the best cinemas in the city, with a 1960s feel to it. Votiv-Kino shows films in original versions on its three screens and also programmes films for the De France (*see p166*). On Sundays, there's a Film-Breakfast: €9.50 buys breakfast and a film.

Open-air cinemas

Freiluftkino Krieau
2, Trabrennbahn Krieau (729 17 43/www. krieau.com). Tram N. **Open** July, Aug from 9pm. **Tickets** €7.50. **No credit cards**. **Map** p249 K6.
Celebrating its tenth anniversary this year, this open-air cinema is held in the old Krieau trap racing course in the Prater. A mixture of classic and contemporary films is screened, but films in English are only shown on Thursdays.

Kino unter Sternen
2, Augarten-Park (tickets 0800 664 040 from 3pm daily/www.kinountersternen.at). Tram 5. **Open** late June-mid Aug. **Tickets** €7.50; €32.50 5 tickets. **No credit cards**. **Map** p243 F4.
Six weeks of open-air cinema on a huge screen in the shadow of the Augarten flak tower. Classic films, as well as a theme-based selection, are all shown in original version on a giant screen. Nearby a variety of food stalls set up along a tree-lined avenue, adding to the festive atmosphere. Umbrellas and blankets are provided in case of bad weather. Note that early booking and insect repellent are essential.

DVD & video stores

Alphaville
4, Schleifmühlgasse 5 (585 1966/www.alphaville.at). U1, U2, U4 Karlsplatz/tram 62, 65/bus 59a. **Open** 10am-10pm Mon-Sat; 2-7pm Sun. **No credit cards**. **Map** p247 E8.
In 2007, Alphaville celebrated its tenth anniversary with a massive party in the Gartenbaukino. Run by dedicated cinephiles from a cool store on the arty Schleifmühlgasse, Alphaville has over 8,000 films on DVD, with all the latest UK and US series. Quite simply Vienna's best video store.

Bookshop Satyr Filmwelt
1, Marc-Aurel-Strasse 5 (535 5326). U1, U4 Schwedenplatz/tram 1, 2, 21, N/bus 2a. **Open** 10am-7.30pm Mon-Fri; 9am-5pm Sat. **Credit** AmEx, DC, MC, V. **Map** p251 E6.
Opposite Pickwicks (*see below*), this bookshop specialises in film and stocks a good variety of biographies, posters and scripts, plus DVDs and soundtracks.

Pickwicks
1, Marc-Aurel-Strasse 10-12 (533 0182/www. pickwicks.at). U1, U4 Schwedenplatz/tram 1, 2, 21, N/bus 2a. **Open** 11am-10pm Mon-Fri; 10am-10pm Sat; noon-8pm Sun. **No credit cards**. **Map** p251 E6.
Vienna's oldest English-language video/DVD rental store is also the largest, mainly due to lack of quality control. Having moved the merchandise into the cellar, the ground floor is now a cosy café and bookstore.

My Vienna Peter Morgan

London born screenwriter **Peter Morgan** (whose screenplay for the 2006 British film *The Queen* was nominated for an Oscar) is a regular visitor to Vienna. When he's in town, he resides in style with his in-laws, the formidable Schwarzenberg dynasty.

'There are, of course, many Viennas. Vienna of the Cold War – Slavic and Eastern, Baroque Amadeus Vienna with powder wigs, waltzes and kitsch, fin de siècle Freud Vienna with bearded men, doctors and smoke-filled cafés, and WWII Vienna of the *Anschluss*, bowing its head in shame. All these identities fight for attention as you walk through the city, preferably inside the 1st district, within the Ring. That's when I'm happiest in Vienna, I suppose. Walking. Savouring a city divided into four identities.

'I love the useless shops, selling old buttons, antique watches, medals from fallen soldiers. The forgotten squares – the Fransiskanerplatz – with the alcoholics coming twice a day to be fed in the monastery; Das Kleines Cafe,

unchanged, unchanging. A stone's throw away is Das Immervoll, owned by a part-time actor with a baritone voice – my favourite Viennese restaurant.

'I love the Albertina Kirche, the Palmenhaus restaurant, the Loos Bar. I love Judenplatz, the cobbled streets, the Salzamt coffee house with its unreconstructed waiters, the Café Havelka, the smell of the smoke and the newspapers on wooden frames.

'But most of all, if I'm honest, I love leaving Vienna. Not because I dislike it; on the contrary, but because staying there too long feels like a bad idea. Bad for your health (it's terribly melancholic), and because being there too long feels like going backwards.

'Above all I love leaving Vienna because coming and going is so blissfully easy. High on my list on what I like about the place, bizarre as it may sound, is the airport – and the roads that lead to and from it. Empty. Comfortable – and for anyone accustomed to air travel in and out of the UK or the US in the 21st century, almost like another time.'

Galleries

Vienna's booming contemporary art scene is one of Europe's most vibrant.

Erwin Wurm's installation 'House Attack' at **MUMOK**. *See p85*.

Despite the moaning of museum directors desperate for more space and gallery owners lamenting the dearth of serious Austrian collectors, contemporary art is flourishing in Vienna. One clear sign is the fact that Francesca von Habsburg, daughter and heiress of the steel baron and obsessive art collector Hans Heinrich Thyssen-Bornemisza, chose to open her **TBA 21 Thyssen-Bornemisza Art Contemporary** showroom in a Baroque city palace in Vienna's 1st district rather than in her native London. The local art crowd flock to her openings in the hope of an audience with the 'archduchess', but whatever her personal agenda may be, von Habsburg's high profile does draw international attention to Vienna.

The popularity of the MuseumsQuartier (MQ) is another positive sign. Whether the broader public actually gets beyond its shops and bars and into the galleries is a moot point, but the constant series of installations and events in the MQ's public areas does its bit to expose the uninitiated to the arts. In 2005, MUMOK's exhibition of domestic private collections proved that solvent art lovers do exist in Vienna, though they prefer to keep out of the spotlight. Slowly, however, they are beginning to acquire the sort of kudos that art patrons in the Anglophone world have long enjoyed.

The ViennAfair (*see p158*) is a chance for these shy creatures to mingle with artists, curators and dealers. Since its foundation in 2005, it has specialised in Southern and Eastern European art. The 26 galleries from Skopje to Bratislava that took part in 2007 are sponsored by the Erste Bank. As this financial institution expands eastwards, it collects art in the countries where its new branches are located. Corporate collecting is a relatively new phenomenon in Austria, though one notable exception is the pioneering Essl collection that celebrates its 35th anniversary in 2007.

Fortunately, it's not only the champagne quaffers of the art world who are on a roll. The Viennese off-scene is showing strong signs of life too, with a glut of artist-run galleries, exhibitions and festivals. These include temporary occupations such as the old courthouse that 'space invasion' (www.spaceinvasion.at) used to exhibit newcomers, or permanent initiatives like the non-commercial *dreizehnzwei* space (www.dreizehnzwei.net) that specialises in media art. More and more independent art festivals take place in the city. Soho in Ottakring (*see p159*) was the first among them, staging art in shops and public spaces around the Brunnenmarkt.

Not at all square: **Christine König**. *See p175.*

And what do these organisers of alternative art spaces do when they feel the chill wind of time blowing? They become regular art dealers, of course. In the last two years, several new gallery owners in their thirties started successfully showing their own generation while at the same time cultivating new collectors.

INFORMATION

Check the weekly *Falter* for the best overview of current exhibitions. On the net, useful sites include Artmagazine (www.artmagazine.cc) and the Esel initiative (www.esel.at), while kunstnet (www.kunstnet.at) focuses on individual gallery programmes. They are only available in German. The best source of information in English is the website www.basis-wien.at, a regularly updated archive of the contemporary art world.

Otherwise look out for flyers in art-friendly cafés and bars, such as Schikaneder (*see p167*); Joanelli (*see p199*); fluc, rhiz (*see p194*); Topkino (*see p167*), plus those located within the MQ.

Public galleries

Art, some of it exquisite, is also on display at the Albertina (*see p69*), Kunsthistorisches Museum (*see p77*), MAK (*see p119*), Secession (*see p99*), Belvedere (*see p91*), Leopold Museum (*see p85*), Liechtenstein Museum (*see p102*) and MUMOK (*see p85*).

BA-CA Kunstforum

1, Freyung 8 (537 33 36/www.ba-ca-kunstforum.at). U3 Herrengasse. **Open** 10am-7pm Mon-Thur, Sat, Sun; 10am-9pm Fri. **Admission** €8.70; €4.40-€7.30 concessions. **No credit cards. Map** p250 E6.

Owned by Austria's most ubiquitous high street bank, the popular Kunstforum proffers a menu of itinerant, blockbusting exhibitions generally featuring male painters like Chagall or de Kooning, or else themed shows with titles like 'Eros in modern art'. With the main gallery attracting a largely middle-aged audience, work by younger, contemporary artists is relegated to a former strong room in the basement called Tresor.

Bawag Foundation

1, Tuchlauben 7a (534 53 226 55/www.bawag-foundation.at). U3 Herrengasse. **Open** 10am-6pm Mon-Sat. **Tours** 5pm Thur; 3pm Sat. **Admission** free. **Map** p250/1 E6.

Another bank-sponsored inner-city exhibition space, Bawag concentrates on big contemporary names with an emphasis on photography and film. Recent shows to have drawn plaudits include the satirical site-specific installation the *Welfare Show* by the Danish duo Elmgreen & Dragset, the Candice Breitz video portraits of John Lennon fans and Rodney Graham's witty fakes.

Essl Museum

An der Donau- Au, 1 3400 Klosterneuburg (02243 37050/www.sammlung-essl.at). S4 from Spittelau to Weidling-Klosterneuburg/U4 Heiligenstadt, then bus 239. **Open** 10am-6pm Tue, Thur-Sun; 10am-9pm Wed. **Admission** €7; €3.50-€5 concessions; free 6-9pm Wed. **No credit cards.**

Unusually in a country where art collectors tend towards anonymity, Agnes and Karl-Heinz Essl have invested the profits of their DIY empire in a splendid building on the outskirts of Vienna to house their substantial, but rather incoherently assembled collection of post-1945 Austrian and international art. Sniffed at by art snobs, the Essls have been collecting for 35 years and invite internationally renowned curators to oversee their shows. Combine a visit here with a walk along the Danube and a trip to Klosterneuburg monastery.

Generali Foundation

4, Wiedner Hauptstrasse 15 (504 9880/http:// foundation.generali.at). U1, U2, U4 Karlsplatz/tram 62, 65. **Open** 11am-6pm Tue, Wed, Fri-Sun; 11am-8pm Thur. **Admission** €6; €4.50 concessions. **Credit** MC, V. **Map** p250 E8.

Located in a converted former hat factory, the Generali insurance company's art space is one of Vienna's most imposing and prestigious. Exhibiting selected works from its large collection of conceptual art from the 1960s and '70s, Generali set a high standard for corporate collections by rediscovering works that combine the political with an intensely personal approach. Much of the credit should go to ambitious director Sabine Breitweiser for

presenting the collection in a contemporary setting. Expect to see artists such as Valie Export, Adrian Piper, Hans Haacke, Allan Sekula, Gustav Metzger and the ubiquitous Heimo Zobernig. Lately, there's been a stronger focus on Eastern Europe with artists like Július Koller and Edward Krasinski. The first show each year is supervised by an external curator and often turns out more experimental. There's also a media library of literature and rare videos.

Kunsthalle project space

4, Treitlstrasse 2 (521 89-33). U1, U2, U4 Karlsplatz/tram 1, 2, D, J. **Open** 4pm-midnight Tue-Sat; 1-7pm Mon, Sun. **Admission** free. **Map** p250 E8.

Architect Adolf Krischanitz designed this diaphanous rectangle – one that doesn't easily lend itself to exhibitions. The project space houses shows of very mixed

My Vienna Francesca von Habsburg

After her riotous London years hanging out with Steve Strange and singing backing vocals on Visage's iconic 'We Fade to Grey', Francesca married Karl von Habsburg, moved to Vienna and opened a gallery to house her growing collection of contemporary art.

'In many ways, Vienna is a little known capital with many, many secrets that would take several lifetimes to appreciate. At the heart of the city are its coffee houses. Sitting at the right table in the right café is as important as a good accessory. Something immaterial that makes all the difference! I'd recommend Café Anzengruber (*see p198*) as it's hip with the art crowd and on the same street as most of the good

galleries. Among the Austrian artists I really like are Siegrun Appelt, Brigitte Kowanz, Hans Schabus, Markus Schinwald and Heimo Zobernig. In fact, wherever you are in Vienna, you'll stumble over contemporary art in the most unexpected locations, but don't miss the Generali Foundation, the Bawag Foundation and the TBA 21 Thyssen-Bornemisza Art Contemporary Foundation. Ironically all run by women (myself included!), these small private foundations are Vienna's chapels to contemporary art.

'If I'm shopping in the 1st district, I always stop for a quick snack and a *Pfiff* (mini beer) at the classic Polish Trzesniewski (*see p120*). For dinner, the new and very stylish Ein Wiener Salon (*see p121*) is a must with its set menu and enormous portraits of Empress Maria Theresia and Emperor Franz I. It's very small so book early. Also new on the scene, with really great food for low prices and a cool atmosphere is Zum Roten Elefanten (*see p126*).

'Vienna is also the city of the Habsburgs so make sure you see the Imperial Treasury in the Hofburg (*see p64*). It is now widely publicised by a new campaign that proudly announces "We have no more emperors but we do have their jewels", which I find hilarious! Seeing the crown of the Holy Roman Emperor at close range is really a unique experience.

'People never give enough time to Vienna. I always end up doing a fraction of all this with my guests, who always promise to come back when they have more time, overwhelmed by a city full of art and extraordinary architecture.'

Let's stick together – Vienna's gallery clusters

It's a weekday evening, yet there are crowds of carefully dressed people in the street. Everybody seems to know one another, with young and old sipping glasses of wine and engaging in a shared interest. Yes, it's opening night in one of the three art gallery clusters that have formed in Vienna since 2000. Since the art market crash and gallery closures of the 1990s, a new spirit of cooperation has conquered the endemic grumbling of the Viennese. These shared party-like openings, pioneered in New York City's Soho, are the way the art dealers currently drag in the crowds.

Ample spaces and low rents have always been a magnet for the arts. When Georg Kargl opened his gallery on Schleifmühlgasse off the Naschmarkt in 1998, the street was a run down druggy thoroughfare. But the art dealer saw there was more to this quarter. Like in the 1970s, when Kargl detected the value of long-neglected Jugendstil furniture, he recognised the cultural history of the so-called Freihausviertel, once a huge worker's tenement with a theatre, where in 1791 Mozart's *Magic Flute* was premiered. Kargl persuaded several colleagues to become his neighbours. Today, the erstwhile psychedelic passage is all fancy design emporia and chic flower shops, vintage boutiques and cafés – not to mention four flourishing galleries:

Kargl, **König**, **Senn** and **Engholm Engelhorn**. And the Anzengruber next door remains the art crowd's favourite watering-hole.

Close to the MuseumsQuartier another huddle of galleries has developed along Eschenbachgasse. The pioneers **Meyer Kainer**, **Krobath Wimmer** and **Janda** have been followed by **Mezzanin** and **Steinek** in the last two years. While Eschenbachgasse's strongest player Meyer Kainer brings international art stars to Vienna and features Austria's most successful exports, its neighbours watch out for interesting newcomers. Krobath Wimmer is already harvesting the fruits of its belief in young conceptual art and Janda's female painters are attracting a lot of heat. Mezzanin managed to develop from an alternative gallery to a highly professional spot and even after 25 years in the business Silvia Steinek still has a fresh eye for individualists.

Long-established contemporary art galleries in Vienna live on in the big old apartment galleries of Seilerstätte in the Innenstadt. And for a while they reacted nervously to the collectivism of their competitors, with their NYC-style brightly lit, big windowed shop premises. Since **Insam** and **layr:wüstenhagen** moved in close by, however, they have sunk their differences and united under the banner of Seilerstätte: at the last opening, nine galleries took part.

quality, from the animation films of Nathalie Djurberg or Steven Cohen's provocative performances to group shows from distant countries like Ukraine or Georgia. In cooperation with the University of Applied Arts, an annual competition for art students takes place. The restaurant/bar with its terrace is one of Vienna's most likeable alfresco spots.

Kunsthalle Wien

7, Museumsquartier, Museumsplatz 1 (infoline 52189-33/office 52189-1201/www.kunsthallewien. at). U2 Museumsquartier. **Open** 10am-7pm Mon-Wed, Fri-Sun; 10am-10pm Thur. **Admission** €7.50; €6 concessions. **No credit cards.** Map p250 D7.
Living in a box proved more successful than residing in a Baroque palace: during the decade or so when it camped out in a prefab on Karlsplatz, the Kunsthalle was the brightest rising star in Vienna's contemporary art constellation, earning itself an excellent international reputation. Unfortunately, its present location in the MQ is easy to miss and it has to compete for visitors with the neighbouring MUMOK. Today, it tries to raise attendances with theatrical blockbuster shows such as its own 'Superstars' or the Liverpool Tate's 'Summer of Love', as well as cultivating its reputation among a more informed art audience with individual shows by the likes of Eva Hesse or Louise Bourgeois. Such a double-edged strategy may work for a large museum like Tate Modern, but the Kunsthalle is often criticised for it. Its fortunes were briefly revived by the second edition of 'Lives and works in Vienna' in 2005, selected by foreign curators. However, the presence of the MUMOK is tempting the Kunsthalle to abandon its former interest in Austrian artists in favour of contemporary art from Korea and Mexico.

Künstlerhaus

1, Karlsplatz 5 (587 9663/www.k-haus.at). U1, U2, U4 Karlsplatz/tram 1, 2, D, J. **Open** 10am-6pm Wed, Fri-Sun; 10am-9pm Thur. **Admission** €12; €10 concessions. **No credit cards.** Map p251 E8.
Founded in 1861, this institution is the public face of the stuffy Künstlervereinigung (Society of Artists), whose members exhibit on the second floor. Currently badly in need of renovation, the Künstlerhaus is waiting for a handsome prince to awaken it. In the past, this was done by young idealistic curators with shows on themes as varied as electronica, designer strategies, fashion labels and megalomania in architecture, all on a shoestring budget.

TBA 21 Thyssen-Bornemisza Art Contemporary

1, Himmelpfortgasse 13/9 (513 9856/www.tba21. org). U1, U3 Stephansplatz. **Open** noon-7pm Tue-Fri; noon-6pm Sat, Sun. **Admission** free. Map p251 E7.
'I've got it in my genes,' claims Francesca von Habsburg, daughter of art collector Hans Heinrich Thyssen-Bornemisza, who could not resist assembling a collection of her own. Not only does she acquire cutting-edge work by Doug Aitken, Olafur Eliasson or Janet Cardiff, she also sponsors events like the puppet rock opera *Don't Trust Anyone over Thirty* by Dan Graham and Tony Oursler or the Danube boat trip that brought Kutlug Ataman's video installation *Kuba* to various spots in the former Habsburg empire. Von Habsburg resides on the top floor of the palatial building that houses her constantly growing collection.

Private galleries

1st district

Charim Galerie

1, Dorotheergasse 12 (512 0915/www. charimgalerie.at). U1, U3 Stephansplatz. **Open** 11am-6pm Tue-Fri; 11am-2pm Sat. **No credit cards.** Map p250 E7.
Myriam Charim's interests range from Viennese actionists Günter Brus, Otto Muehl and Herrmann Nitsch to contemporaries such as filmmaker Edgar Honetschläger or Documenta11 participant and photographer Lisl Ponger, who explores ethnocentric views of other cultures. Her collection also includes old and new works by feminist performance artist Valie Export. Among her young charges are the Ukrainian Ivan Bazak and the Czech Daniel Pitin.

Galerie Dana Charkasi

1, Fleischmarkt 11 (699-10498 865/www. dana-charkasi.com). U1, U4 Schwedenplatz. **Open** 11am-2pm Mon, Wed, Fri; 4-7pm Tue, Thur. **No credit cards.** Map p251 F6.
Dana Charkasi comes from an art-collecting family that owned works by Schiele and still owns the tourist-trap restaurant Griechenbeisl. One would not expect to find a contemporary art space in such kitsch surroundings, but the stairs lead to a selection of witty, young Vienna-based artists such as Susanne Schuda and Kamen Stoyanov, both of whom are on their way up.

Galerie Ernst Hilger

1, Dorotheergasse 5 (512 5315/www.hilger.at). U1, U3 Stephansplatz. **Open** 10am-6pm Tue-Fri; 10am-4pm Sat. **No credit cards.** Map p250 E7.
Ernst Hilger runs three separate entities in and around a building just off Graben. On the ground floor Hilger contemporary promotes younger artists. Next door he consorts with multinational Siemens in a so-called 'ArtLab' of rather mixed quality. The first-floor main gallery trades primarily in art that sells itself: canvases, objects and prints from Warhol and Picasso to Mel Ramos and Mimmo Rotella.

Galerie Grita Insam

1, An der Hülben 3 (512 5330/www.galeriegrita insam.at). U3 Stubentor. **Open** noon-6pm Tue-Fri; 11am-6pm Sat. **No credit cards.** Map p251 F7.
Grita Insam runs one of Vienna's oldest contemporary spaces – her 'information gallery' was the first attempt in the city to promote audio and early media art. Working tirelessly for over three decades, Insam opened a beautiful new space in 2005 where she

Herbert Hinteregger at
Georg Kargl Fine Arts. *See p176*

represents international names such as photographer Candida Höfer or conceptual-art-pioneers Art & Language as well as new local talents, like the ubiquitous artist, DJ and fanzine editor Christian Egger.

Galerie Hohenlohe & Kalb

1, Bäckerstrasse 3 (512 9720/www.galeriehohenlohe. at). U4 Schwedenplatz. **Open** 11am-6pm Mon-Fri; 11am-3pm Sat. **No credit cards. Map** p251 F6.
Since 1999, ex-artist Theresa Hohenlohe has established herself with a spirited new programme that showcases younger Austrian artists such as Franz Kapfer, Jutta Strohmaier and Roland Kollnitz, and evergreens like the German painter Albert Oehlen. Keeping close ties to Documenta boss Roger Buergel provides the gallery with the best advice.

Galerie Krinzinger

1, Seilerstätte 16 (513 30 06/www.galerie-krinzinger.at). U1, U3 Stephansplatz. **Open** noon-6pm Tue-Fri; 11am-4pm Sat. **No credit cards. Map** p251 E/F7.
For over 35 years, restless gallery owner and art fair expert Ursula Krinzinger has shown established Austrian avant-garde artists (Günter Brus, Rudolf Schwarzkogler), 'new painting' (Hubert Schmalix, Siegfried Anzinger) and, more recently, US West-Coaster Chris Burden and the Dutch Atelier van Lieshout. Since his international breakthrough, phones ring daily requesting Erwin Wurm's photographic *One-Minute Sculptures.* Thematic shows and works by younger artists are exhibited at Schottenfeldgasse 45, home of Krinzinger Projekte.

Galerie Krobath & Wimmer

1, Eschenbachgasse 9 (585 7470/www.krobath wimmer.at). U2 Museumsquartier. **Open** 1-6pm Tue-Fri; 11am-3pm Sat. **No credit cards. Map** p250 D8.

Having moved from a small art-shop-cum-gallery to premises in the opulent Palais Eschenbach, Helga Krobath and Barbara Wimmer support artists such as Documenta12 participant Florian Pumhösl and freshly appointed academy professor Dorit Margreiter. And besides these highly successful neo-conceptualists, pop art practitioners such as Ugo Rondinone or Julian Opie are also shown.

Galerie Martin Janda

1, Eschenbachgasse 11 (585 7371/www.martin janda.at). U2 Museumsquartier. **Open** 1-6pm Tue-Fri; 11am-3pm Sat. **No credit cards. Map** p250 D8.
Martin Janda looks for artists whose work reflects their social and cultural milieu. The works shown range from the installations of Vienna-based Chinese artist Jun Yang to the ironic photographic performances of conceptualist Július Koller. Beside gifted sculptor Werner Feiersinger and Swiss 'explosion specialist' and video artist Roman Signer, female painters such as Adriana Czernin and Maja Vukoje also feature prominently.

Galerie Meyer Kainer

1, Eschenbachgasse 9 (585 7277/www.meyer kainer.at). U2 Museumsquartier. **Open** 1-6pm Tue-Fri; 11am-3pm Sat. **No credit cards. Map** p250 D8.
From the Vanessa Beecroft extravaganza in the Kunsthalle to Austrian Heimo Zobernig's first solo show at the MUMOK or the riotous boy band Gelitin at the Venice Biennale, expect Christian Meyer and Renate Kainer (former partners of Georg Kargl) to have their fingers in the pie. A star-spangled programme includes Austria's most bankable artist, Franz West, as well as pop artists Yoshitomo Nara, Sarah Morris and Raymond Pettibon. The gallery's newcomers Martina Steckholzer and Siggi Hofer both hail from the South Tyrol.

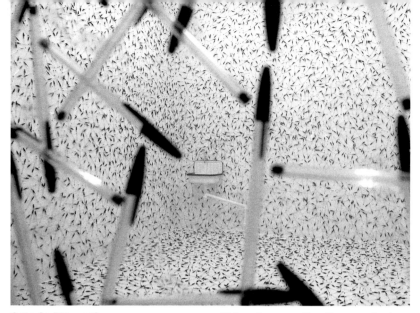

Galerie Mezzanin

1, Getreidemarkt 14/Ecke Eschenbachgasse (526 4356/ www.mezzaningallery.com). U2 Museumsquartier. **Open** 1-6pm Tue-Fri; 11am-3pm Sat. **No credit cards. Map** p250 D8.

Endless successions of ants, pipes and cables emerge from Peter Kogler's computer, an Austrian artist who became famous in the 1990s for huge print installations (one covers a car park at Vienna airport). The gallery shows Kogler alongside younger Viennese artists such as Anna Jermolaewa, who uses toys in her videos, or painter Katrin Plavcak, who takes unsettling motifs from internet footage.

Galerie Nächst St Stephan Rosemarie Schwarzwälder

1, Grünangergasse 1 (512 1266/www. schwarzwaelder.at). U1, U3 Stephansplatz. **Open** 11am-6pm Mon-Fri; 11am-4pm Sat. **No credit cards. Map** p251 F7.

This attractive, well-lit 19th-century apartment lies on the site of the first commercial gallery in Vienna. Opened in 1923 by Otto Kallir and then reopened in 1954 by the art-loving Catholic priest Monsignor Otto Mauer, it became notorious as a post-war meeting place for the avant-garde movements that sparked Viennese Actionism in the 1960s. The new owner, Rosemarie Schwarzwälder, turned it into a space devoted to contemporary painting and photography, with works by Herbert Brandl, Helmut Federle, James Welling and Jörg Sasse.

Galerie Steinek

1, Eschenbachgasse 4 (512 8759/www.galerie. steinek.at). U2 Museumsquartier. **Open** 1-6pm Tue-Fri; 11am-3pm Sat. **No credit cards. Map** p247 E8.

The gallery recently moved to Eschenbachgasse, where it competes for the attention of collectors with four other spaces. From the provocative drawings of Italian artist Carol Rama to the poetic conceptualism of American Robert Barry or the performance photos of Beijing artist Rong Rong, Steinek offers insights into artists who invariably have strong characters – this gallery is always good for a surprise and is sometimes breathtaking

layr:wüstenhagen contemporary

1, An der Hülben 2 (524 5490/www.layr wuestenhagen.com). U3 Stubentor. **Open** 11-6pm Tue-Fri; 11am-4pm Sat. **No credit cards. Map** p251 F7.

After running a tiny alternative space for over two years, charming devils Emanuel Layr and Thomas Wüstenhagen proudly inaugurated their serious new gallery in 2005 with the youngest cast of artists in town. Like the artist group Mahony, most are children of the mid 1970s and share an ironic sense of humour among other traits. There are always two shows to see: one in the regular gallery and another – of a more experimental nature – in the so-called 'garage'.

4th district

Christine König

4, Schleifmühlgasse 1a (585 7474/www.kunstnet.at/ koenig). Tram 62, 65/bus 59a. **Open** 11am-7pm Tue-Fri; 11am-3pm Sat. **No credit cards. Map** p247 D8.

One of the established stars of Vienna's gallery scene, König's programme promotes local heroes G.R.A.M., Johanna Kandl and the young drawing addict Constantin Luser, as well as more established figures such as Vienna-Group-member Gerhard Rühm and internationally acclaimed names including Kara Walker, Werner Büttner and Jimmie Durham. **Photo** *p170.*

Engholm Engelhorn Galerie

4, Schleifmühlgasse 3a (585 7337/www.engholm engelhorn.com). Tram 62, 65/bus 59a. **Open** 11am-7pm Tue-Fri; 11am-3pm Sat. **No credit cards. Map** p247 D8.

Kerstin Engholm shows young, conceptually challenging artists from all forms of media. Names to watch out for here include light-and-sound installation artist Angela Bulloch, Constanze Ruhm and UK artists Darren Almond and Mark Hosking. There is also a strong focus on painting which is presented in group shows that are called 'saloons', regularly covering quality German work by Hendrik Krawen or Dirk Skreber.

Gabriele Senn Galerie

4, Schleifmühlgasse 1A (585 2580/www.galerie senn.at). Tram 62, 65/bus 59a. **Open** 11am-6pm Tue-Fri; 11am-3pm Sat. **No credit cards. Map** p247 D8.

With strong links to the German art market, Gabriele Senn was responsible for introducing Cosima von Bonin, Kai Althoff and Georg Herold to Vienna, as well as presenting younger Austrians Bernhard Fruehwirth, Marko Lulic and Barbara Mungenast to the world. Much of it's highly stylised; don't let yourself be intimidated by the formalistic, cryptic art works that Dennis Loesch and Josphine Pryde specialise in.

Georg Kargl Fine Arts

4, Schleifmühlgasse 5 (585 4199/www.georg kargl.com). Tram 62, 65/bus 59a. **Open** 11am-7pm Tue, Wed, Fri; 11am-8pm Thur; 11am-3pm Sat. **No credit cards. Map** p247 D8.

What looks like a smart shop front is in fact the entrance to a deceptively large sky-lit basement space. Kargl is undoubtedly the main player in the Viennese art world, both as a personality and for his work at the now-defunct Galerie Metropol. He exhibits seriously saleable art by Gerwald Rockenschaub, Herbert Hinteregger, Mark Dion, Elke Krystufek, Thomas Locher or Cerith Wyn Evans. Younger artists like Carol Bove or Andreas Fogarasi are shown in the so-called Georg Kargl BOX, a 40sq m (430sq ft) space beside the main entrance that consists of an ingenious frontage and interior designed by prized American artist Richard Artschwager. **Photo** *p174.*

6th district

Galerie Amer Abbas

6, Schadekgasse 6-8 (585 2613/www.kunst buero.at). U3 Neubaugasse/bus 13a. **Open** 3.30-7.30pm Wed-Fri; 1-3pm Sat. **No credit cards. Map** p246 C8.

For a long time owner of the popular multi-purpose arts space kunstbuero, Amer Abbas has recently decided to concentrate more on art fairs and collectors. With his excellent instinct for emerging artists, this native Iraqi has discovered the likes of Gelatin, Marcin Maciejowski and Pavel Braila.

Galerie Andreas Huber

6, Capistrangasse 3 (586 0237/www.galerie andreashuber.at). U2 Museumsquartier. **Open** 2-6pm Tue-Fri; 11am-3pm Sat. **No credit cards. Map** p247 D8.

After successfully co-directing the non-commercial gallery offspace, Andreas Huber opened a 'real' gallery off Mariahilfer Strasse in 2005. Showing the work of his peers (thirtysomethings) has proved fruitful for Huber, who promotes artists with a feminist agenda such as Carola Dertnig and Kaucyila Brooke, as well as Academy graduate Leopold Kessler, who makes witty and boyish interventions in public space.

Galerie Knoll

6, Gumpendorfer Strasse 18 (587 50 52/www. kunstnet.at/knoll). U2 Museumsquartier. **Open** 2-7pm Tue-Fri; 11am-3pm Sat. **No credit cards. Map** p250 D8.

A pioneer in building links between Vienna and Central and Eastern Europe, Hans Knoll set up the first private gallery in post-1989 Eastern Europe, in Budapest. So it is no surprise that the Hungarian artists Ákos Birkás, Csaba Nemes and Ivica Capan are frequently displayed here. Knoll organizes art-trips to Russia every year and ships home provocative works by post-communist art collectives such as AES+F and Blue Noses.

7th district

Galerie Hubert Winter

7, Breitegasse 17 (524 0976/www.galeriewinter.at). U2, U3 Volkstheater. **Open** 11am-6pm Tue-Fri; 11am-2pm Sat. **No credit cards. Map** p250 D7.

For over 35 years Hubert Winter has been introducing international artists such as Lawrence Weiner, Haim Steinbach or Fred Sandback. He also exhibited 1980s newcomers such as Brigitte Kowanz and Franz Graf, and accompanied them to stardom – or at least to a job at the Academy of Fine Arts. These days, a younger range of Viennese artists, including 'walking artist' Michael Höpfner or the gifted humourist Catrin Bolt, as well as international newcomers like the Chinese Lei Xue, are shown.

Momentum Photography Editions

7, Karl-Schweighofer-Gasse 12 (228 8893/www. momentum.co.at). U2, U3 Volkstheater. **Open** 11am-7pm Tue-Fri; 11am-5pm Sat. **No credit cards. Map** p250 D7.

Specialising in affordable editions, the three young photo aficionados Valerie Loudon, Moritz Stipsicz, Anthony Hauninger opened their own gallery in 2006. All fields of photography from art to fashion or sport are featured, but Momentum's major ambition is to get more attention for Austrian photography. The gallery reproduces series by great photo-reporters like Erich Lessing and Barbara Pflaum, as well as singular works by artists such as Elke Krystufek or Andreas Bitesnich. Prominent names – among whom are Nan Goldin, Marie-Jo Lafontaine or Jürgen Teller – also feature.

Gay & Lesbian

A low-key scene that occasionally lets off steam.

Two days a year, Vienna transforms itself into a loud, self-confident gay city. Should your visit coincide with either the Life Ball AIDS fund-raiser or the Rainbow Parade, you'd probably think you'd stepped into some perv paradise. Sadly, the other 363 days are a rather more pedestrian affair. While Vienna's 'queer quarter', districts 4 and 6 on either side of the Naschmarkt, offers an ever-growing choice of bars for gay men, lesbians are very poorly served, with numerous locations recently closing.

In an enthusiastic attempt to court the pink euro, the Vienna tourist board's *Queer Vienna* pamphlet lists bars and saunas, and hails the gayness of historic figures such as Prince Eugène of Savoy and the architects who built the Staatsoper. Violence against gays and police harassment are extremely rare in Vienna and both the Life Ball and the Rainbow Parade are important dates in the straight calendar.

Cafés & bars

See also p125 Motto and *p140* Operncafé Hartauer Zum Peter.

Alte Lampe
4, Heumühlgasse 13 (587 3454/www.altelampe.at). U4 Kettenbrückengasse, **Open** 8pm-1am Wed, Thur, Sun; 8pm-3am Fri, Sat. **No credit cards.** **Map** p247 D8/9.
Although Vienna's oldest gay bar continues to attract all ages, bears are its most prominent regulars. For over 50 years, the Alte Lampe has provided a rustic, wood-panelled refuge for the city's queer folk – shame they can't get someone to tune the old piano.

Café Berg/Löwenherz Bookshop
9, Berggasse 8 (café 319 5720/bookshop 317 2982-1/www.loewenherz.at). Tram 37, 38, 40, 41, 42. **Open** *Café* 10am-1am daily. *Bookshop* 10am-7pm Mon-Thur; 10am-8pm Fri, 10am-6pm Sat. **Credit** *café & bookshop* MC, V. **Map** p243 D/E5.
This stylish café/bookstore sits on the hilly Berggasse just up the road from Sigmund Freud's former residence. Soon to celebrate its 15th anniversary, the Berg's friendly staff serve great breakfasts, lunches and dinners, and its well-stocked gay bookstore is worth a browse.

Café Savoy
6, Linke Wienzeile 36 (586 7348). U4 Kettenbrückengasse. **Open** 5pm-2am Mon-Fri; 9am-2am Sat. **No credit cards.** **Map** p247 D8.

This classic café has an authentic camp interior consisting of chandeliers, feathers and gigantic old mirrors. Apart from Saturday afternoons when a mixed clientele seeps in from the Naschmarkt, it's pretty much dominated by men of all ages. **Photo** *p178.*

Café Willendorf/Rosa Lila Villa
6, Linke Wienzeile 102 (587 1789/www.villa.at). U4 Pilgramgasse. **Open** 6pm-2am daily. **No credit cards.** **Map** p247 D8.
What began as a squat in the 1980s is now Vienna's most prominent gay institution. Within its pink and purple exterior, the Rosa Lila Villa houses a bar/restaurant (Café Willendorf) with a shady ivy-clad courtyard and facilities for discussions and counselling. Open to folk of any sexual orientation, the clientele is predominantly gay and lesbian.

Eagle
6, Blümelgasse 1 (587 2661/www.eagle-vienna.com). U3 Neubaugasse. **Open** 9pm-4am daily. **No credit cards.** **Map** p246 C8.
You'll need to buzz to get into this popular late-night men-only bar. Known locally as the world's only leather bar without leather, it has videos and an active darkroom with individual cabins.

Felixx
6, Gumpendorfer Strasse 5 (920 4714/www.felixx-bar.at). U2 Museumsquartier. **Open** 7pm-3am daily. **No credit cards.** **Map** p247 D8.
Felixx pulls in a young, dressy clientele. Recently done out, it features 1980s-style high benches and tables with chandeliers providing low-lighting. Meals are available but it's worth checking out the neighbouring Zum Roten Elefanten (*see p126*).

Frauen Café
8, Lange Gasse 11 (406 3754/www.frauencafe.com). Tram 46, J. **Open** 7pm-midnight Tue-Thur; 7pm-2am Fri, Sat. **No credit cards. Map** p246 C6/7.
Now in its 30th year, this grande dame of Vienna's lesbian scene is currently the only women-only spot in the city. Small and cosy and open to straight women, the Frauen Café offers reasonably priced drinks and friendly service.

Lo:sch
15, Fünfhausgasse 1 (895 9979/www.lmc-vienna.at). U6 Gumpendorfer Strasse. **Open** 10pm-2am Fri, Sat. **No credit cards. Map** p246 A9.
The club house of LMC, Vienna's Leather and Motorbike Community. Given that strict dress codes apply at this men-only leather and fetish bar, it's advisable to check the events section of the website. Not for the faint-hearted.

Mango Bar
6, Laimgrubengasse 3 (587 44 48/www.mango bar.at). U4 Kettenbrückengasse/bus 57a. **Open** 9pm-4am daily. **No credit cards. Map** p247 D8.
At both Felixx and this cruisey, crowded bar for young guys you can get free tickets for Why Not? Just ask at the bar – the staff are very friendly and the place is always so lively you might stay.

Nightshift
6, Corneliusgasse 8 (586 23 37). U3 Neubaugasse/ bus 13a,14a. **Open** 10pm-6am daily. **No credit cards. Map** p246 C9.
The place for those who failed to pick someone up in the Eagle (it's just around the corner), with videos and a lively darkroom with individual cabins.

Sling
4, Kettenbrückengasse 4 (586 2362/www.sling.at). U4 Kettenbrückengasse. **Open** 3pm-4am daily. **No credit cards. Map** p247 D9.
This hi-tech cruising bar has long opening hours and a variety of facilities that include darkrooms, glory holes, what they call a 'piss cinema' and shower facilities. There's also a good bar with free lube and condoms, and an on-the-house breakfast from 2am.

Stiefelknecht
5, Wimmergasse 20 (545 2301). Tram 62, 65. **Open** 10pm-2am Mon-Thur, Sun; 10pm-4am Fri, Sat. **No credit cards. Map** p247 D10.
A serious leather bar with slings, swings and so on. Dress the part. Strictly men only.

Village Bar
6, Stiegengasse 8 (585 1180/www.village-bar.at). U3 Neubaugasse/bus 13a. **Open** 7pm-3am daily. **No credit cards. Map** p247 D8.
Vienna's hottest American-style gay bar has good cocktails, cheap shots and themed nights. It gets very crowded at weekends.

Clubs

Why Not? is Vienna's only exclusively gay dance joint. The popular Heaven night (www.heaven.at) is now held at the Camera Club (*see p199*) on the first and third Saturday of the month. Subzero, an underground labyrinth at Siebensterngasse 27 in the 7th district (www.subzero.at) is currently home to queer:beat while the exotic Homoriental nights take place at good venues such as Badeschiff (*see p196*), Aux Gazelles (*see p198*) and Ost Klub (*see p193*). Check www.gayboy.at to keep abreast of the latest gay-driven club nights.

Why Not?
1, Tiefer Graben 22 (925 3024/www.why-not.at). U2 Schottentor, U3 Herrengasse. **Open** 22-open end Fri, Sat. **Admission** free before midnight. **No credit cards. Map** p250 E6.
This popular town-centre bar-disco is generally patronised by younger guys (women too). There's a subterranean dance floor and separate bars with a lounge area with lots of red plush and darkroom.

Café Savoy. *See p177.*

Cruising areas

Cruising in Vienna is mostly safe and police seem to turn a blind eye. The Rathauspark – on the left-hand side as you face the Rathaus, past the fountain – is the most popular turf in spring and summer. Summer is also best for the Donauinsel. Serious cruising goes on at the Toter Grund area beside Steinspornbrücke, a long trek down river along the Neue Donau. Take the U1 to VIC, then bus 91a to the Roter Hiasl stop, or rent a bike.

Stations such as Stephansplatz and Alte Donau of the U1 line are daytime cruising areas. The Albertina passage that runs beneath the Ring from the Staatsoper to Café Aida (a peculiar mixture of old Viennese, tourists, gay men and rent boys) has a bit of traffic. The Venediger Au near the Prater big wheel and the Schweizer Garten beside Südbahnhof are less popular and more risky.

Events

Life Ball
9, Porzellangasse 32-33 (595 5600/www.lifeball.org). Held at the end of May or early June, this annual AIDS fund-raising event has established itself as a glamorous, celebrity event. Although tickets tend to disappear within an hour of going on sale, it's worth checking out what's happening around the Rathaus.

Rainbow Parade
www.regenbogenparade.at. **Date** late June. Vienna's wild and wonderful Pride event has been marching round the Ringstrasse since 1996.

Identities – Queer Film Festival
www.identities.at.
This biennial gay and lesbian film festival held at cinemas throughout Vienna will return in June 2009.

Media

Vienna Gay Guide
www.gaynet.at.
A city map for gay tourists, indicating hotels, restaurants, bars, clubs, saunas, shops and cruising areas around town. Available by post from the website.

Xtra
www.xtra-news.at.
The most established of Vienna's gay publications has a calendar of events, classified ads, columns, bar listings and more politics than its competitors.

Saunas

Kaiserbründl
1, Weihburggasse 18-20 (513 3293/www.gay sauna.at). U1, U3 Stephansplatz. **Open** 2pm-midnight Mon-Thur; 2pm-2am Fri; 1pm-2am Sat; 1pm-midnight Sun. **Admission** (per day, incl locker) €16; €10 after 9pm Mon-Thur & concessions. **Credit** AmEx, DC, MC, V. **Map** p251 E7.
Built in 1870 by the Persian ambassador as a gift to his son, these marvellous Moorish-style baths must be among the most beautiful gay bathhouses in the world. The painter Stefan Riedl (a gay artist who supervised the restoration of the baths) added some splendid erotic wall paintings alongside the intricate mosaics. You'll find relaxation rooms, cruising areas, cabins, a darkroom, a Finnish sauna, massage, a solarium and a new bar area. The clientele is on the older side these days, but the Kaiserbründl remains the crowning glory of gay Vienna.

Sauna Frisco
5, Schönbrunner Strasse 28 (entrance Rüdigergasse) (920 2488/www.frisco.at). U4 Pilgramgasse. **Open** 3pm-midnight Mon-Thur; 3pm Fri-10pm Sun non-stop. **Admission** €8; €16 weekends. **No credit cards. Map** p247 D9.
Directly opposite Motto, Vienna's newest gay sauna is a cosy affair with steam baths, video and food.

Sport Sauna
8, Lange Gasse 10 (406 7156/www.sportsauna.at). Tram 46. J. **Open** 3pm-1am Mon-Thur; 3pm Fri-1am Mon non-stop. **Admission** €8 Mon-Wed & concessions; €11 Thur, €15 all weekend (Fri-Sun). **No credit cards. Map** p246 C7.
Popular with the younger crowd, this sauna has a steam bath, bar, videos and cabins, but the decoration is unbelievably cheesy.

Arts & Entertainment

Music: Classical & Opera

More than Mozart.

A visitor to Vienna in 2006 would have been forgiven for thinking that Wolfgang Amadeus Mozart was the only composer who ever lived or worked in the city. Vienna turned itself inside out to honour the 250th anniversary of Mozart's birth, putting on one of the largest series of tributes ever dedicated to the memory of a composer. The festivities kicked off with the unveiling of the Mozarthaus Wien (*see p59*) and continued with innumerable concerts, exhibitions, symposia, plays and a plastering of the great man's moniker on every conceivable item and surface. The inevitable backlash that set in could best be summed up with the piece entitled *I Hate Mozart*, which premièred in November 2006 at Theater an der Wien. But now that Mozart fever has run its course, visitors to Vienna can once again take full advantage of the sheer variety of classical music that the city has to offer. (At least until 2009, when it's Haydn's turn (*see p187* **2009 – All hail Haydn!**). After all, any city that can claim Mozart, Beethoven and Schubert as past residents has an unmatched claim to be at the centre of the musical universe.

In keeping with this extraordinary tradition, there is music to suit every possible taste on offer. If you prefer an orchestral concert, the **Wiener Philharmoniker** or **Wiener Symphoniker** are likely to be performing, and if you're specifically interested in early and Baroque music, the **Concentus Musicus**, conducted by Nikolaus Harnoncourt, is at your service. High-calibre chamber ensembles such as the **Alban Berg Quartet** also call Vienna their home and the city positively basks in solo recitals by top-notch instrumentalists and singers. Contemporary music is represented by the formidable **Klangforum Wien**.

This is not to say, however, that every performance is a gem. The downside to the historical awe accorded Vienna and its music is a certain complacency. This can manifest itself in many ways: from a lacklustre performance 'good enough for the punters', to a feeling emanating from cloakroom staff that 'you should be grateful just for the experience'. Then again, perhaps we should.

TICKETS & INFORMATION

Concert information is available from tourist offices (*see p232*), in listings magazines such as *Falter* and on information columns scattered all over the city. Advanced tickets are available from the outlets mentioned below. At some major venues, tickets and prices are divided into five categories; in descending order of expense, these are: G (gala), P (première), A, B and C. Vienna also hosts festivals with classical music and opera throughout the year (*see pp158-161*).

Österreichische Bundestheaterkassen

1, Operngasse 2 (514 44 7880/7881/7882/credit card bookings 513 1513/www.bundestheater.at). U1, U2, U4 Karlsplatz/tram 1, 2, D, J. **Open** 8am-6pm Mon-Fri; 9am-noon Sat, Sun, public holidays; 9am-5pm first Sat of the month. **Credit** AmEx, DC, JCB, MC, V. **Map** p250 E7/8.

The State Theatre Booking Office has tickets available for the Schauspielhaus, Staatsoper, Volksoper, Burgtheater and Akademietheater. (Each theatre also has its own box office – see individual listings for details). Tickets for the Staatsoper and Volksoper go on sale one month before the date of performance and can be booked by telephone with a credit card one day after the advanced sale begins. Lines are open 10am-9pm daily; English is spoken. You can also order tickets online.

Vienna Classic Online

www.viennaclassic.com. **Credit** AmEx, DC, MC, V.

Easy to navigate, this online ticket agency covers all the big and most of the smaller venues, offering tickets for opera, concerts, theatre, musicals and some special events. Search by venue, category or date.

Wiener Staatsoper

1, Herbert von Karajan Platz 1 (514 44-7810/www. wiener-staatsoper.at). U1, U2, U4 Karlsplatz/tram 1, 2, D, J. **Credit** AmEx, DC, JCB, MC, V. **Map** p250 E7.

Tickets for the Staatsoper can be purchased at the box office in the foyer from 9am until two hours before the performance Mon-Fri, Sat 9am-noon, and from the information office in the arcades at the Staatsoper from 9am until one hour before the performance, or on Saturday from 9am-5pm. Many of the costumed ticket sellers on the square tout tickets to sold out or otherwise hard to see performances, but be warned – they usually come at a hefty price.

Musikverein. See p182.

Wien-Ticket

6, Linke Wienzeile 6 (588 30-529/phone bookings 58 885/www.wien-ticket.at). U1, U2, U4 Karlsplatz (exit Secession). **Open** 10am-9pm daily. **Credit** AmEx, DC, MC, V. **Map** p250 D8.

This daytime box office of the Theater an der Wien and the Raimund Theater also sells tickets for all other venues. Last-minute tickets for Theater an der Wien are available one hour before curtain. The Raimund Theater also offers standing room two hours before curtain for €2.50.

Wien-Ticket Pavillon

1, Herbert-von-Karajan-Platz (no phone). U1, U2, U4 Karlsplatz/tram 1, 2, D, J. **Open** 10am-7pm daily. **Credit** AmEx, DC, MC, V. **Map** p250 E7.

This booth is located next door to the Staatsoper. It supplies tickets for most venues.

Main venues

Orchestral, opera & operetta

Kammeroper

1, Fleischmarkt 24 (box office 513 6072/www. wienerkammeroper.at). U1, U4 Schwedenplatz/ tram 1, 2. **Open** *Box office* noon-6pm Mon-Fri; noon-7.30pm (on performance days); 4-7.30pm Sat (only on performance days). **Tickets** €15-€48; €5 standing. **Credit** AmEx, DC, MC, V. **Map** p251 F6.

Ruled with an iron hand from its inception in 1953 by founder Hans Gabor, the Kammeroper, which is dedicated to smaller-scale opera productions, floundered a bit after his death in 1994 but picked up when his widow, Isabella Gabor, and Holger Bleck took over the reins in 2000. The accent is now on per-

The mighty **Staatsoper**.

forming works that are neither included in the repertoire of the bigger houses, nor likely to be produced by the independent companies. The highly successful summer season, which was at one time held amid the mock-Roman ruins in the park of Schönbrunn Palace has moved back to the 1st district under the banner of 'The Vienna Summer Opera Festival'. The permanent home of the Kammeroper is a tiny Jugendstil theatre on the Fleischmarkt. The small space brings the action up close and personal. Besides the Kammeroper itself, Gabor also instituted the Belvedere International Singing Competition, held every summer, usually in July.

Konzerthaus

1, Lothringerstrasse 20 (box office 242 002/infoline 242 00-100/www.konzerthaus.at). U4 Stadtpark/ tram D. **Open** *Box office* 9am-7.45pm Mon-Fri; 9am-1pm Sat and 45mins before start of performance. **Tickets** €15-€120. **Credit** AmEx, DC, JCB, MC, V. **Map** p251 F8.

A massive and much needed renovation was completed on the Konzerthaus in 2000, returning the Grosser Saal, Mozartsaal and Schubertsaal to their previous glory and adding another hall on the lower level. Rather mundanely named the New Hall, this has been put to good use continuing the Konzerthaus tradition of promoting new music. The Konzerthaus also features three further rooms, the Schönbergsaal, the Alban Berg Saal and the Wotruba Salon, as well as a much-lauded restaurant.

As for the music, the Wiener Symphoniker and Concentus Musicus both play here and contemporary classical music is featured every autumn for four weeks (usually in November) when the Konzerthaus stages 'Wien Modern', Vienna's premier festival of new music, dedicated to promoting post-1945 composition. Often the Konzerthaus ventures beyond classical music with regular jazz and world music offerings. Among recent artists were Nick Cave, Lambchop, Jan Garbarek and Marisa Monte.

Musikverein

1, Bösendorferstrasse 12 (505 8190/www. musikverein.at). U1, U2, U4 Karlsplatz/tram 1, 2, D, J. **Open** *Box office* 9am-8pm Mon-Fri; 9am-1pm Sat. Closed 1 July-15 Aug. **Tickets** €16-€90; €4-€6 standing. **Credit** AmEx, DC, JCB, MC, V. **Map** p251 E8.

If you've ever joined the millions worldwide who watch the New Year's Day concert on TV, you've already seen the Vienna Philharmonic's unofficial main home, the opulent Musikverein. The magnificent main hall of this building is more than merely a pretty face, though: it's also an acoustic miracle. The ceiling above its 1,750 seats isn't joined to the walls, but hangs freely to allow for better vibration; there is also an entire room underneath that polished wooden floor for the same reason. The smaller 660-seat Brahmssaal is no less ornate, and it is used for chamber concerts and recitals. Four further halls, prosaically named after the materials used in their constructions, were built beneath the building in 2001-04 to designs by Austrian architect Wilhelm Holzbauer. Tickets to a Saturday afternoon or Sunday morning Vienna Philharmonic concert are among the hottest in town; as for the 1 January event, you must have your written request for the following year in by 2 January. Like the Staatsoper, the Musikverein offers standing room tickets, but here you can buy them at the normal box office up to three weeks in advance. The best buy is a seat in the last few rows of the parterre. These are raised, adding a panoramic view to that incredible sound. **Photo** *p181.*

Radiokulturhaus

4, Argentinierstrasse 30a (box office 501 70/377/ café 503 74 04/backstage tour 877 99 99/www. radiokulturhaus.orf.at). U1 Taubstummengasse. **Open** *Box office* 2-7pm Mon-Fri; 60mins before performance Sat, Sun. *Café* 9am-midnight Mon-Fri; Sat, Sun and holidays subject to performance times. **Tickets** €16-€24. **Credit** AmEx, DC, MC, V. **Map** p247 E8/9.

A three-part complex housing the Grosser Sendesaal, home of the Vienna Radio Symphony Orchestra, the Klangtheater Ganzohr ('all ears'), now used mostly for radio plays, and the Radio Café. The Grosser Sendesaal hosts everything from classical, jazz and New Age music to cabaret, exhibitions and spoken theatre. The Radio Café is poorly designed and has neither old-world charm nor modern flair, but offers a varied mixture of evening entertainment in a casual atmosphere and boasts a top-notch chef.

Schlosstheater Schönbrunn

13, Schloss Schönbrunn/Schönbrunner Schlossstrasse (711 55-0/www.musik-theater-schoenbrunn.at). U4 Schönbrunn. **Open** *Box office* from 1hr before performance. **Tickets** €18-€48; €7 standing. **No credit cards.**

Opened in 1749 to entertain the court of Maria Theresia, this is the oldest working theatre in Vienna, and the closest you'll come to the inside of a gilded music box. Napoleon caught a couple of performances here in 1809 while in town doing a bit of conquering. Nowadays, it's rented out to a variety of ensembles and interested parties, including the nearby University of Music and Performing Arts.

Staatsoper

1, Herbert von Karajan Platz 1 (51 444-2960/2959/ tours 51 444-2606/www.wiener-staatsoper.at). U1, U2, U4 Karlsplatz/tram 1, 2, D, J. **Open** *Evening box office* from 1hr before performance. **Tickets** *Gala performances* (G) €18-€254; *Premières* (P) €11-€220; (A) €10-€178; (B) €9-€157; (C) €7-€125; €2-€3.50 standing. **Credit** AmEx, DC, JCB, MC, V. **Map** p250 E7.

The State Opera House, or Staatsoper, was built in 1861-69 according to plans by the architects August Siccardsburg and Eduard van der Nüll. The neo-Renaissance-style structure initially met with ferocious criticism from the local public, who called it the 'sunken crate' and the 'stone turtle'. Siccardsburg never designed again and died of a weakened heart; Van der Nüll killed himself. Neither lived to see the opera house officially opened, on 25 May 1869, with a performance of *Don Giovanni*. However, the citizenry eventually took the building to its heart, to the extent that after 1945, when the Staatsoper had been almost completely destroyed, the Viennese painstakingly reconstructed it. During the reconstruction, the Staatsoper company took up residence in the Theater an der Wien, where the legendary Vienna Mozart Ensemble came into being.

Many men have overseen this pinnacle of musical and operatic achievement over the years – great conductors such as Richard Strauss, Karl Böhm, Clemens Krauss and Herbert von Karajan. It was, however, Gustav Mahler, director from 1897 to 1907, who left the most significant mark on the Staatsoper, simultaneously changing opera itself in ways that are now taken for granted. Dimming the audience lighting during the performance, shortening intermissions to 15-20 minutes and seating late arrivals only after the prologue or first intermission were all radical innovations brought in by Mahler.

The current director, Ioan Holender, announced in February 2007 that he would not renew his contract when it expired in August 2010, causing much speculation over possible successors, who include star tenor Neil Shicoff, conductors Franz Welser-Möst and Christian Thielemann, and Zurich Opera Intendant Alexander Pereira. Holender himself said he favours Burgtheater director Klaus Bachler as his successor, but Bachler is due to take over as head of the Bavarian State Opera in Munich in 2008. If things move with the usual Viennese *Gemütlichkeit* it may take until 2010 to come up with a final candidate.

The *Magic Flute* at the **Staatsoper**.

Arts & Entertainment

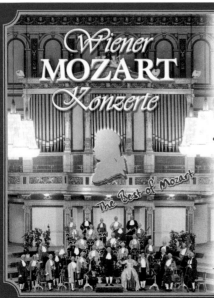

The Staatsoper has one of the largest opera reper-toires in the world (some 70 different productions each year), achieved thanks to a combination of a long season (1 Sept-30 June) and a rotation system that calls for a different opera every day of the week. Although this occasionally plays havoc with the quality of the performances, it does enable visitors to see many different works in a short period of time and keeps native opera lovers busy checking out the latest cast changes. One of the more inspired cast-ings of 2007 saw Montserrat Caballé as the Duchesse de Crakentorp join Juan Diego Flórez and Natalie Dessay in a much heralded production of Donizetti's *La Fille du Régiment*. Opera phenomenon Anna Netrebko, also appeared that season, making a grand entrance at the Opernball, then trilling along-side Roberto Alagna in a new production of Massenet's *Manon*. No matter who's singing, the Wiener Philharmoniker, under the stage name 'Das Orchester der Wiener Staatsoper', provides a lus-cious accompaniment from the pit.

Good seats at the Staatsoper go quickly. Often the only way to get a ticket is by buying one from the touts. Another option, for those with strong legs, is a bargain standing-room ticket (567 of them). You can normally get them 80 minutes before curtain, at the window marked *Stehplätze*; queues can be long. The view from the standing-room area at the back of the stalls is excellent, but it's worth the exhaust-ing climb to the gallery for the best sights and sounds in the house.

Tours of the Staatsoper building are provided almost daily – for exact times, check the website or phone – and are available in seven languages (English, French, German, Italian, Japanese, Russian and Spanish), with the tour lasting 40-45 minutes. However, note that from Tuesday to Sunday the Staatsoper tour is only available in combination with tours of the new State Opera Museum and/or the Austrian Theatre Museum (*see p70*); ticket costs vary depending on the combination chosen but range from €5-€8 (children €2-€5).

Theater an der Wien

6, Linke Wienzeile 6 (58 830-660/tickets 588 85/ www.theater-wien.at). U1, U2, U4 Karlsplatz/bus 59a. **Open** *Box office* 10am-7pm daily. **Tickets** €11-€140; €7 standing. **Credit** AmEx, DC, MC, V. **Map** p250 D8.

This 1,200-seat treasure is most famous for hosting the premières of Beethoven's *Fidelio* (1805), Strauss Jr's *Die Fledermaus* (1874) and *Wiener Blut* (1899). Beethoven actually lived here during preparations for the presentation of his only opera. Since its open-ing in June 1801, the theatre has also seen many per-formances of *The Magic Flute* (if not the première of that piece, as is often claimed). From 1983 to 2005, it was part of the Vereinigte Bühnen Wien com-pany, which used it mainly as a venue for large-scale musicals. On 8 January 2006, the theatre returned to being a permanent opera house with an inaugural concert conducted by Plácido Domingo.

Volksoper

9, Währingerstrasse 78 (51 444-3670/www. volksoper.at). U6 Währingerstrasse-Volksoper/tram 40, 41, 42. **Open** *Box office* 8am-6pm Mon-Fri; 9am-noon Sat, Sun. *Evening box office* from 1hr before performance.* **Tickets** €4-€150; €1.50-€2 standing. **Credit** AmEx, DC, JCB, MC, V. **Map** p242 C4.

The traditional role of the Volksoper has been as Vienna's flagship operetta house and the venue offers over 100 performances in that genre every year. Added to this are musicals, modern dance and concerts by the Volksoper orchestra, as well as some operas. Robert Meyer, a well-known Burgtheater actor who will take over direction of the Volksoper as of the 2007/08 season, said that it's 'the only the-atre in Vienna in which operetta, opera, musicals and dance are equally cultivated'. It certainly takes its role as 'The People's Opera House' to heart; offer-ing in one four-week period 30 performances: three operas, two children's performances, a Zarzuela, two musicals, a ballet evening to music from Queen and three operettas, including Kurt Weill's *Der Kuhhandel* (Arms and the Cow), directed by David Poutney in co-production with the Bregenz Festival and Opera North.

The house itself has a functional exterior and a stark, plain, almost astringent interior design, some-what relieved by the plush red decor. The acoustics are also a little dry, especially at the sides. Don't even think of sitting in the back row of a box: you'll hear little and see nothing. On the plus side, the Volksoper is more affordable than the Staatsoper and tickets are easier to obtain. The 72 standing-room tickets (bal-cony or stalls) are a bargain and under-27s can buy unsold tickets 30 minutes before the performance for as little as €8. The standard is generally high, even if the occasional evening disappoints. The Volksoper ensemble seems to have more rehearsal time and fewer 'stars for the evening' than its much grander colleague across the city, which tends to add to (rather than subtract from) the final result.

Other venues

Arnold Schönberg Center

3, Palais Fanto, Zaunergasse 1-3 (712 1888/www. schoenberg.at). Tram D. **Open** 10am-5pm Mon-Fri. **Tickets** *Exhibitions* €6; *Concerts* free-€14. **Credit** DC, MC, V. **Map** p251 F8.

Opened in April 1998, the non-profit Schönberg Center encompasses an archive, a library, a concert hall, an exhibition hall and seminar rooms. Its mis-sion is to promote interest in and knowledge of Schönberg and the Viennese school of the early 20th century, and related music. The 200-seat hall is used for a plethora of events, and note that performances often include a free pre-lecture or discussion.

Bösendorfersaal

4, Graf Starhemberggasse 14 (504 6651). Tram 62, 65. **Open** *Box office* 9am-4pm Mon-Thur; 9am-2pm Fri. From 7pm onwards on concert days only. **Tickets** free-€20. **Credit** DC, MC, V. **Map** p247 E9.

Arts & Entertainment

A permanent exhibition of pianos gives you something to look at in the intermission at this small concert venue. The room has nice acoustics, but poorly placed columns and a low ceiling make for unfortunate sight lines. Various small-scale recitals take place here, by performers from students to professionals. All have one thing in common: great pianos.

Jugendstiltheater

14, Baumgartner Höhe 1 (911 2492-93/tickets through various agencies depending upon event/ www.jugendstiltheater.co.at). Bus 48a. **Open** *Box office* from 1hr before performance. **Tickets** €15-€35; €10 concessions. **Credit** AmEx, DC, MC, V.
Located in the grounds of the Steinhof psychiatric hospital (*see p104*), this Otto Wagner-designed masterpiece is a regular Wiener Festwochen venue and is used for unusual productions by Vienna's independent opera companies. Despite the lack of renovation, the theatre is very atmospheric and well worth the trek out to the 14th district.

MuseumsQuartier

7, Museumsplatz 1 (524 3321/www.mqw.at/ www.halleneg.at). **Map** p250 D7.
This major addition to Viennese culture is largely devoted to the visual arts, but it does incorporate two halls that are sometimes used for operas, classical concerts and musical theatre: the stirringly named Hall E and the smaller, no less winningly dubbed Hall G. The former is a modern space with

Haus der Musik. *See p187.*

state-of-the-art acoustics and a variable audience capacity (from 377 to 1,800). Hall G can be found on the lower level. With up to 380 seats and similarly excellent acoustics, it is perfect for chamber works and song recitals. *See also p83.*

Odeon

2, Taborstrasse 10 (216 5127/www.odeon-theater. at). **U1, U4 Schwedenplatz/tram 21, N.** **Open** *Box office* from 6pm until start of performance Tue-Sat. *Ticket line* 10am-6pm Mon-Fri. **Tickets** €15-€40. **No credit cards.** **Map** p251 F6.
Used for everything from classical concerts to theatre, the Odeon is the former 19th-century corn exchange. Although it lacks permanent seating or a stage, performances by Jeunesse and Wien Modern, among others, take place here. It's not plush, but the voluminous space makes a big impression.

Ensembles & associations

Alban Berg Quartet

Konzerthaus, 1, Lothringerstrasse 20 (24 200-0). **Map** p251 F8.
In a city saturated with music of all kinds, an Alban Berg Quartet concert is still an event not to be missed. Sadly, violist Thomas Kakuska passed away in 2005, but Günter Pichler, Gerhard Schulz and Valentin Erben have been joined by Isabel Charisius in presenting the string quartet repertoire, old and new, with the unsurpassed combination of intelligence and intuition, technical perfection and artistic freedom that is the group's trademark.

Concentus Musicus Wien

Konzerthaus, 1, Lothringerstrasse 20 (24 200-0). **Map** p251 F8.
One of the world's premier ensembles for Alte Musik, early to Baroque music from the 13th to the 18th centuries. It's impossible to separate the Concentus Musicus from its founder and musical guru, Nikolaus Harnoncourt. Together, the man and the group have succeeded in making once-dusty Baroque music come alive on original instruments.

Jeunesses Musicales Austria

Konzerthaus 1, Lothringerstrasse 20 (505 6356/ www.jeunesse.at). U4 Stadtpark/tram D. **Kartenbüro (ticket office)** *1, Bösendorferstraße 12, in the Musikverein building 505 63 56).* **Open** 9am-7.30pm Mon-Fri. **Tickets** €7-€36; €7-€18 under-26s; €5-€7.50 standing. **Credit** DC, MC, V. **Map** p251 F8.
Jeunesses organises over 600 concerts and events throughout Austria every year, celebrating its 60th season in 2008/09. Its initial aim is to provide music for young people, but its concert programmes, presented in Vienna at various venues including the Musikverein and the Konzerthaus, are of such exceptional quality that music lovers of all ages vie for tickets, which sell out quickly.

Klangforum Wien

5, Diehlgasse 51 (521 67-0/www.klangforum.at).

2009 – All hail Haydn!

After Mozart's anniversary in 2006, 2009 sees another major memorial year for classical music with the 200th anniversary of the death of Joseph Haydn. Festivities will centre around Eisenstadt, the capital of the province of Burgenland, where Haydn lived for over 40 years, the Lower Austrian town of Rohrau, Haydn's birthplace, and Vienna, where he was a member of the Vienna Boys Choir until his voice broke and he was dismissed for misbehaviour. Haydn also spent his apprenticeship years in Vienna and married in Stephansdom, although perhaps not taking his vows too much to heart. As he said: 'My wife is unable to bear children and therefore I was not indifferent towards the attractions of other women.' Nevertheless, the couple stayed together until Maria Anna Aloysia died in 1800, living most of that time in and around the city of Eisenstadt, where Haydn was employed by a succession of Esterházy princes. He returned to Vienna later in life to write some of his best-known works, including *The Creation* and *The Seasons*, and died there at home on 31 May 1809.

The Haydn Festival Eisenstadt will focus on the universality of Haydn's music and its significance worldwide – an effort which would no doubt be applauded by the man himself, who once humbly asserted, 'my language is understood throughout the world'. To this end, one of the musical highlights of the year will be the World Creation on 31 May 2009, with performances of *The Creation* taking place across the globe with Adam Fischer conducting in Eisenstadt, Lorin Maazel in New York and performances in Tokyo, Sydney, Athens, London and Boston among others.

Closer to home, in Haydn terms, 'The Phenomenon of Haydn, 1732-1809', will illustrate the significance of Haydn's music on the international stage during the period he served as the Royal Director of Music to the court of Prince Esterházy. The exhibition will open in Eisenstadt on 31 March, Haydn's birthday, and continue until 11 November 2009. A number of events are planned to accompany the exhibition including guided organ tours and 'Sacred Haydn' (all twelve masses by Joseph Haydn performed in churches throughout Eisenstadt).

Once a month, a day-long bus tour entitled 'On the trail of Joseph Haydn' will begin in Vienna, taking in Haydn's birthplace in Rohrau, the Esterházy castle, the Haydn Houses in both Eisenstadt and Vienna, ending with a concert in the Festsaal of the Austrian Academy of Science where he made his last public appearance on 27 March 1809 during a performance of *The Creation*, conducted by Antonio Salieri. To join a tour, contact Elite Travel Agency (258 1674-0, www.elitetours.at).

The festival website is www.haydn2009.at.

Since it was founded in 1985 by Swiss composer Beat Furrer, this 'soloist ensemble' has become a leading force in New Music worldwide. Klangforum Wien's democratic approach encourages co-operation between interpreters, conductors and composers, a policy mirrored in the stylistic variety of its varied repertoire. This ranges from classical modern to works of up-and-coming young composers, with space for experimental jazz and free improvisation.

Radio Symphonieorchester Wien (RSO)

Radiokulturhaus, 4, Argentinier Strasse 30a (5017 0377/www.rso-wien.orf.at).
In the capable hands of conductor-in-chief Bertrand de Billy since September 2002, the Vienna Radio Symphony Orchestra has a penchant for unearthing the new, the unknown or the almost forgotten – this is both its forte and the reason for its relative obscurity. However, the RSO's high level of musicianship, combined with a 'this is being taped' awareness on the part of the players, makes for excellent performances. You'll find the RSO performing on its home turf in the Radiokulturhaus, at the Musikverein, the Konzerthaus and, from 2007, at the Theater an der Wien as the resident opera orchestra.

Wiener Philharmoniker

Musikverein, 1, Bösendorfer Strasse 12 (505 6525/ www.wienerphilharmoniker.at).
The 140-member Vienna Philharmonic Orchestra has financed and managed itself since 1908 (it was actually founded in 1842). This is important, as it allows the orchestra the freedom to make decisions uninfluenced by contemporary fashions. For instance, it gave up approximately €180,000 in state subsidies in order to retain its right to run things as it sees fit, including remaining virtually all male. As well as presenting a full season of concerts between September and mid June at the Musikverein, including the New Year's Day Concert, the Philharmonic performs each summer at the Salzburg Festival, tours widely, and is the house orchestra of the Staatsoper, under the alternative title of Orchester der Wiener Staatsoper. The Wiener Philharmoniker's history is documented in two rooms at the Haus der Musik (*see p60*).

Arts & Entertainment

Wiener Sängerknaben (Vienna Boys' Choir)

2, Obere Augartenstrasse 1 (216 3942/www.wsk.at).
Undoubtedly one of Vienna's most prestigious exports, these little cherubs in blue-and-white sailor suits are the darlings of Austria. The boys' musicianship and general professionalism are at an indisputably high level, but at times they seem a bit jaded – more red-eyed than rosy-cheeked. It's scarcely any wonder, with their schedule. They have a regular gig at the Burgkapelle (9.15am every Sunday and on religious holidays during the school year).

Wiener Symphoniker

6, Lehárgasse 11 (589 7951/www.wiener-symphoniker.at).
Known as Vienna's 'second' orchestra, the Wiener Symphoniker might be internationally in the shadow of the Philharmoniker but has a long and impressive history. The orchestra presents some 200 concerts a year, mostly in the Konzerthaus and the Musikverein.

Independent opera companies

None of the *Freigruppen*, or independent companies, has a permanent home. Here are the two most prominent and easily accessible.

NetZZeit

www.netzzeit.at. **Tickets** through the Konzerthaus (242 002/www.konzerthaus.at).
NetZZeit (Network Time) has dedicated itself to promoting and presenting contemporary works. One of its attempts to include the audience in the proceedings was entitled *Rauschkonzert* ('inebriation concert') and involved the audience drinking their 'after show drinks' before the performance, leading the tipsy public to feel freer to join in.

Neue Oper Wien

www.neueoperwien.at. **Tickets** through Wien-Ticket (58 885/www.wien-ticket.at).
Of the four main ensembles in Vienna, New Opera Vienna is the most successful in terms of number and size of productions per year. Its ability to put on full scale productions of modern works is perhaps due to its penchant for co-productions with more established, traditional groups.

Musical theatres

Raimund Theater

6, Wallgasse 18-20 (59 977/www.musicalvienna.at).
U6 Gumpendorfer Strasse. **Open** Box office 10am-1pm, 2-6pm daily. **Tickets** €10-€95; €2.50 standing. **Credit** AmEx, DC, MC, V. **Map** p246 B9.
The Raimund opened in 1893 as a theatre for the middle classes in what was then an outer suburb of Vienna. Only spoken drama was presented until 1908, when director Wilhelm Karczag introduced opera and operetta. In 2004, it staged the disastrous *Barbarella*,

but 2006 saw the world première of the very successful *Rebecca* based on the Daphne du Maurier book and Hitchcock film. *Rudolf*, a musical about the life of the Crown Prince, is next in line of succession.

Sacred music

A visit to Sunday Mass is a fine way to combine architectural, musical and spiritual sightseeing. As well as the Burgkapelle, in the 1st district, the Augustinerkirche, Karlskirche, Minoritenkirche, Michaelerkirche and Stephansdom are all worth a visit.

Burgkapelle

1, Schweizerhof (533 9927/www.bmukk.gv.at).
U3 Herrengasse/tram 1, 2, D, J. **Open** Box office 11am-3pm Mon-Thur; 11am-1pm, 3-5pm Fri; 8.15am-9.15am Sun. **Tickets** €5-€29. **No credit cards.** **Map** p250 D8.
The Wiener Sängerknaben (Vienna Boys' Choir) performs here every Sunday and on religious holidays at 9.15am except during the summer (late June to mid September). Check the website for the musical programme. Tickets must be booked in advance.

Traditional Vienna

If you're looking for the definitive performance of *Eine Kleine Nachtmusik*, don't bother with these places. Nevertheless, they provide a good opportunity to enjoy some nice tunes in beautiful surroundings. Their standard varies, but those listed below are the most popular.

Hofburg: Festsaal, Zeremoniensaal & Redoutensaal

1, Heldenplatz (Festsaal & Zeremoniensaal); Josefsplatz (Redoutensaal) (587 2552/www.hofburgorchester.at). U3 Herrengasse.
Performances May-Oct 8.30pm Tue, Thur, Sat. **Tickets** €39-€52. **Credit** MC, V. **Map** p250 D7.
Artistes from the Staatsoper and Volksoper perform in the historic rooms of the Habsburgs' imperial palace, producing by far the best music at these venues. There are two box offices (one for each Platz), which open one hour before each concert. It's best to book by phone. None of the halls has numbered seating, so get there early to ensure a good spot.

Wiener Kursalon

1, Johannesgasse 33 (512 5790/www.soundof vienna.at). **Open** 8.30am-8.30pm daily.
Performances 8.15pm daily. **Tickets** €38, €47, €54; €90 (VIP). **Credit** AmEx, DC, JCB, MC, V. **Map** p251 E7.
The Wiener Kursalon once hosted the famous promenade concerts of the Strauss dynasty. The Salon Orchestra 'Alt Wien' (Old Vienna) performs an all-Strauss programme that includes ballet and operetta; it runs every day from late March through to the end of February. The Kursalon building itself is worth a look, as is the Strauss statue nearby.

Arts & Entertainment

Music: Rock, Roots & Jazz

Spoiled for choice.

For lovers of what the authorities disdainfully call U-Musik (*Unterhaltungsmusik* or 'entertainment music'), Vienna offers a diverse and convivial scene. Reacting vigorously against the opulence and conservatism of the city's classical heritage, Vienna's music-makers are a truly innovative and creative bunch, and have been hugely influential in the fields of dance and electronica. Meanwhile, the city is bursting at the seams with venues of every size and stripe, ensuring that there is something worth seeing most nights. Vienna is a regular stopping-off point for touring British and American bands, who are rewarded for their efforts by knowledgeable and enthusiastic audiences. In return, the punters reap the benefits of well-managed venues with excellent acoustics and sightlines, reasonable ticket and bar prices, friendly staff and unobtrusive security. This overall charm is in part due to the fact that several key venues, such as Flex, Porgy & Bess and Szene Wien, are partially subsidised by the city council. Last but not least, the extensive public transport network will whisk you to and from the gig in no time.

ON THE DECKS

In the mid 1990s, Vienna's dance scene held clubbers rapt with a velvety, downtempo sound that mirrored the city's dawdling, pastoral lifestyle, exemplified by Kruder & Dorfmeister's seminal 1998 album *The K&D Sessions*. Yet K&D and their peers always tended to shun the limelight, and inhabited the bar and the club rather than the live venue. A decade on, K&D remain relatively anonymous, releasing music on their own G-Stone label and making occasional appearances on the global DJ circuit.

Today, Vienna's dance and electronica scene remains one of the most vibrant in Europe, helped by the city's relatively small size and the fact that, as Christof Kurzmann, owner of the Charhizma label and co-founder of the rhiz music bar, says, 'everybody knows everybody.' The scene has diversified, though, since its peak of activity in the 1990s. Patrick Pulsinger and Erdem Tunakan's once feted Cheap Records is no longer as influential, while the adventurous Mego label, which in the '90s put out a slew of challenging laptop improv from the likes of Pita

Austria's own Falco died in 1998.

(Peter Rehberg), Fennesz and Farmers Manual, has morphed into Editions Mego, concentrating more on archival releases than new music. But Rehberg and Fennesz remain active, their Vienna roots showing in their constant quest for the perfect digital sound.

Meanwhile, other Vienna-based artists are maintaining the city's reputation for creative and original work. Imprints like Klein and Mosz serve up a steady diet of engaging fare, from the soulful post-rock of Sofa Surfers to the frankly bizarre beat-driven crooning of Louie Austen. Folks such as Kurzmann, Bernard Fleischmann and Radian turn out polished, cerebral electronica for the *Wire*-reading crowd, while poppier grooves come courtesy of one-woman electro project Gustav and the slinky Austrian-French duo Saint Privat.

Arts & Entertainment

Ost Klub. *See p193.*

HONKING HORNS

Vienna has swung to the pulse of jazz since the early years of the last century, and these days hosts a varied selection of clubs hosting both Austrian and international artists. The pick of these is **Porgy & Bess**, which consistently books high quality modern and avant-garde performers. The man behind it, Mathias Rüegg, is also the founder of the Vienna Art Orchestra, an internationally renowned jazz ensemble.

Porgy's closest rival in the live jazz stakes, **Birdland**, is the baby of Austria's most famous jazz musician, keyboardist Joe Zawinul. Born in Vienna, Zawinul moved to the US in the late '50s, where he played with Miles Davis before co-founding the influential jazz fusion outfit Weather Report. Although still based in the US, Zawinul performs regularly at the club that bears the name of his most famous composition.

Vienna also boasts Material Records, a well-established and active jazz label founded by the highly acclaimed guitarist Wolfgang Muthspiel. A frequent performer in the city, Muthspiel never allows his technical skill to overcome his assured melodic instincts. Besides Muthspiel, Material's varied roster also includes gifted fellow travellers Helgi Jonsson and Rebekka Bakken.

TURBO FOLK

'The Balkans begin in Vienna,' so Metternich is supposed to have said, and the claim is borne out by the rapid growth in popularity of south-eastern European music in the city over the past few years. Wild, intoxicating and unblushingly sexy, yet with an undercurrent of melancholy,

the Balkan music vogue is an antidote to the cool formalism of electronica, owing much to current migration trends and the popularity of the movies of Emir Kusturica. Since 2004, the annual Balkan Fever festival (*see p159*) has brought many of the region's best performers to Vienna, while the exuberant **Ost Klub** provides a year-round showcase for this compelling variety of folk music.

DARK ENTRIES

Routinely ignored by the mainstream media, the goth and post-industrial scene thrives in Vienna, its denizens forming loose networks and alliances with like-minded souls across Europe. Bands like Der Blutharsch and Novy Svet, and labels such as Hau Ruck and Klanggalerie, deliver music of uncompromising solemnity to their legions of black- and camo-clad followers. Visit www.gothic.at for the lowdown on gigs, get-togethers and cemetery picnics.

JINGLE JANGLE

Austria has no great tradition of guitar-based rock, although fans are well served by the many bands who include Vienna in their touring schedules. Established home-grown bands such as Naked Lunch and Garish have recently been joined by the superb A Life, A Song, A Cigarette, whose folk and country-tinged debut album *Fresh Kills Landfill* was a highlights of 2006.

WHAT'S GOING ON

Gigs in Vienna, especially those by visiting British and American acts, can and do sell out well in advance, so plan ahead to avoid disappointment.

Arts & Entertainment

Fortunately, there are several ways to make sure you're not greeted by the *Ausverkauft* ('sold out') sign when you arrive at the venue. The weekly *Falter* (published every Wednesday) carries detailed music listings both by day and by artist, so it's easy to find out who's playing when and where. Flyposters advertising upcoming events cover every available urban surface, while bars and record shops creak under the weight of flyers and handbills. Finally, the Jugendinfo information centre gives out lists of events at many venues, and sells tickets for them as well.

Venues

All In

9, Währinger Gürtel, Stadtbahnbögen 90-91 (406 30 75/www.allinbar.com). U6/tram 43 Alser Straße. **Open** 6pm-2am Tue-Thur; 6pm-4am Fri, Sat; 10am-8pm Sun. **Admission** free-€5. **Credit** DC, MC, V. **Map** p242 B5.
A relatively new arrival on the lively Gürtel scene, All In distinguishes itself from its neighbours by its artfully designed interior, expensive cocktails and hipster clientele. Jazz, funk and hip hop gigs weekly.

Arena

3, Baumgasse 80 (info 798 85 95/bar 798 33 39/www.arena.co.at). U3 Erdberg. **Open** *Summer* 2pm-late daily. *Winter* 4pm-late daily. **Admission** free-€40. **No credit cards. Map** p248 J9.
Operating under the banner 'Love music, hate fascism', this former slaughterhouse is a reliable purveyor of gigs by established alternative acts – recent visitors have included John Cale, the Yeah Yeah Yeahs and Jarvis Cocker – and a favourite hangout

of the punk, drum 'n' bass and techno crowds. It has a large courtyard where open-air gigs take place and non-mainstream films are shown in the summer. A 2005 facelift preserved the Arena's industrial ambience and its iconic brick smokestack.

B72

8, Hernalser Gürtel, Stadtbahnbögen 72 (409 2128/www.b72.at). U6/tram 43 Alser Straße. **Open** 8pm-4am daily. **Admission** free-€15. **No credit cards. Map** p246 B6.
Popular, compact little spot on the Gürtel, with regular club nights and occasional live acts spanning a range of styles from reggae to indie and alt-country. Black Dice and the Willard Grant Conspiracy have recently played here. The split level interior gives a fine view of the stage from upstairs.

Birdland

3, Landstraßer Hauptstraße 2 (info 219 63 93/tickets 58 885/www.birdland.at). U3, U4 Landstraße. **Open** 6pm-2am Mon-Sat. **Admission** €15-€40. **Credit** MC, V. **Map** p248 G7.
Located in the plush environs of the Hilton Hotel, and with ticket prices to match, Birdland is Viennese jazz legend Joe Zawinul's way of giving something back to the city – albeit thanks to a large municipal subsidy. While the acoustics are superb, visibility is poor and the atmosphere can be a little sterile. Drinks too are pricey by local standards. The programming also has been rather unadventurous of late, with middle-of-the-road supper-club acts edging out anything that might frighten the horses.

Blue Tomato

15, Wurmsergasse 21 (985 5960/www.blue tomato.cc). U3 Johnstraße. **Open** 7pm-2am Mon-Sat. **Admission** free-€15. **No credit cards.**

A great find – a tiny, informal jazz and improv club occupying the back room of a relaxed and friendly local bar. The programming is mostly accomplished local musicians of the modern variety, but occasionally a real legend like sax maestro Peter Brötzmann turns up to shake the walls.

Café Carina

8, Josefstädter Straße 84 (406 4322/www.cafe-carina.at). U6/tram J, 33 Josefstädter Straße. **Open** 6pm-2am Mon-Sat. **Admission** free. **No credit cards. Map** p246 B6.

Grungy Gürtel hangout, handily placed right next to the U-Bahn. Most nights feature gigs by local bands, but they have to compete for attention with the pool table at the back. There's a picturesque old-style bar, and an internet terminal in case you get bored.

Café Concerto

16, Lerchenfelder Gürtel 53 (406 4795/www.cafe concerto.at). U6 Josefstädter Strasse/tram 5, 33, J. **Open** 4pm-late Tue-Sat. **Admission** free-€12. **No credit cards. Map** p246 B7.

A popular after-hours joint opposite the Carina, where you can hear anything from jazz, Celtic, and klezmer to folk and light rock on most nights (from 9pm). Gigs are held in the cellar, a bizarre cave-like space decked out in fake rocky walls. Staff are friendly, drinks are cheap and the bands, well, unpredictable.

Chelsea

8, Lerchenfelder Gürtel U-Stadtbahnbögen 29-31 (407 9309/www.chelsea.co.at). U6 Josefstädter Strasse/tram J, 33. **Open** 6pm-4am Mon-Sat; 4pm-3am Sun. **Admission** free-€15. **No credit cards. Map** p246 B7.

Long established anglophile venue that draws the crowds with a potent mix of British, European and American alternative rock acts, including a sprinkling of 'name' artists (Buzzcocks, Mark Eitzel, Jarboe). The Chelsea's pounding sound system and hospitable layout (four arches, four bars) make for a convivial night out.

Derwisch

16, Lerchenfelder Gürtel 29 (corner Hasnerstrasse) (492 6110/www.cafederwisch.com). U6 Thaliastrasse/ tram 46. **Open** 2pm-2am daily. **Admission** free-€15. **No credit cards. Map** p246 B7

Completely unmarked and hidden away in the courtyard of a dilapidated Gürtel tenement, this improvised cellar offers rousing live Balkan music on Fridays and the odd gig during the rest of the week. If the vibe's right, expect lots of sweaty, table-top dancing.

Flex

1, Donaukanal/Augartenbrücke (533 7525/www. flex.at). U2, U4 Schottenring. **Open** 8pm-4am daily. **Admission** €3-€20. **No credit cards. Map** p243 E5.

Justly the most revered club in Vienna, Flex boasts an awesome sound system and a diverse programme of DJs spinning anything from indie and techno to house and downbeat. Dub Club on Mondays is the time to catch itinerant international DJs and the odd member of the G-Stone posse, while Fridays showcase alternative rock sounds under the London Calling banner. Live acts of the calibre of the Decemberists and Arcade Fire also feature, frequently selling the place out. Although currently surrounded by building work, Flex is attractively located on the southern bank of the Donaukanal – a great place to chill on warm summer evenings. Inside, the venue's distressed sci-fi appearance and the huge sounds coming from the PA add up to a vital live experience.

Fluc

2, Praterstern 5 (no phone/www.fluc.at). U1 Praterstern. **Open** 6pm-2am daily. **Admission** free-€15. **No credit cards. Map** p244 G5.

Now back in a new location after a year's absence due to construction work, Fluc is rapidly becoming Vienna's primary venue for cutting-edge and experimental live music. Situated on the edge of the Prater fairground, it's actually two venues, both of which host regular live events as well as DJs. The Fluc proper (where entry is always free) is housed in an unprepossessing prefab, while the Fluc-Wanne is an underground space hewn from a former pedestrian subway. These unconventional surroundings are mirrored by Fluc's adventurous programming spanning avant rock, improv, Japanese noise and laptoppery.

Gasometer/BA-CA Halle

11, Guglgasse 8 (96 096/www.ba-ca-halle.at). U3 Gasometer. **Admission** around €30. **Credit** MC, V. **Map** p249 K10.

A 3,000-capacity hall located in the Gasometer complex, a sympathetic redevelopment of four massive gas tanks into a living, working, shopping and entertainment zone. This is the best venue to catch mid-ranking acts from the UK and USA on tour; Bloc Party, Nine Inch Nails and the Scissor Sisters have all dropped in. The acoustics, views and atmosphere are all above average for this type of venue.

Jazzland

1, Franz-Josefs-Kai 29 (533 2575/www.jazzland.at). U1, U4/tram 1, 2 Schwedenplatz. **Open** 7pm-2am Mon-Sat. **Admission** €10-€18. **No credit cards. Map** p251 F6.

Tiny cellar club positioned under Vienna's oldest church, the Ruprechtskirche. The programming is similarly venerable, with swing and trad jazz by local and American musicians the norm. Established since 1972, the place also offers an extensive Austrian food menu. They don't take reservations, so arrive early if you want to be sure of a table.

Metropol

17, Hernalser Hauptstraße 55 (407 77 407/www. wiener-metropol.at). U6 Alserstraße/tram 9, 43. **Open** 8pm-midnight Mon-Sat. **Admission** €11-€35. **Credit** AmEx, DC, MC, V. **Map** p242 A5.

Originally a music hall, Metropol is an attractive theatre approached from the street through a leafy courtyard. Inside it's pleasant and spacious, yet small enough to create a lively atmosphere. Sadly, however, Metropol has lost the plot as far as booking artists goes, with the odd big MOR name such as the Dubliners popping up among a succession of lacklustre rock and roots acts.

Ost Klub

4, Schwarzenbergplatz 10 (505 62 28/www.ost-klub. at). Tram D. **Open** 6pm-4am Thur-Sat. **Admission** €5-€15. **No credit cards. Map** p251 F8.

Ost Klub currently offers the steamiest night out in the city. The nightly programme of live acts features both bands from countries east of Vienna and many, such as the stirring vocalist Fatima Spar and Bulgarian accordionist Martin Lubenov, who are now resident here. While much of the music can be categorised as 'Balkan', you're just as likely to be shaking your ass to Russian disco or Hungarian ska. With a good main stage and a network of smaller rooms to get your breath back, the Ost is vibrant, attitude-free and reasonably priced. **Photo** *p190.*

Planet Music

20, Adalbert-Stifter-Straße 73 (332 4641/ www.planet.tt). U6 Handelskai then 10 min walk/ tram N. **Admission** €15-€30. **No credit cards. Map** p243 F1.

This tired venue in an inaccessible part of town serves up a dubious array of tribute acts and 'battle of the band' contests. However, recently things have perked up somewhat with gigs by the Shout Out Louds and the mighty Wrens but heavy metal still most definitely predominates.

Porgy & Bess

1, Riemergasse 11 (512 88 11/www.porgy.at). U3 Stubentor/trams 1, 2. **Open** 7.30pm-late daily. **Admission** €5-€25. **Credit** MC, V. **Map** p251 F7.

Arguably the finest live music venue in Vienna, Porgy & Bess is far and away the best place to hear modern jazz, blues and world music. This stylish club makes an immediate and favourable impression with its handsome split level interior and friendly, enthusiastic vibe. The programming is second to none, with the likes of Anthony Braxton, Evan Parker, Living Colour and Roy Ayers all playing in early 2007.

Reigen

14, Hadikgasse 62 (894 0094/www.reigen.at). U4 Hietzing. **Open** 6pm-4am daily. **Admission** €10-€20. **No credit cards.**

Another venue specialising in jazz and blues, Reigen is unfavourably located on a thunderous main road. Once you're inside, however, there's a cosy performance space. If you're hungry, pop out to the adjacent Café Wunderer.

rhiz

8, Lerchenfelder Gürtel, Stadtbahnbögen 37-38 (409 2505/www.rhiz.org). U6 Josefstädter Strasse/tram J. **Open** 6pm-4am Mon-Sat; 6pm-2am Sun. **Admission** free-€10. **No credit cards. Map** p246 B6/7.

Feted as the temple of Viennese electronica, rhiz is all plate glass, bare brickwork, and visible ducts and wiring. The challenging musical programme may disturb the uninitiated. It's not all white

Fluc.

noise, though, and you might hear jazz and a spot of alt country. In summer it's a lot less earnest, and the terrace is frequently packed.

Sargfabrik
14, Goldschlagstraße 169 (988 98 111/www. sargfabrik.at). Tram 52 Diesterweggasse. **Admission** €5-€25. **No credit cards.**
Slightly awkward to get to by public transport, Sargfabrik is well worth the effort. It's a housing co-operative with a theatre and café-restaurant attached; the theatre has regular gigs by biggish world and jazz performers, as well as cabaret, performance art and events for children.

Shelter
20, Wallensteinplatz 8 (961 9195/www.shelter.at). Tram 5. **Open** 8pm-2am Tue-Sat. **Admission** free-€8. **No credit cards. Map** p243 E3.
Popular indie dive, with a frequently rammed front bar and a low-ceilinged, garishly painted back room where bands play. Entry is often free, there's Guinness and Strongbow on draught, and table football and pinball machines round out the fun.

Stadthalle
15, Vogelweidplatz 14 (98 100/www.stadthalle. com). U6 Burggasse. **Admission** up to €70. **Credit** AmEx, DC, MC, V. **Map** p246 A7.
The Stadthalle is the place where big name acts (Muse, Red Hot Chili Peppers, the reformed Police) play when they come to Vienna. Two separate halls, the romantically named Hall D and Hall F, dispense the usual bland trappings of arena rock.

Szene Wien
11, Hauffgasse 26 (749 3341/www.szenewien. com). U3 Zippererstraße. **Admission** €11-€25. **No credit cards.**
Vienna's longest established and most reliable medium-sized rock venue, the Szene consistently attracts top quality UK and US acts on tour. Recent highlights have included Peter Hammill, Sunn O))) and Sparklehorse. The auditorium is box-like, but the acoustics are great, the bar serves simple, reliable food, and there's a large unkempt garden at the back.

Tunnel
8, Florianigasse 39 (405 3465/www.tunnelvienna.at). Tram J. **Open** 9am-2am daily. **Admission** free-€5. **No credit cards. Map** p246 B6.
Pleasant, studenty cellar bar with cosy booths to sit in. Live rock and jazz are on the syllabus most evenings, although the music tends to take a back seat to drinking and socialising.

Tüwi
19, Peter-Jordan-Straße 76 (47 654 2010/http:// tuewi.action.at). Bus 10A, 40A. **Open** *Café* 8am-10pm Mon-Fri during university term times, later on concert days. **Admission** free-€5. **No credit cards. Map** p242 A2.
Tüwi is a Vienna one-off, bizarrely located in an imposing Altbau in the genteel environs of the 19th district. By day a vegetarian café and slacker

hangout, by night it turns into an uncompromising punk and hardcore venue. Bands regularly annoy the neighbours into the small hours, and there's a seated area outside where you can retreat when the sonic onslaught gets too much.

Vorstadt
16, Herbststraße 37 (495 0198/www.vorstadt.at). U6 Burggasse. **Open** 5pm-2am Mon-Sat; 10am-2am Sun. **Admission** free-€12. **No credit cards. Map** p246 A7.
Civilised local set-up with good food, leafy courtyard and a separate room where performances take place. The varied programme includes jazz, soul, blues and Balkan music.

WUK
9, Währinger Straße 59 (401 21/www.wuk.at). U6 Währinger Straße/tram 40, 41, 42 Spitalgasse. **Open** 11am-2am Mon-Fri; 5pm-2am Sat, Sun. **Admission** free-€25. **No credit cards. Map** p242 C4.
The WUK (Werkstätten- und Kulturhaus) is a huge (12,000 sq m/130,000 sq ft) 19th-century brick-built cultural centre with workshops and exhibition space arranged around a gorgeous ivy-clad courtyard. Music is high on the agenda, with local bands rehearsing in the basement and regular gigs by cult names, plus club nights in the main hall.

Festivals

For details of **Jazz Fest Wien**, **Balkan Fever** and the **Donau Festival**, see the Festivals chapter; *pp158-161.*

Konfrontationen
Festival office: Jazzgalerie Nickelsdorf, Untere Hauptstraße 13, 2425 Nickelsdorf (02146 2359/ www.konfrontationen.at). **Dates** mid July.
Held in the unlikely surroundings of a *Gasthaus* close to the Hungarian border, Konfrontationen is a three day celebration of challenging performances from the world's leading avant jazz and free improvising musicians. Artists of the calibre of AMM, Cecil Taylor and Phil Minton all made the journey here. An Arcadian courtyard bedecked with vines provides an appropriately distinctive setting for this unique event. (€35 for a day ticket, €85 for a weekend pass).

Wiesen
Festival office: Hauptstraße 140, 7203 Wiesen (02 626 81648/www.wiesen.at). **Dates** various throughout the summer.
If the weather's fine, an open-air gig in Wiesen, 60km (37 miles) south of Vienna in the state of Burgenland, is an enticing proposition. Originally a three-day jazz festival, Wiesen has branched out in recent years with numerous other weekends devoted to pop, rock and reggae as well as a smattering of one-off gigs. The festival site is pleasantly pastoral yet well equipped, and there are buses back to Vienna after the last encore.

Nightlife

No attitude, no threats, kooky venues – and cheap drinks.

Mess around in a boat: **Badeschiff**. *See p196.*

For all their geeky interest in the various subgenres of the dance scene, the Viennese are not exactly known as clubbing folk. Notoriously bad movers, and allergic to premium prices and dress codes, local night birds are an undemanding lot, happy with an unusual location and interesting sounds at a volume that permits conversation. If you're not a full-on fashionista, one of the joys of Vienna is that drinks prices vary little between daytime cafés and clubs. That said, Vienna does have a handful of pricey, modish venues, such as **Passage** and **Volksgarten**, that are always packed to the rafters.

More than clubs, Vienna is about DJ bars. Outside the 1st district, Vienna's nightlife action is focused on four main areas. Just beyond the Ringstrasse lie Karlsplatz and the Naschmarkt, with bars and clubs such as **Schikaneder** and **Club U**. From here you're a step away from Mariahilfer Strasse, bisecting the 6th and 7th districts – the home of everything from cocktail spots and gay bars to several of the city's most fashionable clubs and lounges, such as **Bar Italia Lounge** and **Café Leopold**. The third major node is conveniently concentrated along the busy Gürtel ring road, in the arches beneath the U6 U-Bahn line, between the stations Thalia Strasse and Alser Strasse. If you're here in summer, head for the banks of the Danube Canal where you can lounge in a deckchair at **Strandbar Herrmann**, splash in the pool on the **Badeschiff** and check out Vienna's best club, the legendary **Flex**.

Given the ephemeral and promoter-powered nature of club events, we only list venues with regular opening hours. For a more up-to-date picture, consult the omnipresent flyers, and the middle pages of local listings paper *Falter*, which prints the weekly goings-on of around 60 selected nightspots. For a peek into the club music scene, www.playfm.at streams DJ sets from various local venues.

See *p192* for **Flex**, *p193* for **Porgy & Bess**.

American Bar (Loos Bar)

1, Kärntner Strasse 10 (512 3283). U1, U3 Stephansplatz. **Open** noon-4am daily. **Credit** AmEx, DC, JCB, MC, V. **Map** p251 E7.

Known locally as the Loos Bar after the architect Adolf Loos, who designed the place in 1908, this tiny modernist gem cunningly uses mirrors to give an illusion of space. The cocktails may be pricey, but it's not every day you can sup in an architectural masterpiece. Note that gawpers will be ejected unless they order a drink.

Badeschiff

1, Donaukanal, between Schwedenbrücke & Urania (513 0744/www.badeschiff.at). U1, U4 Schwedenplatz/tram 1, 2. **Open** *May-Oct* 8am-midnight daily (Laderaum club all year 10pm-4am daily). **Admission** €5. **No credit cards.** **Map** p251 F6.

Vienna now has a Parisian-style ship with a pool moored on the Danube canal near Schwedenplatz. During the day, folks come to sun themselves, eat, drink or have a swim. Note that in high summer, there's a €5 charge to get on the ship, which gets you a swim or a rebate on your tab. Later at night, in the *Laderaum* (hold), feisty club music is provided by Sofa Surfers and other local heroes. **Photo** *p195*.

Nocturnal nibbles

If you're peckish in the early hours, the Naschmarkt area is your best bet for a bite.

Café Bendl

1, Landesgerichtsstrasse 6 (408 3087). U2 Rathaus/tram J. **Open** 6am-2am Mon-Thur; 6pm-4am Fri, Sat; 6pm-2am Sun. **No credit cards. Map** p250 C/D6.

Toasted a darker shade of brown by years of cigarettes, this is a semi-subterranean cave serving a menu of soups, stews and other Austrian fillers.

Café Drechsler

6, Linke Wienzeile 22 (581 2044/www. cafedrechsler.at). U1, U2, U4 Karlsplatz, U4 Kettenbrückengasse/bus 59a. **Open** 3am-2am Mon-Sat. **No credit cards. Map** p250 D8.

This renowned asylum for insomniacs, stall-holders, tramps, ball-goers and party people has been given a modern but sensitive shake-up by Sir Terence Conran, no less. *Pictured.*

Robert Goodmann

4, Rechte Wienzeile 23 (967 44 15/www. goodmann.at). U4 Kettenbrückengasse. **Open** 4am-10am daily. **No credit cards. Map** p247 D8.

Eating until 8am and dancing until 10am to anything from German crooners to commercial hip hop and reggae.

Broadway Piano Bar

1, Bauernmarkt 21 (0664 587 4861/www.broadway bar.at). U1, U3 Stephansplatz. **Open** 9pm-late Tue-Sat. **Admission** (music supplement) free-€12. **Credit** AmEx, MC, V. **Map** p251 E6.

The enchanting Broadway seems straight out of the 1930s, though it's only been open for some 22 years. Step inside and, amid the candlelight and ageing plush, there'll be someone tinkling on a Bösendorfer that takes up a quarter of the whole space. Run by Bela Koreny, a refugee from 1956 Hungary, the bar has seen appearances from the likes of Leonard Bernstein and Billy Joel and continues to run a varied programme featuring chansons, jazz duos, classical soloists and theatre monologues.

Café Alt Wien

1, Bäckerstrasse 9 (512 5222). U1, U3 Stephansplatz. **Open** 10am-2am daily. **No credit cards. Map** p251 F6.

A good café during the day and a fine drinking establishment after dark, with nicotine-stained ceilings, poster-covered walls and a general air of Paris circa 1968. The clientele is a mixture of students and gregarious elderly Bohemians. If you can get a table, try ordering the legendary goulash.

Club U

1, Otto Wagner Pavillon, Karlsplatz (505 9904). U1, U2, U4 Karlsplatz. **Open** Club 10pm-4am daily. **No credit cards. Map** p250 E8.

Located beneath one of Otto Wagner's railway pavilions, Club U doubles as a coffee house and alfresco bar (day) and an arty club environment (night), both downstairs and on the upper terrace. The decks are manned daily by purveyors of anything from drum 'n' bass to punky techno.

First Floor

1, Seitenstettengasse 5 (533 2523). U1, U4 Schwedenplatz. **Open** 7pm-4am Mon-Sat; 8pm-3am Sun. **Credit** AmEx, DC, MC, V. **Map** p251 F6.

Squeezed in beside the dives that make up the concentration of pubs and clubs that are rather misleadingly known as the Bermuda Triangle, this is one of Vienna's few truly great bars. Designed by the feted Eichinger oder Knechtl design team, using original fittings and panelling from the Kärntner Strasse's 1930s Mounier Bar, First Floor is a highly seductive nook with minimal lighting emanating from a fishless aquarium behind the bar. Other signs of excellence can be found in the friendly staff, who mix great drinks, and the good music.

Manolos

1, Volksgartenstrasse 1 (526 2082/www.manolos.at). U2, U3 Volkstheater/tram 1, 2, 46, 49, D, J. **Open** 6pm-2am Mon-Sat. **Credit** MC, V. **Map** p247 D7.

Vienna's top Latin bar is the elegant Manolos, run by a chirpy Mexican of the same name. It's right beside parliament, and Austrian MPs can be spotted tucking into the spicy tapas and vintage tequilas. The joint livens up when bands playing the whole palette of Latin music kick in.

Passage

1, Burgring, corner Babenbergasse (961 8800/ www.sunshine.at). Tram 1, 2, D, J. **Open** 8pm-4am Tue, Wed; 9pm-4am Thur; 10pm-6am Fri, Sat. **Admission** €10-€13. **Credit** AmEx, DC, JCB, MC, V. **Map** p247 D7.

With its long queues waiting to get in, sniffy doormen, funky interior and pricey drinks, Passage is the nearest that Vienna gets to a proper big city clubbing vibe. Located in a former subway beneath the Ringstrasse, it's a fairly bare space that mutates via all manner of lighting effects. Name DJs such as Rainer Trüby, Dorfmeister and Kenny 'Dope' Gonzales occasionally show but accessible throbbing house is normally the dish of the day.

Pavillon im Volksgarten

1, Burgring (532 0907). U2, U3 Volkstheater. **Open** May-Oct 11am-2am Mon-Thur, Sun; 11am-4am Fri, Sat. **No credit cards. Map** p250 D7.

This beautiful 1950s folly is a delight on a summer evening. You can enjoy floodlit boules along with a fine view of the illuminated Neue Burg, to a selection of laid-back tunes. Admission is usually free, but entrance is charged for the oversubscribed Techno Café on Tuesday nights. Through the winter of 2006/07, it was used as a restaurant.

Planter's Club

1, Zelinkagasse 4 (533 33 9315/www.plantersclub. com). U2, U4 Schottenring/tram 1, 2. **Open** 5pm-4am daily. **Credit** AmEx, DC, MC, V. **Map** p250 E5.

Leather armchairs and potted palms give Planter's the air of a British colonial club. The clientele is dominated by thirtysomething suited types who bop around to DJ Samir's rare grooves and soul stompers. The bar staff are highly competent and serve superb drinks, such as the vintage rums.

Shambala

1, Robert-Stoltz-Platz 1 (588 90 7000/www.le meridien-vienna.com). U1, U2, U4 Karlsplatz/tram 1, 2, D, J. **Open** 10am-1am daily. **Credit** AmEx, DC, JCB, MC, V. **Map** p247 E7.

The achingly cool bar at Le Meridien hotel will probably scare off a lot of Viennese with its spectacular lighting effects and glassed-off smooching niches. If you're not fazed by the setting, a fine evening of cocktails and lounge music can be had here.

Volksgarten

1, Burgring 1 (532 4241/www.volksgarten.at). U2, U3 Volkstheater/tram 1, 2, D, J. **Open** 9.30pm-late Mon-Wed; 11pm-late Thur-Sat. **Admission** €5-€15. **Credit** AmEx, DC, MC, V. **Map** p251 D7.

Vienna's best-loved party complex has a magnificent location. Despite the high-tech renovation of the main dancefloor, the Banane, a curved salon overlooking the garden, retains its gorgeous 1950s fittings. The broad menu of dance genres attracts all comers. Drinks are expensive. The opening times we give above are rough guidelines and tend to vary according to managerial whim, so it's best to consult the website or look carefully at the flyers.

Arts & Entertainment

2nd district

For **Fluc**, see p192.

A Bar Shabu

2, Rotensterngasse 8/Glockengasse (0650 544 5939).
U1 Schwedenplatz, then tram 21, N. **Open** 5pm-late
Mon-Fri, Sun; 7pm-late Sat. **Credit** AmEx, DC, MC,
V. **Map** p251 F6.

Formerly a taxi drivers' hangout, the Shabu serves
local cognoscenti a selection of 15 absinthes in a
relaxed, somewhat dishevelled interior. Further
draws are good sounds and a bar billiards table, and
be sure to check out the tiny 'Japanese room'.

Bricks

2, Taborstrasse 38 (216 3701/www.bricks.co.at).
Tram N. **Open** 8pm-4am daily. **No credit cards.**
Map p243 F4.

This dimly lit, arched basement bar has been a late-
night stalwart for years. Though in need of a technical and aesthetic overhaul, Bricks has good vibes, zero
attitude and a kaleidoscopic musical programme that
still features DJ Elk's legendary '60s night.

3rd district

Strandbar Herrmann

3, Herrmannpark (beside Urania) (0650/718 04 01/
www.strandbar-herrmann.at). U1, U4 Schwedenplatz
(exit Urania). **Open** May-Oct 10am-2am daily.
Admission free. **Credit** MC, V. **Map** p251 G6.

Voted second best bar in the world by *Condé Nast
Traveller* in 2006, the Herrmann gets its name from
its location in the canal-side Herrmannpark, which
commemorates Emanuel Herrmann (1839-1902),
inventor of the picture postcard. And it's a bit like
being beside the seaside here. The promontory
where the Wien river enters the Danube Canal has
been covered with sand and strewn with deckchairs.
No bathing but plenty of sunbathing, eating and
chilling to great sounds until 2am.

4th district

For **Schikaneder**, see p167.

Café Anzengruber

4, Schleifmühlgasse 19 (5878 2979). U1, U2, U4
Karlsplatz/bus 59a. **Open** 5pm-2am Mon; 11am-2am
Tue-Sat. **No credit cards. Map** p247 E8.

A favourite spot with the art crowd from the
Schleifmühlgasse galleries. Dusty, charming art covers the walls and the atmosphere is pleasantly old
world; as an added bonus the food is good too. It's
perfect for afternoon intimacies as well as more boisterous entertainment later on.

Roxy

4, Operngasse 24/Faulmanngasse (961 8800). U1,
U2, U4 Karlsplatz/tram 1, 2, D, J/bus 59a. **Open**
10pm-4am daily. **Admission** €5-€10. **Credit** AmEx,
DC, JCB, MC, V. **Map** p250 E8.

This central late-nighter sports a plush interior and
tiny dancefloor. It's often packed to the seams when
the odd Vienna Scientist, Sofa Surfer or foreign guest
does the honours on the decks.

Silverbar

*4, Wiedner Hauptstrasse 12 (589 18036/www.das
triest.at).* **Tram** 62. **Open** 6pm-2am Mon; 7pm-3am
Tue-Sat; 4pm-midnight Sun. **Credit** AmEx, DC, MC,
V. **Map** p247 E9.

Located in the Conran-designed Das Triest (*see p45*),
this is one of Vienna's best-loved hotel bars, with
lounge sounds, leather snugs and excellent drinks.

6th district

For **Topkino**, see p167. For **Ra'mien**,
see p126.

Aux Gazelles

6, Mariahilfer Strasse 1b (Rahlgasse 5) (585 6645/
www.auxgazelles.at). U2 Museumsquartier. **Open**
11am-2am Mon-Thur; 10am-4am Fri, Sat.
Admission (club nights) free-€10. **Credit**
AmEx, DC, MC, V. **Map** p250 D8.

With its restaurants, bars, tea lounges and Moroccan
steam bath, this gargantuan Moorish labyrinth
always seemed a bit too ambitious for Vienna.
Having ditched its original Ibiza-esque music policy, Aux Gazelles now pulls in a particularly mixed-
nationality crowd with full on Balkan beats, Oriental
dance music and the odd live act from the genre. The
Friday and Saturday club nights feature DJs from
far afield places such as Turkmenistan.

Bar Italia Lounge

*6, Mariahilfer Strasse 19-21 (585 2838/www.bar
italia.net). U2 Museumsquartier, U3 Neubaugasse.*
Open 6.30pm-3am Mon-Sat. **Credit** DC, MC, V.
Map p246 C8.

Beneath the cool Bar Italia is this even icier designer
basement. Good food, professional service and fine
cocktails come in an intimate setting, with a competent DJ pool, overseen by Café del Mar favourite DJ
geb-el providing a house/lounge soundtrack.

Jenseits

*6, Nelkengasse 3 (587 1233). U3 Neubaugasse/bus
13a.* **Open** 9pm-4am Mon-Sat. **No credit cards.**
Map p246 C8.

The period chintz and velvet interior appears to con-
firm the legend that Jenseits ('the beyond') was once
a brothel. It remains a wonderfully retro environment for a couple of drinks and the odd waltz round
the tiny dancefloor. The music is an always appealing blend of vintage soul and funk, lounge sounds
and chansons. Come early to avoid the crush.

Joanelli

6, Gumpendorfer Strasse 47 (0650 311 8404).
U3 Neubaugasse. **Open** 6pm-2am Mon-Sat. **Credit**
AmEx, DC, MC, V. **Map** p247 D8.

Vienna's oldest ice-cream saloon is now a hip, but
totally unpretentious, bar. Much loved by the arty

Rotes Bar. *See p200.*

crowd, the Joanelli is a stylish set-up with good wines and beers, a chilled soundtrack and the odd bite to eat. Plans are afoot to restart the sale of ice-cream.

7th district

Blue Box

7, Richtergasse 8 (523 2682/www.bluebox.at). U3 Neubaugasse/bus 13a. **Open** 5pm-2am Mon; 10am-2am Tue-Thur, Sun; 10am-4am Fri, Sat. **No credit cards. Map** p246 C8.
One of Vienna's first DJ bars when it opened over 20 years ago, Blue Box still spins tunes from electronica to swing every night. However, it is looking a tad threadbare, and the thick clouds of smoke and sometimes relentless music are drawbacks.

Café Leopold

7, Museumplatz 1 (523 6732/www.cafe-leopold.at). U2 Museumsquartier. **Open** 10am-2am Mon-Thur, Sun; 10am-4am Fri, Sat. **Credit** AmEx, DC, MC, V. **Map** p250 D7.
Rather appropriately built into the Leopold Museum (*see p85*), Café Leopold remains the MuseumQuartier's most happening nocturnal venue, featuring some of the best spinners in town – among them Joyce Muniz, Karl Möstl and DJ DSL. Live acts also take place with innovative London-based New Yorker Joe Driscoll appearing in mid 2007. The place is a glass fish tank, pleasantly appointed but far too small to accommodate the crowds that besiege it, especially at weekends.

Camera

7, Neubaugasse 2 (523 3063/www.camera-club.at). U3 Neubaugasse/bus 13a. **Open** 9.30pm-late Thur-Sat. **Admission** €10. **No credit cards. Map** p246 C8.

Marjane Satrapi's acclaimed graphic novel *Persepolis* recounts how she bought her first bag of grass at the Camera in the mid 1980s. The dealers have now been replaced by various local posses such as the Icke Micke gang who bring DJs playing electro clash, hip hop and general feel-good party sounds.

Donau

7, Karl Schweighofergasse 10 (523 8105). U2, U3 Volkstheater/tram 49. **Open** 9pm-4am Mon-Sat; 9pm-2am Sun. **Admission** free. **No credit cards. Map** p247 D7.
The neo-classical arches of the Donau have long been a favourite of the Vienna club scene. Now trading almost exclusively in electro, minimal techno and clicky pop, the lighting by Doctor Flash puts the fine interior to good use.

Europa

7, Zollergasse 8 (526 3383/www.hinterzimmer.at). U3 Neubaugasse/bus 13a. **Open** 9am-4am daily. **Credit** AmEx, DC, MC, V. **Map** p246 C8.
One of the few places in town where you can eat, drink and chill out until the early morning, Europa attracts a young, clubby crowd day and night. Behind the steel door lies the Hinterzimmer, a miniscule back-room club hosting regular DJ nights.

Nachtasyl

6, Stumpergasse 53 (596 9977). U3 Zieglergasse. **Open** 8pm-4am daily. **No credit cards. Map** p246 B9.
Plastered with peeling posters and handbills, this rather dingy cellar has a conspiratorial vibe dating back to when it was a meeting place for Czechs and other refugees from communist regimes. Even Vaclav Havel once showed up. The 'Night Asylum' now provides refuge for a varied clientele, offering

DJ sets and the odd eclectic act often hailing from owner Jiri's native Czech Republic. Understandably, the reasonably priced local tipple is a bottle of Budweiser with Becherovka chasers.

Rotes Bar

7, Neustiftgasse 1 (521 11 218/www.volkstheater.at). U2, U3 Volkstheater. **Open** end of performance to 1am daily (table reservations 2-6pm daily on 0699 150 15013). **Admission** free-€7. **No credit cards.** **Map** p250 D7

The interior of the Volkstheater's Red Bar is a glorious show of crystal chandeliers and heavy velvet curtains over a marble floor. By opening this gem for live music of various genres, DJs, readings and dining, the theatre is subsidising its other operations. But it's a great addition to Viennese nightlife. **Photo** *p199.*

Shultz

7, Siebensterngasse 31 (522 9120). U3 Neubaugasse. **Open** 9am-2am Mon-Thur; 9am-3am Fri, Sat; 5pm-2am Sun. **Credit** AmEx, DC, MC, V. **Map** p246 C8.

A spacious 1960s-style bar in a splendid Jugendstil building, Shultz is one of the rare breed of designer bars in Vienna. Cocktails are the mainstay. Music is a pleasing blend of cool funk and lounge.

Wirr

7, Burggasse 70 (929 4050/www.wirr.at). Bus 48a. **Open** 10am-2am Mon-Thur, Sun; 10am-4am Fri, Sat. **Credit** AmEx, DC, MC, V. **Map** p246 B7.

This bar-club has become the extended front room of the alternative crowd, one that's full of mismatched sofas and thrift shop tat. Ventilation is now considerably better in the downstairs dancehall, where some of Vienna's best nights are held – for example, the Treasure Isle vintage reggae sessions. Check the website for details.

8th district

For **B72** *see p191,* for **Chelsea** and **Café Carina,** *see p192,* and for **rhiz** *see p193.*

Más!

8, Laudongasse 36 (403 83 24). Tram 5, 43, 44/bus 13a. **Open** 6pm-2am daily. **Credit** AmEx, DC, JCB, MC, V. **Map** p246 B6.

Mercifully free of Tex-Mex tat, this voluminous designer Mexican bar/restaurant is one of Vienna's most spectacular locations. While the food is good of its ilk, the real pleasure lies in sipping a mojito at the long bar (with its vast illuminated tortoise-shell backdrop), watching the formation dancing of the Latino bar staff and tapping your feet to the Fania tracks.

Miles Smiles

8, Lange Gasse 51 (405 9517). U2 Rathaus/tram J. **Open** 8pm-2am Mon-Thur, Sun; 8pm-4am Fri, Sat. **Admission** free. **No credit cards.** **Map** p250 C6.

A typically laid-back Viennese venue. The name betrays the owner's weakness for jazz; occasionally live soloists or duos appear, especially during JazzFestWien (*see p160).*

9th district

For **WUK,** *see p194.*

Café Stein

9, Währinger Strasse 6-8/Kolingasse 1 (319 7241/ www.cafe-stein.com). U2 Schottentor/tram 1, 2. **Open** 7am-1am Mon-Sat; 8am-1am Sun. *Stein's Diner* 7pm-1am Mon-Sat. **No credit cards.** **Map** p250 D5.

No longer the height of modernity, the Stein still pulls in students from the nearby university faculties, as well as media trash, models and clubbers. The food is generally excellent, though drinks are a little expensive and staff can be a bit humourless. The neighbouring Stein's Diner boasts a lot of red leather, low lights and occasional DJs.

Summerstage

9, Rossauer Lände (315 5202/www.summer stage.co.at). U4 Rossauer Lände. **Open** May-Sept 5pm-1am Mon-Sat; 3pm-1am Sun. **No credit cards.** **Map** p243 E4.

A loose grouping of various restaurants sets up shop along this stretch of the Danube Canal in summer. Here you can eat and drink alfresco much later than the usual 11pm. Why the organisers bother arranging a lame programme of jazz, boules and art to pull in punters is a mystery – the waterside location is a sufficient draw. Booking is strongly advised.

12th district

U4

12, Schönbrunner Strasse 222 (817 1192/www.u-4.at). U4 Meidlinger Hauptstrasse. **Open** 10pm-late daily. **Admission** €4-€10. **Credit** AmEx, DC, MC, V. **Map** p246 B10.

U4 has been a cornerstone of Viennese nightlife for over two decades – Kurt and Courtney showed up, Prince and Sade played aftershow gigs and Falco, Austria's most successful pop export, namechecked it. Totally revamped in 2006, it is now covered in black graphite and equipped with modern ventilation and a powerful new sound system. As it tries to attract the very broadest of audiences, it's worth consulting the schedule – you may end up with a night of tacky German Schlager music. Approach with care!

Zoo

12, Schönbrunner Strasse 175 (no phone/www.the zoo.at). U4, U6 Längenfeldgasse. **Open** 10pm-late Fri, Sat. **Admission** free-€10. **No credit cards.** **Map** p246 B10.

Operating since mid 2006, the Zoo is a spacious new club located just beyond the Gürtel in the 12th district. Up to now, it's specialised in reggae-related sounds and drum 'n' bass, usually at weekends but with the odd mid-week session. And in June 2007, it finally gave the locals a taste of what dubstep is about with two nights featuring, among others, Loefah, Benga and Boxcutter. Junglist Ed Rush was also a recent visitor. Good vibes, good prices and some very uncompromising music.

Sport & Fitness

Acres of green space and top facilities.

Sport in Austria is serious business, with Austrians committed to a host of sporting activities ranging from traditional skiing to football and the recent craze for Nordic walking. Vienna is (somewhat surprisingly) a paradise for fitness freaks and outdoor enthusiasts. While moderate mountains and wooded nature are easily reachable by public transport, there are also plenty of good places within the city – notably Donauinsel (*see p88* **Down by the river**) and the Prater (*see p90*) – to walk, run, cycle or in-line skate. On the spectatorial front, all eyes will be on Austria when it co-hosts the UEFA Euro 2008 Championships with Switzerland (*see p205* **Euro 2008**).

Major stadia

Ernst-Happel-Stadion

2, Meiereistrasse 7 (728 0854). U1 Praterstern, then tram 21, bus 80a. **Map** p249 K7.
The 53,000-seater Ernst-Happel-Stadion (formerly the Prater Stadium) is Vienna's largest, and named after the Austrian football player and coach who died in 1992. It's the main venue for international football matches, and big domestic and European fixtures, as well as some concerts.

Stadthalle

15, Vogelweidplatz 14 (981 000/www.stadthalle. com). U3 Schwegler Strasse, U6 Burggasse/Stadthalle/tram 6, 19, 18, 49/bus 48a.
Map p246 A7.
The Stadthalle hosts sporting events as varied as ice hockey (including the World Championship) and ice-skating, dance, tennis and indoor football, as well as concerts and other non-sporting events.

Spectator sports

Football

Vienna's two Bundesliga teams, Austria and Rapid Vienna, have the heated rivalry of any teams sharing the same city. Traditionally, Austria plays a more technical, intellectual game, while Rapid takes a more traditional, fighting approach. Sold-out games are a rarity in Vienna, so getting last-minute tickets is no problem. National team games are played at the Ernst-Happel-Stadion (*see above*). For tickets (around €30) contact the Austrian Football Federation (727 180/www.oefb.at).

Austria Memphis Franz-Horr-Stadion

10, Fischhofgasse 10-12 (688 01 50-301/tickets 219 55 19/www.fk-austria.at). U1 Reumannplatz, then tram 67/bus 15a. **Tickets** €5-€21. **Credit** (internet sales only) DC, MC, V.
Recent structural work has increased this tumble-down stadium's capacity to 11,800.

Rapid Vienna Gerhard-Hanappi-Stadion

14, Keisslergasse 6 (info 910 010/www.skrapid.at). U4 Hütteldorf. **Tickets** average €15. **Credit** AmEx, DC, MC, V.
Rapid is the biggest club in Austria and plays in a stadium named after its former player Gerhard Hanappi, who also designed it. The capacity is 19,600. Tickets are also available from branches of Bank Austria-Creditanstalt.

Horse racing

The Prater (*see p90*) is the location of flat-racing and trotting tracks.

Wiener Galopp-Rennverein (Viennese Galloping Race Association)

2, Freudenau/Rennbahnstrasse 65 (728 95 31/www.freudenau.at). U3 Schlachthausgasse, then bus 77a. **Open** Sept & May; check website for specific dates. **No credit cards.** **Map** p249 M9.
One of Europe's oldest racetracks, Freudenau boasts splendid belle époque wrought-iron stands but a very irregular racing programme. There are two main events annually.

Wiener Trabrenn-Verein (Viennese Trotting Association)

2, Nordportalstrasse 274 (728 00 46/www.krieau.at). U3 Schlachthausgasse, then bus 83a, 84a/U1 Praterstern, then tram 21. **Open** 2pm most Sat. Closed July, Aug. **No credit cards.** **Map** p244 J5.
The Krieau track has Europe's first steel and concrete grandstand, built in 1912 by a student of architect Otto Wagner. There's regular racing for most of the year. It's used in summer as an open-air cinema.

Participation sports

Boating

The Alte Donau is the more popular site for sailing; pedal boats and other craft can also be rented there and on the Neue Donau.

Sailing School Hofbauer

22, An der oberen Alten Donau 191 (204 3435/ www.hofbauer.at). U1 Kagran. **Open** *Apr-Oct* 9am-dusk daily. **Rates** phone for details. **No credit cards. Map** p245 M2.
Sailing classes in English are available at the Kagran location of the Hofbauer. You'll need photo ID as a deposit. All kinds of boats and windsurfers are available for hire.

Wolfgang Irzl Segel-und Surfschule

22, An der oberen Alten Donau 29/Florian Berndlgasse 33-34 (203 6743/www.irzl.at). U1 Alte Donau. **Open** *Mid Apr-Sept* 10am-8pm daily. **Rates** €14/hr sailing boat; €7/hr rowboat; €10.50/hr pedal boat; €15/hr motorboat; €11/hr windsurf; €7/hr surfbike. **No credit cards. Map** p245 M2.
Offers both sailing and windsurfing classes, as well as all manner of craft for hire. ID and €10 are required as a deposit.

Bowling

Brunswick Bowling

2, Prater Hauptallee 124 (728 0709/www.us-play.com). Tram N. **Open** 10am-1am Mon-Thur; 10am-2am Fri, Sat; 9am-1am Sun. **Rates** €3-€4.50 per person. **Shoe rental** €2. **Credit** AmEx, DC, MC, V.
Brunswick Bowling offers 32 lanes and *Big Lebowski*-inspired Thursday-night club sessions with name DJs spinning records (in winter).
Other locations 17, Schumanngasse 107 (486 4361).

Chess

Playing chess was a popular pastime during the great years of Vienna's café culture at the start of the 20th century, and the city still supports dozens of clubs that meet regularly today. **Café Museum** (*see p138*) is the best-known café for a pick-up chess game. You can also play at **Café Sperlhof** (*see p140*).

Climbing

Kletterwand am Flakturm

6, Esterházypark (585 47 48/info 513 8500). U3 Neubaugasse/bus 13a, 14a, 57a. **Open** *Apr-Oct* 2pm-dusk daily. **Rates** €12 adults for 1hr 30min; €2.50 children. **No credit cards. Map** p246 C8.
Scale this imposing flak tower built by the Nazis during World War II. There are 25 climbing routes that go up to 34m (111ft), with climbing difficulties ranging from four to eight. Inexperienced climbers can get instruction or a safety spotter – call to reserve.

Cycling

Generally flat and with over 700 kilometres (435 miles) of bike paths in the city and surrounding areas, Vienna is excellent for cyclists. In town, bike lanes are pretty safe and convenient – they are often on the pavement. Popular spots for cycling include the Prater, along the Donaukanal and around the Alte and Neue Donau, and on the Donauinsel (*see p88* **Down by the river**), with bike rental at many spots near the river. The Hauptallee boulevard through the Prater is popular for cycling, skating, jogging and strolling. You can also circle the Ring on a bike path. For out of town cycling, head west along the Danube.

Bikes can be taken on the U-Bahn and local S-Bahn trains from 9am to 3pm and after 6.30pm Monday to Friday, after 9am on Saturday and all day Sunday and holidays. Bicycles must go in carriages sporting a bike symbol and require a half-price ticket. They can be taken on trains marked with a bicycle symbol on the timetable; outside Vienna's central transport Kernzone (Zone 100), which covers the entire city, bikes require a special ticket. Only folding bikes can be taken on trams, and they are not allowed at all on buses.

Fahrradverleih Skaterverleih Copa Cagrana

22, near the Reichsbrücke bridge, close to the Schuhski shop, on the east side of the Neue Donau in the Copa Cagrana (263 5242/0664 345 8585/www. fahrradverleih.at). U1 Donauinsel. **Open** *Mar, Oct* 9am-6pm daily. *Apr, Sept* 9am-8pm daily. *May-Aug* 9am-9pm daily. **Rates** from €5/hr, €25/day city bike; €7.50/hr, €38/day mountain bike; €7/hr, €30/day in-line skates. **No credit cards. Map** p244 J3.
This place is centrally located for Donauinsel and river route exploration. All sorts of bikes are available for hire, including tandems, rickshaws and bikes for the handicapped that can be pedalled with the hands. Rent a bike for a four-hour period and you'll get one hour free. Photo ID and a deposit are required.

Pedal Power Radverleih

2, Ausstellungsstrasse 3 (729 7234/www.pedal power.at). U1 Praterstern. **Open** *Apr-Oct* 9am-7pm daily. **Rates** (24-gear bicycle) from €5/hr, €4/hr concessions; €27/day, €21/day concessions. **Credit** AmEx, DC, MC, V. **Map** p244 H5.
Bikes come with locks and a map, and staff will provide advice on routes. The store can drop off and pick up bikes from hotels.

Golf

There are about 15 clubs in and around Vienna.

Golf Club Wien

2, Freudenau 65a (0222 728 9564/www.gcwien.at). U3 Erdberg, then bus 77a. **Open** daylight hours daily. *Office* 8.30am-12.30pm, 2-6pm daily. **Fee** €70/person/round. **No credit cards.**
The Vienna club is Austria's oldest, founded in 1901, although the current course was built after World War II on the site of former polo grounds. An 18-hole site, it cuts through the Freudenau horse racetrack.

Non-members can play during the week (all day Mon-Thur; until 1pm Fri) if they are members of another club and have a minimum 28 handicap.

Golf und Sport Club Fontana

Fontana Allée 1, Oberwaltersdorf (02253 606 401/www.fontana.at). By car, A2 exit Baden, turn right and follow signs for Oberwaltersdorf. **Open** all year (weather permitting). **Fee** €150 Mon-Fri; €175 Sat, Sun. **Credit** AmEx, DC, MC, V.

Twenty kilometres (12 miles) south of Vienna lies this residential/golf complex owned by Austro-Canadian billionaire Frank Stronach. Although the whole thing smacks of *The Truman Show*, the course itself is a blinder and hosted the comeback tournament of the PGA European Tour in 2007. Visitors must belong to an accredited club.

Health & fitness

Club Danube

3, Franzosengraben 2-4 (798 8400/98 8405/ www.clubdanube.at). U3 Erdberg. **Rates** €20 1-day pass; €14 2-hr card. **Credit** DC, MC, V. **Map** p249 K10.

The club is in the same building as U3 Erdberg, so take the lift in the station to the seventh floor. With over ten locations in Vienna and uncomplicated day membership, Club Danube is the most accessible to visitors of the fitness clubs in Vienna, offering a wide range of activities and facilities, including exercise classes, tennis, squash, badminton, sauna and solarium, all at reasonable prices.

Other locations throughout the city.

Holmes Place Lifestyle Club

1, Wien Börseplatz, Wipplingerstrasse 30 (533 97 9090/www.holmesplace.at). U2 Schottentor. **Open** 6.30am-11pm Mon-Fri; 9am-10pm Sat, Sun. **Rates** phone for details. **Credit** AmEx, DC, MC, V. **Map** p250 E6.

This branch of the Holmes Place chain is one of the most luxurious health clubs in Vienna, with all the usual facilities, including a swimming pool. If you are a member of Holmes Place in the UK or else-where, you can get half-price day membership at both Vienna locations. Otherwise you need to know a member in Vienna and pay full price.
Other locations 20, Wien Kaiserwasser, Wagramerstrasse 17-19 (263 89 89).

John Harris

1, Nibelungengasse 7 (587 3710/www.johnharris fitness.at). U1, U2, U4 Karlsplatz. **Open** 6.30am-11pm Mon-Fri; 9am-9pm Sat, Sun. **Rates** €25.50 1-day pass. **Credit** AmEx, DC, MC, V. **Map** p250 D7/8.

The facilities at the John Harris club include weights, cardiovascular machines, aerobics and dance class-es, solarium, massage, sauna, jacuzzi, t'ai chi class-es and a swimming pool. For putting in some serious training, however, there's a 25m (82ft) pool at the Strobachgasse branch. If you belong to a club with IHRSA affiliation, the discounted pass is €15.
Other locations 5, Strobachgasse 7-9 (544 1212).

Wellness Park Oberlaa

10, Kurbadstrasse 16 (6800 99700/www.oberlaa.at). U1 Reumannplatz, then tram 67. **Open** *Racket sports* 8am-10pm Mon-Fri; 8am-9pm Sat, Sun. *Fitness centre* 7.30am-11pm Mon-Fri; 7.30am-10pm Sat, Sun. **Rates** *Racket sports* €28/day. *Fitness centre* €17/day. *Thermal pool* €18.35/day. **Credit** DC.

Thoroughly renovated in 2006, this massive all-purpose 'wellness' complex has a fitness centre with weights and machines, aerobics and other classes, a sauna and massage rooms. In addition it has 13 indoor and five outdoor tennis courts, as well as 14 squash courts and 15 badminton courts, five indoor and outdoor thermal pools, two children's pools, three whirlpools, and men's, women's and mixed saunas, as well as a solarium and massage, herbal and eucalyptus rooms.

Hiking

Hiking is extremely popular among Austrians. For a touch of the woods and mountains, the **Wienerwald** (Viennese woods) (*see p214*) to the north-west of the city is a good place to explore. Equally, the area around the spa towns **Baden** and **Bad Vöslau** (*see p214*), which are worth a visit themselves, to the south of the city is also great for day trips. Trails are pretty well marked and the free tourist office map is enough to orient you. For a detailed map of the Wienerwald with hiking and bike routes, purchase a copy of Freytag & Berndt's *Wienerwald Wanderatlas* for €13.90.

Another place for a hike is the **Donau-Auen national park**, created in 1996, which spreads east from the Danube near Vienna (www.donauauen.at). The nearest section to Vienna of these Danube wetlands can be reached by taking the U1 to Kagran, then bus 93a to the Danzergasse stop.

If you fancy a good long walk without transport hassles, head for the Prater (U1 Praterstern or terminus of tram N).

Ice-skating

Try an outdoor skating rinks to get Vienna's winter wonderland feel. Or, if you fancy something closer to nature and have your own skates, head out to the Old Danube for a skate on the river (U1 Alte Donau). From late January to early March, an outdoor ice-skating rink opens in **Rathausplatz** (*see p79*).

Wiener Eislaufverein

3, Lothringerstrasse 22 (713 6353). U4 Stadtpark. **Open** *Late Oct-early Mar* 9am-8pm Mon, Sat, Sun; 9am-9pm Tue, Thur, Fri; 9am-10pm Wed. **Admission** €8; €3-€6 concessions. *Boot rental* €5.50. **No credit cards.** **Map** p251 E/F8.

This centrally located open-air rink also has a Punsch bar for an after-skate drink.

In-line skating

The outdoor sites listed for cycling are popular with in-line skaters too, though it's also not uncommon in Vienna to see someone doing their grocery shopping on skates. There's a small ramp area for skaters in the Prater near the Riesenrad. There are other skate rental places on the Donauinsel. *See also p202* Fahrradverleih Skaterverleih Copa Cagrana.

Skatelab

2, Engerthstrasse 160-178 (214 9565). U1 Vorgartenstrasse/bus 11a. **Open** *Nov-Apr* 2-9pm Tue-Fri; 10am-8pm Sat, Sun. **Admission** €7.50; €4-€5.50 concessions. **No credit cards.** **Map** p244 H3.

This indoor in-line-skating rink has a street course with obstacles, mini-ramps and videos for skaters who can't wait for good weather. You have to bring your own skates, but (free) skateboards are available.

Jogging

Jogging is a popular pastime in Vienna and the city has a safe-enough vibe so that runners shouldn't feel afraid. For a pleasant run close to the centre, try the path along the Donaukanal. The Prater Hauptallee is the city's most popular stretch, but joggers also like the Augarten in the 2nd district and the grounds of the Belvedere in the 3rd district. For a competitive race, the main event in town is the **Vienna Marathon** in May (*see p159*).

Euro 2008

'Expect emotions' was the mistranslated motto officially unveiled by Austrian FA president Friedrich Stickler at a launch at Vienna City Hall in January 2007, exactly 500 days before football's UEFA European Championships kicks off. Euro 2008, under the somewhat slicker German slogan 'Erlebe Emotionen' ('Experience Emotions'), will take place in eight cities across co-hosts Austria and Switzerland between 7 and 29 June. Vienna, home of the national Ernst-Happel-Stadion (*see p201*) in the Prater Park, will stage seven matches, including the final.

With the exception of the 53,000-capacity Ernst-Happel-Stadion and the 42,000-capacity St Jakob-Park in Basle, all grounds only hold around 30,000 people each, the bare minimum for what is the world's third largest sporting event after the Olympic Games and the FIFA World Cup. Nearly 600,000 fans from 142 countries submitted ticket applications to www.euro2008.com at midnight on 31 March 2007. All 31 matches are massively oversubscribed. Individual national associations will be able to sell tickets to their fans after the group draw in December 2007.

Up until then, some 50 European countries will have played a seemingly endless qualifying tournament to produce 14 teams to join the two host countries in June 2008. England is expected to make it despite highly criticised setbacks in Croatia and Israel, while Scotland and Northern Ireland have upset the form book by notching unexpected wins over France, Spain and Sweden.

As for the hosts, Austria have never even qualified for the European finals before, so hosting the tournament was the only way to ensure participation. Defeat in recent years to minnows Canada, Hungary and, most disgracefully, the Faroe Islands, hardly fill local fans with confidence. Meanwhile, the domestic game is struggling, not least in Vienna. A revival by Austria Vienna, thanks to the generosity of Austro-Canadian billionaire Frank Stronach, came to an abrupt halt when Stronach pulled out and key players left in droves. Champions in 2006, the Violets were mired mid-table in 2006/07. Record title-holders Rapid are still popular but trail way behind the new force in the league, Salzburg, backed and rebranded by energy-drink billionaire Dietrich Mateschitz. FC Red Bull Salzburg, wearing the logo of the canned product instead of Salzburg's traditional violet, and playing at the Bulls Arena, attracted the managerial talent of Giovanni Trapattoni and Lothar Matthäus to win the league by a country mile in April 2007. It's doubtful that this success will extend to European competition in 2007 to 2008 though – Austrian league football is played by Central European journeymen and also-rans.

The last decent player Austria produced, former Rapid star Andreas Herzog, was the figure Euro 2008 marketeers chose to dress up and drive one of Vienna's two new branded trams at the D-Day-500 launch. Equally underwhelming has been the naming of the inevitable inane mascots, Trix and Flix ('a vital part of the understanding of the whole event,' according to Swiss tournament director Christian Mutschler). In Vienna, match-day shenanigans will close the Ringstrasse between Hofburg and the Rathaus to accommodate the bars, stands and big screens of the 'Fan Mile' – another Germany 2006 innovation that the Austrians hope will put a shine on things, whatever happens on the field.

Skiing

With over 60 per cent of the terrain classified as being 'alpine landscape', Austria is rightly thought to be the home of modern alpine skiing. Indeed, almost half the population practise downhill, cross-country skiing or snowboarding. One-day package trips from Vienna are an easy way to sample this most Austrian of activities. Many travel agencies offer one-day bus trips to ski slopes from December to March – try Columbus Reisebüro (1, Dr-Karl-Lueger-Ring 8, 534 110). Austrian Railways also offers an all-inclusive day trip. Dieters Schizug ('Dieter's ski train') runs at weekends and holidays from early December to early March and includes a round-trip train ride, transfers to the slopes and a one-day lift ticket at Semmering area sites. Check with travel agencies at Vienna train stations or phone 5800 34247. *See also pp219-220.*

Hohe Wand Wiese

14, Mauerbachstrasse 172-174 (979 1057). U4 Hütteldorf, then bus 249, 449. **Open** *Dec-Mar* 9am-9.30pm Mon-Fri; 9am-10pm Sat, Sun. **Rates** €6 10-ride lift ticket; €13 1-day pass; €9 half-day pass (from 1pm). **No credit cards.**

A good local skiing site. Hohe Wand Wiese has snow cannons ready once there's a deep-enough natural base, but season opening may be delayed until there's sufficient snow.

Swimming & bathing

The banks of the Danube, either side of the Neue Donau channel, are the nearest Vienna gets to a beach. Take the U1 to Donauinsel, and walk until you find a suitable spot. Topless sunbathing is generally acceptable, but head downstream for the nude spots (marked FKK on maps). Two stops further on the U1, the **Alte Donau** (*see p88* **Down by the river**) has paying beach clubs such as the vast Gänsehäufel (take the U1 to Kaisermühlen-Vienna International Centre, then bus 90a, 91a or 92a to Schüttauplatz), which has both swimming pools and beaches, and a peaceful nudist area. On the opposite bank the best bet is the Bundesbad Alte Donau. The city also has a formidable stock of indoor and outdoor pools. Many of the older baths are period gems, worth a visit in themselves. For details of all Vienna's bathing facilities in English, visit www.wien.gv.at/english/leisure/bath.htm.

Amalienbad

10, Reumannplatz 23 (607 4747). U1 Reumannplatz. **Open** 9am-6pm Tue; 9am-9.30pm Wed-Fri; 7am-8pm Sat; 7am-6pm Sun. **Admission** (full day) €4.50, €3.50 concessions; €3.50 2.5hr session. **No credit cards.**

Amalienbad is a beautiful Jugendstil indoor baths complex with solarium, massage, towel service, foot and cosmetic treatments, and a restaurant. On top of that, there are men's, women's and mixed sessions in the two large sauna rooms.

Krapfenwaldbad

19, Krapfenwaldgasse 65-73 (320 15 01). Bus 38a. **Open** *May-Sept* 9am-8pm daily. **Admission** (full day) €4.50, €3.50 concessions; €3.50 after 1pm. **No credit cards.**

Vienna's poshest swimming pool has a magnificent setting high above Grinzing, with stupendous city views. Run by the council since 1923, it has period-piece wooden changing rooms, Mediterranean pines, wooden loungers and two pools. It gets packed on summer weekends.

Schönbrunnerbad

Schönnbrunner Schlosspark (817 5353). U4 Schönbrunn. **Open** *Apr, May, Sept* 8.30am-7pm daily. *June, July, Aug* 8.30am-10pm daily. **Admission** (full day) €9; €7 from 1.30pm; €4 from 5pm. **No credit cards.**

This privately run pool in the gardens of the Schönbrunn palace was rebuilt and opened to the public in 1975. Signposted from the U-Bahn station, it's a stiff but agreeable walk through the woods to get there. Today, late opening hours make it popular with young singles but small children can paddle safely in an area divided from the main pool.

Strand Bad Alte Donau

22, Arbeiterstrandbadstrasse 91 (263 6538). U1 Alte Donau. **Open** *May-mid Sept* 9am-8pm Mon-Fri; 8am-8pm Sat, Sun. **Admission** (full day) €4.50; €3.50 concessions; €3.50 after 1pm. **No credit cards.**

This bathing spot on the old Danube is a favourite with yummy mummies and their children. The old poplar trees give wonderful shade in the heat of the summer and there's a gorgeous 1950s pavilion selling ice-cream and hotdogs.

Tennis

Vienna has dozens of tennis courts. Look at the *Gelbe Seiten* (Yellow Pages) under 'Tennishallen'. Wellness Park Oberlaa (*see p204*) also has a large number of courts.

Tennis Point Vienna

3, corner of Baumgasse & Nottendorfergasse (799 9997/www.tennispoint.at). U3 Erdberg. **Open** 7am-11pm daily. **Rates** phone for details. **No credit cards. Map** p248 J9.

A complex with ten indoor tennis courts, six badminton courts and two squash courts.

Tennis Wien Leistungszentrum

2, Wehlistrasse 320 (726 2626/www.tenniswien.at). U1 Praterstern, then tram 21/bus 80b, 83a. **Open** 8am-9pm Mon-Fri; 8am-8pm Sat, Sun. **Rates** phone for details. **Credit** DC.

Nine indoor, 11 outdoor courts and tennis classes. There's also a restaurant, sauna and shop.

Theatre & Dance

Theatre is still at the centre of the Viennese whirl.

Tanzquartier Wien. *See p208.*

The Viennese have a love/hate relationship with the theatre. Apart from identifying with a great theatrical tradition, they also have a personal stake in it: a significant proportion of taxpayers' money has traditionally subsidised the performing arts, and the heads of the state theatres are government appointees. The large, sophisticated audience that Vienna's theatre culture has engendered over the centuries regards the stage as a vital fixture in social life, far and beyond mere entertainment. Theatres are often the setting for furious debates on the nation's cultural politics – for example, the occasion when protesters piled into the plush Burgtheater and Volkstheater in 2000 to hear intellectuals from home and abroad react to the news that Jörg Haider's Freedom Party had entered the governing coalition. Controversial directors, programming and productions are discussed as earnestly as political scandals, and people take sides in the arguments regardless of whether they have ever actually set foot in the theatre in question.

While overall funding remains generous by European standards, the 2004 Theaterreform blew a chill wind through the rehearsal rooms and foyers of Vienna's smaller venues, sending many of them to the wall. Nevertheless it did engender a new sense of urgency that has produced some interesting new models such as the **3raum – Anatomietheater**.

The Viennese are on the whole disdainful of spectacle, so global blockbuster touring troupes are generally confined to peripheral venues. At the core of the scene is reliable, well-crafted theatre, ranging from classical to experimental. Young playwrights, directors and actors are fostered at venues such as the great classical **Burgtheater** and its worthy dependencies **Akademietheater** and **Kasino am Schwarzenbergplatz**. The **Schauspielhaus** as well as the **Volkstheater** and now even the crusty **Theater in der Josefstadt** regularly host new work from Eastern Europe, the Middle East and elsewhere, while the **Tanzquartier Wien** pursues an experimental, interdisciplinary 'performance' programme, which renders formal distinctions between artistic genres superfluous.

It's worth checking out the late-night improvisations by the English Lovers group (www.english-lovers.at) and some fine theatre jams at **Theater in der Drachengasse** and **Ensembletheater**. There is also a large enough ex-pat audience in Vienna to have supported two English-language theatres, the **English Theatre** and **International Theatre**, for many years.

Every month, the tourist information office puts out a calendar (*Program*) of cultural events, but the most comprehensive listings and reviews are in the programme section of

Red star Vienna: **Volkstheatre**.

the weekly paper *Falter*. Most of Vienna's theatres are closed in July and August. The Wiener Festwochen (*see p160*) running from mid May through June, is the highlight of Vienna's theatre calendar. It features an outstandingly broad selection of international premières and contemporary productions of new and classic works. The new festival series forumfestwochen (www.festwochen.at) focuses on young directorial talent, primarily from Eastern Europe.

Dance

Contemporary dance now has an established base for itself in Vienna. Located in the MuseumsQuartier, the multifunctional dance centre **Tanzquartier Wien** (TQW) begins its seventh season in September 2007. Director Sigrid Gareis runs a densely packed, rigorous programme of local and international experimental performances, theoretical discussions, interdisciplinary projects, and training for young professional dancers. Despite attacks at home on its experimental theory-based programming, the TQW is the object of great interest, admiration and envy from many abroad and has seen a consistent rise in its audiences. More traditional ballet is provided by the talented dancers of the Staatsoper and Volksoper ballet company who appear to be reacting well to the influence of new director Gyula Harangozó.

A very active fringe scene of local companies keeps dance on the programme of numerous smaller venues. **dietheater Künstlerhaus** hosts the fine imagetanz festival of small

contemporary dance works every March and October. ImPulsTanz (mid July to mid August; *see p160*), a high-quality, broad-based international dance festival, showcases seminal contemporary pieces, as well as the work of young choreographers. The festival also offers numerous workshops from beginner to professional levels in nearly every conceivable form of movement and dance, by top artists and trainers from all over the world.

Tanzquartier Wien

7, Museumsplatz 1 (581 3591/www.tqw.at). U2 Museumsquartier, U2, U3 Volkstheater/tram 49. **Box office** 10am-8pm Mon-Fri; 10am-7pm Sat; from 1hr before evening performance. **Tickets** €11-€22. **Credit** AmEx, DC, MC, V. **Map** p250 D7.
Vienna's first facility dedicated exclusively to dance. The ambitious local and international experimental performance programme usually runs from Thursday to Saturday, and changes nearly every week. Performances generally take place in Halle G, in the Kunsthalle building next to the lava-grey MUMOK. Dance workshops, theoretical discussions and symposia are held in the TQW studio spaces near the Leopold Museum. **Photo** *p207*.

Theatre

Main venues

The Burgtheater, Akademietheater and Kasino am Schwarzenbergplatz are all under the Burgtheater's management. Tickets may be obtained at its ticket office, and also through the Österreichische Bundestheaterkassen (*see p180*). On Tuesdays, many theatres charge half price for tickets.

Akademietheater

3, Lisztstrasse 1 (info 51444-4140/tickets 51444-4740). U4 Stadtpark/tram 71, D. **Box office** see Burgtheater; from 1hr before evening performance. **Tickets** €7-€44. **Credit** AmEx, DC, MC, V. **Map** p251 F8.
The 500-seat Akademie was taken over in 1922 by the Burgtheater, at the request of the actors, for staging chamber works. Visitors to the city often overlook the Akademietheater in favour of the more famous Burgtheater, but visually and acoustically, it is a thrilling setting for drama, albeit without the pomp of the big house. Check out the austere 1950s Kantine, where actors and theatre-goers mingle over a goulash and a beer (*see p124* **Canteen scene**).

Burgtheater

1, Dr-Karl-Lueger-Ring 2 (info 51444-4145/tickets 51444-4440/www.burgtheater.at). U2, U3 Volkstheater, U2 Schottentor/tram 1, 2, D. **Box office** 8am-6pm Mon-Fri; 9am-noon Sat, Sun; from 1hr before evening performance. **Tickets** €7-€48. **Credit** AmEx, DC, MC, V. **Map** p250 D6.
The Burgtheater has upheld its status as the great standard-bearer of classical theatre in the German-speaking world since it opened its doors in 1888. Like many Ringstrasse edifices, the building itself was blighted by functional defects and had to be remodelled shortly after completion to improve its appalling acoustics and poor visibility. A joke at the time claimed that 'In Parliament you can't hear anything, in the Rathaus you can't see anything and in the Burgtheater you can neither see nor hear anything'. Today, the theatre is a fabulous historical monument, but what happens on stage is usually anything but antiquated. The Burgtheater's outstanding ensemble is a magnet for such innovative directors as Martin Kusej, Karin Beier and Jan Bosse, whose profound reconsiderations of classic works and treatments of the latest plays by Austrian

3raum -
Anatomietheater.
See p210.

leviathans such as Peter Handke and Elfriede Jelinek make for compelling theatre. The 60-seater Vestibül space in one of the wings has often been a launching pad for young directorial talent. No regular performances are held in July and August, but guided tours are available all year round. The Burgtheater seats 1,175 with standing room for 85.

Kasino am Schwarzenbergplatz

3, Schwarzenbergplatz 1 (51444-4830). Tram 1, 2, D. **Box office** see Burgtheater; from 1hr before evening performance. **Tickets** varies. **No credit cards.** **Map** p251 F8.
Many young directors have launched their careers in this most extravagant of small theatre spaces in Vienna. The marble-clad Kasino was originally the residence of Franz Josef's depraved brother, Archduke Ludwig Viktor. With seating for a maximum of 200, it has been used by the Burgtheater since the 1970s for up-close experimental work.

Schauspielhaus

9, Porzellangasse 19 (317 0101/www.schauspielhaus.at). U4 Rossauer Lände/tram D. **Box office** 4-6pm Mon-Fri. *Performance nights* from 2hrs before performance. **Tickets** €16; €10 concessions. **Credit** AmEx, DC, MC, V. **Map** p243 D4.
Co-directors Barrie Kosky, the enfant terrible of Australian theatre, and Israeli Airan Berg produced some great author-based theatre here that consolidated loyal audiences. Their legacy has been recognised with the appointment in 2007 of former Burgtheater dramaturge Andreas Beck as their successor. The German has little good to say about the current state of Austrian theatre so the ball is now firmly in his court.

Theater in der Josefstadt

8, Josefstädter Strasse 26 (42 700-300/www.josefstadt.org). U2 Rathaus/tram J. **Box office** 10am until performance starts Mon-Fri; 1pm until performance starts Sat, Sun. **Tickets** €4-€63. **Credit** AmEx, DC, MC, V. **Map** p246 C6.
Built in 1788 and given a neo-classical flourish by Josef Kornhäusel in 1822, the theatre is one of Vienna's oldest and best. It was immortalised in a scene from Carol Reed's *The Third Man* where Joseph Cotton dozes off while watching Harry Lime's girlfriend perform in an operetta, and this reputation for boredom has stuck until recently. However, the appointment of new director Herbert Föttinger in 2006 unleashed a quiet revolution in the form of stage versions of the Dogma movie *Festen*. Hopefully this will not alienate his bread and butter audience. The theatre reopens in October 2007 after renovation: first-time visitors will be impressed by the raising of the ornate chandeliers as the lights dim.

Volkstheater

7, Neustiftgasse 1 (info 523 35 01-0/tickets 524 7263/7264/www.volkstheater.at). U2, U3 Volkstheater/tram 49/bus 48a. **Box office** 10am until performance starts Mon-Sat. **Tickets** €7.50-€38. **Credit** AmEx, DC, MC, V. **Map** p250 D7.

When the Volkstheater was built in 1889, its brief was to present German dramatists to a wider public than the Burgtheater. Today's repetoire is full of plays in translation such as the 2006 production of Lars von Trier's *Dogville*. Renamed the 'Strength Through Joy Theatre' by the Nazis, its current director Michael Schottenberg incurred the wrath of the heritage authorities when he dismantled the so-called Hitlerzimmer, a reception room prepared for the Führer that he never actually set foot in. With its brown walls restored, it is now used for discussions, monologues and chamber pieces related to the period. To the time of writing the most visible achievements of Schottenberg's tenure have been off stage – the opening of the Rotes Bar (*see p200*) and the Soviet-style illuminated red star on the roof.

Smaller venues

For details of the Odeon, *see p186*.

dietheater Wien

Konzerthaus *3, Lothringer Strasse 20 (tickets 587 0504/www.dietheater.at). U4 Stadtpark/tram D.* **Box office** 4.30-7pm Mon-Sat. **Tickets** varies. **No credit cards. Map** p251 F8.
Künstlerhaus *1, Karlsplatz 5 (tickets 587 0504/ www.dietheater.at). U1, U2, U4 Karlsplatz/tram 1, 2, D, J.* **Box office** 4.30-7pm Mon-Sat; from 1hr before evening performance. **Tickets** varies. **No credit cards. Map** p251 E8.
Dietheater Wien operates from two small theatres at the Konzerthaus and the Künstlerhaus (capacity 80 and 200 respectively). At the time of writing, plans are underfoot to relaunch it under a new name. Although the name is as yet unknown, the theatres will definitely be run by Berliners, Haiko Pfost and Thomas Frank, who promise lots of interdisciplinary shenanigans.

3raum – Anatomietheater

3, Beatrixgasse 11 (ticket reservations 0650-323 33 77/www.3raum.or.at). U4 Stadtpark/tram O. **Box office** telephone/online reservations. **Tickets** varies. **No credit cards. Map** p248 G7
In April 2006, the operating theatres of the former faculty of veterinary science morphed into an atmospheric off-scene location. Masterminded by Hubsi Kramar, an influential figure on the Viennese scene, the 'three room theatre' is a broad forum that features theatre, cabaret and live music. By renting space out to a variety of groups and performers, as well as holding film screenings and running an agreeable bar, it is likely to be around for a while. **Photo** *p209*.

English Theatre

8, Josefsgasse 12 (402 12 60-0/www.english theatre.at). U2 Rathaus/tram J. **Box office** 10am-5pm Mon-Fri. *Performance days* 5-7.30pm Sat. **Tickets** €19.50-€38. **Credit** MC, V. **Map** p246 C7.
Founded in 1963, the English Theatre has carved a reputation for quality among the Anglophile and expat communities by bringing good West End and Broadway productions to its small space in Vienna.

Anthony Quinn, Larry Hagman and Leslie Nielsen have all trod its boards, and works such as *The Red Devil Battery Sign* by Tennessee Williams and Albee's *Three Tall Women* had their Austrian premières here. Recent highlights included performances by Chicago comedy troupe the Second City and Jeffery Hatcher's *A Picasso* that starred local darling Nicole Beutler in his first English role.

Ensembletheater

1, Petersplatz 1(tickets 535 3200/evenings 533 2039/ www.ensembletheater.at). U1, U3 Stephansplatz. **Box office** 2pm-6pm Mon-Fri; from 1hr before evening performance. *Advance ticket sales 1, Marc-Aurel-Strasse 3/6.* **Tickets** €9-€18. **Credit** DC, MC, V. **Map** p251 E6.
This centrally located former 1950s jazz dive has vaulted cellars and an inviting bar area serving drinks until 1am. The accent is on 20th-century works with a political bent.

International Theatre

9, Porzellangasse 8 (319 6272/www.international theatre.at). Tram D. **Box office** 11am-3pm Mon-Fri, 11am-2pm Sat. *Performance nights* 6-7.30pm. **Tickets** €20-€24; €14 concessions. **Credit** MC, V. **Map** p243 D4.
Having celebrated its 30th anniversary in 2004, this youthful, gung-ho bunch of expats managed to survive the Theaterreform. Its second theatre, the Fundus, located nearby at Müllnergasse 6a, is famous for its annual performances of *A Christmas Carol*.

Rabenhof

3, Rabengasse 3 (712 82 82/www.rabenhof.at). U3 Kardinal Nagl Platz/bus 74a. **Box office** 2-6pm Tue-Fri. *Performance nights* 6pm until performance starts. **Tickets** €12-€24. **Credit** MC, V. **Map** p248 H9.
Located in the enormous Rabenhof council project (*see p112* **Monolithic city**), the theatre often holds cabaret-style attractions involving an irreverent mixture of trash, intellectualism and agit prop.

TAG (Theater an der Gumpendorfer Strasse)

6, Gumpendorferstrasse 67 (tickets 586 5222/ www.dastag.at). U3 Neubaugasse/bus 13a. **Box office** 4pm until performance time. **Tickets** €9-€17. **No credit cards. Map** p246 C8.
Following the retirement of the founders of Gruppe 80, one of Vienna's leading ensemble theatres, the venue was taken over in January 2006 by three groups: Theater Kinetis, L.U.S.Theater and established improv company urtheater.

Theater in der Drachengasse

1, Drachengasse 2/Fleischmarkt 22 (tickets 513 1444/www.drachengasse.at). U1, U4 Schwedenplatz. **Box office** 3.30-7pm Tue-Sat. **Tickets** €16; €10 concessions. **Credit** V. **Map** p251 F6.
This tiny space presents avant-garde chamber works, in various languages. Look out for the itinerant English Lovers improvisation group playing every second and last Friday of the month at the bar.

Trips Out of Town

Leopoldsberg. *See p112.*

Getting Started

Between the woods and the water.

Semmering. *See p219.*

It's not hard to leave the city behind. Within an hour or less of Vienna, you can be enjoying breathtaking countryside: vineyards, the Danube, the Alpine foothills or the Vienna Woods, with much of this easily accessible by excellent public transport. Those with a yen for the east can explore Slovakia, Slovenia, Hungary and the Czech Republic – all no more than two hours' drive away.

The Austrian Tourist Board is so organised that even Austrians use it. Its staff book hotels that often include extras such as a ski pass or wine tasting. The main office for the trips described on pages 214-220 is the Lower Austria Tourist Information in Vienna, where phones are usually answered promptly and correct information is provided in English. The website also yields useful travel material. For detailed information about areas or tours, phone the regional offices below.

Austrian Tourist Information
0810 10 18 18/www.austria.info.at.

Lower Austria South Alpine Region/Semmering
Bahnhof Semmering (02664 8452/www. semmeringbahn.at). **Open** 9-11.30am, 1.30-4.30pm daily.

Lower Austria Tourist Information
53610 6200/www.niederoesterreich.at.

Vienna Woods Region Tourist Information
Hauptplatz 11, Purkersdorf (02231 621 76/ www.wienerwald.info). **Open** 9am-5pm Mon-Fri.

Wachau-Nibelungengau Tourist Information
Schlossgasse 3, Spitz (02713 30060 60/www. wachau.at). **Open** 8.30am-4.30pm Mon-Thur; 8.30am-2.30pm Fri.

By boat

It's easy to travel by boat to Bratislava, Budapest and the Wachau in summer – vessels leave either from beside the Reichsbrücke on the Danube or beside the Marienbrücke on the Danube Canal. Bicycles are allowed, but passengers should state their intention to bring them when booking a ticket.

DDSG Blue Danube

Booking and information: 2, Handelskai 265 (58 880-0/www.ddsg-blue-danube.at). U1 Vorgartenstrasse. **Open** 9am-6pm Mon-Fri; 10am-4pm Sat, Sun, holidays. **Map** p242 J4. *City centre ticket office: beside Schwedenbrücke (218 701 05). U1, U4 Schwedenplatz.* **Open** 8am-4.30pm daily. **Credit** DC, MC, V. **Map** p249 F6.

Not only is the Donaudampfschifffahrtsgesellschaft (DDSG) one of the longest words in the German language, it is also Vienna's leading passenger ship service for destinations up and down river – even as far as the Black Sea. Its excellent website in English provides full details of schedules and fares for trips to Budapest and the Wachau. The DSGG's latest acquisition is the *Twin City Liner*, a Norwegian-built catamaran that cuts the trip down to 1hr 15mins. Operating daily from early April to late October and at weekends during winter, the service has been so successful that early booking is essential. It can be done at www.twincityliner.com.

By bike

To cycle out of town, hit the Danube Bike Trail and either head south towards Budapest or, even better, north towards Klosterneuberg and the Wachau. For more information, *see p214*. For bike hire firms within Vienna, *see p202*.

By train

Fast, reliable Austrian Railways is the main public transport system for travelling outside Vienna. There are four types of train: *Schnellzüge* are the fast trains with few stops, *Eilzug* trains are slightly more ponderous, and the Intercity and Eurocity only travel between major conurbations. Only the *Schnellzüge*, IC and EC take reservations. With train schedules changing frequently, it's best to consult times with the ÖBB information service (*see below*). Staff speak English. You can buy a ticket on the train or in the station. It's almost always cheaper to buy a train ticket in conjunction with other public transport, so if you arrive by U-Bahn, tram or bus, show your ticket to the conductor.

ÖBB Austrian Railways

05 1717/www.oebb.at. **Credit** AmEx, DC, MC, V. The excellent ÖBB website now has an excellent search facility where you simply tap in the details of your departure point and destination, and then hit search. There are three different railway stations serving the area around Vienna:

Westbahnhof (U3, U6 Westbahnhof).
Serves the western regions including trains to Melk.
Südbahnhof (tram D/bus 13a).
Serves the southern region including trains to Schneeberg and Semmering.
Franz-Josefs-Bahnhof (U4 Friedensbrücke/tram D, 5, 33).
Serves the Danube valley including trains to Klosterneuburg and Krems.

By bus

Given the quality of Austrian railways, especially out of Vienna, Austrians rarely travel by bus. These are mainly used by Eastern Europeans travelling home.

Eurolines Austria

3, Erdbergstrasse 202 (798 2900/www.eurolines.at). U3 Erdberg. **Open** *Reservations* 6.30am-8.30pm Mon-Fri; 6.30-11.30am-4.30-8.30 pm Sat, Sun, holidays. **Credit** AmEx, DC, MC, V.
You can reach a myriad of destinations in the East, as well as Western European capitals, with the Eurolines service. There are six buses daily to Bratislava, taking 1hr 30mins. Budapest has four buses daily and the journey takes 3hrs 45mins.

Postbus

Information 71 101/www.postbus.at.
More remote areas of Austria can be reached by this underfunded service and in winter they travel to ski areas near Vienna such as Semmering. Phone Postbus for details.

By car

The Austrian motorways are four to six lanes wide and fast. A road tax sticker (*Pickerl*) is required for all cars using the motorways. Valid for one month or one year, the sticker can be bought at the borders and at most Trafik shops. Fines can be heavy if drivers are caught without a *Pickerl*.

Getting out of Vienna is easy: just follow the Ringstrasse to find all the roads and signposts you need. The A2 takes you south to Graz; the S6, a well-posted motorway, goes to Semmering. The Rax turn-off is at Gloggnitz, follow route 27 to Reichenau and Payerbach. For Schneeberg, leave the A2 at Wiener Neustadt, following route 26 to Puchberg.

To Bratislava, follow signs to Schwechat airport on the A4. Just beyond the airport, take route 7. The A4 goes all the way to Budapest.

To the Wachau: take the A1 to Melk, then drive down either side of the River Danube to Krems, returning along route 3 over Stockerau and Klosterneuburg.

The Vienna Woods

The city's miraculous green belt inspires composers, soothes the Viennese and continues to frustrate developers.

The Vienna Woods, or Wienerwald, inspired Schubert, Beethoven, Mozart, Strauss and Schönberg, and still makes Viennese hearts sing. Few cities have the luxury of protected natural reserves so close. The Woods cover an enormous area of forests, hills and wilderness – 1,250 square kilometres (483 square miles) in all – and form a verdant horseshoe running west from the Danube round to the southern reaches of the city. The northern section is easily accessible by public transport from the city centre. To get to the southwestern reaches adjoining towns such as Baden and Mödling, it's a longer trek passing through the unlovely developments of Vienna's south side.

HIKING & MOUNTAIN BIKING

Along with the Prater and the Danube Island, the Wienerwald is a Viennese playground for hiking, mountain biking, picnicking and wine-fuelled Heurigen outings. Trams D, 38 and 43 will whisk you to the nearest sections but if you fancy a more challenging ramble, consult www.wien.at/english/leisure/hiking where 12 selected routes close to Vienna are listed in English with maps. Throughout the Wienerwald there are over 40 mountain-biking paths, all well signed (the woods are plastered with informative signposts), covering more than 900 kilometres (560 miles) of the Woods. Bike-trail maps are shown on www.mbike.at. All info is in German, but click on the region, then 'alle Strecken' to view maps; alternatively, pick up a map from the Vienna Woods tourist office (see p212) or at bicycle rental services (see p202). The only downside of the woods is the presence of ticks carrying Lyme disease and central European encephalitis.

Baden bei Wien

Once the Empire's most fashionable spa resort, Baden today is a genteel provincial town full of pastel-coloured Biedermeier and neo-classical buildings and fussy parks, all bathed in the smell of its sulphurous waters. Illustrious residents included Beethoven, who composed his *Ninth Symphony* at Rathausgasse 10, and, an artist of rather different stripe, one Leopold von Sacher-Masoch, whose classic *Venus in Furs* is set in Baden.

The Badner Bahn tram takes you from the Staatsoper in Vienna to Baden's small Hauptplatz in an hour. Here you'll find many of the town's historic monuments: the early 17th-century plague column, Kornhäusel's neo-classical Rathaus, and the Kaiserhaus, former summer residence of Franz II. North of Hauptplatz is the Kurpark, the old spa complex, the main bath house of which is now Austria's largest, most grandiose casino. This and Baden's hot thermal baths are the town's main attractions. Try the waters at the open-air art deco **Kurstrandbad** (Helenenstrasse 15-21) or covered **Römerthermebad** (Brusattiplatz 4).

Baden is an excellent starting point for touring the southern and western Vienna Woods, but its hotels and restaurants are all pretty pompous. At **Casino Baden** (Kaiser Franz Ring 1, 02252 44496) you can eat, sleep and gamble. Beethoven's favourite was the magnificent **Grand Hotel Sauerhof** (Weihburggasse 11-13, 02252 41251). (There are more modest restaurants around Hauptplatz.)

Try to get to the whimsically named **Gumpoldskirchen**, just a few miles outside Baden. As the most famous wine-growing village south of Vienna, it's packed with great Heurigen, especially along Wienerstrasse and Neustiftgasse. Otherwise take the stiffish walk to **Veigl Hütte** (Oberen Beethoven-Wanderweg 40, 02252 62702) for views of the vineyards and Vienna.

Tourist information

Baden Tourist Board

Brusattiplatz 3 (02252 22600-600/www.baden.at). **Open** *May-Sept* 9am-6pm Mon-Fri; 9am-2pm Sat. *Oct-Apr* 9am-5pm Mon-Fri.

Heiligenkreuz & Mayerling

Driving from Baden to Heiligenkreuz will take you through the Helenental, the valley of St Helena. One of the most beautiful valleys in the Woods, it was the inspiration for Beethoven's *Pastoral Symphony*. Napoleon thought it so gorgeous he wanted to end his days here, although in fact he died in a different St Helena.

Mayerling (02258 2275, www.mayerling. info) became a household name after the 1935

film, starring Charles Boyer, dramatised the tragedy that took place in Crown Prince Rudolf's hunting lodge. In 1889, the heir to the throne and his 17-year-old mistress, Baroness Maria Vetsera, died in a mysterious double suicide. Emperor Franz Josef converted the lodge into a convent of atonement of the Carmelite nuns, so there's not much to see, but it's still popular with tourists.

A few miles away lies **Heiligenkreuz Abbey** (02258 8703, www.stift-heiligenkreuz. at). The Cistercian abbey blends elements of the Romanesque, Gothic and Baroque periods, and its name (Holy Cross) derives from the relic of the cross that Leopold V brought here. The complex houses a number of treasures. The basilica, begun in 1135, is the oldest example of ribbed vaulting in Austria. A 150-year gap between the construction of the three Romanesque naves and the Gothic presbytery makes the church especially interesting. The chapter house, a Babenberg burial place, contains Austria's oldest ducal tomb. The tragic Maria Vetsera is buried in the village cemetery. There's a decent restaurant in the complex; otherwise try **Hanner** in Alland (Mayerling 1, 02258 2378), in the coolly designed hotel of the same name. It has a wonderful garden.

Mödling

About 20 minutes from Vienna by S-Bahn, Mödling is an idyll in the woods. Back in 1818, its quiet elegance, spa waters and forested landscape lured Beethoven. He spent two summers in the **Hafner House** at Hauptstrasse 79 (02236 24159, visits by appointment), where he wrote the *Diabelli Variations* and the famous *Missa Solemnis*. The other famous composer associated with Mödling is Arnold Schönberg. Between 1919

and 1925, he lived in an elegant house at Bernhardgasse 6, which now houses a small museum; it's used for concerts organised by the Arnold Schönberg Center (*see p185*). Mödling's **Stadtbad**, or swimming baths (Badstrasse 25, 02236 22335), were built in 1928, but the Bauhaus style is diminished by water slides and bouncy castles. The facilities are good though. **Babenbergerhof** (Babenbergergasse 6, 02236 22246) is a decent place to eat.

From Mödling there are around 85 kilometres (53 miles) of marked hiking trails through woodland to **Burg Liechtenstein**, a castle built by Hugo de Liechtenstein in 1136 and restored in the 19th century. Beside this magical folly is the neo-classical Liechtenstein Palace (1820), now a private retirement home.

In neighbouring Hinterbrühl is the **Seegrotte** (Grutschgasse 2a, 02236 26364, www.seegrotte.at), a gypsum mine that was accidentally flooded in 1912 during a blasting operation and is now Europe's largest underground lake. In World War II, the Nazis pumped the grotto dry and assembled the fuselage of the world's first jet fighter on the site. Boat tours run from here. In the village, **Höldrichsmühle** (Gaardnerstrasse 34 02236 262740, www.hoeldrichsmuehle.at) is a hotel/ restaurant in an old mill patronised by Schubert, where he reputedly wrote his famous lied *The Linden Tree*.

Off the B11 between Hinterbrühl and Heiligenkreuz lies the **Sparbach** nature park (www.naturpark-sparbach.at) which has deer, wild boar and adventure playgrounds.

Tourist information

Mödling Tourist Information

Elisabethstrasse 1 (02236 26727/www.moedling.at). **Open** 9am-5pm Mon-Fri.

The Danube Valley

Fortresses, monasteries and terraced vineyards – the Wachau is the Danube's most bucolic stretch.

After numerous attempts to regulate its flow and alleviate the danger of flooding, the Danube at Vienna appears straight and relentless. However, 100 kilometres (62 miles) upstream, the river follows a meandering course through the narrow Wachau Valley, forming a stunningly picturesque ensemble of steeply, terraced vineyards and hills crowned with fortresses, monasteries and ruins. A UNESCO World Heritage Site since 2000, the Wachau was commended for its 'outstanding riverine landscape' along the 35-kilometre (22-mile) stretch between the towns of Melk and Krems.

The 550 or so castles and fortified monasteries – such as the monumental Stift Klosterneuburg and Stift Gottweig – that overlook the Danube on its passage through Lower Austria testify to the river's importance as a trade route between east and west, and to the violent disputes that this provoked. Capitalising on the mild climate, the locals developed a prosperous agriculture by planting vast vineyards, and the peach and apricot orchards that fill the valley floor. Visitors flock

here in the spring to witness the ethereal beauty of the blossoming apricots and throughout the year to enjoy the Wachau's fine wines and excellent restaurants.

Accessible and well organised for tourists, the Wachau's most important towns, Melk and Krems, can be reached by train in just over an hour from Vienna, or by boat in three hours (*see p213*). Spend a night or two at one of the area's small hotels or restaurants with rooms.

One of the most enjoyable ways to experience the Danube Valley is by bike. The Danube Bike Path follows the river for 1,300 kilometres (808 miles) from Donaueschingen in Germany to Budapest. The path (which is quite flat) takes in 258 kilometres (160 miles) of Lower Austria, and there are plenty of Heurigen, picturesque villages and accommodation to break your journey. Bikes can be hauled on to the trains and boats going up and down the Wachau, and good maps of the region are provided free by Lower Austria Tourist Information (*see p212*); ask them about bicycle hire too. For boat trips see DDSG Blue Danube Boat Trips (*see p213*).

Some of the scenes...

Klosterneuburg

A short bus or train ride upriver from Vienna lies the historic Danube town of Klosterneuburg, with its arresting 12th-century Augustinian monastery. The Baroque domes and neo-Gothic spires of **Stift Klosterneuburg**, sandwiched between the Danube and the Vienna Woods, mark it out as one of Austria's wealthiest and oldest. During the reign of Karl IV, a Spanish-bred Habsburg, plans were made for a large imperial palace along the lines of Madrid's El Escorial, but funds ran out and only one of the four inner courtyards was semi-completed. The whole complex was extensively renovated in 2006, with a new entrance via the Sala Terrena. You can wander through most of the monastery but to see the Verdun Altarpiece in the Leopoldskapelle, an astonishing winged altar completed in 1181 by Nicolas of Verdun, a guided tour is obligatory (Stiftsplatz 1, 02243 411 212, www.stift-klosterneuburg.at).

Other sights in Klosterneuburg include **Essl Museum** (*see p170*), an enjoyable collection of contemporary art and, in a similar vein, the **Haus der Künstler** and the newly opened **Gugging Museum** in the grounds of the Gugging Psychiatric Clinic in the nearby village of Maria Gugging.

On the way to Gugging the same bus passes the village of Kierling, where at Hauptstrasse 187, Franz Kafka died of tuberculosis in 1924 while correcting proofs of his short story collection *A Hunger Artist*. The small memorial room with books and photos can be visited (8am-noon, 2-5pm Mon-Fri, 02243 444323) but it isn't the actual room where he died.

Museum Gugging/ Haus der Künstler

Hauptstrasse 2, 3400 Maria Gugging (0664 8490 695/www.gugging.org). U4 Heiligenstadt or Klosterneuburg-Kierling train station then bus 239. **Open** *May-Sept* 10am-6pm Tue-Sun; *Oct-Apr* 10am-5pm Tue-Sun. **Admission** €7; €5 concessions. **No credit cards**.

Between the late 1950s and the 1980s, psychiatrist Leo Navratil encouraged his patients to paint and draw; some, such as Johann Hauser and August Walla, became internationally hailed exponents of 'Art Brut', their work exhibited in 200 museums and galleries all over the world. The façade and interior of the building where these artists lived (Haus der Künstler) are a riot of colour. Nine active patients/artists currently live there and visitors to the house are encouraged. In 2006, the Gugging Museum was opened to showcase the marvellously repetitive, detailed work of the Gugging artists.

Krems

The historic centre of Krems, 70 kilometres (43 miles) northwest of Vienna, marks the entrance to the Wachau. Made up of three formerly separate settlements – Krems, Und and Stein –

...along the beautiful Danube.

it became a wealthy wine-growing town in the 13th century, evident from well-appointed late-medieval and late-Gothic buildings such as the Pfarrkirche and Piaristenkirche in the cobbled streets north of its main drag, Landstrasse.

Apart from a stop at the tourist office (*see below*), you can jump the appropriately named Und district and head for Krems Stein, the town's most atmospheric medieval quarter. The main Steiner Landstrasse is a delightful parade of Renaissance townhouses that periodically opens on to cobbled squares with views of the Danube. The centrepiece is the 13th-century Minoritenkirche, the oldest church of the mendicant Minorite order north of the Alps. It now serves as the **Kremser Klangraum** for sound installations and contemporary music concerts during events such as the off-kilter Donaufestival (*see p158*). Stein also boasts the Kremser Kunstmeile (the Krems 'Art Mile') which runs parallel to the Danube from Kloster Und to the Steiner Landstrasse. Here are museums and galleries such as the **Kunsthalle Krems** (www.kunsthalle.at) and the **Karikaturmuseum** (www.karikatur museum.at) among other institutions dedicated to architecture and literature.

Krems offers some seriously good eating. Try the **m.kunst.genuss** in the Kunsthalle, or **Salzstadl** (Donaulände 32, 02732 70312), a fine old Gasthaus with live jazz and pleasant rooms to rent. In the small alleys above Steiner Landstrasse, delightful Heurigen, such as **Hambock Erich** (Kellergasse 31, 02732 84568) have views of the Danube and the distant **Stift Göttweig**. Around six kilometres (three-and-a-half miles) south of Krems, this splendid Baroque complex, built by Johann Hildebrandt, originally dates from 1083. Its restaurant also has fine vistas of the valley (02732 855 81-0, www.stiftgoettweig.or.at).

Tourist information

Wachau-Nibelungengau Tourist Information

Schlossgasse 3, Spit (02713 30060 60/www. wachau.at). **Open** 8.30am-4.30pm Mon-Thur; 8.30am-2.30pm Fri.

Dürnstein

Nine kilometres (five miles) upriver from Krems, the tiny walled town of Dürnstein, with its striking powder-blue and white Baroque tower, is one of the Wachau's most idyllic images. However, the town owes its good fortune to that fact that Richard the Lionheart was imprisoned in its now ruined castle by Archduke Leopold V. This and the ensuing

legend of Blondel (Richard's French minstrel), who discovered his master's whereabouts by singing his way through central Europe, have given Dürnstein a steady stream of British visitors since the dawn of modern tourism. Today, it's also a favourite spot for Austrians to tie the knot.

Good eating and comfortable rooms are available at, you guessed it, **Gasthof Sänger Blondel** (Dürnstein 64, 02711 253, www.saengerblondel.at, open Apr-Oct).

Weissenkirchen & Spitz

As well as a gorgeous riverside location and a backdrop of terraced vineyards, Weissenkirchen also has a lovely network of cobbled streets. On the main square, the **Wachaumuseum** (02715 2268, open April-Oct), a display of folk arts and oil paintings of the Wachau, is housed in the 16th-century Teisenhoferhof. **Raffelsbergerhof** (02715 2201, www.raffelsbergerhof.at, open mid Apr-Nov) is an atmospheric hotel in an old vaulted shipmaster's residence.

Spitz an der Donau, six kilometres (three-and-a-half miles) upstream from Weissenkirchen, is a slightly larger town with lovely, strollable streets. At the **Schifffahrtsmuseum** in the Baroque Schloss Erlahof (02713 22 46), the show of Danube sailing craft gives an idea of life in pre-tourist Wachau. Wine is the lifeblood of Spitz and in a good year the town's 2,000 inhabitants produce 56,000 litres (12,320 gallons). The are plenty of Heurigen in Spitz; try the streets Radlbach and In der Spitz.

Melk

The town cowers in the shadow of its abbey, **Stift Melk** (3390 Melk, 02752 555, www. stiftmelk.at), perched on a cliff over the Danube. The abbey is huge – 17,500 square metres (188,370 square feet) in area. Its side façade is an incredible 1,115 metres (3,695 feet) long. Once the residence of the Babenberg family, it has been a Benedictine monastery since 1089. Master builder Jakob Prandtauer built the abbey in its present form in the 18th century. The marble hall and the library, with their high, tiered ceilings, are astonishing. For food, the best bet is the **Stiftsrestaurant** (02752 52555) inside the monastery walls.

Five kilometres (three miles) outside Melk lies magnificent castle **Schloss Schallaburg** (3382 Schallaburg, 02754 6317, www.schalla burg.at). It's a compendium of architectural styles: Romanesque, Gothic, Renaissance and Mannerist. Even the floor is a riot of mythological figures and fantastic creatures.

Trips Out of Town

Southern Alpine Region

The last flourish of the Alps is an outdoor paradise.

Take the train to **Semmering**.

Although the Alps peter out south of Vienna, snowy peaks are within easy reach of the capital. The border between Lower Austria and Styria, the last Alpine hiccup before the land flattens out towards the great Hungarian plain, lies only 90 kilometres (60 miles) south of the city. The area is the source of the city's good drinking water and a magnificent outdoor amenity for city dwellers. During the habitually overcast Viennese autumns and winters, city dwellers don their boots and lederhosen and set off early to catch some rays on the slopes of Rax, Schneeberg and Semmering.

These three mountains are perfect for a spot of *wandern* – the relaxed Austrian version of mountain hiking. All three have trains, gondolas or ski lifts working year-round that will take you a fair way up the mountain-side, while adventurous hikers and climbers can follow well-marked trails. For alpine skiing, Semmering is well equipped for day trippers. Schneeberg and Rax also have extensive cross-country trails. Semmering is the favourite port of call with day and weekend trippers from Vienna, who like to put up in the monumental Panhans grand hotel, take a trip on the historic Semmering Railway and stroll the valleys.

Travelling further afield to Rax or Schneeberg, taking in Reichenau and Semmering on the way back to Vienna, is easiest by car.

SKIING

In winter, people descend on sedate Semmering for downhill and cross-country skiing at one of two ski areas. The 1,318-metre (4,326-foot) **Hirschenkogel** is within walking distance of all Semmering's hotels and has both artificial snow and a floodlit ski-piste. There's also a gentle children's slope; toboggans can be hired from the ski rental shop. In Spital am Semmering, ten kilometres (six miles) further on, is the less crowded **Stuhleck**, which has 20 kilometres (12 miles) of pistes and its own floodlit run (open 6-9pm Mon-Sat). Cross-country ski routes can be obtained from the tourist office.

Semmering-Hirschenkogel

Semmering (02664 8038/snowline 02664 2575/ www.hirschenkogel.at). **Open** *Pistes* 8.30am-4pm Mon-Fri; 8am-4pm Sat, Sun. **Cost** *Day card* €28.50; €15 children. *Half day* €23.50; €13 children. *Day pass for all 3 local ski regions* €31; €15.50 children. **Credit** AmEx, DC, MC, V.
Facilities include an eight-person gondola, a four-seater chairlift and a help lift on the Panhans side.

Semmering

Until 1854, Semmering was an undisturbed mountain pass. Then Carl Ritter von Ghega's Semmering Railway succeeded in connecting this Alpine wilderness to Vienna. Never before had it been so easy to reach the mountains (nowadays, direct trains leave frequently from Südbahnhof). The first railway to become a UNESCO World Heritage site, the Semmering stretch is admired as a feat of engineering and for its functional beauty. The train meanders along a series of 31 viaducts and tunnels amid beautiful Alpine scenery.

Over the following 20 years, Semmering, with its mild weather and stunning views of the mountains Schneeberg and Rax, gained in popularity. In 1882, the first villas were built on the edge of the mountain, and in 1889 the original 44-room Panhans was opened. By 1900, the Panhans had become a massive grand hotel, its guest book from 1900 to 1938 reading like a roll-call of high society. Emperor Franz Josef, Austro-Hungarian aristocracy, writers, artists, actors and intellectuals from Europe and America all lived it up here (there's even a photograph of Josephine Baker riding a sled outside the hotel). Requisitioned by the Nazis during World War II, the Panhans became popular with Rommel and Göring. After the war, Semmering never regained its place in society, and the hotel closed in 1969. However, in 1994 the **Panhans** (Hochstrasse 32, 02664 8181, www.panhans.at) reopened, having been refurbished to something approaching its former glory. Since then, Semmering has blossomed. Thousands of well-marked walks start from both the Panhans and the **Panoramahotel Wagner** (Hochstrasse 267, 02664 25120, www.semmering.cc). Smaller than the Panhans, the Wagner has wonderful views, Swedish-designed rooms, a top restaurant and that surprising rarity in the country – a no-smoking policy.

The new **Zauberberg** (magic mountain) cable car (02664 8038/www.zauberberg.at) takes you up Semmering's Hirschenkogel peak (1,340 metres/4,400 feet). Popular with hikers and mountain bikers, there are numerous gentle descents that pass by welcoming mountain huts where meals are served.

Tourist information

Wiener Alpen in Niederösterreich

Schlossstrasse 1 Katzelsdorf (02622 78960/www.wieneralpen.at). **Open** 8.30am-4pm Mon-Fri.
The very friendly English-speaking staff at this regional tourist office can advise on daily excursions and will also provide maps.

Mount Rax

Mount Rax (2,007 metres/6,587 feet) is a great place to experience the Alps without having to travel too far from Vienna. It's well signposted and has an unusually large, 34-kilometre (21-mile) plateau, dotted with eight mountain refreshment huts – all with superb views.

You can get most of the way up Rax with little effort. Following the signs to the Rax-Seilbahn in Hirschwang, you reach the **Rax Gondola** (Reichenau-Hirschwang, 02666 52497, www.raxseilbahn.at), which climbs 1,547 metres (3,280 feet) in eight minutes. A 30-minute walk takes you to the **Ottohaus** (1,644 metres/5,395 feet) for refreshment. For a more vigorous hike, drive beyond the Rax Gondola to Prainer Gscheid, where you can park and take the trail for a few hours towards **Karl Ludwighaus** (1,804 metres/5,920 feet), then up to the top of Rax.

From Payerbach, you can travel the five kilometres (three miles) to Hirschwang on the **Höllentalbahn**, one of the world's oldest functioning narrow-gauge railways (02666 524 2312, www.lokalbahnen.at/hoellentalbahn).

Just above Payerbach is the chalet that architect Adolf Loos built in 1929 for Viennese industrialist Paul Khuner. Today, the **Looshaus** is an attractive hotel/restaurant (02666 52911, www.looshaus.at). The dining room, with a vast window, is the chalet's most awesome feature and staff will guide you to the neighbouring Mostheuriger where deceptively strong semi-fermented cider is served.

Tourist information

Reichenau/Rax Tourist Office

Hauptstrasse 63, 2651 Reichenau/Rax (02666 528 65//www.reichenau.at). **Open** 9am-4pm Mon-Fri.

Schneeberg

Schneeberg is Vienna's 'local' mountain and, at 2,075 metres (6,810 feet), the highest peak in Lower Austria. It stands just outside Wiener Neustadt on the A2 motorway south. As a result of its accessibility, Schneeberg tends to be more crowded than Rax. A railway line compounds its popularity; a steam engine and the green and yellow dappled **Salamander train** (02636 3661-20, www.schneebergbahn.at) leave from the town of Puchberg am Schneeberg to carry visitors nine-and-a-half kilometres (six miles) to Hochschneeberg (1,795m), near the summit. Trains operate from late April until early December; full ascents take 50 minutes with the Salamander and 80 minutes with the steam train.

Directory

Features

Directory

Getting Around

By air

Flughafen Wien-Schwechat

General flight information 7007 22233/www.viennaairport.com. Vienna's international airport lies south-east of the city on the Ostautobahn (direction Budapest). The above phone number is the central infoline, which will connect you to the service you require.

TO AND FROM THE AIRPORT

Getting to and from the airport by public transport is easy – it's a 20-minute ride by bus or train from the centre of town. The **airport shuttle buses** operate two routes: to/from the City Air Terminal (Schwedenplatz/corner Marc-Aurel-Strasse) and from Vienna's Westbahnhof, via Südbahnhof (it takes 35 minutes from Westbahnhof). The fare is €6 one way, €11 return per passenger, including luggage (children up to six free, six-15 years €3 one way, €5.50 return). Tickets are available from vending machines or the driver. Buses run about every half hour. **By train**, the Schnellbahn 7, from Wien Nord, via Wien Mitte, runs every half hour costing €3 one way. For more information, phone 05 17 17-1. A faster, more expensive way to get to and from the airport is the **CAT (City Airport Train)**. It takes 16 minutes and costs €9 one way, €16 return per passenger (online purchases €8 one way, €15 return). Children up to 15 years travel free if accompanied by an adult. Luggage can be checked in from 24 hours to 75 minutes prior to departure.

If you take a **taxi**, use airport taxis rather than standard ones as they charge a cheaper flat rate. C+K Airport Service (444 44) and Airport Driver (22822) charge a

one-way rate of €27. On arrival in the airport, the C+K stand is directly to the left of the arrivals hall; drivers are usually immediately available. **Limousines** and a selection of large and small vans are available from Airport Service Mazur (7007 36422), but they need to be reserved in advance.

City Airport Train (CAT)

Wien Mitte/Landstrasse (25 250/www.cityairporttrain.com). **Credit** AmEx, DC, MC, V.

Vienna Airport Lines (Airport Shuttle Bus)

24hr phone service 700 732-300. **Credit** (at the automat machines only) AmEx, MC, V.

Airlines

Air Berlin/Fly Niki *reservations 0820 737 800/ www.airberlin.com*
Austrian Airlines *reservations 05 17 89/www.aua.com*
British Airways *reservations 79 567567/www.britishairways.at*
Delta Airlines *reservations 795 67023/www.delta.com*
Lufthansa *reservations 0810 1025 8080/www.lufthansa.at*
Tyrolean Airways (Austrian Airlines Group) *05 17 89/ www.tyrolean.at*

By rail

Trains are used for most domestic travel within Austria, and travelling on them is a very pleasant experience. Timetables can be picked up from the information office at any station.

There are all sorts of special services available, such as a pick-up for customers with confirmed reservations, where a reserved taxi or hotel representative meets you at the train station or accommodation (usually free); or the 'Haus zu Haus' luggage service, which picks up and delivers your bags (up to three bags, maximum 25kg per bag),

charging €14.90 for one bag, €19.90 for two, €24.90 for three. It is especially useful for skiers not wanting to lug equipment around.

If travelling west towards Salzburg or Tyrol, try to take a 'Panorama' compartment, a first-class car with huge windows that are perfect for viewing the fabulous scenery.

There are three main train stations: **Westbahnhof** for trains to the west, to cities such as Salzburg, Frankfurt, London and Paris; **Südbahnhof** for Bratislava, Budapest, Prague, Venice and Rome; and **Franz-Josefs-Bahnhof** for north-western Austria and Prague. For all reservations and information call the number below.

ÖBB (Austrian Railways)

05 17 17/www.oebb.at.

By bus

Vienna has no central bus station. All buses arriving or leaving the city now stop at different stations throughout the city.

Infocenter postal & railroad buses

711-01/www.postbus.at. **Open** 7am-8pm daily.

Vienna has excellent public transport and is an easy city to get around. A public transport day ticket can be used on any of the trams, buses or U-Bahn lines that zigzag and encircle the city centre. Forget taking a car into the 1st district as parking spaces are rare and garages are expensive.

Public transport is safe, reliable and fast, and it goes almost everywhere. The **Eastern Region Transport Association (VOR)** is a network of eight zones covering a huge area that includes Vienna and surrounding towns. The central zone is known as the Kernzone (zone 100). There are trams, buses and five U-Bahn lines that run until midnight, with Nightline bus services running overnight. Maps of Vienna's transport system, as well as timetables, can be obtained at any U-Bahn station.

Fares & tickets

Tickets can be bought at U-Bahn stations and at tobacconists for €1.70 or on board buses and trams for €2.20. They are valid for one hour on all three modes of transport. Most U-Bahn stations have multilingual vending machines that sell tickets and dispense change. Validate your ticket upon starting a journey by sliding it into the small blue validation machines located at the entrance to each U-Bahn line, and on all buses and trams.

U-Bahn stations are barrier free so the system operates on trust. Plain clothes inspectors operate, so fare dodging could mean a fine of €70. Take note that the dumb-tourist routine doesn't work. Once you validate your ticket, keep it in case you get checked.

If you are going to be in Vienna for more than a day, public transport costs can be reduced by purchasing monthly (€49.50), weekly (€14) or three-day cards (€13.60). The last of these lasts 72 hours from the time of validation. Various daily tickets include the 'Vienna Shopping Card' 8am-8pm (€4.60) and the '24 hours Vienna' ticket, lasting 24 hours from validation (€5.70).

There are also strip tickets (*Streifenkarten*), valid for four trips (€6.80; one punch per journey) or eight days (one punch per day, valid until 1pm the day after – €27.20). Strip tickets can be used by groups, with one punch per person.

Another option is the Vienna Card (€18.50). It is valid for 72 hours, and it also entitles you to discounts at museums, galleries and restaurants.

Children up to the age of six can travel free all year round, and children up to the age of 15 can travel free on Sundays, public holidays and Austrian school holidays. Otherwise they can travel with half-price tickets,

which can be purchased on the tram (€1.10), on the bus (€1.10) or at the vending machines (90¢) at U-Bahn stations.

All senior citizens (women over 60, men over 65, not only Austrians) can travel with a two-journey half-price ticket (€2.30; one punch per journey). They must travel with ID proving their age. All transport tickets or cards are valid for the Nightline bus service.

Transport Information Offices

Vorverkaufsstellen der Wiener Linien
General information (7909/100/www.wienerlinien.at). **Open** 6am-10pm Mon-Fri; 8.30am-4.30pm Sat, Sun.
There are offices located at selected U-Bahn stations across the city. Those at Stephansplatz, Karlsplatz and Westbahnhof are open 6.30am-6.30pm Mon-Fri; 8.30am-4pm Sat, Sun. Those at Landstrasse (Wien Mitte), and Volkstheater are open 6.30am-6.30pm Mon-Fri. All accept credit cards (AmEx, DC, MC, V) and provide information plus tickets for the buses, trams and U-Bahn.

U-Bahn

The underground is reliable, quick and comfortable. Routes are self-explanatory, and you'll find pamphlets in English available in most U-Bahn information offices. Routes on maps are colour-coded (U1 is red, U2 is purple, U3 is orange, U4 is green and U6 is brown) with all station signs in the same colours. Doors don't automatically open on the U-Bahn, so pull the handle sharply or press the lighted button.

Local trains

The S-Bahn and Lokalbahn are the local and fast railways that run in Vienna and further afield. The Badner Bahn connects Vienna and the town of Baden.

If you are taking an S-Bahn within Vienna, you don't have to purchase another ticket, but if you travel outside zone 100, you'll need an additional ticket depending on how many zones you are travelling in. You can find this out by looking at the bull's eye zone map posted in all stations.

Trams

Vienna has a great system of trams, or *Strassenbahnen*, that will take you everywhere within the city and its outskirts. All tram stops are clearly marked, with timetables. Every stop is announced by name, with corresponding connecting lines and most central stops now have electronic displays showing how long you have to wait. Tram line numbers or letters stand alone, for example 2, D, J.

Buses

Buses go to all the places that trams can't. Their stops look just like the tram stops and also have maps and timetables clearly displayed. Bus lines are identified by numbers ending with an 'a' or by three-digit numbers, for example 13a, 149, 234.

Bus information

Details about timetables and fares are provided by Transport Information Offices, *see above*.

Nightline

Vienna rolls up its pavements at midnight but safe, reliable Nightline buses run from 12.30am to 5am on the half hour on 22 routes. All transport tickets or cards are valid for Nightlines.

Taxis

Vienna's taxis are reliable and not too expensive. Hailing them on the street sometimes works, but taxi ranks are clearly marked. Phoning for a taxi often takes less than three minutes' waiting time. A small tip or 'rounding off' of the fee is expected. There's a basic rate on weekdays (€4.50 for pick-ups) plus a per-kilometre charge. On Sundays, public holidays and at night (1-6am) both the basic fare and per-kilometre rate go up. There's also a waiting charge.

Taxi phone numbers

31 300/60 160/81 400.

Driving

Like everything else in Austria, driving is highly regulated and relatively safe. You are required

Directory

by law to carry all documents, driving licences and luminous waistcoats on you in case you are stopped. Speed limits are 30-50km/h (18-31mph) in residential areas, 100km/h (62mph) on country roads and 130km/h (80mph) on motorways. Spot checks are common in Austria, and so are breath tests. Take extra care at tram stops when passengers alight.

Breakdown services

Austria has two 24-hour major breakdown services. The service is free for members; however, non-members can call on their services and pay by cash or credit card. These charges can be reimbursed if you have motor insurance that covers you for Austria.

ARBÖ

15, Mariahilfer Strasse 180 (24hr emergency hotline 123/office 891 21-0/www.arboe-wien.at). Tram 52, 58. **Open** 9am-6pm Mon-Fri; 9am-noon Sat. **Credit** AmEx, DC, MC, V. **Map** p250 D8.

ÖAMTC

1, Schubertring 1-3 (24hr hotline 120/office 711 990/www. oeamtc.at). Tram 1, 2, D, J. **Open** 9am-6pm Mon-Fri; 9am-noon Sat. **Credit** DC, MC, V. **Map** p251 F7.

Fuel stations

All international petrol stations take credit cards; local stations may not. Those listed below are open 24 hours.

BP

1, Morzinplatz 1. **Map** p251 F6.
3, Erdberger Lände 28-30. **Map** p248 G7.
19, Heiligenstädterstrasse 46-48. **Map** p243 D1.

Shell

22, Wagramerstrasse 14. **Map** p245 K2/3.

Parking

Parking in most areas of the 1st district is a nightmare and the police are quick to ticket and tow, costing anything from €23 to €165 – so avoid it wherever possible.

Districts 1-9 and 20 have blue zones (*Kurzparkzonen*), where you purchase parking vouchers

(*Parkscheine*) at tobacconists. In the 1st district you can park for up to 90 minutes, 9am-7pm Mon-Fri, and Saturday as marked. In other districts you can park for up to two hours, 9am-8pm Mon-Fri, and Saturday as marked. Look for designated parking spaces marked with blue lines. Vouchers come in 30-, 60- and 90-minute increments. Car parks are marked with a blue P and display the number of spaces available. Remember to pay at the vending machines before removing your car.

Vehicle hire

Renting a car is a fairly standard procedure in Austria, but do specify if you plan to drive into eastern Europe.

Autoverleih Flott

6, Mollardgasse 44 (597 3402/ www.flott.at). U4 Margaretengürtel. **Open** 7am-6pm Mon-Fri; 7am-noon Sat. **Credit** AmEx, DC, MC, V. **Map** p246 C10.

Avis

1, Opernring 3-5 (town office 587 6241/24hr reservation hotline 0800 0800 8757/www.avis.at). U1, U2, U4 Karlsplatz/tram 1, 2, D, J. **Open** 7am-6pm Mon-Fri; 8am-2pm Sat; 8am-1pm Sun. **Credit** AmEx, DC, MC, V. **Map** p250 E7.

Europcar

1, Schubertring 9 (town office 714 67 17/airport 7007-326 99/ www.europcar.at). Tram 1, 2, D, J.

Open *Town office* 7.30am-6pm Mon-Fri; 8am-1pm Sat; 8am-noon Sun. *Airport office* 7.30am-11pm Mon-Fri; 8am-7pm Sat; 8am-11pm Sun. **Credit** AmEx, DC, MC, V. **Map** p248 J8.

Hertz

1, Kärntner Ring 17 (512 8677/www.hertz.at). U1, U2, U4 Karlsplatz/tram 1, 2, D, J. **Open** 7.30am-6.30pm Mon-Fri; 9am-4pm Sat, Sun. **Credit** AmEx, DC, MC, V. **Map** p251 E8.

Cycling

Vienna is a great city for cyclists, as long as you avoid main roads and tram lines. By 2010, there will be around 800km (500 miles) of bike paths in the city. The bike path around the Ringstrasse is a lovely way to tour the city without getting lost. The Danube canal bike path is another good way of crossing the city and the ramp beside the Prater bridge will take you to Vienna's largest car-free cycling area. Full information and a map of all city bike paths are available at www.wien.gv.at/english/leisure/bike.htm or in a booklet produced by the Tourist Office. For bike rental, *see p202*.

Walking

Vienna is a very walkable city, although jaywalking could result in a fine. Beware the change in normally placid Austrians when they get behind the wheel.

Travel advice

For up-to-date information on travel to a specific country – including the latest news on safety and security, health issues, local laws and customs – contact your home country government's department of foreign affairs. Most have websites packed with useful advice for would-be travellers.

Australia
www.smartraveller.gov.au

Canada
www.voyage.gc.ca

New Zealand
www.safetravel.govt.nz

Republic of Ireland
http://foreignaffairs.gov.ie

UK
www.fco.gov.uk/travel

USA
http://travel.state.gov

Resources A-Z

Addresses

House and building numbers, and door numbers, follow the street name (for instance, Alserbachstrasse 54/9). Numbers are even on one side of the street and odd on the other. *Strasse* (street) is often abbreviated to Str. Smaller streets (usually all side streets off a bigger street) are called *Gasse* (Webgasse, for example). Addresses are preceded by the district number, for example, Wittgenstein-Haus is at 3, Parkgasse 18, meaning number 18 Parkgasse, in the 3rd district.

Age restrictions

The legal age for drinking and smoking is 16 and for driving 18. The age of consent for heterosexual sex is 14, for homosexual 16.

Business

Conventions & conferences

Austria Center Vienna
22, Bruno-Kreisky-Platz 1 (260 69-0/www.acv.at). U1 Vienna International Centre.

Hofburg Congress Centre & Redoutensaele Vienna
1, Heldenplatz (5873 6660/www. hofburg.com). Tram 1, 2, D, J. **Map** p250 D7.

Reeds Messe Wien
2, Messeplatz 1 (7272 0/www. messe.at). U1 Praterstern. **Map** p250 D7.

Couriers

DHL
3, Steingasse 8 (0820-550 505/ www.dhl.at). Tram 71. **Open** 8am-7.45pm Mon-Fri; 8am-12.30pm Sat. **Credit** AmEx, DC, MC, V. **Map** p248 H9.

UPS
Express Counter, 1, Walfischgasse 6 (512 88 55/service hotline 0810

00 66 30/www.ups.com). U2 Karlsplatz Oper/tram 1, 2, D, J. **Open** 8am-6pm Mon-Fri. **Credit** AmEx, MC, V. **Map** p251 E8.

Office hire & secretarial services

Regus Business Centres

1, Schottenring 16 (53 712-0/www.regus.com). U2 Schottentor/tram 1, 2, D. **Map** p250 D6.
1, Parkring 10 (516 33-0). Tram 1, 2. **Map** p251 F7.
6, Mariahilfer Strasse 123 (59 999-0). U3 Neubaugasse. **Map** 246 C8.
All **Open** 8am-5pm Mon-Fri. **Credit** AmEx, DC, MC, V. Regus provides office space to rent, plus all kind of related business services (secretary, phone, fax machines and so on).

Translators & interpreters

UNIVERSITAS - Österreichischer Übersetzer - und Dolmetscherverband

Austrian Association of Translators and Interpreters
19, Gymnasiumstrasse 50 (368 60 60/www.universitas.org). U6 Nussdorfer Strasse. **Map** p242 C3. The Association will provide all the necessary information regarding translating or interpreting services and connect you with a suitable translator or interpreter.

Useful organisations

Austrian Chamber of Commerce

4, Wiedner Hauptstrasse 63 (05 90 900/www.wko.at). Tram 62, 65. **Open** 8am-4pm Mon-Thur; 8am-3.30pm Fri. **Map** p247 E10.

British Embassy Commercial Section

3, Jauresgasse 12 (716 13 6161/www.britishembassy.at). Tram 71. **Open** 9am-1pm, 2-5pm Mon-Fri. **Map** p247 F8.

A directory of British companies in Austria is kept here.

US Chamber of Commerce

9, Porzellangasse 35 (319 575/infoline 0900 833 933/ www.amcham.or.at). Tram D. **Map** p243 D4.
A directory of US firms, subsidiaries, affiliates and licensees in Austria is available for members for €30 and non-members for €40. It can be ordered directly by fax or email.

Women's Career Network (WCN)

1, Mahlerstrasse 3, 2nd floor (966 29 25/www.wcnvienna.org). U1, U2, U4 Karlsplatz/tram 1,2, D, J. **Map** p251 E7.
Affiliated with the American Women's Association, this network acts as a resource and support network for women seeking to develop their careers in Austria. It offers bi-monthly meetings, a newsletter and members' directory.

Consumer

If you have questions about your rights as a consumer, contact the organisation below:

Consumer Information Association (VKI)

6, Mariahilfer Strasse 81 (58 877-0/www.konsument.at). U3 Neubaugasse. **Open** 9am-4pm Mon-Fri. **Map** p246 C8.

Customs

Austria is part of the EU, so provided you purchased them in another EU state, you can bring limitless goods into the country as long as they are for personal use. Guidelines are given as follows: 800 cigarettes, 400 cigarillos, 200 cigars, 1kg tobacco; 10 litres spirits, 20 litres fortified wine; 90 litres wine (or 60 litres sparkling wine) and 110 litres beer. The same quantity of goods can be taken out of Austria, provided you are entering another EU state.
When entering from a non-EU country or when purchasing in

duty-free shops within the EU, you can bring: 200 cigarettes or 100 cigarillos or 50 cigars or 250g tobacco; 2 litres wine and 1 litre spirits; or 2 litres spirits or 2 litres champagne; and 50g perfume and 250ml eau de toilette, and 500g coffee and 100g tea.

Items subject to import and/or export control include: controlled drugs, weapons, indecent material, certain plants, meat, meat products and products of animal origin such as hides, skin, eggs, milk and dairy products (however, 1kg per person of fully cooked meat/meat products, in cans or hermetically sealed containers is permitted).

VAT refunds can be claimed by travellers with destinations in non-EU countries. You can get the necessary forms from stores where you bought the items. Allow an extra 15 minutes at the airport to queue and process your refund.

Disabled

In general, Vienna is a relatively easy city to get around and most U-Bahn stations are equipped with lifts. Bus drivers will bring out ramps for wheelchair users, but only the new trams are low enough to allow access.

Several organisations provide specific advice. The Vienna tourist office has a guide for handicapped people in English and the municipal website www.wien. gv.at has a section entitled 'Vienna for visitors with disabilities', where you'll find extensive information on hotels, sightseeing, restaurants, theatres and cinemas.

Bizeps

523 8921/www.bizeps.or.at.
Open 10am-4pm Mon-Thurs; 10am-1pm Fri.
A multilingual support group run by and for people with disabilities.

Fahrtendienst Gschwindl

810 4001. **Open** 6am-6pm Mon-Fri.
Taxis equipped to transport wheelchairs, with a flat-rate charge of €28 to destinations within Vienna.

Information on the U-Bahn for the blind

7909 41300.
Open 8am-3pm Mon-Fri.

Drugs

Although no drugs, either soft or hard, are allowed in Austria, possession of marijuana seeds is not illegal. On the other hand, prescription drugs such as sleeping pills, sedatives and Prozac are considered illegal in large quantities. Should you bring any of these drugs into Austria, bring your prescription to avoid the risk of confiscation.

For the past decade or more, the Austrian drugs authorities have been fighting a problem of dealers pushing hard drugs. Many dealers operate under the noses of police surveillance, concentrated in places such as at the Kettenbrückengasse U4 station, the tunnels leading to Karlsplatz and certain stations on the U6 U-Bahn.

Vienna's strong social system means there is a network of social workers, doctors and psychologists ready and willing to help addicts get off their habits. Three-quarters of the city's 7,000 or so addicts are in some form of drug therapy, and strict rent control means that most of them aren't homeless.

Drugs laws are complicated, but basically, possession of a small amount of soft drugs will result in a slap-on-the-wrist type caution, or *Anzeige*, from the police, but probably nothing more. Punishment varies but can include obligatory therapy and, for Austrians, loss of driver's licences. However, with the government adopting harsher law and order policies, more punitive punishments seem to be likely in the future.

Drogenberatungstelle

6, Esterhazygasse 18 (24hr hotline 586 0438-0/www.vws.or.at). Bus 13a, 14a. **Open** 4-8.30pm Mon; 2-8.30pm Tue-Sun. **Map** p246 C9.
Advice and help with drug problems.

Electricity

The current used in Austria is 220v, which works fine with British 240v appliances. If you have US 110v gadgets, it's best to bring the appropriate transformers. Plugs have two pins, so bring an adaptor.

Embassies & consulates

Australian Embassy

4, Mattiellistrasse 2-4 (506 74/ www.australian-embassy.at). U1,U2, U4 Karlsplatz. **Open** 8.30am-4.30pm Mon-Fri. **Map** p251 E8.

British Consulate

3, Jaurèsgasse 10 (716 13-5151/ www.britishembassy.at). Tram 71. **Open** 9.15-10.15am, 2-3pm Mon-Fri for consular and passport enquiries. **Map** p247 F8.

British Embassy

3, Jaurèsgasse 12 (716 13-0/ www.britishembassy.at). Tram 71. **Open** 9am-1pm, 2-5pm Mon-Fri. **Map** p247 F8.

Canadian Embassy

1, Laurenzerberggasse 2 (3rd floor) (5313 83000/www. kanada.at). U1, U4 Schwedenplatz/tram 1, 2. **Open** 8.30am-12.30pm, 1.30-3.30pm Mon-Fri. **Map** p251 F6.

Irish Embassy

3, Landstrasse Hauptstrasse 2, (715 4246) U4 Landstraße Hauptstraße . **Open** 9.30-11.30am, 1.30-4pm Mon-Fri. **Map** p251 F6.

South African Embassy

19, Sandgasse 33 (320 6493/ www.southafrican-embassy.at). U4 Heiligenstadt/bus 38a. **Open** 8.30am-noon Mon-Fri.

US Consulate

1, Parkring 12a (31339-7537/ www.usembassy.at). U3 Stubentor/ tram 1, 2. **Open** Visas 8-11.30am Mon-Fri. Phone enquiries 9.30-11.30am Mon-Fri. **Map** p251 F7.

US Embassy

9, Boltzmanngasse 16 (31 339-0/ www.usembassy.at). Tram 37, 38, 40, 41, 42. **Open** 8.30am-noon, 1-4.30pm Mon-Fri. **Map** p243 D4.

Emergencies

Beware: *Ambulanz* means emergency room or outpatient clinic, and *Rettung* means ambulance. *See also p227* Health.

Ambulance

Rettung (144).

Fire
Feuerwehr (122).

Police
Polizei (133).

For information about HIV/AIDS, see right.

Hosi
2, Novaragasse 40 (216 6604/www.hosiwien.at). U1 Praterstern. **Map** p251 G5.
A political meeting point for gay activists. Regular events include: open house (from 7pm Tue); lesbian group (7pm Wed); coming out groups (from 7pm Thur) and occasional dance nights for women (7pm Fri).

Rosa Lila Tip
6, Linke Wienzeile 102 (Gays 585 4343/Lesbians 586 8150/ www.villa.at). U4 Pilgramgasse. **Open** *Info evenings for lesbians 5-8pm Mon, Wed, Fri. Info evenings for gays 5-8 pm Mon, Wed, Sat; 7-8pm Fri* **Map** p246 C9.
Counselling, discussion groups and advice for gays and lesbians.

Most doctors in the Austrian Health Service (*Krankenkasse*) speak English. Hospital care is divided between general care (*allgemeine Klasse*) or private (*Sonderklasse*). Treatment is available for citizens of all countries that have reciprocal treaties with the Austrian Krankenkasse – in effect most European states. Britain has a reciprocal arrangement with Austria so that emergency hospital treatment is free when you show a British passport. Technically, seeing doctors, dentists or getting treatment at outpatient departments is also free. However, receiving free medical treatment can involve bureaucracy, so it's best for non-EU citizens to take out full health insurance. Few hospitals will accept credit cards.

Holders of the European Health Insurance Card (EHIC) will be treated free at any hospital listed below or with any doctor who takes patients from *Alle Kassen* (all insurance funds). Branches of the Wiener Gebietskrankenkasse (regional insurance fund) can inform you which doctors take the EHIC. Check the website below.

Wiener Gebietskrankenkasse
10, Wienerbergstrasse 15-19 (601 22-0/www.wgkk.at). U6 Meidling/ bus 7a, 10a, 15a. **Open** 7.30am-2pm Mon-Wed, Fri; 7.30am-4pm Thur.

Accident & emergency

There are many A&E hospitals (*Unfallspitäler*) listed under hospitals (*Krankenhäuser*) in the white pages of the phone book. The following hospitals accept emergencies 24 hours a day, seven days a week.

Allgemeines Krankenhaus (AKH)
9, Währinger Gürtel 18-20 (40 400-0/www.akh-wien.ac.at). U6 Michelbeuern. **Map** p242 B5.
The largest hospital in Europe, the AKH is affiliated with the University of Vienna. It is your best option in central Vienna.

Lorenz Böhler Unfall Krankenhaus
20, Donaueschingenstrasse 13 (33 110-0/www.ukhboehler.at). U6 Dresdnerstrasse. **Map** p243 F2.

Sankt Anna Kinderspital
9, Kinderspitalgasse 6 (401 70-0/ www.stanna.at). U6 Alser Strasse/ tram 43, 44. **Map** p242 B5.
This friendly, hectic children's hospital has doctors on hand 24 hours a day to check out high fevers, rashes or worse.

Complementary medicine

The pharmacies listed below specialise in homeopathy.

Apotheke Kaiserkrone
7, Mariahilfer Strasse 110 (526 2646/www.kaiserkrone.at). U3 Zieglergasse. **Open** 8am-6pm Mon-Fri; 8am-noon Sat. **Credit** MC, V. **Map** p246 C8.
Vienna's most reliable address for homeopathy. Appointments can be made here with specialists.

Internationale Apotheke
1, Kärntner Ring 17 (512 2825/ www.internationale-apotheke.at). U1, U2, U4 Karlsplatz/tram 1, 2, D, J. **Open** 8am-6pm Mon-Fri; 8am-noon Sat. **Credit** AmEx, DC, MC, V. **Map** p251 E8.
Specialists in all types of homeopathic treatments.

Contraception & abortion

Outpatient Clinic for Pregnancy Help
1, Fleischmarkt 26 (24 hour hotline 512 9631-250). U1, U4 Schwedenplatz/tram 1, 2. **Open** 8am-5pm Mon-Fri; 8am-3pm Sat. **Map** p251 F6.
Pregnancy tests, birth-control advice and abortion counselling.

Dentists

Austrians have good dental care, but only some costs are covered by the state system. Many Austrians skip across the border to Hungary, where they can get the same treatment for a third of the cost. Dentists (*Zahnärtzte*) are listed in the phone book and the majority speak English.

University Dental Clinic
9, Währinger Strasse 25a (4277-67001). Tram 37, 38, 40, 41, 42. **No credit cards. Map** p250 D5.
The university emergency dental clinic is open Mon-Fri, but only for a few hours. Phone for times.

Doctors

If you need an English-speaking doctor, phone 513 95 95 (24 hour hotline). The British Embassy (716130) can also provide you with a list of English-speaking doctors. Take your EHIC card or private insurance documents with you.

HIV/AIDS

AIDS-Hilfe Wien
6, Mariahilfer Gürtel 4 (599 37/ www.aids.at). U6 Gumpendorfer Strasse/tram 6, 18. **Open** 4-7pm Mon, Wed; 9am-noon Thur; 2-5pm Fri. **Map** p246 B9.
For tests, results and counselling.

Directory

Opticians

See p154.

Pharmacies

Often sporting wonderful biblical names such as 'Heilige Geist' (Holy Ghost) or 'Auge Gottes' (The Eye of God), pharmacies (*Apotheken*) in Vienna are found throughout the city. They are signposted with a red serpentine 'A'. Normally open 8am-noon, 2-6pm Mon-Fri; 8am-noon Sat, many no longer close at lunchtime.

Pharmacies have a rota system at night and on Sundays, and all display a sign indicating the nearest one open.

Medicine Delivery Service

Medikamentenzustelldienst *89 144.*
For €19 this 24-hour service will pick up and deliver medicines from pharmacies.

Helplines

Alcoholics Anonymous

3, Barthgasse 7 (799 5599/ www.anonyme-alkoholiker.at). U3 Schlachthofgasse. **Open** 6-9pm daily. **Map** p248 J9.
A number of English-speaking groups meet regularly, two evenings and two days a week.

Viennese Children & Youth Protection

Wiener Kinder-und Jugendanwaltschaft
9, Sobieskigasse 31 (1708). U6 Nussdorferstrasse/tram 37. **Open** 9am-5pm Mon-Fri. **Map** p242 C3. English spoken.

Women's Emergency Centre

Frauen Notruf der Stadt Wien *71 719.*
Council funded rape crisis centre with counselling in English.

ID

There is no law obliging citizens to carry means of identification. However, if the police want to check your passport and you don't have it with you, they may insist on accompanying you to wherever you've left it.

Internet

For such a traditional city, Vienna has embraced the internet with remarkable gusto. Restaurants, bars and businesses habitually have homepages and these are often extremely well constructed and maintained.

Broadband access is widely available throughout the city and is common in hotels, and there's wireless access at many cafés across town. For information on public internet access, see www.wien.gv.at/english/edp/wlan. htm. Internet access is available at the call-centres that line virtually every Viennese street. www.helge.at/wlan has a list of numerous locations – mostly cafés – with free WLAN access.

Left luggage

At the airport, left luggage is in the entrance hall across from the rental cars and costs €2.70 per day, depending on the size of luggage. All major credit cards are accepted.

In the larger train stations in Vienna, there are no longer any left luggage offices, but you are able to leave your luggage in a locker (€2).

Legal help

If you run into legal trouble, contact your insurers or your national consulate (*see p226*).

Libraries

Austrian National Library

1, Heldenplatz (53 410-252/ www.onb.ac.at). Bus 2a, 3a. **Open** *Oct-June* 9am-9pm Mon-Fri; 9am-12.45pm Sat. *July-Sept* 9am-4pm Mon-Fri; 9am-12.45pm. **Map** p250 E7.
Browse the catalogue, select what you want and pick the books up the next day to take to the reading room. There's a varied choice of English titles.

Städtische Büchereien

7, Urban-Loritz Platz 2a (4000-84 500/www.buechereien.wien.at). U6 Burggasee/bus 48a. **Open** 11am-7pm Mon-Fri; 11am-5pm Sat. **Map** p246 B8.

Vienna's public libraries have an excellent collection of books, tapes and CDs. This splendid central branch, with panoramic city views, has just inherited the British Council's collection after its sad demise in 2007.

Lost property

To trace possessions left on a tram or bus, phone the General Information Office (790 943-500); for those left on a train, phone Südbahnhof (5800 22 222). Each bus and tram has a station where lost property is taken. After one week, everything is removed to the central police lost and found office. Go in person, with plenty of patience.

Central Lost & Found

Zentrales Fundamt
18 Bastiengasse 36-38 (4000-8091). Tram 41. **Open** 8am-3.30pm Mon-Wed, Fri; 8am-5pm Thur. **Map** p250 D5.

Media

Press

International newspapers and magazines are widely available from kiosks, street sellers and tobacco stores all over Vienna but no actual papers or periodicals in English are published here.

A disproportionate number of titles on sale in Austria belong to the ever-expanding News Group. Led by the enterprising Fellner brothers, its publications tend to resemble buy-by-post catalogues.

Radio

Despite the emergence of private radio stations after the broadcasting laws in 1997, none have seriously challenged the hegemony of state broadcasting.

The state-run ÖRF's station, Österreich 1 (92.0 FM, 87.8 FM), offers a blend of classical, jazz and opera music, including concerts and other cultural programmes. Radio Wien (89.9 and 95.3 FM), one of ÖRF's regional stations, has pop, news, weather and traffic. Ö3 (99.9 FM) is a slick commercial station.

For visitors, the ÖRF-run FM4 is still the best option,

broadcasting indie/dance music 24 hours daily (103.4 FM), in English from 1am to 2pm, with English-language news on the hour from 6am to 7pm.

Radio Austria International (6,155kHz, 5,945kHz, 13,730kHz) is ÖRF's short-wave station designed by the government to be the 'voice of Austria' abroad. It has news and information and an English, Spanish and Russian service.

Probably the best bet for more diverse programming is Radio Orange (94 FM), which features soul, hip hop, jazz and African music.

Television

Since the 2001 Private TV Law created a framework for terrestrial commercial TV, only one licence has so far been granted. ATV is a grim collage of reruns, bad movies and *The Lugners*, an Osbournes-inspired chronicle of a society building contractor, best known for inviting Pamela Anderson and more recently Paris Hilton to the Opera Ball. Austrian TV therefore consists of two state-run national channels, ÖRF1 and ÖRF2 (www.orf.at). Other channels are available only via cable or satellite.

Money

In January 2002, Austria switched to the euro (€). One euro is made up of 100 cents. There are seven banknotes – €5 (grey), €10 (red), €20 (blue), €50 (orange), €100 (green), €200 (yellow-brown) and €500 (purple) – and eight coins – 1 cent, 2 cents, 5 cents, 10 cents, 20 cents, 50 cents, €1 and €2.

ATMs

Hole-in-the-wall machines are dotted around throughout Vienna and have a lit sign with two horizontal green and blue stripes. The specific cards that each machine takes are marked and there's a choice of languages. Note that the machines don't give receipts. There are also a few automatic currency-converting machines, stating 'Change/Cambio' with instructions in English, that will accept foreign banknotes.

Banks

The best place to exchange money is in a bank, as it will give you a better rate. You'll also save money by exchanging a larger sum in one go, as there is often a minimum commission charge.

Most banks open 8am-12.30pm and 1.30-3pm during the week, extended to 5.30pm on Thursday. A few banks, such as the main BA-CA bank on Schottengasse and the Die Erste Bank on Graben 21, do not close for lunch. Some banks, generally at railway stations and airports, stay open longer.

Bureaux de change

City Air Terminal

U3, U4 Wien Mitte. **Open** 8am-12.30pm, 2-6.30pm daily.

Opera/Karlsplatz

U1, U2, U3, U4/tram 1, 2, D, J. **Open** 8am-7pm daily.

Südbahnhof

Tram D. **Open** 6.30am-10pm daily.

Westbahnhof

U3/tram 5, 6. **Open** 7am-10pm daily.

Credit & debit cards

Compared with western Europe, Budapest and Prague, Vienna is not a credit card-friendly town. Many of the smaller hotels and restaurants do not take credit cards, and retail credit card percentages are very high compared with the rest of Europe. Debit cards marked with Visa or Maestro (Mastercard) symbols can be used, but with a signature rather than a PIN number.

American Express

1, Kärntnerstrasse 21-23 (512 400-40). U1, U3 Stephansplatz. **Open** 9am-5pm Mon-Thur; 9am-4pm Fri. **Map** p251 E7. Holders of the card can use the company's facilities here, including the cash advance service.

Lost/stolen cards

If you lose your credit card, or it has been stolen, phone one of the emergency numbers listed below. All lines are open 24 hours daily.

American Express 0800 900 940. **Diners Club** 501 350. **MasterCard** 0800 218 235. **Visa** 711 11 770.

Tax

Non-EU citizens can reclaim value-added tax (*Mehrwertsteuer*, or MwSt) on goods purchased in the country. Ask to be issued with a Tax-Free shopping cheque (or U34 form) for the amount of the refund and present this, together with the receipt, at the refund office at the airport.

Natural hazards

Austria's only natural hazards are Lyme disease and Central European encephalitis (CEE), or tick-borne encephalitis. Both are transmitted by infected ticks, but the former is an easily treatable bacterial infection. CEE, however, is a viral infection of the central nervous system with no known cure. Both are highly prevalent in forested areas of Central Europe such as the Vienna Woods, particularly from April to October. The risk of CEE should not be exaggerated as over 90% of tick bites are harmless. If infection does take place, flu-like symptoms appear one to three weeks later, normally lasting two to four days. Only around one in 250 cases actually leads to encephalitis.

Opening hours

From Monday to Friday, shops in Vienna are now legally allowed to open between 6am and 7.30pm and until 9pm on two days. On Saturdays, 6pm is the latest closing time. With the exception of bakeries, all shops are closed on Sunday and public holidays apart from those located in railway stations (try Wien Nord or Franz-Josephs-Bahnhof). In practice these longer opening hours are only operative in commercial areas such as Mariahilfer Strasse and the 1st district. Many smaller shops still close for lunch.

Police stations

The emergency number for the police is 133. The police are generally straightforward, and speak English. Police stations (*Polizeiwachzimmer*) are marked with a red-and-white sign and some of the most central are: 1, Am Hof 3 (313 10-213 10); and 1, Stephansplatz (U-Bahn Station) (313 10-213-70).

Central Police HQ
1, Schottenring 7-9 (313 100). U2 Schottentor. **Map** p250 D5.

Postal services

The postal service is efficient and easy to use and most workers speak English. Post boxes are painted bright yellow and sport a two-ended horn, often mounted on walls. An orange stripe denotes that the box will still be emptied at weekends.

For more information, call the Post Office 24-hour hotline (08100 10100).

All post offices offer express mail and fax services. Look in the phone directory's white pages under *Post- und Telegraph-enverwaltung* for locations of post offices and their opening times, or go to www.post.at. The following post offices all have extended opening hours.

Franz-Josefs-Bahnhof
9, Althanstrasse 10.(0577 677 1090) Tram 5, D. **Open** 7am-8pm Mon-Fri; 9am-2pm Sat, Sun. **Map** p243 D3.

Main Post Office
1, Fleischmarkt 19 (0577 677 1010). U1, U4 Schwedenplatz/ tram 1, 2. **Open** 6am 10pm daily **Map** p251 F6.

Südbahnhof
10, Wiedner Gürtel 1b.(0577 677 1103) Tram D. **Open** 7am-8pm Mon-Fri; 9am-2pm Sat, Sun. **Map** p247 F10.

Westbahnhof
15, Europaplatz. (0577 677 1150) U3, U6 Westbahnhof. **Open** 7am-10pm Mon-Fri; 9am-8pm Sat, Sun. **Map** p246 B8.

Poste restante

Poste restante facilities are available at any post office, but only the main post office (*see above*) has a 24-hour service. Letters should be addressed to the recipient 'Postlagernd, Postamt' –

along with the address of the particular post office. They can be collected from the counter marked *Postlagernde Sendungen*. Take your passport.

Public holidays

New Year's Day (1 Jan); **Epiphany** (6 Jan); **Easter Monday**; **May Day** (1 May); **Ascension Day** (6th Thur after Easter); **Whit Monday** (6th Mon after Easter); **Corpus Christi** (2nd Thur after Whitsun); **Assumption Day** (15 Aug); **Austrian National Holiday** (26 Oct); **All Saints' Day** (1 Nov); **Immaculate Conception** (8 Dec); **Christmas Day** (25 Dec); **St Stephen's Day** (26 Dec).

Religion

Because of Vienna's musical heritage, many people attend church simply to enjoy the music on offer. Look out particularly for details of Sunday Mass at the Augustinerkirche, Karlskirche, Minoritenkirche, Stephansdom and Michaelerkirche. The acclaimed Vienna Boys' Choir sings Mass at the Burgkapelle on Sundays and religious holidays at 9.15am, except from July to mid September, but to hear the choir you must pay both a concert fee and have a bag thrust under your nose for donations. If you can't arrange seats on the chapel floor, don't bother with the balconies – many of them have obscured views.

Anglican

Christ Church
3, Jaurèsgasse 17-19 (714 89 00).Tram 71. **Map** p251 F7. Sunday services at 8am and 10am; members of Viennese choirs are often invited as guest singers. It runs a great second-hand bookshop at Salesianergasse 20 (open 9.30am-4pm Tue-Thur; 9.30am-noon Fri, Sat).

Judaism

City Synagogue
1, Seitenstettengasse 4 (535 0431-412). U4 Schwedenplatz. **Map** p251 F6.
In order to be admitted, you must show your passport.

Mormon

Church of Jesus Christ & Latter Day Saints
19, Silbergasse 1 (367 5647). Tram 38/bus 10a.

Protestant

International Baptist Church
6, Mollardgasse 35. U4 Margareten Gürtel. **Services** 11.30am 12.30pm Sun.

United Methodist Church
15, Sechshauser Strasse 56 (604 53 47). Bus 57a. **Services** 11.15am Sun. **Map** p246 A10.

Roman Catholic

St Augustin
1, Augustinerstrasse 3 (533 7099). U1, U2 Karlsplatz. **Mass** 11am, 6.30pm Sun. **Map** p250 E7.

St Stephan's Cathedral
1, Stephansplatz 3 (515 52). U1, U3 Stephansplatz. **Map** p251 E6.

Votivkirche
9, Rooseveltplatz 8 (4085 05014). U2 Schottentor. **Mass** 11.15pm Sun. **Map** p250 D5.

Safety & security

Vienna is one of the safest cities in Europe. Many people, including women, don't think twice about walking alone in most districts, even at night. Public transport is generally safe. The opening up of the borders with eastern Europe, however, has begun to have an effect. An increasing amount of pick-pocketing and petty crime is occurring in tourist locations, so take precautions in crowded areas. A few places to steer clear of: Karlsplatz station is notorious as a drugs centre; the Prater at night is known for pickpockets.

Smoking

Austrians are among the heaviest smokers in western Europe. Politicians have dithered on the subject and no change to the law is likely before 2008.

Study

Language classes

Berlitz

1, Graben 13 (512 8286/ www.berlitz.at). U1, U3 Stephansplatz/bus 1a. **Open** 8am-8pm Mon-Fri. **No credit cards. Map** p250 E6.
Individual, intensive and evening courses in German.
Other locations 6, Mariahilfer Strasse 27 (586 5693); 10, Troststrasse 50 (604 3911).

Cultura Wien

1, Bauernmarkt 18 (533 2493/www.culturawien.at). U4 Schwedenplatz/bus 1a, 3a. **Open** 9am-6pm Mon-Fri. **No credit cards. Map** p251 E6.
Offers intensive four-hour classes taught daily, and evening classes two days a week in courses lasting four and eight weeks. There's a good summer programme for younger students.

Inlingua

1, Neuer Markt 1 (512 2225/www.inlingua.at). U1, U3 Stephansplatz. **Open** 9am-6pm Mon-Fri. **No credit cards. Map** p250 E7.
Four-hour-a-day intensive courses are run in sessions lasting two weeks or longer. Inlingua also offers evening courses in business German twice a week. Classes are limited to three to six students.

University of Vienna

9, Universitätscampus-Altes AKH Alser Strasse 4, Hof 1.16 (4277-24101/www.univie.ac.at/wihok) Tram 43, 44. **Open** *July-Sept* 8.30am-4pm Mon-Fri; *Oct-June* 9am-4pm Mon-Fri; 9am-6.30pm Tue. **No credit cards. Map** p242 C5.
Cheap nine- or 12-week courses in German for foreigners.

VHS Polycollege

5, Stöbergasse 11-15 (54 666 100/www.polycollege.ac.at). Bus 12a,14a, 59a. **Open** 8.30am-7.30pm Mon-Fri; 8.30am-12.30pm Sat. **No credit cards. Map** p247 D10.
The Volkshochschulen are Vienna's adult education colleges. They offer a wide range of language courses, as well as many others including cookery, photography and yoga. The Polycollege is the most dynamic of the 18 that operate in Vienna. For a full list, go to www.vhs.at.

Universities

Club International Universitaire (CIU)

1, Schottengasse 1/Mezzanine (533 6533/www.ciu.at). U2 Schottentor/tram 1, 2, D. **Open** 9am-8pm Mon-Fri by appointment. **Map** p250 D6.
Apart from organising lectures, debates, social events and trips, this focal point of international student activity in Vienna also offers help and advice on many matters to foreign students.

Open University

1, Fischerstiege 10-16 (533 2390/www.open.ac.uk)). U1, U4 Schwedenplatz. **Open** 9am-5pm Mon-Fri. **Map** p251 E6.
A complete English curriculum is offered in the humanities and social sciences, as well as a selection of Masters degrees and postgraduate programmes in management and business studies.

Webster University

22, Berchtoldgasse 1 (269 9293/www.webster.ac.at). U1 Vienna International Centre/tram 90, 91/bus 92a. **Map** p245 L4.
A fully accredited private American university recognised in Austria, with BA, MA and MBA programmes in English. Subjects include international relations, management, computer science and psychology.

Telephones

Since deregulation in the late 1990s, you can now make cheap calls worldwide from privately run phone shops all over the city. Telephone boxes are plentiful, and calls can also be made from most post offices. Mobile use is high, with virtually as many phones as inhabitants.

Directory inquiries

Austria, EU countries, neighbouring countries from Austria (11 88 77).
World (0900 11 88 77).
Mobile phones (0800 664 664).
Telegrams (0800 100 190).

Telekom Information

0800 100 100.
Information about the wide range of telephone tariffs in Austria.

Making a call

To make an international call, dial the country code, city code and telephone number. A few country codes are: Australia 61, Germany 49, Hungary 36, India 91, Ireland 353, Japan 81, New Zealand 64, South Africa 27, UK 44, USA/Canada 1.

All telephone numbers in Austria have prefixes, which are usually printed in parentheses. To make a call to Vienna from elsewhere in Austria, dial 01 and then the number. To phone Vienna from abroad, dial 00 43, followed by 1 and then the number. To dial an Austrian mobile phone from abroad (usually 0676, 0699, 0650 or 0664 numbers), dial 00 43, then the number without the 0.

Many general city numbers only have four digits. Austrian telephones have direct-dial extensions that are often placed at the end of the telephone number, preceded by a hyphen.

Public telephones

Smartly designed though rarely used, public telephone booths, many with internet terminals, are all over Vienna. A local call costs a minimum of 20¢.

Information operator

11 88 77

Mobile telephones

A mobile telephone is called a Handy, a nifty English word that Austrians are disappointed to learn isn't used in Britain. As there is plenty of competition, you can get your mobile phone free and just pay for your calls plus your monthly line rental.

Drei

0800 30 30 00/www.drei.at.

Mobilkom/A1

0800 664 664/www.A1net.at.

One

277 28-3040/www.one.at.

Telering

0800 650 650/www.telering.at.

Directory

T-Mobile

0676 2000/www.t-mobile.at.

Time

Austria is on Central European Time, which means it is an hour ahead of Britain. Like Britain, Austria puts its clocks forward an hour on the last Sunday of March and puts them back an hour on the last Sunday of October.

Tipping

There are no fixed rules about tipping, but in a restaurant it is customary either to give a ten per cent tip or to round up the bill. Announce the total sum to the waiting staff as they take your money – they will normally pocket the tip and then return your change.

Taxi drivers normally receive an extra ten per cent over the metered fare, and €1 per bag is normal for porters and bellhops. Tipping is common in Austria, so an extra €1 or €2 for workers, hairdressers or any services will never hurt.

Toilets

There are 330 public toilets in Vienna, all marked by a large WC sign. Some are open 24 hours a day, others vary but are generally open from 9am to 7pm daily. Public toilets with attendants cost 50¢, but at least they are clean. The WC on the Graben is worth a visit for the art nouveau decor. Other usefully located WCs are in the Opernpassage and Rathauspark. U-Bahn stations have toilets, but not all are open all the time.

Tourist information

City Hall Information

(Rathaus) 1, Friedrich-Schmidt-Platz 1 (52 550-0). U2 Rathaus/tram 1, 2, D. **Open** *Phone enquiries* 8am-6pm Mon-Fri; 8am-4pm Sat, Sun. **Map** p250 D6. Although not a tourist office, the City Hall does provide a number of maps and brochures in English. Phone for details of opera performances, ticket sales and museum hours.

Vienna Tourist Board

1, Albertinaplatz 1 (24 555/www.vienna.info). U1, U2, U4 Karlplatz/tram 1, 2, D, J. **Open** 9am-7pm daily. **Map** p247 E7.

Youth Information Vienna

1, Babenbergerstrasse 1 (1799/www.wienxtra.at). U2 Museumsquartier/tram 1, 2, D, J. **Open** noon-7pm Mon-Sat. **Map** p250 D7.

Visas & immigration

Citizens of other EU countries have the right to enter Austria and remain for an indefinite period of time. However, anyone staying in Austria in a private house or apartment for more than 60 days is technically required to register with the Magistratisches Bezirksamt, although this is not enforced (*see below* Residence permits).

Officials at Austria's road and train borders with eastern Europe tend to be particularly fierce if you are holding a passport from an eastern European state.

A visa is not required for US citizens for stays of up to three-months in length; at the end of a six-month stay you must leave the country if you do not have a residence permit.

Residence permits

If you are planning on staying in Austria for more than 60 days, you'll need to register with the Magistratisches Bezirksamt (of your district) to obtain a *Meldezettel* – a confirmation of where you live. A *Meldezettel* is requested for everything from renting a flat to applying for a library card. Buy the forms at any tobacconist and locate the Bezirksamt in your area (in the phone book under *Magistratisches Bezirksamt/Meldeservice*). Bring your passport with you.

If you specify a religious affiliation in the 'Religion' section of the form you may be automatically registered as a member of that particular church and therefore liable to church taxes. Religion is taken very seriously in Austria, so shrugging

off their demands won't work. Religious orders are entitled to a percentage of your salary unless you are registered as ORB.

If you change address, you'll need to de-register at your current Magistratisches Bezirksamt and re-register in the new one.

When to go

Vienna's rather mild continental climate, hot in summer and cold in winter, is growing milder and hotter by the year. Wind can often make the temperature seem lower than it really is. During the winter the city sometimes ices over. During summer rain is frequent. The best time to go is May-June and September-October.

Women

For the Women's Career Network (WCN), *see p225*.

American Women's Association (AWA)

1, Singerstrasse 4/11 (966 29 25/www.awavienna.com). U1, U4 Karlsplatz/tram 1, 2. **Open** 10am-4pm Mon, Tue, Thur, 10am-3pm Fri. **Map** p251 E7.
A non-profit organisation to help English-speaking women living in Vienna.

Working in Vienna

Citizens of the European Economic Area are exempt from the bureaucratic requirements of obtaining work permits. If you're not a citizen of the EEA, then gaining a permit is a hassle. You will need a work permit (*Arbeitsgenehmigung*) unless you are specifically exempt according to the law governing the employment of foreigners (*Ausländerbeschäftigungsgesetz*).

However, if you marry an Austrian, life immediately becomes much easier. But even so, in order to work, you must have a residence permit (*Aufenthaltsbewilligung*) and a written confirmation from the regional Labour Office (*Arbeitsmarktservice*) that certifies your work permit exemption. Look in the phone book 'white pages' under 'Arbeitsmarktservice' to find the closest office to you.

Further Reference

Books

Ilse Barea *Vienna*
Readable historical account of the city from the Baroque era to World War I by a Viennese émigrée.

Thomas Bernhard *Cutting Timber*
Vituperative novel portraying contemporary Viennese artistic and literary circles. It shows the author, Bernhard, at his trademark maniacal and misanthropic best.

Bill Bryson *Neither Here nor There*
Includes a flippant but perspicacious account of his Vienna sojourn as a teenage backpacker in Europe.

Elias Canetti *The Tongue Set Free*
The author spent his formative school days in Vienna before World War II. Fond memories of the Tunnel of Fun at the Prater, and a family friend who spoke of Bahr and Schnitzler and was 'Viennese if for no other reason than because she always knew, without great effort, what was happening in the world of the intellect'.

George Clare *Last Waltz in Vienna*
A moving account of the ominous pre-*Anschluss* years through the eyes of a young middle-class Jew.

Françoise Giroud *Alma Mahler: or the Art of Being Loved*
A racy defence of Alma's talents, scathing on Gustav Mahler's attempts to stifle her musical career.

Brigitte Hamann *Hitler's Vienna*
Grim, fascinating and essential reading about pre-war Vienna in an unsatisfactory translation.

Peter Handke *The Goalkeeper's Fear of the Penalty*
Austria's most celebrated contemporary novelist. His work does not deal specifically with Vienna.

Ingrid Helsing Almaas *Vienna; A Guide to Recent Architecture*
Pocket-sized, opinionated and well illustrated.

Allan Janik and Stephen Toulmin *Wittgenstein's Vienna*
Tracing the aesthetic and literary background to Wittgenstein's life. Rendered in clogged prose and plagued with typos.

Elfriede Jelinek *The Piano Teacher*
Filmed by Michael Haneke, it catches the stifling atmosphere of 1950s Vienna. Numerous other works by the 2004 Nobel Prize winner are available in English.

William M Johnson *The Austrian Mind: An Intellectual and Social History 1848-1938*
Dry but thorough American work conveniently subdivided.

John Lehmann and Richard Bassett *Vienna, A Travellers' Companion*
Eye-witness accounts, letters, stories of Vienna.

Eva Menasse *Vienna*
Much acclaimed Jewish saga by debut novelist.

Jan Morris *50 Years of Europe: An Album*
Several illuminating pieces on Vienna show Morris's barely disguised contempt for the city.

Frederick Morton *A Nervous Splendour: Vienna 1888-89* and *Thunder at Twilight: Vienna 1913-14*
Engrossing dramatised accounts of the end of Habsburg Vienna. The first centres on the Mayerling affair and the latter on events prior to World War I.

Robert Musil *The Man without Qualities*
Impressive in size and reputation: the kind of book you really should read, but never get round to (you could just read chapter 15, for its account of the intellectual revolution).

Hella Pick *Guilty Victim*
Semi-personal account of modern Austria by a Jewish exile from Vienna.

Christoph Ransmayr *The Dog King*
An absurd, beautifully written tale about the horrors of war, set in a fictional Alpine town.

Joseph Roth *Radetzky March* and *The Emperor's Tomb*
Roth's finest novels chronicle the decline of the Empire. Splendid new translations by Michael Hofmann.

Joseph Roth *The String of Pearls*
The Shah of Persia visits Vienna, demands the services of a countess, and gets a look-alike whore instead. Lots of doomed characters and scenes in coffee houses.

Paul Strathern *Wittgenstein in 90 Minutes*
Summary of Wittgenstein's life and philosophy ('If people did not sometimes do silly things, nothing intelligent would ever get done').

Georg Trakl *Selected Poems*
For serious and professional melancholics.

Stefan Zweig *The Royal Game*
The influence of Freud and the early psychoanalysts is impossible to miss.

Stefan Zweig *The World of Yesterday*
Fascinating explanation of the key role the Jews played in the artistic development of Vienna.

Websites

www.aardvark.at/metro
Unofficial website of the U-Bahn and tram network, also includes some interesting anecdotes.

www.austria.org Austrian press and information service based in Washington, DC.

www.bmaa.gv.at Austrian Foreign Ministry site.

www.ethermagazine.at Superior ex-pat site with good concert tips.

www.falter.at Vienna's best listings paper. In German.

www.mqw.at Full details of events at the MuseumsQuartier.

www.tiscover.com Features on leisure and holidays.

www.viennahype.at An official tourist info site aimed at young visitors, designed by the Lomographic Society.

www.vienna.info Vienna Tourist Information site.

www.vienna.metblogs.com Entertaining blog site with off-the-wall comments. In English.

www.virtualvienna.com An enjoyably amateurish site by Vienna's expat community.

www.wien.gv.at Municipal site with general info on Vienna. Excellent historical pieces too.

www.wienguide.at Walking tours in the city.

Index

Advertisers' Index

Please refer to the relevant pages for contact details

Place of interest and/or entertainment	
Railway stations	
Parks	
Hospitals	
U-Bahn stations	U
S-Bahn stations.	Ⓢ
Churches	✚
Area name	WÄHRING

Maps

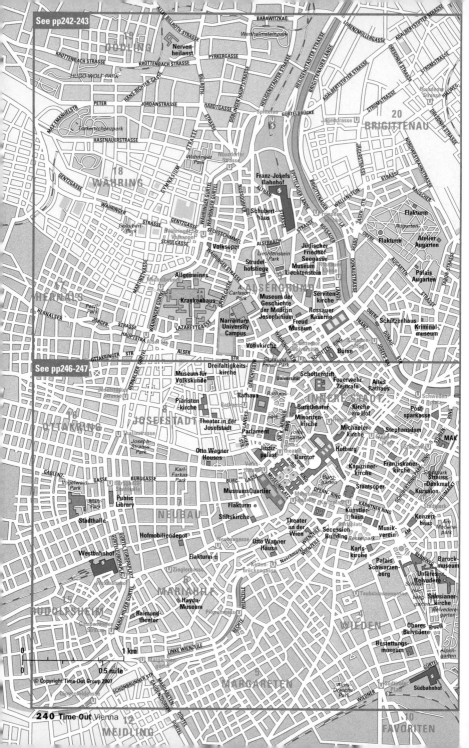

BARAWITZKAG.

DÖBLING

WÄHRING

HERNALS

OTTAKRING

JOSEFSTADT

NEUBAU

RUDOLFSHEIM

MARIAHILF

BRIGITTENAU

ALSERGRUND

INNERE STADT

WIEDEN

MARGARETEN

MEIDLING

FAVORITEN

© Copyright Time Out Group 2007

1 km
0.5 mile

FLORIDSDORF

DONAUTURMSTRASSE

ARBEITERSTRANDBADS TRASSE

WAGRAMER STRASSE

DONAUSTADT-STRASSE

Donauturm

Donaupark

Alte Donau

ERZHER?OG KARLSTR.

Alte Donau

UNO City
(Vienna International
Centre)

WAGRAMER BRÜCKE

Kaiserin-Vienna
Int. Centre

WAGRAMER STRASSE

DONAUSTADT

Donau

Neue Donau

HANDELSKAI

INDUSTRIESTRASSE

DRESDNER STRASSE

ENGERTHSTRASSE

Gänsehäufel
Baths

NORDBAHNSTRASSE

Alte Donau

AM KAISERMÜHLENDAMM

REICHSBRÜCKE

LABORSTRASSE

AM

Donau

Neue Donau

Ungarische Strasse

Neubau

STRASSE

HEINESTRASSE

LASALLE

Praterstern Wien-Nord

Venediger

Prater-
museum

Wien
Nord

AUSSTELLUNGSSTRASSE

Riesenrad

HAIDGASSE

Strauss
Museum

Planetarium

Nestroyplatz

Urania

HANDELSKAI

Donauinsel

LEOPOLDSTADT

SCHÜTTELSTRASSE

Kunsthaus
Wien

Krieau
(Racecourse)

WEISSGERBER

Hundert-
wasser-Haus

Spenadl-
Wiese

Lagerwiese

Arenawiese

METTE

Ernst-Happel-
Stadion

City-Air-
Terminal

Landstr. Wien Mitte

Wittgenstein-
haus

Jesuitenwiese

Prater

ERDBERGER

Hundewiese

Rochus-
markt

SCHÜTTELSTRASSE

STADION-

Arenberg

Flakturm

Portois
& Fix

Rennweg

Strassenbahn
museum

Unterer-Prater

ERDBERGERBRÜCKE

HANDELSKAI

RENNWEG

LANDSTRASSE

SCHLACHTHAUS-

Lusthaus

Botanischer
Garten Der
Universität

BAUMGASSE

Erdberg

SIMMERINGER LÄNDE

OSTAUTOBAHN

LANDSTRASSE

Schweizer

20er
Haus

Garten

Heeresgeschichtliches
Museum

RENNWEG

Gasometer

SIMMERING

Vienna by Area

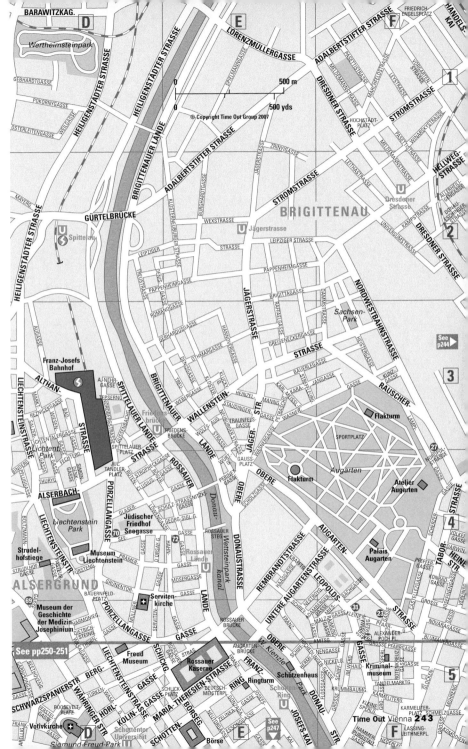

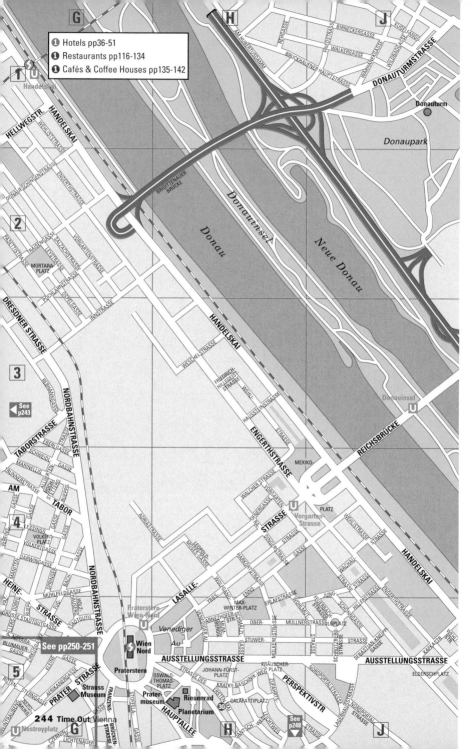

Hotels pp36-51
Restaurants pp116-134
Cafés & Coffee Houses pp135-142

1

DONAUTURMSTRASSE

Handelskai

Donauturm

Donaupark

HELLWEGSTR.

HANDELSKAI

Donauinsel

2

Donau

Neue Donau

MORTARA PLATZ

DRESDNER STRASSE

HANDELSKAI

3

See p243

WESCHELSTRASSE

FRIEDRICH-HILLEGEIST-STRASSE

WEILL-STRASSE

HAUPTSTRASSE

Donauinsel

REICHSBRÜCKE

TABORSTRASSE

NORDBAHNSTRASSE

ENGERTHSTRASSE

MEXIKO-

AM

TABOR

WALCHER-STRASSE

PLATZ

4

LESSINGG

VOLKERT PLATZ

VORGARTEN STRASSE

U Vorgarten-Strasse

HANDELSKAI

HEINE

STRASSE

NORDBAHNSTRASSE

LASALLE-

MAX-WINTER-PLATZ

MÜLLNERSTRASSE

PLATZ

AUSSTELLUNGSSTRASSE

Fraterstern Wien Nord

U

Venediger Au

Wien Nord

AUSSTELLUNGSSTRASSE

PERSPEKTIVSTR

See pp250-251

5

Praterstern

OSWALD-THOMAS-PLATZ

JOHANN-FÜRST-PLATZ

ELDERSCHPLATZ

Strauss Museum

Prater-museum

Riesenrad

Planetarium

PRATER STRASSE

HAUPTALLEE

See p248

Nestroyplatz

G

H

J

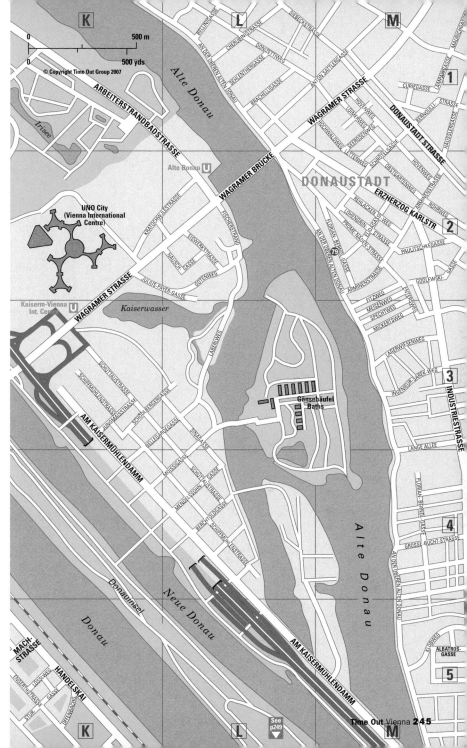

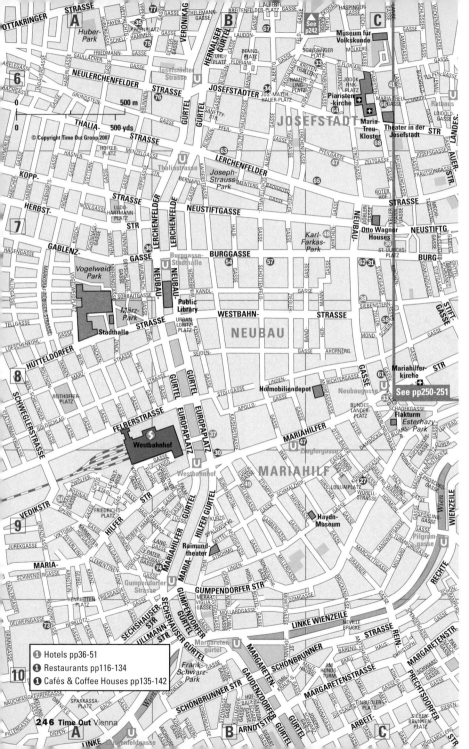

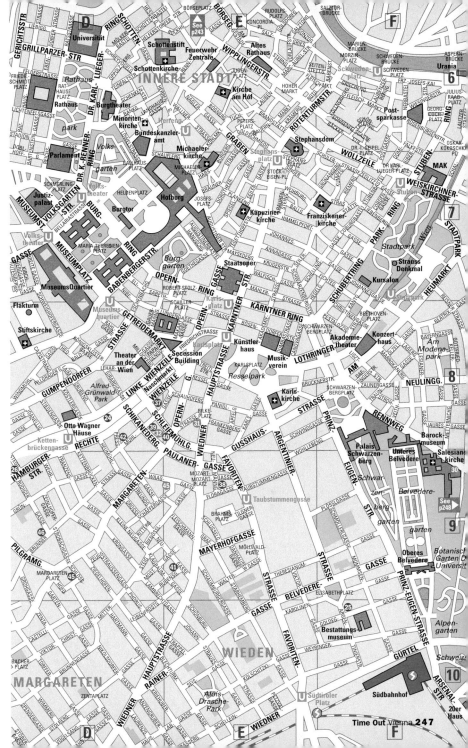

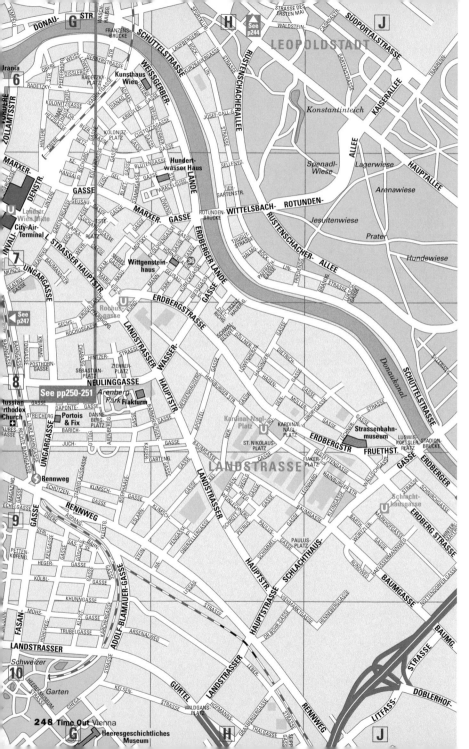

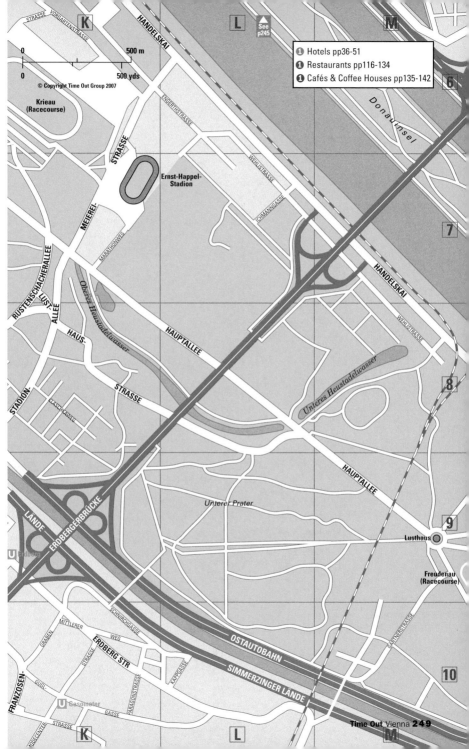

STRASSE VORGARTENSTRASSE

K

L

M

HANDELSKAI

See p245

6

0   500 m

0   500 yds

© Copyright Time Out Group 2007

Donauinsel

Krieau
(Racecourse)

ENGERTHSTRASSE

STRASSE

WEHLISTRASSE

MEIEREI

Ernst-Happel-
Stadion

ICHMANNGASSE

7

HANDELSKAI

RUSTENSCHACHERALLEE

MARATHONWEG

Oberes Heustadelwasser

HAUPTALLEE

WEHLISTRASSE

LUST-

ALLEE

HAUS-

Unteres Heustadelwasser

8

STRASSE

STADION-

KASCHAWEG

HAUPTALLEE

ERDBERGERBRÜCKE

Unterer Prater

LÄNDE

9

U Erdberg

Lusthaus

Freudenau
(Racecourse)

GÄRTNERSTRASSE

SCHNIRCHGASSE

MITTLERER

WEG

OSTAUTOBAHN

GRABEN

ERDBERG STR

STRASSE

PARADINISTRASSE

KAPPGASSE

SIMMERZINGER LÄNDE

FRANZOSEN-

BUSI-

10

U Gasometer

GASSE

STRASSE

MÖDERNTOR-

❶ Hotels pp36-51
❶ Restaurants pp116-134
❶ Cafés & Coffee Houses pp135-142

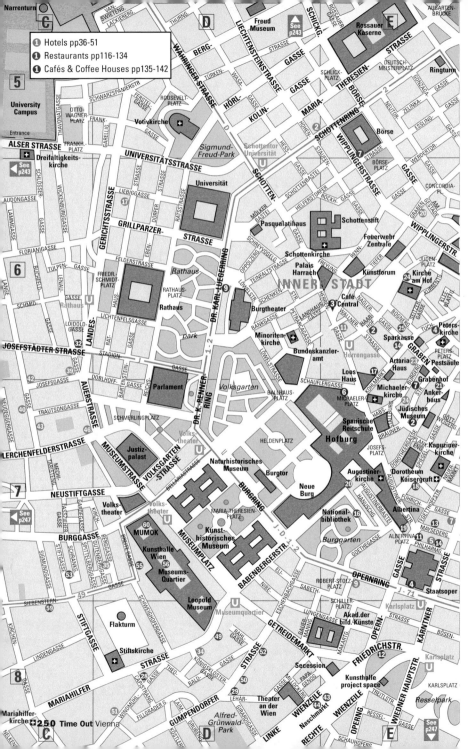

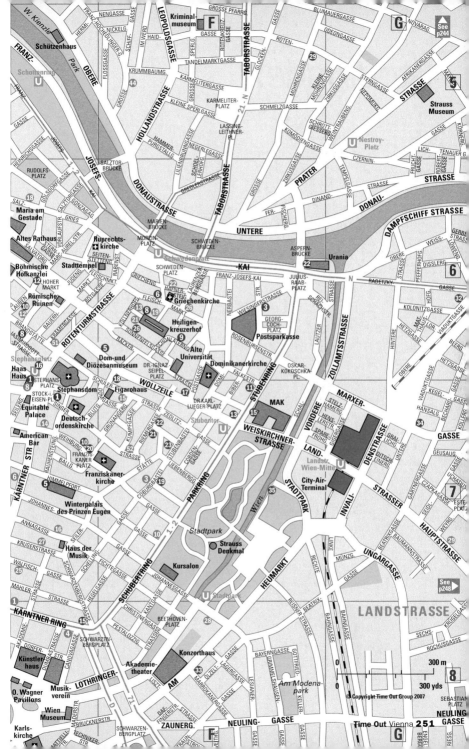

Steet Index

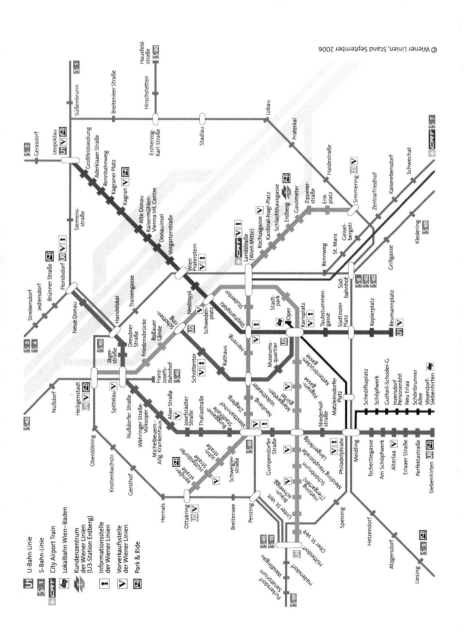

© Wiener Linien, Stand September 2006